Education in the
New Latino Diaspora

Recent Titles in
Sociocultural Studies in Educational Policy Formation and Appropriation
Bradley A.U. Levinson and Margaret Sutton, Series Editors

Policy as Practice: Toward a Comparative Sociocultural Analysis of Educational Policy
Margaret Sutton and Bradley A.U. Levinson, editors

Education in the New Latino Diaspora

Policy and the Politics of Identity

Edited by

Stanton Wortham, Enrique G. Murillo Jr., and Edmund T. Hamann

Sociocultural Studies in Educational Policy
Formation and Appropriation, Volume 2

ABLEX PUBLISHING
Westport, Connecticut • London

Library of Congress Cataloging-in-Publication Data

Education in the new Latino diaspora : policy and the politics of identity / edited by
Stanton Wortham, Enrique G. Murillo Jr., and Edmund T. Hamann.
    p. cm.—(Sociocultural studies in educational policy formation and appropriation,
  ISSN 1530–5473 ; v. 2)
    Includes bibliographical references and index.
    ISBN 1–56750–630–5 (alk. paper)—ISBN 1–56750–631–3 (pbk. : alk. paper)
    1. Hispanic Americans—Education.   I. Wortham, Stanton Emerson Fisher, 1963–   II.
  Murillo, Enrique G.   III. Hamann, Edmund T.   IV. Series.
  LC2669.E39   2002
  371.829'68073—dc21   2001022914

British Library Cataloguing in Publication Data is available.

Library of Congress Catalog Card Number: 2001022914
ISBN: 1–56750–630–5
        1–56750–631–3 (pbk.)
ISSN: 1530–5473

First published in 2002

Ablex Publishing, 88 Post Road West, Westport, CT 06881
An imprint of Greenwood Publishing Group, Inc.
www.ablexbooks.com

Printed in the United States of America

The paper used in this book complies with the
Permanent Paper Standard issued by the National
Information Standards Organization (Z39.48–1984).

P

In order to keep this title in print and available to the academic community, this edition
was produced using digital reprint technology in a relatively short print run. This would
not have been attainable using traditional methods. Although the cover has been changed
from its original appearance, the text remains the same and all materials and methods
used still conform to the highest book-making standards.

Contents

Foreword by *Bradley A. U. Levinson*   vii

Acknowledgments   xiii

1. Education and Policy in the New Latino Diaspora   1
   Edmund T. Hamann, Stanton Wortham, and *Enrique G. Murillo Jr.*

2. Reinventing *Educación* in New Latino Communities:
   Pedagogies of Change and Continuity in North Carolina   17
   Sofia Villenas

3. Recent Language Minority Education Policy in Georgia:
   Appropriation, Assimilation, and Americanization   37
   Scott A.L. Beck and *Martha Allexsaht-Snider*

4. *¿Un Paso Adelante?* The Politics of Bilingual Education, Latino
   Student Accommodation, and School District Management in
   Southern Appalachia   67
   Edmund T. Hamann

5. The New Paths of Mexican Immigrants in the United States:
   Challenges for Education and the Role of Mexican Universities   99
   *Víctor Zúñiga, Rubén Hernández-León, Janna L. Shadduck-
   Hernández,* and *María Olivia Villarreal*

6. Gender and School Success in the Latino Diaspora   117
   Stanton Wortham

7. Fragmented Community, Fragmented Schools: The
   Implementation of Educational Policy for Latino Immigrants   143
   Elias Martinez

8. Lowrider Art and Latino Students in the Rural Midwest   169
   Karen Grady

9. Policy Design as Practice: Changing the Prospects of
   Hispanic Voices   193
   Michael Brunn

10. How Does It Feel to Be a *Problem*?: "Disciplining" the
    Transnational Subject in the American South   215
    Enrique G. Murillo Jr.

11. The New Latino Diaspora and Educational Policy   241
    Margaret A. Gibson

Index   253

About the Editors and Contributors   261

Foreword

Bradley A.U. Levinson

Not long ago I was taking a flight to Mexico out of the Indianapolis Airport, and the gentleman checking me in—white, fiftyish, a little paunchy—asked me for my proof of citizenship. As I showed him my birth certificate and driver's license, apologizing for my expired passport, he seized the occasion to announce:

Some of these Mexicans, you know, you wouldn't believe what they show me, sometimes an Indiana driver's license and nothing else. . . . There's times I want to just call immigration and send them back in a U-Haul or something, the same way they came over. And you wouldn't believe it. They're totally illiterate. Those boxes full of clothes that they take with them [for selling down in Mexico], they can't even read the Spanish, let alone the English. These people, I tell you, they don't care about education. They're just here for a buck.

I tried a feeble rejoinder, commenting that I knew a lot of Mexican families in Indiana that cared deeply about their children's education. As he was punching in my data, he just grunted a response. Eyeing the line behind me, I decided not to press the issue. I walked away to find some coffee before my flight.

Starbucks loomed before me. I went in wondering to myself what made this man think that I would be sympathetic to his lament. He must have seen me as white and assumed I would share a racial, perhaps a patriotic, concern. He didn't stop to think that my travel to Mexico might indicate a familiarity with, perhaps even a fondness for, Mexican people and culture. I was at the Starbucks counter now, presumably a new key symbol of corporate consumer domination. Yet Latino music was playing on the sound system, and Spanish voices were jockeying in the back. A Latina woman with a strong accent took my order, and I sat down to watch her banter with two fellow Spanish-speaking employees.

After a little while, I started up a conversation in Spanish, and eventually I related to her and a coworker the comments made by the man at the airline counter. The woman, around 40 years of age, was disturbed, and spoke about the difficulty of encountering such attitudes and assumptions among the "Americanos." She sensed that many long-time residents harbored such ill will. Yet her twenty-something male coworker found a grain of truth in the man's attitude. Born in Texas and moved to Indiana a few years prior, this young man criticized some of the more newly arrived Mexican men: "A lot of them are just here to make some quick money and go home. They don't really care about learning English or respecting the laws. Some of them even get 'wives' here when they already have wives and families back home. They tend to give all of us a bad name."

My experience at the airport highlighted several of the social dynamics explored by the authors of the fine book before you. A racially dominant local resident attempted to "bond" with me, a perceived fellow-dominant, by casting aspersions on the intentions and educational achievements of a racial-linguistic minority relatively new to Indiana. Moreover, he assumed that all the brown-skinned, Spanish-speaking folks he saw were Mexican, and failed to note the national and regional diversity within this group. Meanwhile, two recently arrived members of the group he viewed as homogeneous actually held conflicting views about the actions and intentions of "their people." Perhaps because of generational differences, or differences in their experience of incorporation into U.S. life, these two Starbucks employees could not agree about the meaning of the man's comments. This is just a small snapshot of the complex, ever-shifting nature of social relations in the New Latino Diaspora.

As the 2000 millennium came and went with vigorous fanfare, and while most celebrated the moment amidst fireworks and champagne, a quieter transformation received far less attention. By most accounts, the decade of the 1990s witnessed a fundamental demographic shift in the continental United States. New immigrant minorities, especially Latino immigrants, began to settle in impressive numbers outside the major urban centers and agricultural corridors they had previously occupied. The immigrants have been drawn to the relative security of new jobs in meat processing and other light industry. They have been fleeing either from the drugs, gang violence, and overt racism of the largest U.S. inner cities or from the limited economic opportunity of their Latin American nations. In any case, these Latinos have effectively participated in the creation of a New Latino Diaspora in the cities, small towns, and dispersed counties of the northeast, the southeast, the midwest, and the mountain west.

What kinds of new social relations and cultural identities have emerged in these regions of the New Latino Diaspora? As fundamental sites of socialization and cultural transmission, public schools can reveal a great deal about such relations and identities. Schools are places where fundamental values and assumptions about cultural difference get played out in varying policies and practices, and where school actors—teachers, administrators, students, and their parents—develop strategies in response to one another and to prevailing policies. As institutions that "mediate" relationships between immigrant households and broader political-economic structures (Lamphere, 1992), schools often crystallize the kinds of conflicts and accommodations around cultural differences occurring in other spheres of local and national society. That is why the outstanding collection of essays brought together by Stanton Wortham, Ted Hamann, and Enrique Murillo is so timely and important. By providing us a glimpse into the politics of identity and educational policy in the New Latino Diaspora, these authors throw light onto a series of broader cultural questions emerging in the new American millennium. Allow me to identify just a few of this book's many illuminations.

As Latinos move into new parts of the rural and semirural United States and carve out a social niche for themselves, their identities shift or consolidate, weaken or strengthen, depending on the particular contexts of action. Most Latinos find promising economic prospects tied to anxious or hostile social conditions. In response to expressions of racism, cynicism, or indifference—the local efforts at "disciplining the transnational subject" so compellingly described by Murillo—Latinos enact various strategies along a continuum of accommodation and resistance. They may try to "blend in" or "stand firm" or feign incomprehension. In this book, we find many such strategies. Among the most poignant are the expressions of creative cultural adaptation among Latinas in a New England town, analyzed by Wortham, or the acts of cultural resistance and self-affirmation captured by Grady in the "lowrider art" of Midwest high school ESL (English as a Second Language) students. In most of these analyses, we also find local schools struggling to meet the varying needs of Latino newcomer children and adolescents. Sometimes the struggles are in good faith, whereas at other times they betray a kind of benign or even hostile neglect.

It's not only just a question of whether and how we can reform our schools to best meet the educational needs of new Latino immigrants, to help create a more multicultural public sphere that's respectful of difference, but it's also about how long-standing residents can learn from and draw upon the educational traditions of the new Latinos. For instance, with their concept of *buena educación*, elucidated by Sofia Villenas in her study of a North Carolina town, new Latinos contrast a broader practice of moral education—of cooperation, solidarity, honesty, hard work, and respect for elders—to the prevailing notions of education they find in the schools there. Not only do these Latinos suggest a critique of prevailing conceptions and institutions, but they also present a potential contribution. As the United States matures toward a more inclusive conception of public

values, studies such as that by Villenas hold out the promise of a model of recip-
rocal cultural integration rather than the long-standing model of unilateral assimilation. To be sure, new Latinos must learn to abide by certain prevailing
practices and beliefs—in substantive equality before the law, for instance, and ultimately, the U.S. constitution—and that implies a certain kind of assimilation.
Yet Latinos' strong educational traditions also hold out the promise of further
enriching the sociocultural fabric of region and nation.

Another strength of this book is the way it permits the reader to appreciate
the complex interplay of "official" and "unofficial" policy practices. We see the
will to govern of authorized policy makers and power holders, including teachers and school administrators in alliance with local elites. On the other hand,
we see the creative response, the appropriation or rejection of such official policy initiatives by the Latino subjects to whom they are fundamentally directed.
Many of the articles in the book thus focus on Latino students and families
and their own identity formation in the new Diaspora. This is the traditional
focus of ethnographic research. Yet, importantly, other chapters highlight the
official policy processes by which Latino students are defined, "managed," and
presumably served. In Michael Brunn's piece, for instance, we see teachers and
administrators struggling to define a language policy that ostensibly empowers
Latino newcomers for school achievement, but that in reality enforces a highly
restrictive Anglo norm. Then there are the wonderfully interlocking accounts
and reflections produced by scholars who had different roles to play in the creation and documentation of educational policies for new Latino immigrants in
northern Georgia. In three separate articles, Zúñiga et al., Beck and Allexsaht-
Snider, and Hamann each demonstrate the potential pitfalls but also the great
promise of concerted policy efforts rooted in good research and goodwill across
international borders.

Finally, the authors represented in this volume come from distinct cultural
backgrounds and research traditions, and this is part of what lends the book its
strength. We have both "outsiders" and "insiders"—scholars who are Latino
themselves, but with different immigration or ethnic histories within the United
States; and Euro-American scholars, some of whom have studied the immigration dynamic or taught immigrants themselves through long careers, and others
who've been rather recently attracted to the subject. We also have Mexican nationals who view U.S. immigration from the view of the sending country. The
various personal histories and subjectivities of the authors—and the various ways
they engaged in their research projects—allow them to speak to and about different problems. This internal diversity therefore makes the book especially rich
and yet, though rooted in solid qualitative research methods, the studies reported
by these authors share a common concern for the rights and dignity of Latino
newcomers.

The New Latino Diaspora is here to stay. Before long it won't even be very new. This book provides us with an important set of insights about how we can study and improve the educational prospects for newcomers and old-timers alike.

REFERENCE

Lamphere, Louise, ed. 1992. *Structuring Diversity: Ethnographic Perspectives on the New Immigration.* Chicago: University of Chicago Press.

Acknowledgments

The editors would like to thank various people for their support and contributions to this volume. Sofia Villenas and Enrique Murillo did the first work theorizing the New Latino Diaspora, as part of the North Carolina Public Sphere project at the University of North Carolina, Chapel Hill, and all of us have benefited from their initial work on the phenomenon. Edmund Hamann and Sofia Villenas organized a session on the New Latino Diaspora at the annual meetings of the American Anthropological Association in 1997, at which several of us began to present our work on the topic. Norma González, Marki LeCompte, Marcelo Suárez-Orozco, and Enrique Trueba have provided insights and encouragement in our conversations with them about the topic and the volume. Bradley Levinson and Margaret Sutton saw potential in our work and have provided support and editorial guidance through the process, Betty Deane did an exemplary job in preparing the manuscript, and Jane Garry has been a supportive editor. We would also like to thank the Latino newcomers and established residents in each of the research sites who enabled our presence, who tolerated our observation and scrutiny, and who took time to answer our questions. Our thoughts are with them as they forge new identities and shape the character of local democracies wherever they settle.

1

Education and Policy in the New Latino Diaspora

Edmund T. Hamann, Stanton Wortham, and Enrique G. Murillo Jr.

THE NEW LATINO DIASPORA

Increasing numbers of Latinos (many immigrant, and some from elsewhere in the United States) are settling both temporarily and permanently in areas of the United States that have not traditionally been home to Latinos—for example, North Carolina, Maine, Georgia, Indiana, Arkansas, rural Illinois, and near resort communities in Colorado.[1] Enrique Murillo and Sofia Villenas have called this the New Latino Diaspora (Murillo and Villenas, 1997). Newcomer Latinos are confronted with novel challenges to their senses of identity, status, and community. Instead of arriving in settings, like the Southwest, where Latinos have lived for centuries, those in the New Latino Diaspora arrive in unfamiliar places where long-term residents have little experience with Latinos. In the New Diaspora, then, Latinos face more insistent questions about who they are, who they seek to be, and what accommodations they merit—questions that are asked both by themselves and by others.

These questions about identity often get addressed through formal and informal policies of mediating institutions (Lamphere, 1992; Levinson and Sutton, 2001)—notably schools (Goode et al., 1992)—which are key sites for the enactment of status hierarchies and other scripts for interethnic interaction. In these New Latino Diaspora sites, the scripts for interethnic interaction are contradictory, emergent, and very much in flux, but their consequences are often predictable. Anglo hosts are often suspicious of Latino newcomers, and few Latino Diaspora schools so far are able to help Latino schoolchildren overcome the economic and social barriers they face. The most common educational accommodation to their needs is to pull them out of content classes for ESL work, a practice that often disrupts their acquisition of content knowledge.

Preliminary data on schooling in the New Latino diaspora—high school completion rates, representation in higher school tracks, etc.—are not encouraging. New Latino Diaspora students are often placed in less-preferred spaces—sometimes literally in closets. And they are often taught by less credentialed teachers, who are themselves stigmatized by peers through an academic "caste system" that looks down on bilingual/ESL education (Grey, 1991).

The emergent patterns in the New Latino Diaspora seem similar to the unsatisfactory Latino experiences in the Southwest and in cities such as Chicago and New York, but we do not have much data. We know a lot about the education of U.S. Latinos in such areas as the Southwest (e.g., Foley, 1990; Vasquez et al., 1994; Suárez-Orozco and Suárez-Orozco, 1995; Romo and Falbo, 1996; and Valdés, 1996) and Chicago (e.g., Guerra, 1998). But, with the partial exception of some studies that emerged from the Changing Relations Project (e.g., Grey, 1991), the literature includes very little about the educational experiences of newcomers in the New Latino Diaspora. Nor are there any comparative analyses of the overlaps and dissimilarities in educational policies and experiences in New Latino Diaspora locales. This volume provides data on these issues.

The nine substantive chapters in this volume present ethnographic case studies from various New Latino Diaspora locations in order to explore how Diaspora Latinos find themselves constructed by members of the receiving communities and how they assert their identities in response. Because the authors of the chapters variously identify as Anglo, Chicano, Latino, and/or Mexican national (and differ along other key dimensions as well), the collection presents a polyvocal perspective on the New Latino Diaspora.

The New Latino Diaspora represents a unique sociohistorical location. Like most immigrants and many other U.S. Latinos, most New Diaspora Latinos regularly face racism and the burdens of being working class and speaking a minority language. They confront a segmented labor market that they are usually expected to enter only "from the bottom" (Spener, 1988). Unlike the majority of immigrants arriving in the United States at the beginning of the twentieth century, however, many of the Latino newcomers are coming directly to rural locations that are unaccustomed to outsiders of any type, or that have conceptualized difference only in dichotomous terms into which the newcomers do not readily fit (e.g., white and black). And in some cases, despite the challenges and obstacles that they face, members of the New Latino Diaspora do not face conditions where anti-Latino discrimination is deeply endemic— because the Latino presence is too new. Because of the unique conditions they face, Diaspora Latinos do not easily fit most models of minority children in school. The chapters in this volume describe both familiar and unfamiliar predicaments and opportunities faced by Diaspora Latinos as they move into rural America outside the Southwest.

EDUCATION AND POLICY

The contributors to this volume focus on institutional settings, like schools, in which Latinos adopt identities and have identities imposed on them. But education and schooling are not seen as fully synonymous here (e.g., Hansen, 1990; Borofsky, 1987). As Levinson and Holland explain:

Anthropologists have long recognized the existence of culturally specific and relative definitions of the educated person. Although the degree to which cultural training is formalized, situated at a remove from the activities for which it is intended, and provided on a mass scale may vary, anthropologists recognize all societies as providing some kind of training and some set of criteria by which members can be identified as more, or less, knowledgeable. Distinct societies, as well as ethnic groups and microcultures within those societies, elaborate the cultural practices by which particular sets of skills, knowledges, and discourses come to define the truly "educated" person. (1996, 2)

In the cases presented here, what knowledge and skill are sought after varies according to one's perspective. Host community members (typically Anglos) and newcomer Latinos often differ in their views of education. Both see schooling as a vehicle for education, and there is some overlap in their goals for schooling (e.g., English literacy skill acquisition, graduation). There are also some differences. Though few acknowledge it, host community members often distinguish between what constitutes an "educated" Latino and an "educated" Anglo. An "educated" Latino, for instance, may be constructed as one who knows how to work hard and not complain, whereas an educated Anglo may know how to shape a corporate vision and engineer profitable practices.

Latino newcomers also bring cultural identities, experiences, and ways of knowing to their new locations. Using these, they create models of what knowledges, skills, and dispositions are worthy of respect and have utility. As Villenas shows in her chapter, the resulting construction of what it means to be educated matches neither the construction of educated that was extant in the Mexican city or village of origin, nor the constructions of educated offered by the new host society.

Bringing their own dynamic, hybrid visions of education, Latino newcomers often confront a contradiction in their host communities. They encounter an ideology that values equal treatment and self-determination. On the other hand, the

practices through which host communities respond to newcomers often conflict
with these values. Some members of host communities overtly denigrate the
newcomers and fantasize about returning to a pre-Latino state; many do not.
Even most of these, however, nonetheless participate in educational policies and
practices that often label and constrain Latino students.

Borrowing from Levinson and Sutton (2001) and Shore and Wright (1997),
we treat policy as more than just formal dictates and resource allocations sent
from above. Policy also includes locally created and contested action. Four of
Levinson and Sutton's arguments inform this book:

- Policy serves as a legitimating charter for the techniques of administration and as an operating manual for everyday conduct; it is the symbolic expression of normative claims
  worked into a potentially viable institutional blueprint. Instead of separating them entirely, we examine policy formation and implementation as a dynamic, interrelated
  process. (2)
- In all the scholarly discourse around policy, there is little evidence of the sociocultural
  perspective: a locally informed, comparative account of how people make and engage
  with policy. (6)
- In the processes of policy formation, problems are constructed for solution and thus the
  needs of individuals and societies become subject to authoritative definition. (17)
- Among public policy arenas, educational policy is unique in its power to determine who
  has the right to become an "educated" person. (17)

Policies, both formal and improvised, start as the identification of problems.
They embed constructions of the status quo, beliefs that the status quo is inadequate, and theoretical propositions about how specific actions will bring
changes. A common element of the sites considered here is that the presence of
Latino newcomers was constructed as a problem. Once policies are articulated,
they start to delimit understandings of how the problem can be solved. Con-
ceptualizing newcomers as problems in particular ways (e.g., they need to be
Americanized, they have deficits which need to be remedied, they should be
given little support because they are stealing our jobs, they need to learn English), host communities articulate views of who the Latinos are and what types
of treatment they deserve.

Newcomers, too, engage in formal and informal policy formation. They construct views of themselves and Anglos, partly in response to Anglos' constructions of them. Using Levinson and Sutton's inclusive construction of the idea of
policy, even such acts as dropping out or sending one's children back to Latin
America to be raised by relatives (e.g., Hagan, 1994; Trueba, 1999) are a type of
educational policy. As they explain (2001, 5), "Even outright resistance to a policy can be seen as a kind of [appropriated version of policy] insofar as it incorporates a negative image of policy into schemes of action." The chapters in this

volume describe various cases of the interplay between Latino and Anglo construals of "the problem" in New Latino Diaspora sites.

SCHOOLING, THE POLITICAL ECONOMY, AND THE PUBLIC SPHERE

Educational policy at the local level is always challenged by demographic change. In the New Latino Diaspora, these challenges almost always involve local businesses' "externalization of indirect costs" (Hackenberg, 1995, 238) and the "Latinization of low-wage labor" (Griffith, 1995, 129). The businesses that lure newcomer labor to the Latino Diaspora have left it to the existing social service infrastructure—such as schools, health care providers, municipal offices, etc.—to negotiate the added costs and complications of serving new populations (González Baker et al., 1999, 99). Externalization of indirect costs can cause resentment on the part of service providers, though more often than not those sentiments are directed at the newcomers rather than at the businesses precipitating the changes. Along with this resentment often come overt acts of newcomer exploitation, such as landlords overpricing substandard housing because of housing shortages and employers' use of fear to intimidate workers from seeking medical assistance or workman's compensation for work-related injuries and illness. Most of the chapters describe, or at least hint at, such dynamics across the Latino Diaspora.

In the case of Latino newcomers, many who speak Spanish as a first and sometimes only language, an immediate necessity is communication. This might mean hiring bilingual paraprofessionals for the school setting. Typically, however, the changes and needed responses are much more profound, extending beyond school sites into the larger community and proving to be much more complex than just a need for language interpreters. San Miguel (1987, xv) has claimed that the acrimonious debates about bilingual education (perceived as accommodation to Latinos) need to be replaced by a focus on schools' unwillingness or inability to meet the diverse needs of Mexican-descent children.

Latino students, parents, and laborers in the New Latino Diaspora bring to their encounter with established residents beliefs about their own identities, about the identities and beliefs of established residents, and about the political economy in which they are intertwined. Tied to these are cultural beliefs about child rearing, household responsibility, and family values. As Valdés (1996), Delgado-Gaitan (1990), Vásquez et al. (1994), Villenas (this volume), and others have noted, Latino parents frequently have different conceptualizations of parent and school responsibilities than the middle-class Anglos who set most U.S. public school policy. In general, schooling in traditional Latino Diaspora locations has not been responsive to Latinos and has not encouraged Latino parental input into schooling (e.g., San Miguel, 1987, 217). Nor have Latino newcomers' skills been consistently appreciated and used as building blocks for subsequent education.

In the Southwest and other areas with a higher density of Latinos, there have been important exceptions to the generally inadequate treatment educational institutions have given to Latinos. For example, the Latino parent involvement group described by Delgado-Gaitan (1990) provides newcomer parents with an opportunity for authentic input into the schooling of their children. The high schools described by Lucas et al. (1990) and some of the districts described by Dentler and Hafner (1997) are responsive to newcomer Latino student needs. The "funds of knowledge" work at the University of Arizona (Moll et al., 1992; González et al., 1995; Moll and González, 1997) has helped educators build on students' existing skills and knowledge. All these examples could be instructive for educational policies and policy implementation in the New Latino Diaspora, but so far they have not been adopted.

If "best practices" that lead to high achievement among Latinos are known (e.g., Lucas, 1997; Walqui, 1999), why is it that they are so inconsistently pursued? The answers are complex. Shor's (1986) cynical observation that schooling in a capitalist society is "successful" to the extent that it conveys to students stratified expectations would suggest that schools do not want to remedy inadequacies in the education available to Latino newcomers. A quite different explanation could claim that the problems of any inadequate current practice are ephemeral, that they will be remedied as soon as educators learn what is needed. Several chapters in this volume do describe how host schools struggled to find resources and knowledge as the process of demographic change unfolded, but this cannot suffice as an explanation. Something also seemed to interfere with educators' efforts to find the best practices noted earlier, or kept them from feeling that these were viable, in their communities. In many cases this interference came from host community stereotyping of Latinos.

Established residents in New Latino Diaspora locales are influenced by various large-scale projects for and against newcomers. For example, national debates about bilingual education and its purported implications for cultural identity are known to many host community residents, and inform their reactions to newcomers, even though their understanding of bilingual education is generally limited. Concerns about illegal immigration and job displacement also inform some host community responses to newcomers. As Suárez-Orozco summarizes: "Anti-immigrant sentiment—including the jealous rage that 'illegals are getting benefits instead of citizens like my friend'—is intertwined with an unsettling sense of panic in witnessing the metamorphosis of 'home' into a world dominated by sinister aliens" (1998, 296–297).

Furthermore, ostensibly sympathetic responses to newcomers often do not lead to more favorable outcomes, because they can be less sympathetic than they first appear.[2] The proimmigration script described by Suárez-Orozco (1998) is common in New Latino Diaspora locales (e.g., Hamann, 1999). In that script Latino newcomers are constructed as hardworking, loyal, religious, family oriented, and willing to take work no one else wants. The script simultaneously reiterates the mythology of the United States being attractive and fair to immigrants, a view espoused by many host community members, and one that rationalizes assimilative projects. But the alleged virtues of immigrants also constrain, as they deny newcomers the prerogative to complain about working conditions, inadequate housing, and racism at school, and to seek work and opportunities that others do want (because to do so would be disloyal and confrontational).

THE PERSPECTIVES OF NEWCOMERS

Informed by the "funds of knowledge" (Moll et al., 1992; González et al., 1995, Moll and González, 1997) that they bring with them to their new contexts, as well as the habits and experiences of immigrants who have preceded them to the new site (Hagan, 1994), Latino newcomers adopt various beliefs and behaviors once they arrive in New Latino Diaspora communities. They may imagine themselves as part of their new community (Chavez, 1994; Anderson, 1983), or feel detached and tentative, or actively excluded from it. Schools can be key sites for the construction of community identity and inclusion (e.g., Pugach, 1998; Peshkin, 1994; Bissinger, 1991), but they can also be sites that exclude Latino newcomers through the persistence of nonresponsive policies and the failure to build on newcomers' existing funds of knowledge.

Many newcomers resist both the virulent and "benevolent" forms of racism they encounter by affirming their own identities as immigrants or minority group members. (Benevolent racism refers to the policies and practices of those who allege good intentions but whose actions have discriminatory consequences [Villenas, 2001; see also the chapters by Villenas and Wortham, this volume].) For some newcomers, affirmation of identity involves a rejection of majority values and institutions, i.e., what Ogbu (1987) calls the cultural inversion model. At the school level, many "pushed-out" (Trueba, 1991) Latino students would fit in this category. Although rejecting majority values and institutions might be a healthy response to discrimination, with respect to identity development and cultural preservation such a stance often leaves minority students vulnerable to serious economic and social problems.

Some Latino newcomers manage to affirm their own cultures without overtly rejecting majority values and institutions. Pugach (1998) describes students in a New Mexico border town who create a Latino model of school success that is nonetheless accepted by the mainstream. In some cases, however, managing to become bicultural means conforming to majority practices in school but affirming immigrant ones at home. This is akin to the strategy pursued by Sikh students in Britain documented by Hall (1995) and the strategy attempted by the Portuguese immigrant students studied by Becker (1990; cf. also Gibson, 1997).

Becker notes, however, that newcomers' attempts at situational manipulation of ethnic identity—for example, attempting to have a mainstream rather than immigrant identity at school—were not always recognized by members of non-newcomer groups. Teachers and non-Portuguese students continued to compartmentalize the Portuguese newcomers as immigrants and to articulate negative stereotypes about them. Despite the immigrant students' use of accentless English at school, their imitation of popular clothing styles, and other efforts to reject their stigmatized immigrant identity, they were identified as having limited potential and limited school aspirations. Grady's chapter describes how students' bids for acceptance can vary according to the topic of the class, with art, a subject that embraces self-expression, proving to be more receptive than others. Wortham's chapter describes how gender can influence both the bids for acceptance that are attempted, as well as the way they are received.

Some newcomers react to racism by internalizing negative stereotypes of their home cultures. They try to assimilate to the mainstream culture, using a replacement orientation—with new cultural competencies permitting abandonment of their original culture (e.g., Keefe and Padilla, 1987).

Whatever strategy they adopt, newcomers' identity maintenance and construction projects do not occur in isolation from Anglos' attempts to uphold the "mainstream" cultural order. The majority often "racializes" immigrant groups. Historically, this racializing has often meant identifying immigrants as biologically distinct and inferior, but if such overtly racist ideologies have largely lost favor, the social construction of immigrants as less deserving and/or as missing knowledge, lacking skills, and being inferior remains powerful, if tacit. The application of a cultural deficit ideology to Latinos has been criticized in the research literature for at least 30 years (e.g., Carter, 1970; Erickson, 1987; Vasquez, et al., 1994), but according to Valdés (1996) and Valencia (1997), it still remains commonplace among many mainstream educators. In their chapter, Beck and Allexsaht-Snider note that a cultural deficit ideology is consistent with a colonialist ideology, with the colonizer assuming all their attributes are superior to those of the colonized. In accordance with the racializing process and the promulgation of cultural deficit ideologies, members of the mainstream, individually and through the institutions they lead, often exclude newcomers from positions of power in the workplace, the community, and the schools.

As migration streams feeding Diaspora locations mature (Massey et al., 1987; Tienda, 1989), newcomers attracted by employment often settle in and bring their families to Diaspora locations without feeling attached to their new loca-

tion (Anderson, 1983; Chavez, 1994). Political involvement and residential sta-
bility are more likely if newcomers imagine themselves as part of their new community, but that is difficult to accomplish and often resisted by local Anglos.
Limited housing options, financial vulnerability, and (for some) the risk of
deportation all contribute to residential mobility.

Meier and Stewart (1991) have found that Latino students' performance at
school correlates with both the community political power of Latinos and their
presence as instructors and administrators. The implications of this finding for
New Latino Diaspora locations are dramatic, as newness to community, lack of
citizenship, and other factors inhibit Latino newcomers' political participation.
Because of Latinos' recent arrival in the region and their lack of political power,
nearby teacher-training institutions usually have developed few Latino-oriented
recruiting initiatives and student support networks. This limits the regional supply of Latino educators and helps perpetuate the dynamic described by Meier
and Stewart.

Unlike past generations of immigrants, members of the New Latino Diaspora
are often close enough to home and connected enough to robust transnational
labor movements that it is easy for them to retain strong ties to their home countries (Hagan, 1994). Guerra (1998) even suggests that many Latinos now live in
"transnational communities"—communities that cannot be adequately defined
using a single geographic reference, or even a single nation. In the case of Mexican newcomers, lingering sending-community ties are facilitated by the Mexican
government's formal attempts to remain salient to expatriates through programs
like such as *Mexicanos en el Extranjero* (Mendez Lugo, 1997; Goldring, 1998).
Those in migrant sending communities who depend on financial remittances
also have a stake in keeping newcomers connected to their sending communities.

The circumstances of displacement from sending communities, the use of
geographically diverse family and fictive kin networks as an economic risk-
minimization strategy (Stark, 1991), and the uncertainty of economic and cultural opportunities in the receiving community further explain enduring ties to
home communities (Ainslie, 1999; Gutiérrez, 1999). Such ties can influence
newcomers' educational aspirations and can compel natives of host communities to construct the newcomer population as temporary and in need of only
minimal help. Thus a final dilemma faced by Latino newcomers in the New
Latino Diaspora is the ambiguity of whether they are migrants or immigrants,
an ambiguity that many newcomers themselves express.

The chapters in this book examine the construction of cultural identity in the
New Latino Diaspora by examining educational policymaking, interpretation,
and implementation. We focus on education in a broad sense—including not just
school practice and school district management, but also popular education,

grassroots efforts, and the informal learning that comes from reading newspapers and participating in the public sphere. The chapters vary in their primary focus, with some considering gender, some focusing on families and households, others on K–12 schools, others on school districts and state departments of education, and still others on formal and informal public community life.

We use ethnography to focus on day-to-day interethnic interaction and to describe host community members' construction of a Latino "Other" (and Latinos' contributions to and resistance against this construction). Using such ethnographic descriptions, the chapters illuminate how policy mandates have consequences for Latinos and non-Latinos at the local level. The chapters describe the local processes by which official and de facto policies are created and responded to. Thus these chapters provide a basis for what Delgado-Gaitan and Trueba (1991) refer to as the ethnography of empowerment, where ethnographic data becomes the rationale for the reform of policy and practice.

The chapters differ on a number of dimensions, among them authors' identities. Although all the authors are now affiliated with institutes of higher education, several had other affiliations when they carried out their fieldwork or gained entry to the field sites. Beck worked for Georgia's Migrant Education program; Martinez assisted with a school district's Title VII grant; Brunn helped a school district create a language policy for newcomers; Zúñiga, Hernández, Shadduck, and Villarreal all worked for the Mexican university partner that offered a range of services to two Georgia school districts; and Hamann made his first foray into his research site as a Title VII grant-writer.

Geography is another source of difference among the chapters. Three look at Georgia, two at North Carolina, one at northern New England, two at the rural Midwest, and one at the Rocky Mountains. Yet geography is also a source of similarity, as all the studies except Beck and Allexsaht-Snider's describe rural locations (their study describes a state department of education so it does not have fixed site). The largest site described in this volume is a city of 25,000.

The economies of the communities studied are superficially different, with Latino newcomers attracted to work opportunities in the resort industry in the Rockies; meatpacking in Illinois, Indiana, New England, and North Carolina; and a diversity of industries in Georgia, most notably carpet mills. Yet the economic niches in each of these sites are similar: The work is tedious, hazardous, and low-paying. An insufficient number of established community members are willing to take such work, so the work becomes ethnically typed or marked (Tienda, 1989) with the collective identity of the Latino newcomers tied to the low-status occupations most hold.

Deriving policy recommendations from her ethnographic work with Latino parents, in Chapter 2 Villenas describes Latina mothers' confusion and frustration with the public schools their children were attending, including the mismatch between values and ideologies at home versus at school. She describes how Latina mothers' views of parenting are changing, but through innovation and not assimilation. Her chapter then sketches how school policies and practices would need to change to be more accommodating to Latino parents and students.

In Chapter 3, Beck and Allexsaht-Snider describe the Georgia Department of Education's statewide response to the growing presence of Latino newcomers in Georgia. Their chapter draws on Beck's five years of work with the federally funded but state-administered Georgia Migrant Education program, to give an account of how political changes in the Georgia Department of Education undermined many Latino students' chances at a full education.

Chapters 4 and 5 describe a partnership between two northwest Georgia school districts and a private university in Mexico, from very different perspectives. Edmund Hamann investigates the "window of policymaking opportunity" that opened when one of the Georgia districts conceded it was not sure how to respond to rapid demographic change. He describes how a binational partnership was created between the school district and a Mexican university. Hamann describes "alternative policymaking moments," when stakeholders who usually are not positioned to influence schooling on a large scale suddenly have the chance to be policy makers.

Víctor Zúñiga, Rubén Hernández-León, María Olivia Villarreal, and Janna Shadduck-Hernández describe their experiences as Mexico-based university professors who were asked to help two Georgia school districts create educational policies for Latino newcomers. Their chapter chronicles their successes and struggles in facilitating a public forum for Latino newcomer families, so that those families could more readily represent their needs and interests to school personnel. Also considered is the prospect of Mexican universities assisting U.S. school districts in general, and in the Latino Diaspora in particular.

Wortham's contribution in Chapter 6 is the only chapter set in northern New England. After noting the frequent disparity between the individualistic orientation of most American schooling and the household/familial orientation of most Latino newcomers, Wortham considers the different ways male and female Latino adolescents construct personal identities and how these different gendered identities affect those students' school success. U.S. school policy and practice seem to provide a liberating opportunity for many female Latinas in Wortham's study, but it seems to limit the horizons of the males.

In Chapter 7 Martinez describes an atypical New Latino Diaspora site, one that is located in a state that has long been host to Latinos (Colorado), but in a community that has not. He describes some educators' attempt to implement an "ideal" transitional bilingual education program. In this case, district policies and unforeseen circumstances led to a less than ideal program that had negative educational consequences for the Latino newcomers. His chapter illustrates well how the community context that Latino newcomers confront enables the creation of a separate and inadequate school experience for newcomer children.

Based on her ethnographic research with Latino immigrant students at a high school in rural Indiana, Grady describes in Chapter 8 how these students resisted the official assimilationist curriculum by acquiring an alternative text on *Lowrider Arte* (a magazine of art inspired by the longtime Chicano tradition of customizing "low-rider" automobiles, one that affirms a Chicano aesthetic). She then describes how this resistance was validated by the school when a mainstream art teacher embraced students' involvement with lowrider art.

In Chapter 9 Brunn describes his experiences facilitating a rural Illinois district's attempt to develop a language policy. His account of how Latino parents and students were integrated into a formal policy development process, and of the resistance put up by some educators who were skeptical of its recommendations, illustrates both the challenge and the promise of inclusive policy formation in the New Latino Diaspora.

Enrique G. Murillo Jr.'s Chapter 10 returns to several of the themes broached in this introduction—particularly the role of racialized political economy—by looking at the virulently anti-immigrant construction of Latino newcomers in a North Carolina community where the only accepted identity of immigrants was as labor. Murillo then describes how the local poultry industry's quest to remain "globally competitive" and its dependence on immigrant labor for work "no one else wants" has dehumanized Latinos in this town. His conclusions draw together and contextualize many findings from the preceding chapters.

The volume ends with summative Chapter 11, which was prepared by Margaret Gibson.

NOTES

1. The term Latino can be defined expansively to include anyone of descent or origin from territories under the neocolonial (and sometimes overtly colonial) yoke of the Monroe Doctrine (Hayes-Bautista and Chapa, 1987)—that is, nearly all of Latin America and the Caribbean. We use that definition here. However, most members of the New Latino Diaspora were born in or trace their origins to Mexico and Central America. Newcomers from Cuba, the Dominican Republic, and South America seem mostly to be heading to locales with long-established Latino populations—e.g., Miami and New York—though there are exceptions to this trend (for example, Dominican immigrants in Rhode Island, Colombians in Georgia).

2. Prevalent as patronizing, colonial, and ultimately racist viewpoints may be, however, we must clarify that established members of host communities can act with grace and sincerity toward Latino newcomers. There are those who accept and promote an "additive view of acculturation" (Gibson, 1997, 441) and who thereby ameliorate the social and economic burdens of being a Latino newcomer without trying to convert or condescend

toward the newcomer community. It is just that the pool of those who do well by new-comers is smaller than those who mean well.

REFERENCES

Ainslie, Ricardo C. 1999. "Cultural Mourning, Immigration, and Engagement: Vignettes from the Mexican Experience." In *Crossings: Mexican Immigration in Interdisciplinary Perspective*. Marcelo M. Suárez-Orozco, ed. Pp. 283–300. Cambridge, MA: Harvard University, David Rockefeller Center for Latin American Studies.

Anderson, Benedict. 1983. *Imagined Communities: Reflections on the Growth and Spread of Nationalism*. New York: Verso.

Becker, Adeline. 1990. "The Role of School in the Maintenance and Change of Ethnic Group Affiliation." *Human Organization*. 49(1):48–55.

Bissinger, H.G. 1991. *Friday Night Lights: A Town, a Team, and a Dream*. New York: Harper Perennial.

Borofsky, Robert. 1987. *Making History: Pukapukan and Anthropological Constructions of Knowledge*. New York: Cambridge University Press.

Carter, Thomas P. 1970. *Mexican Americans in School: A History of Educational Neglect*. New York: College Entrance Examination Board.

Chavez, Leo R. 1994. "The Power of the Imagined Community: The Settlement of Undocumented Mexicans and Central Americans in the United States." *American Anthropologist*. 96(1):52–73.

Delgado-Gaitan, Concha. 1990. *Literacy for Empowerment: The Role of Parents in Children's Education*. London: Falmer Press.

Delgado-Gaitan, Concha and Henry Trueba. 1991. *Crossing Cultural Borders: Education for Immigrant Families in America*. London: Falmer Press.

Dentler, Robert A. and Anne L. Hafner. 1997. *Hosting Newcomers: Structuring Educational Opportunities for Immigrant Children*. New York: Teachers College Press.

Erickson, Frederick. 1987. "Transformation and School Success: The Politics and Culture of Educational Achievement." *Anthropology & Education Quarterly*. 18(4):335–356.

Foley, Douglas E. 1990. *Learning Capitalist Culture: Deep in the Heart of Tejas*. Philadelphia, PA: University of Pennsylvania Press.

Gibson, Margaret A. 1997. "Complicating the Immigrant/Involuntary Minority Typology." *Anthropology & Education Quarterly*. 28(3):431–454.

Goldring, Luin. 1998. "The Power of Status in Transnational Social Fields." In *Transnationalism from Below*. Michael Peter Smith and Luis Eduardo Guarnizo, eds. Pp. 165–195. New Brunswick, NJ: Transaction Publishers.

González, Norma, Luis C. Moll, Martha Floyd Tenery, Anna Rivera, Patricia Rendon, Raquel Gonzales, and Cathy Amanti. 1995. "Funds of Knowledge for Teaching in Latino Households." *Urban Education*. 29(4):443–470.

González Baker, Susan, Frank D. Bean, Augustin Escobar Latapi, and Sidney Weintraub. 1999. "U.S. Immigration Policies and Trends: The Growing Importance of Migration from Mexico." In *Crossings: Mexican Immigration in Interdisciplinary Perspectives*. Marcelo M. Suárez-Orozco, ed. Pp. 81–105. Cambridge, MA: Harvard University, David Rockefeller Center for Latin American Studies.

Goode, Judith G., Jo Anne Schneider, and Suzanne Blanc. 1992. "Transcending Boundaries and Closing Ranks: How Schools Shape Inter-relations." In *Structuring*

Diversity: Ethnographic Perspectives on the New Immigration. Louise Lamphere, ed. Pp. 173–213. Chicago: University of Chicago Press.

Grey, Mark A. 1991. "The Context for Marginal Secondary ESL Programs: Contributing Factors and the Need for Further Research." *The Journal of Educational Issues of Language Minority Students.* 9:75–89.

Griffith, David. 1995. "*Hay Trabajo:* Poultry Processing, Rural Industrialization, and the Latinization of Low-Wage Labor." In *Any Way You Cut It: Meat-Processing and Small-Town America.* Donald D. Stull, Michael J. Broadway, and David Griffith, eds. Pp. 129–151. Lawrence: University Press of Kansas.

Guerra, Juan C. 1998. *Close to Home: Oral and Literate Practices in a Transnational Mexicano Community.* New York: Teachers College Press.

Gutiérrez, David G. 1999. "Ethnic Mexicans and the Transformation of "American" Social Space: Reflections on Recent History." In *Crossings: Mexican Immigration in Interdisciplinary Perspective.* Marcelo M. Suárez-Orozco, ed. Pp. 309–335. Cambridge, MA: Harvard University, David Rockefeller Center for Latin American Studies.

Hackenberg, Robert A. 1995. "Joe Hill Died for Your Sins." In *Any Way You Cut It: Meat-Processing and Small-Town America.* Donald D. Stull, Michael J. Broadway, and David Griffith, eds. Pp. 232–264. Lawrence: University Press of Kansas.

Hagan, Jaqueline María. 1994. *Deciding to Be Legal: A Maya Community in Houston.* Philadelphia: Temple University Press.

Hall, Kathleen. 1995. "'There's a Time to Act English and a Time to Act Indian': The Politics of Identity among British-Sikh Teenagers." In *Children and the Politics of Culture.* Sharon Stephens, ed. Pp. 243–264. Princeton, NJ: Princeton University Press.

Hamann, Edmund T. 1999. "Anglo (Mis)Understandings of Latino Newcomers: A North Georgia Case Study." In *Negotiating Power and Place at the Margins: Selected Papers on Refugees and Immigrants,* vol. VII. Juliene Lipson and Lucia Ann McSpadden, eds. Pp. 156–197. Washington, DC: American Anthropological Association.

Hansen, Judith Friedman. 1990. [1979]. *Sociocultural Perspectives on Human Learning.* Prospect Heights, IL: Waveland Press.

Hayes-Bautista, David E. and Jorge Chapa. 1991. "Latino Terminology: Conceptual Basis for Standardized Terminology." *American Journal of Public Health.* 77:61–68.

Keefe, Susan E. and Amado M. Padilla. 1987. *Chicano Ethnicity.* Albuquerque: University of New Mexico Press.

Lamphere, Louise. 1992. "Introduction: The Shaping of Diversity." In *Structuring Diversity: Ethnographic Perspectives on the New Immigration.* Louise Lamphere, ed. Pp. 1–34. Chicago: University of Chicago Press.

Lamphere, Louise, Alex Stepick, and Guillermo Grenier, eds. 1994. *Newcomers in the Workplace: Immigrants and the Restructuring of the U.S. Economy.* Philadelphia: Temple University Press.

Levinson, Bradley A. and Dorothy Holland. 1996. "The Cultural Production of the Educated Person: An Introduction." In *The Cultural Production of the Educated Person: Critical Ethnographies of Schooling and Local Practice.* Bradley A. Levinson, Douglas E. Foley, and Dorothy C. Holland, eds. Pp. 1–54. Albany: State University of New York Press.

Levinson, Bradley A. and Margaret Sutton. 2001. "Policy as/in Practice: Developing a Sociocultural Approach to the Study of Educational Policy." In *Policy as Practice: Toward a Comparative Sociocultural Analysis of Educational Policy.* Westport, CT: Ablex Press.

Lucas, Tamara. 1997. *Into, Through, and Beyond Secondary School: Critical Transitions for Immigrant Youths*. Washington, DC : Center for Applied Linguistics.

Lucas, Tamara, Rosemary Henze, and Ruben Donato. 1990. "Promoting the Success of Latino Language-Minority Students: An Exploratory Study of Six High Schools." *Harvard Education Review*. 60(3):315–340.

Massey, Douglas S., Rafael Alarcón, Jorge Durand, and Humberto González. 1987. *Return to Aztlán: The Social Process of International Migration from Western Mexico*. Berkeley: University of California Press.

Meier, Kenneth J. and Joseph Stewart Jr. 1991. *The Politics of Hispanic Education:* Un Paso Pa'lante y Dos Pa'tras. Albany: State University Press of New York.

Mendez Lugo, Bernardo. 1997. "El Migrante Mexican en EU: De Actor Local a Actor Global." *Mexico and the World* 6(Sept. 97).

Moll, Luis C., Cathy Amanti, Deborah Neff, and Norma González. 1992. "Funds of Knowledge for Teaching: Using a Qualitative Approach to Connect Homes and Classrooms." *Theory into Practice*. 31(1):132–141.

Moll, Luis C. and Norma González. 1997. "Teachers as Social Scientists: Learning about Culture from Household Research." In *Race, Ethnicity, and Multiculturalism: Policy and Practice*. Peter M. Hall, ed. Pp. 89–114. New York: Garland Press.

Murillo, Enrique, Jr. and Sofia Villenas. 1997. "East of Aztlán: Typologies of Resistance in North Carolina Communities." Paper presented at "Reclaiming Voices: Ethnographic Inquiry and Qualitative Research in a Postmodern Age," Los Angeles.

Ogbu, John U. 1987. "Variability in Minority School Performance: A Problem in Search of an Explanation." *Anthropology & Education Quarterly*. 18(4):312–334.

Peshkin, Alan. 1994 [1978]. *Growing Up American: Schooling and the Survival of Community*. Prospect Heights, IL: Waveland Press.

Pugach, Marleen C. 1998. *On the Border of Opportunity: Education, Community, and Language at the U.S.–Mexico Line*. Mahwah, NJ: Lawrence Erlbaum Associates.

Romo, Harriet D. and Toni Falbo. 1996. *Latino High School Graduation: Defying the Odds*. Austin: University of Texas Press.

San Miguel, Guadalupe. 1987. *"Let Them All Take Heed": Mexican Americans and the Campaign for Educational Equality in Texas, 1910–1981*. Austin: University of Texas Press.

Shor, Ira. 1986. *Culture Wars: School and Society in the Conservative Restoration, 1969–84*. Boston: Routledge & Kegan Paul.

Shore, Cris and Susan Wright, eds. 1997. *Anthropology of Policy: Critical Perspectives on Governance and Power*. London: Routledge.

Spener, David. 1988. "Transitional Bilingual Education and the Socialization of Immigrants." *Harvard Educational Review*. 58(2), 133–153.

Stark, Oded. 1991. *The Migration of Labor*. Cambridge: Basil Blackwell.

Suárez-Orozco, Carola and Marcelo Suárez-Orozco. 1995. *Transformations: Migration, Family Life, and Achievement Motivation among Latino Adolescents*. Stanford, CA: Stanford University Press.

Suárez-Orozco, Marcelo M. 1998. "State Terrors: Immigrants and Refugees in the Post-National Space." In *Ethnic Identity and Power: Cultural Contexts of Political Action in School and Society*. Yali Zou and Enrique T. Trueba, eds. Pp. 283–319. Albany: State University of New York Press.

Tienda, Marta. 1989. "Looking to the 1990s: Mexican Immigration in Sociological Perspective." In *Mexican Migration to the United States: Origins, Consequences, and Pol-*

icy Options. Wayne A. Cornelius and Jorge A. Bustamante, eds. Pp. 109–147. San Diego: Center for U.S./Mexican Studies, University of California.

Trueba, Henry T. 1991. "From Failure to Success: The Roles of Culture and Cultural Conflict in the Academic Achievement of Chicano Students." In *Chicano School Failure and Success: Research and Policy Agendas for the 1990s.* Richard R. Valencia, ed. Pp. 151–163. London: Falmer Press.

———. 1999. "The Education of Mexican Immigrant Children." In *Crossings: Mexican Immigration in Interdisciplinary Perspective.* Marcelo M. Suárez-Orozco, ed. Pp. 253–275. Cambridge, MA: Harvard University, David Rockefeller Center for Latin American Studies.

Valdés, Guadalupe. 1996. *Con Respeto: Bridging the Distances between Culturally Diverse Families and Schools, an Ethnographic Portrait.* New York: Teachers College Press.

Valencia, Richard R., ed. 1997. *The Evolution of Deficit Thinking: Educational Thought and Practice.* London: Falmer Press.

Vasquez, Olga, Lucinda Pease-Alvarez, and Sheila M. Shannon. 1994. *Pushing Boundaries: Language and Culture in a Mexicano Community.* Cambridge: Cambridge University Press.

Villenas, Sofia. 1997. "Una Buena Educación: Latino Education and Cultural Conflict in North Carolina." Paper presented at the American Anthropological Association Annual Meeting. Washington, DC.

———. 2001. "Latina Mothers and Small-Town Racism." *Anthropology & Education Quarterly.* 32:3–28.

Walqui, Aída. 1999. *Access and Engagement: Program Design and Instructional Approaches for Immigrant Students in Secondary School.* Washington, DC: Center for Applied Linguistics.

Wortham, Stanton. 1997. "The Unintended Tracking of Latino Schoolchildren in Rural New England." Paper presented at the American Anthropological Association Annual Meeting. Washington, DC.

2

Reinventing *Educación* in New Latino Communities: Pedagogies of Change and Continuity in North Carolina

Sofia Villenas

The small rural town of Hope City,[1] in the center of North Carolina, brings to mind "chicken festivals" and Andy Griffith's Aunt Bea.[2] And yet *taquerías* and *tiendas*[3] are now a new part of this quintessential "American" landscape. Similarly, Spanish with its varied accents is spoken alongside a distinctive Hope City southern English. One hears a new generation of Latino children speaking English and "Spanglish" with regional Southern accents in the elementary schools, the churches, on the streets, and at Latino soccer Saturdays in the park. Indeed, Hope City's recently emerging Latino population (at least 38 percent of the town's total population in 1997) is becoming a dynamic and resilient presence as new cultural forms are forged in a region with no previous history of Latino settlement.

These cultural forms included contested and newly improvised productions of what it means to raise children with *una buena educación*[4]—or well-educated children who have respect, moral values, and loyalty to family. These productions also required resilience in the face of public discussions about Latino as "Other," "problem," and "noncitizen." These constructions were informed by xenophobic racisms that have discursively situated Latinos/as as undeserving and unentitled to public services (see Murillo Jr. this volume and Villenas, 2001). Real material and psychological consequences have followed for Latino families seeking to live, work, and provide an education for their children in Hope City. Additionally, Latino families have also had to be resilient in the face of benevolent racisms (Villenas and Moreno, forthcoming) practiced by some social, health, and education professionals who did seek to provide them with much needed public services (Villenas, 1999, 2001). However, as is often the case with "educative" agencies, the "helping" impulse of the social service professionals was simultaneously constructed within discourses of "lacking," "needy," and "we know what's best." Hence, alleged benevolence was instead disabling as competing definitions of child rearing and family education took center stage in these cultural and ideological struggles.

In this chapter, I draw from my two-year ethnographic study to examine the cultural/racial dynamics and creative resilience of Hope City Latino families in these conflictual debates about Latino family education.[5] Certainly, though professionals and educators most often dominated the public discourse and often gave monolithic definitions of Latino cultures, Latino parents also articulated their own diverse beliefs about and enactments of a good education. This *buena educación* centered steadfastly on moral values such as *respeto* and *buen comportamiento* (good conduct), but it also suggested continuity (tradition) and change, improvisation, and contestation—in short, negotiations that were to occur on their own terms. Beliefs about child rearing are thus examined as a contested terrain with a moral education as its defining core—one that is juxtaposed against a perception of a morally lax U.S. society and constructed in the context of cultural alienation and racism. In the end, I argue that in the conception and implementation of "education" services (i.e., schools, adult education, health and social services), "benevolent" policymakers must move away from articulating policy on behalf of Latino families and from simple generalizations about Latino family life. Rather, Latino parents' agency and their complex articulations and practices of *una buena educación*, as processes of maintaining cultural integrity and community building, must take center stage.

LABOR EXPLOITATION AND CULTURAL CONSTRUCTIONS OF LATINO FAMILIES: FROM WORKERS TO SOCIAL SERVICE CLIENTS

In the mid-1990s, Latino workers, many of whom were undocumented, made up approximately 85–90 percent of the poultry factory workforce in Hope City (Helping Hands[6] organization staff member, cited in Levin et al., 1994). Ninety chickens a minute, or 5,460 chickens per hour, are defrosted, hung, gutted, plucked, cut into pieces, and packaged. At wages from about $6 an hour, it is clear that the high intensity manual labor and high efficiency of the work on the factory line provides rapid capital gains for the owners, yet at the expense of posing serious health risks for the workers (Alanís, 1999; Griffith, 1995). Hand muscle problems such as carpal tunnel syndrome, rheumatism, and cuts from huge knives and machinery, as well as falls on the cold icy floors, all present dangerous working conditions. Hope City Latino residents explained the health dangers they had to worry about to interviewers of *Telemundo*, a Mexican television station:[7] "*Es mucho movimiento con las manos, muchos se enferman de un problema con la muñeca, es un problema bien serio que hace que la gente no pueda usar muy bien las manos*" (It's a lot of movement with the hands, many get health problems with the wrist, it's a very serious problem that makes for people not being able to use their hands well). Another Latino worker further explained: "*Es todo congelado, entonces el movimiento de las manos con el clima donde están trabajando es frío, frío y el agua que están agarrando caliente, caliente, eso hace que produzca reacciones en las manos como calambres*" (Everything is frozen and so the hand movements with the temperature where they're working is cold, cold, and the water they're using is hot, hot, and so that produces reactions in the hands like cramps).

Moreover, Latino poultry workers also asserted that *ilegales* or undocumented workers often had no choice but to do dangerous work at high speeds and intensity—otherwise they lost their jobs. Latinos/as told stories about themselves and other relatives who were injured on the job and consequently fired:[8] "I had a brother who had an accident . . . he was incapacitated for life and what happened, the first opportunity they [the poultry factory management] had they fired him. He worked tacking boxes of chicken and he slipped and fell, he suffered a slipped disc, and so then he was operated on, but he was left with a twitch in his leg and so they gave him disability for life, and supposedly he was going to always work for that company, and at the first opportunity, they fired him and he couldn't do anything about it." It is apparent that the use of Latino workers in the poultry industries of Hope City represented what Murillo Jr. describes as a "perfected form of economic exploitation and violence" (this volume), that is, Latino workers were welcomed as cheap labor but not as human beings with benefits and workers' rights, nor as people/ parents with families of their own who have education and health needs. As an African American resident explained about Latino workers, "They are the new slaves around here."

Many Hope City residents wanted the work and the business that Latinos/as brought, but not the cultural change that came along with the radically altered demographics. In other words, not only was the human being not welcomed, but also the cultural "difference" they represented was kept in check. Thus, there were racial discourses about how Mexicans change and "ruin" neighborhoods. A petition to the board of commissioners which circulated in Hope City, a year or so before I entered the field in 1994, complained about a street that had become "Little Mexico," which was characterized, according to the petitioners, by trash, loose animals, and excessive noise. The petitioners wanted extra police surveillance for "those people." In another example, the drive to "discipline the immigrant Other" (Murillo Jr., this volume) was also at the root of a pamphlet publication sponsored by the mostly non-Latino Hispanic Task Force, which outlined for Latinos/as the "do's and don'ts" of living in the community of Hope City.[9] As a member of an activist organization explained, the pamphlet was recalled after many complaints about its patronizing attitude toward Latinos/as (*Telemundo*, 1997).

The racialization of cultural difference was also keenly felt in the schools, where Latino children had been changing the demographic face of Hope City classrooms. I did not conduct on-site research in Hope City schools and classrooms, but the mothers I worked with spoke about their children's experiences in the schools and their own interactions with teachers. Although parents were grateful and appreciative of teachers' efforts, they also narrated experiences of insensitive as well as caring teachers. Even some of the caring teachers, at best, ignored cultural and language differences.[10] For example, Isabel, a mother of twins, a boy and a girl who were in kindergarten at that time, sadly explained how her children were ignored in the classroom: "*La maestra me dijo que no puede hacer nada por mis hijos que porque no hablan inglés, no entienden, ella no puede saber el conocimiento que tienen, o lo que no saben*" (The teacher told me that she couldn't do anything for my kids because they didn't speak English, they don't understand, she can't know the knowledge they have, or what they don't know). Ironically, university-educated Isabel was closest to the parenting model promoted in the mainstream parent involvement discourse (Lareau, 1989; Valdés, 1996), that is, she did "school-like" activities in the home such as reading to her children, teaching them the alphabet, and doing writing activities. Indeed, her children, like all the other young children of the women I worked with, were talkative, bright, and enthusiastic learners. But, by virtue of speaking Spanish rather than English, her children and other Latino children were denied a good and challenging education because their teacher could not communicate with them and could not build on their existing knowledge base. However, as a county advocate lawyer for Hope City Latinos/as explained, the most disastrous effects were at the high school level, where racism in the form of peer discrimination, institutional tracking, and inferior education for English language learners were rampant. Indeed the majority of Latino students were situated in the lowest tracks, and the unusually high dropout rate was under legal investigation.

Latinos/as as racialized workers and as schoolchildren were thus simultaneously checked, disciplined, and ignored. In addition to their treatment as "worker—not human," they were also discursively situated as clients among health, social service, and adult education professionals. Unlike the treatment of Latinos/as as "workers—not human beings," Latinos as "clients," on the other hand, were framed as needy human beings with race, class, and language differences with needs arising out of their immigrant worker and presumed noncitizen status. Professionals talked about their "plight" as victims of labor abuse and poverty, so that Latinos/as as "clients" were viewed through a needs-based lens. Ironically, in their client role, Latinos/as were again reduced to their plight rather than seen on their own terms as forgers of culture and community.[11]

LATINOS AS CLIENTS

Competing notions of Latino culture and child rearing were at the center of a study conducted in Hope City by Noblit et al. (1995). Interviews with professionals from health and social services, schools, the community college, and the police, were juxtaposed with my interviews of Latino parents and my ethnographic research in the Latino community. We found that the competing definitions of child-rearing practices, especially concerning what is right or appropriate, stemmed from both racializing discourses about difference and from diverse cultural frames of reference. For example, Latino parents approached their practice from the very personal, intimate responsibility to provide a strong moral education to children, teaching them about their roles and responsibilities in the family and community. The service providers, on the other hand, most often saw Latinos/as through the definition of "clients"—that is, through the organizational lens of particular agency concerns. Many of the well-meaning service providers used information from the public domain of child rearing, such as health needs, housing conditions, and questions of abuse or neglect, to talk about Latino families. Unfortunately these conversations about people with particular problems often turned to talk about Latinos/as as "problems" in themselves. In combination with racializing discourses about people who are poor, brown, Third World, and so on, Latino family lifestyles were negatively framed and, most insidiously, discussed in terms of what the parents didn't do, didn't have, or didn't care about (Noblit et al. 1995).

An example from my ethnographic data illustrates this divide between viewing families through agency concerns versus through the meanings families give to their own lives, especially the need to provide a moral education to their children. Lydia, who had recently arrived from Oaxaca with her two young daughters, joined her husband Ricardo to live in a two-bedroom apartment which was shared with two other families. The four of them slept together in one bedroom while the other families slept in the second bedroom and in the living room. Certainly, from a critical Latino activist lens, it becomes important to focus on the housing shortage as it is related to racism and housing discrimination against Latinos. Although this activist stance is extremely important, it risks viewing the family only through the lens of oppression, ignoring dynamic facets of life affirmed by Latinos/as that run alongside their needs. In other words, the "oppression" lens runs the risk of obscuring families' creative productions of culture and meanings. It runs the risk of obscuring what families find important and how they work to define and create joy in their lives.

Yet the "plight" lens becomes even more problematic. From an agency perspective, the focus became one of concern for the plight of people who are poor, as reflected e.g., in their crowded living arrangements. This concern quickly and easily slipped into narrow deficit views of Latino culture and family education. My field notes and reflection journal contain many uncomfortable moments of listening to service providers explain the problems of sanitation, health neglect, and bad "living conditions" in the Latino community (Villenas, 1996). Those conversations regularly turned to talk about these same families who "do not know any better," who were "uneducated," and who had gender relations that were "controlling" and "backward." A deficit and "less than" view of Latino child-rearing practices and family education quickly followed. Indeed, the line between viewing people with "needs" and viewing people with "deficits" is very thin for Latinos/as who are marked in the larger society by their race, class, language (Urciuoli, 1998), and citizenship status.

In returning to Lydia and her family, it is important to understand their cultural and social frame of reference and the meanings they gave to their lives as transnational laborers in the United States, as members of transnational extended families, and as educators of their children. For this family, their living arrangements were not their main concern. After Lydia and her daughters' harrowing travel experience crossing the border without legal documentation, Lydia was extremely happy to have arrived safely in Hope City and to be reunited with her husband Ricardo. Their main concerns now were to educate their daughters to be *noble* (of noble character) and *respetuosas* (respectful of their elders), and to protect them from what they perceived to be the dangers and licentiousness of U.S. society. Lydia explains: *"Veo que los niños de acá andan por la calle, vagan mucho. No me gusta que mis hijas salgan afuera, aveces pienso que los protejo demasiado, pero no me gusta que Karla esté afuera mucho"* (I see that the children here are out in the streets a lot, they loiter. I don't like for my girls to go outside a lot, sometimes I think that I overprotect them but I don't like for Karla to be outside too much). Among other things, Ricardo also said that knowing who they are and where they come from is important, *que no se olviden quienes son sus abuelos* (that they not forget who their grandparents are). In their conversations, Lydia and Ricardo viewed themselves as more than competent parents and as the best educators in their children's lives. According to them, they are the only ones who can teach their children who they are, and to have *respeto*. And they are the only ones who can guard them from the influences of U.S. society. From their lens, their family life is culturally intact (though constantly negotiated), and they must work at keeping it that way in the face of settlement in a culturally foreign terrain and in the face of racism and labor abuse. In contrast, from the point of view of agencies who saw "need," Lydia's family's cultural integrity was questioned in conversations that slipped into lack and deficit.

These conversations about lack and deficit, which were embedded in a "helping" discourse, marked Latino families as clients in racial and class terms. Lipsky (1980) argues that society takes the terms such as "welfare mom" as signals to treat people differently. Hope City newspaper headlines such as "Literacy Void" and "Program Enables Hispanic Women to Become Better Mothers" served as such signals, positioning Latinos/as as inferior. Indeed the zeal with which Latina mothers were solicited for the various health and social services programs unwittingly signaled to the public that Latinas were poor mothers and had poor child-rearing practices. In this manner, their client status worked alongside their brown skin, their Spanish language, their undocumented standing, and their working-class jobs to situate Lydia and her family, and indeed all Latino families, as lacking any cultural integrity and worth as parents/educators. Yet Latinos/as themselves engaged in conversations about education and child rearing outside of the worker and client frames. Latino parents vehemently defined, negotiated, and contested core definitions of *una buena educación* in a manner that went against deficit and needs-based views of their families.

UNA BUENA EDUCACIÓN

Monolithic views of Latino family education need to be replaced by an understanding of the complexity and creativity involved in the expressions, definitions, and practices of *una buena educación*. The education and rearing of children was a contested terrain among Latino families. This was true both with respect to the parents' own upbringing in their home countries and with respect to their beliefs and concerns about raising children in Hope City. The differences did not map on to "country" differences, but rather ran across family ecologies such as the makeup of the family, number of siblings, personalities, formal education, socioeconomic status, environment of upbringing, and rural and urban contexts, to name just a few. Nonetheless, the core of their definitions of education and the families' role in that effort centered on the moral education of their children and the centrality of parents and families in guiding that education.

As other Latino researchers have captured in their representations of Latino education,[12] *respeto* for parents and elders was the most critical element of a moral education. *Respeto* pointed to the primacy of relationships and the valuing of the wisdom of older family members. For children, respect was shown in the way one addressed parents, grandparents, and other adults. As Don Julio, a parent from El Salvador, remarked, "*Pues los consejos principalmente que tienen que respetar a las personas más grandes de edad, más viejos que ellos. . . . No insultar a las personas más viejas de edad que ellos*" (Well, the primary teaching is that [children] have to respect the elders, the people who are older than them). Likewise, Alba, a mother of five children, answered my query about her education in just one statement, "*Que no faltáramos respeto a los mayores,* [pause] *y eso nomás*" (That we not fail to respect our elders, [pause] and that is all). *Respeto* also worked in tandem with the values and morals of being polite, and not lying or stealing. Don Julio asserted that it was important to teach children "*que no agarren lo que no es de ellos*" (to not take what is not theirs), and "*para lo ageno hay que respetarlo, ante todo*" (one must respect what belongs to others first and foremost).

The teaching of a religious faith was also critical in the teaching of a moral education. Ricardo expressed these intertwining elements of *una buena educación,* giving centrality to *respeto*: "I instill in my girls also respect for elders, their language, most of all their language, to not be verbally disrespectful, not to take things that belong to others, . . . their religious education, to teach them to know god, about who is god and all that, and respect for dad and mom, and the grandparents, and most of all for them not to forget who their grandparents are, and, well, to give them the opportunity to study here."

In our conversation, Ricardo focused on *respeto* as he moved to talk about moral conduct, religiosity, respect for one's family, and, finally, schooling. As a parent he sacrificed to give his children the opportunity for formal schooling, something that would be difficult to attain on the *ejido* or the shared communal lands he had worked in Oaxaca.[13] Ricardo saw himself as fulfilling his role as a good parent in teaching his children respect first, and in giving them the opportunities to study in the United States.

Buen comportamiento, or good conduct, is intertwined with respect in terms of comporting oneself with dignity and in a manner that brings respect to the family and community. It includes a hard-work ethic; obedience; cleanliness; comportment in the roles of daughter, son, spouse, father or mother; and the curbing of selfish liberties. In her conversation about her wishes for the future of her boys, Alba repeatedly inserted the words, "*y que se porten bien*" (That they behave properly):

And for my sons, the same, that they be hard workers and that they grow up trying to obtain the things that are the most good in all the world, well how should I tell you. Well as persons, well what more would I wish for than for them *to behave properly,* behave very well, and when they're big and, and if they get to become adult, well to work and *not behave bad* and that they work to earn their money and if they get married well they get married and that *they behave well* with their wives . . . that they grow up and *behave well* as young adults and then later as husbands.

For Alba, her sons' *buen comportamiento* is connected to their future commitments to their roles as working adults, community members, and husbands. Respect for these relationships and for the roles that establish these demonstrates *buen comportamiento.*

Moreover, *buen comportamiento* is also gendered. For girls and women, *buen comportamiento* is connected to virtue in terms of being rooted in *el hogar,* being clean, practicing sexual abstinence until marriage, and in general garnering respect in their roles as little girls, unmarried daughters or single women, and then as wives. Alba echoed the sentiments of many Latina mothers in Hope City, in lovingly expressing how she would like her daughter Elvirita to be when she grew up: "*¿Qué yo más quisiera? Elvirita como niña, pues que cuando sea grande, pues [mira y acarisia a su niña]. ¿Cómo quisiera que fueras pues hija? Toda una niña y luego toda una señorita y luego toda una señora, verdad mija?*" (What would I most want? Elvirita who's a girl, well when she's big that [looks at her daughter and caresses her cheek]. How would I want you to be my daughter, all a little girl and then all a *señorita*, and then all a *señora*, isn't that right, my daughter?).

For Alba then, *buen comportamiento* encompassed a way of life, of living respectfully within the gendered rules of one's particular life stage for the sake of family and community. For girls and young women, this meant living according to one's marital status, guarding one's virginity, and being a good mother. Although western feminists may cringe at these prescribed notions, these lessons must also be understood outside of a simplistic view of women's deference to Latino patriarchy (Villenas, 2001). Racialized mothers teach their daughters both to fit into systems of oppression and to be critical of them (Collins, 1991). These lessons run alongside other *consejos*[14] that both perpetuate and subvert the effects of oppressive patriarchal and capitalist relations on working-class Latina mothers in the United States. As I have written elsewhere, the Latina mothers I worked with in Hope City rearticulated girls' *buen comportamiento* as cultural values rooted in what they perceived to be a "superior" Mexican, Guatemalan, or Salvadoran education (see Villenas, 2001; Villenas and Moreno, forthcoming). In the face of labor exploitation and both benevolent and xenophobic racisms in Hope City, Latina mothers articulated the centrality of *una buena educación* and a commitment to *el hogar*.

Further support for *respeto* and *buen comportamiento* as the defining parameters of a moral education is found not in the monolithic adherence to this education, but rather in its contestations, negotiations, and improvisations. Culture and cultural beliefs about child rearing and family education are not so much a set of shared values as they are a set of oppositions and emergent constructions (Noblit et al., 1995). In other words, it is fruitful to view the articulations of a moral education as what Latinos/as agreed to argue about, or what they have taken to be sufficiently important to engage in "dramatic conversations" about (Bellah et al., 1985). The curbing of hurtful behaviors and vices and the practice of self-discipline and respect were much disputed and struggled over in forging a first-generation community of Latinos/as in Hope City. Indeed, the racialized movement of labor across borders has influenced the ways in which women have been accustomed to rearing children. For example, the costs to working parents are intensified when children are not cared for by a larger community support system, as in their home countries. Alba emphasized in her life history that the children in her homeland are taught by all the people, "*el pueblo les enseña a vivir*" (the people teach the children how to live). Certainly the new social/cultural landscape and the changes in the family brought on by the globalization of capital and dominance of certain cultural forms has created new contestations and new imperatives in the child rearing of Hope City Latino parents.

The following conversation among Alba, Marisela, Lydia, and Rocío illustrates the ways in which parents, and mothers in particular, attempted to understand and make sense of raising children in a new community:

Lydia: In Mexico, you spent more time with the children. . . . The change is more difficult when the children grow up and they get used to life here.

Alba: We wish they could live like how we grew up.

Marisela: It's difficult the change, the schedule, the food. The biggest change they suffer through is at school, with the language. Even though they grow up in our environment, they absorb the customs from here. They'll suffer, humiliated.

Rocío: And the problem for us is that they won't understand us [laughs].

Alba: But then the children will learn the language [English] because they're little.

Marisela: And another difference is that here one works and the mothers neglect their responsibilities.

Rocío: For love, not because a lot of [mothers] neglect their responsibilities.

Alba: It's not to neglect the children but it's to give them everything.

Lydia: But the time that you do give, you make it good [laughs softly].

In their words, these mothers debated the consequences of assimilation and acculturation—*van a sufrir* (they'll suffer); the effects of English language hegemony—*No nos van a entender* (they [the children] won't understand us); the continuity and change of Latino cultural and moral education—*Quisieramos que vivieran como uno se crió* (We wish they could live like how we grew up); and their tenuous but strategic role in this education even as they doubled as working mothers in Hope City factories—*No es para descuidar a los niños, mas bien es para darles todo* (It's not to neglect the children but it's to give them everything). These uncertainties, contestations, and negotiations shaped how *una buena educación* was agreed to be argued about. Yet, as I explain in the next section, the background of these debates became the juxtaposition of their own "moral" education with their perceptions of a dangerous and "licentious" U.S. society.

ESTAR SIEMPRE AL PENDIENTE (TO ALWAYS BE VIGILANT)

Latino parents consistently brought out the themes of *peligro* (danger), *vicios* (vices), and *libertinaje* (licentiousness and lax morals) in our conversations. They expressed their concerns about raising their children in the United States, because they perceived there to be less strictness and more licentiousness in this country, a state of affairs that ran counter to their efforts to teach their children self-discipline and respect for others (Noblit et al., 1995). Yet, what do Latino parents mean when they speak negatively of *libertades* (liberties) and *libertinaje* (licentiousness)? *Doña* Natalia explained that raising children in North Carolina with *una buena educación* goes according to "*la libertad* that you give them." She further explained, "*Si se les da mucha libertad, yo pienso que se perderían . . . pero gracias a dios, siempre han estado a mando de nosotros*" (If you give them a lot of liberties, I think that they will probably be lost . . . but thanks be to God, they [our children] have always been under our will). Likewise, Ernestina explained, "*Yo pienso que los niños necesitan muchos consejos; cuando llegan a cierta edad, porque aquí en este país lo que yo veo que es, mucho problema sobre la droga, agarran mal camino*" (I think that children need a lot of advice, when they reach a certain age because here in this country, what I see is that there is a big problem with drugs, they get on the wrong path).

In their words, parents such as *Doña* Natalia and Ernestina responded to the dangers of society by requiring children to be *al mando*, under the control of parents, and to receive their *consejos*. Parents also had to always be *al pendiente* (vigilante). As Alba explains, "*Aca nomás se está al pendiente de todo con mas preocupaciones, y que llegue el camión por ellos, y estar pendiente que lleguen*" (here one always has to be vigilant of everything, with more worries, that the [school bus] comes for them, and you have to be vigilant that they come home). Parents believed good child rearing entailed curbing liberties, such as hanging out and dating, that would put their children at risk. Mothers in particular feared for their daughters to grow up in a country of moral laxness which competed with their teachings regarding women's virtue and sexuality. For example, Rocío juxtaposed the moral education of her rural town in Mexico with that of the United States: "Well, in Mexico, the advice they give you is, for example, when they start to have boyfriends, 'no, don't be going with your boyfriend [laughs] or you might end up with your *domingo siete* like they say in Mexico when they get pregnant.' And here, well it's normal. . . . And in Mexico it's not the same. Life is very different there. . . . There's it's very rare to see a woman smoking." From Maria's words it is clear that she believed the United States to be morally lax, that is, premarital sex is "normal," and women smoke and drink. Maria's words, however, should not indicate that in Mexico, unmarried girls do not get pregnant, that sexual promiscuity is nonexistent, and that drug and alcohol abuse do not exist. These were certainly very prevalent in their own countries and in their own personal lives. But there are two important points in the parents' descriptions of U.S. society as licentious. The first is simply that these were ideologies defining the parameters of what was to be debated. Again, this is the notion of considering what Latinos/as agree to argue about—or in the case of racialized

Latino mothers, to examine how Latino patriarchy and U.S. racism have shaped what they agreed to argue about. It suffices to look at the cultural differences between something as innocuous as Latin American *telenovelas* and U.S. soap operas to note how virginity and premarital sex are points of debate in the former but not the latter (or at least not under the same assumptions). Moreover, it is also important to note that Maria's comments about Latinas' lowered consumption of alcohol, drugs, and tobacco hold some validity according to research on Latina immigrant women's health (Hayes-Bautista, 2000).

My second point, however, considers not the "truth" of their perceptions, as U.S. and Latin American cultural and moral conduct is much too complex a discussion for this chapter, but rather the source and real effects of Latino parents' strategic assertions of difference.[15] Latino parents' fears, while certainly based on stereotypes often learned through the U.S. media, were also rooted in changing patterns of child rearing in the absence of a community support network and of familiar cultural frames of reference. Their fears also stemmed from the changes in the family, including transnational mothering (Hondagneu-Sotelo and Avila, 1997; Hondagneu-Sotelo, 2000) brought on by migration and new forms of labor participation.[16]

Thus, in the face of their deficit framing in the public sphere as "worker-not human" and/or as "needy client," Latino parents strategically created boundaries, "othering" *los Americanos*, to value their roles as parent-educators, and thus to value their own *buena educación*. As previously argued, labor exploitation and racism structured these education conversations in Hope City (cf. Villenas, 2001). Latina mothers' appropriation of *el hogar* and the teaching of a moral education was practiced alongside the public difficulties they faced (i.e., overcrowded housing, illiteracy, etc.). Indeed, it is unfortunate that the ways in which Latinos/as juxtaposed *una buena educación* with their perceptions of a morally lax U.S. society was missed by service providers who reduced Latino families to their "plight," who reified western-based views of child rearing, and who unwittingly denied Latinos/as their cultural integrity and worth as good parents. Sound parental goals and viable practices were instead misconstrued as problems.

REINVENTING *RESPETO*: PEDAGOGIES OF CHANGE AND CONTINUITY

To be *al pendiente* (vigilant), to give *consejos,* and to enforce discipline in varying ways became crucial for providing *una buena educación* in a culturally alien community, with no previous examples of parents successfully raising southeastern Latino youth. Parents like Neli spoke with confidence, or perhaps worried bravado, "*no importa que se crien acá, van a tener las mismas costumbres de uno*" (it doesn't matter that they're raised here, they'll have our same customs). They struggled with changing and/or re-creating the ways in which they themselves had experienced *educación* in their home countries. *Respeto*, for example, had to be renegotiated in the ways in which parents and children communicated and related to each other. José, a father of three and newly arrived from Colombia, explained that parent-child relationships of his generation were not open and the facts of life were clouded in mystery: "My time was one in which parents weren't as open as they are today, in teaching their children. In other words . . . they didn't have that broad, far reaching scope that exists today to speak to the children. In other words, for us children of a prior generation, everything was a mystery, a mystery that one had to forcefully uncover."

José went on to express how he relates to his children differently, with more open communication, so that the cycle of mystery is broken. Lydia expressed a similar sentiment and need in wanting to establish a different kind of relationship with her children: "*Necesito saber como contestar las preguntas, hablándoles y hacerles entender. Yo no quiero que me tengan miedo si no respeto*" (I need to learn how to answer their questions, talking with them and making them understand. I don't want them to have fear of me, but instead respect). Certainly, as Lydia points out, reinventing *respeto* in parent-child relationships meant doing away with the fear characteristic of previous generations and instilling *confianza* (trust). As Norma explained, in these days and times, *cariño* (love) and *respeto* must be placed alongside *confianza* so that children learn about the facts of life from their parents:

Well, the important thing is love for others, and respect. And the trust to tell me whatever, anything. If it's that they like or don't like what I do or don't do, they should tell me, confide in me. . . . "No" I tell them, "I'm your mother and I'm due respect and love, but I'm also owed trust," I tell them. . . . "Because if you don't tell me, that's the error," I tell my kids "the parents who come from our countries, they don't give their kids the trust the kid needs to confide in them, to express themselves in front of them. . . ." I tell them, "not me, no, that's left to the past." Like I say, I let them, I give them the liberty to express themselves how they want to me. Because, well if one gives them trust, then they'll have the trust to talk to you. . . . I've even advised them about sexuality . . . my husband is embarrassed to do that. I talk to my children.

In her narrative, Norma very eloquently performed how she talked to her children, exemplifying how one needs to speak in order to instill *confianza* in her children. This *confianza* required a give and take from parents and a loosening of authority in communication patterns: "*que me digan a mi lo que sea, cualquier cosa. Si sea que no les guste o que les guste, de lo que hago o de lo que no hago*" ([And the trust] to tell me whatever, anything. If it's that they like or don't like what I do or don't do). Indeed, Norma, like José and Lydia, was breaking away from previous generational patterns of parent-child communication, but doing so while still maintaining children *al mando* and curbing liberties in a licentious U.S. society. Certainly, in Latin America, changes in child rearing and parent-child relationships are also occurring, but the terms and the context for engaging in these "dramatic conversations" (Bellah et al., 1985) are different in North Carolina. An education they had previously taken for granted now needed to be articulated and renegotiated as an urgent response required of them in Hope City, in the face of the cultural assaults on their dignity and integrity as human beings and as parents/educators of a moral education.

CONCLUSION: IMPLICATIONS FOR POLICY

Although members of the Latino diaspora in traditional regions of Latino set-tlement, such as the Southwest, are also reinventing themselves and their family education, Latinos/as in North Carolina and other non-traditional areas of mi-gration are presented with a unique challenge as creators and forgers of new Latino communities. Culturally relevant models of rearing children in rural southern communities were absent for Latino parents settling in Hope City and raising future generations of bicultural Latinos/as. In the context of the southeast where "there is no Alamo to remember, nor occupied territories to claim, nor a legendary Aztlán to recreate" (Murillo and Villenas, 1997), new generations of North Carolinian Latinos/as, or as yet unnamed Chicanos/as, are challenged to reinvent new narratives of group identities and solidarities. Pedagogies of cultural continuity and change, which are collectively determined by North Carolinian Latino parents, are central to reaffirming cultural integrity, including the work of community building and activism awaiting this new generation of southeastern Latino/Chicano youth. In Hope City, negotiation, improvisation, and contesta-tions in the processes of *una buena educación* reaffirmed this cultural integrity in working to resist the cultural denigration and racism that both structured and reinforced the "public difficulties" Latinos/as experienced.

These public difficulties—renamed as labor exploitation, housing discrimina-tion, linguicism (language racism), public health neglect, educational marginal-ization, and so forth—cannot be ignored, even as this chapter calls for attention to the creative resilience and cultural productions emanating from Latino fami-lies. Policymakers in the areas of education, health, and social services are chal-lenged to address the symptoms (and sometimes the root) of structural inequality by understanding and learning from the cultural and social processes of Latino families. Massey, Zambrana, and Bell argue this point:

Policy that seeks to strengthen Latino families rather than debilitate them must be guided by a long-term preventive orientation that places families at the center of the intervention and within the context of their neighborhoods and communities. Furthermore, children must be viewed and treated as part of families. For their optimal growth and development, children require strong, stable and consistent supportive and nurturing relationships. (1995, 202)

However, rather than strengthening families, what we have seen in Hope City is a deficit framing of Latino families on the part of well-meaning providers who sought to "help" Latino parents in their "plight."

Latino parents in Hope City wanted to depart from the *buena educación* traditions that they had grown up with (in other places), but only modestly and on their own terms. Although perhaps few Latino parents would articulate it quite this way, the parents were frustrated by the unnecessary dichotomized choices with which they were confronted—the U.S. way or the Mexico way, English or Spanish, mainstream or deficit, even "school is an opportunity" versus "school is a problem." The changes in the *educación* of their children that they were seeking were no doubt influenced by the ideas in circulation in the Hope City public sphere that they were now a part of, but they hardly matched the deficit and assimilationist frame espoused by well-meaning care providers. Noblit et al. (1995) succinctly summarized the kinds of negative reframings and monolithic views held by Hope City educators and care providers about Latino family life: "The agencies saw Latino families as too large, Latina mothers as not fully competent, Latino men as not participating in child rearing and as 'macho.' The service agencies also saw Latino families as focusing on 'respect for elders' and using corporal punishment to teach this. In the service providers' views, corporal punishment was associated with child abuse. Finally, service providers viewed negatively the role of Latinas (women) as servants of the men, and they judged the use of older siblings to supervise younger siblings as irresponsible." These views disabled Latino families in their relationships with professionals by publicly questioning their cultural integrity and by dismissing them as good and competent educators for their children.

Respecting Latino parents' agency is crucial. That means taking on the easy task of rejecting overt xenophobia when Latinos/as are framed as "workers—not humans," as well as the more difficult task of recognizing and challenging the paternalism and colonialism of benevolent racism when Latinos/as are framed as "clients." It also means not substituting a third script on behalf of Latinos/as— be it a script that promotes traditional Mexican values, an inclusive multiculturalism, or something else. Although I find multicultural respect and equal opportunity to be important and unrealized goals for Hope City, they are not goals that can be realized by edict. Instead, a just vision of education and social change in Hope City requires the legitimate honoring of Latino parents' human agency. It requires respecting their right to guide their children's upbringing and to retain various traditional, coherent goals for their children, even as they modify or question others. At a minimum, this requires replacing the articulation of policy *for* Latino parents with the more restrained articulation of policy *with* the new Latino diaspora.[17]

NOTES

This chapter is written with deep gratitude to the Latino parents of Hope City, to the Hope City activists, and to George Noblit and the research team funded by the Frank Porter Graham Child Development Center at UNC-Chapel Hill. I would like to thank Stanton Wortham and Ted Hamann for their invaluable help and patience.

1. All names of places and peoples are pseudonyms. Enrique G. Murillo Jr. refers to the same town which I call Hope City, with the pseudonym of Sunder Crossings (see Murillo Jr., this volume).

2. Actress Frances Bauvier, who played Aunt Bea in the *Andy Griffith Show*, chose to live out her retirement in Hope City.

3. *Taquerías* is translated as taco stands, and *tiendas* refers to Latino stores.

4. See Levinson, Foley, and Holland's (1996) description of the cultural production of the educated person.

5. I collected data in Hope City from January 1994 through the spring of 1996. Data collection consisted of tape-recorded oral life histories of 21 Latino parents (including those of 11 mothers whom I worked closely with over the two years); participant observations in English as a second language classes, social events, community meetings, school meetings, and church gatherings; and reviews of public documents and newspapers.

6. This organization provides occupational health services to the workers of the major poultry factories in Hope City.

7. *Telemundo* came to Hope City to do a special report centered on North Carolina Mexican migration that was subsequently widely broadcast in Mexico and in the United States. The fact that reporters and cameras from a major Mexican television station were in Hope City went largely unnoticed in the small town's English-speaking community. Latino residents, however, were well aware of the significance of the presence of *Telemundo*. In their interviews, they gave blasting critiques of work conditions at the poultry plants and of the racism they encountered in the town on a daily basis (also see Murillo Jr., 1999).

8. All quotes were originally in Spanish. For a few longer quotes, the editors have removed the Spanish text in order to save space.

9. The Hispanic Task Force had only one Latino member—a professional from South America who did not represent the largely working-class Latino population coming from rural Mexico.

10. It is important to recognize that there were some educators in Hope City schools who truly respected Latinos/as and often went out on a limb to be advocates for Latino family cultural and linguistic rights.

11. Foley gives an example of the "minority despair" discourse and how people are publicly portrayed in their supposed "plight." A picture of two Mesquaki children playing on their front porch was captioned in a newspaper article in the following way: "Mesquaki Indian children in the settlement near Tama, whose eyes reflect the plight and despair of their parents" (1995, 91). Foley showed this newspaper picture to the tribal historian, Jonas Cutcrow, who exclaimed, "Hey, that's my niece and nephew on their grandma's porch!" As Foley recounts it, they both laughed at the surprised look on his nephew's face who was probably wondering what the white guy was doing taking pictures.

12. See Delgado-Gaitan (1992, 1996), Suárez-Orozco and Suárez-Orozco (1995), and Valdés (1996), among others.

13. Primary education in Mexico was practically universally available, though often with limited resources, whereas *secundaria* (secondary/middle school), despite now being mandatory, and *preparatoria* (high school) are less commonly accessible, particularly in rural regions. See Hamann (1999).

14. Concha Delgado-Gaitan (1994) provides an academic definition of *consejos* as cultural narratives, homilies, or narrative advice.

15. I would like to thank Troy Richardson for helping me articulate this point.

16. Many Latina mothers had left one or more of their children in their home countries. Conversely, I also worked with transnational families where the mother was in Latin America and the father was in North Carolina joined by a few children and a trusted sister, aunt, or grandmother who could take on a mothering role.

17. I would like to thank Ted Hamann for his contribution to this conclusion and for rearticulating my thoughts.

REFERENCES

Alanís, Maria Fabiola. 1999. *Michoacanos: Esclavos Tras la Frontera*. Unpublished manuscript. University of Utah, Salt Lake City.

Bellah, Robert N., Richard Madsen, William M. Sullivan, Ann Swidler, and Steven M. Tipton. 1985. *Habits of the Heart*. Berkeley: University of California Press.

Collins, Patricia Hill. 1991. *Black Feminist Thought: Knowledge, Consciousness, and the Politics of Empowerment*. New York: Routledge.

Delgado-Gaitan, Concha. 1992. "School Matters in the Mexican American Home: Socializing Children to Education." *American Educational Research Journal*. 29(3):495–513.

———. 1994. "Consejos: The Power of Cultural Narratives." *Anthropology and Education Quarterly*. 25(3):298–316.

———. 1996. *Protean Literacy: Extending the Discourse on Empowerment*. London: Falmer Press.

Foley, Doug. 1995. *The Heartland Chronicles*. Philadelphia: University of Pennsylvania Press.

Griffith, David. 1995. "*Hay Trabajo*: Poultry Processing, Rural Industrialization, and the Latinization of Low-Wage Labor." In *Any Way You Cut It: Meat-Processing and Small-Town America*. Donald D. Stull, Michael J. Broadway, and David Griffiths, eds. Pp. 129–151. Lawrence: University of Kansas Press.

Hamann, Edmund T. 1999. "The Georgia Project: A Binational Attempt to Reinvent a School District in Response to Latino Newcomers." Unpublished dissertation. University of Pennsylvania, Philadelphia.

Hayes-Bautista, David. 2000. Paper presented at Latinos in the 21st Century titled "Mapping the Research Agenda." Cambridge: Harvard University, David Rockefeller Center for Latin American Studies, April 6–8.

Hondagneu-Sotelo, Pierrette. 2000. "The International Division of Caring and Cleaning Work: Transnational Connections or Apartheid Exclusions?" In *Care Work: Gender, Labor and the Welfare State*. Madonna Harrington Myer, ed. Pp. 149–323. New York: Routledge.

Hondagneu-Sotelo, Pierrette and Ernestine Avila. 1997. "'I'm Here, But I'm There': The Meanings of Latina Transnational Motherhood." *Gender and Society*. 11(5):548–571.

Lareau, Annette. 1989. *Home Advantage*. London: Falmer Press.

Levin, Kimberly, Lia Rolon, Karen Schlanger, Meredith Smith, and Jon Warkentin. 1995. "A Community Diagnosis of the Latino Community in Hope City. Secondary Data Document." School of Public Health, University of North Carolina, Chapel Hill.

Levinson, Bradley A., Douglas E. Foley, and Dorothy C. Holland, eds. 1996. *The Cultural Production of the Educated Person: Critical Ethnographies of Schooling and Local Practice*. Albany: State University of New York Press.

Lipsky, Martin. 1980. *Street Level Bureaucracy: Dilemmas of the Individual in Public Services*. New York: Russell Sage Foundation.

Massey, Douglas S., Ruth E. Zambrana, and Sally Alonzo Bell. 1995. "Contemporary Issues in Latino Families: Future Directions for Research, Policy, and Practice." In *Understanding Latino Families: Scholarship, Policy, and Practice*. Ruth E. Zambrana, ed. Pp. 190–204. Thousand Oaks, CA: Sage Publications.

Murillo, Enrique, Jr. This volume. "How Does it Feel to Be a *Problem?*: Disciplining the Transnational Subject in the American South." In *Education, Policy, and the Politics of Identity in the New Latino Diaspora*. Stanton Wortham, Enrique G. Murillo Jr., and Edmund T. Hamann, eds. Westport, CT: Ablex Publishing Group.

———. 1999. "Growing Pains: Cartographies of Change, Contestation and Social Division in North Carolina." Unpublished dissertation. University of North Carolina, Chapel Hill.

Murillo, Enrique, Jr. and Sofia Villenas. 1997. "East of Aztlán: Typologies of resistance in North Carolina Communities." Paper presented at "Reclaiming Voice: Ethnographic Inquiry and Qualitative Research in a Postmodern Age," Los Angeles.

Noblit, George, Sofia Villenas, Amee Adkins, Gretchen Givens, and Monica McKinney. 1995. "Latino Cultures and Services Study: Perspectives on Children and Families. Final Report." Frank Porter Graham Child Development Center, Chapel Hill, North Carolina.

Suárez-Orozco, Carola and Marcelo Suárez-Orozco. 1995. *Transformations: Migration, Family Life, and Achievement Motivation among Latino Adolescents*. Stanford: Stanford University Press.

Suárez-Orozco, Marcelo and Doris Sommer. 2000. "Becoming Latinos." *David Rockefeller Center for Latin American Studies News*. Spring: 3–5.

Telemundo. 1997. *Jornada en Carolina del Norte*. Mexico City.

Urciuoli, Bonnie. 1998. *Exposing Prejudice: Puerto Rican Experiences of Language, Race, and Class*. Boulder: Westview Press

Valdés, Guadalupe. 1996. Con Respeto: *Bridging the Distance between Culturally Diverse Families and Schools*. New York: Teachers College Press.

Villenas, Sofia. 1996. "The Colonizer/Colonized Chicana Ethnographer: Identity, Marginalization and Co-optation in the Field." *Harvard Educational Review*. 66(4):711–731.

———. 2000. "Latina Womanist Pedagogies in Transborder Settlement: Mother/Daughter Teachings of *Valerse Por Si Misma*." Symposium paper presented at the annual meeting of the American Educational Research Association. New Orleans, April 24–28.

———. 2001. "Latina Mothers and Small Town Racisms: Creating Narratives of Dignity and Moral Education in North Carolina." *Anthropology and Education Quarterly*. 32(1):3–28.

Villenas, Sofia, Donna Deyhle, and Laurence Parker. 1999. "Critical Race Theory and Praxis: Chicano(a)/Latino(a) and Navajo Struggles for Dignity, Educational Equity, and Social Justice." In *Race Is . . . Race Isn't: Critical Race Theory and Qualitative Studies in Education.* Laurence Parker, Donna Deyhle, and Sofia Villenas, eds. Pp. 31–52. Boulder: Westview Press.
Villenas, Sofia and Melissa Moreno. Forthcoming. "To *valerse por si misma* (be self reliant): Between Race, Patriarchy, and Capitalism, Latina Mother/Daughter Pedagogies in North Carolina." *International Journal of Qualitative Studies in Education.*

3

Recent Language Minority Education Policy in Georgia: Appropriation, Assimilation, and Americanization

Scott A.L. Beck and Martha Allexsaht-Snider

This chapter provides a case history of language minority educational policy in the New Latino Diaspora. Policy development for English language learners is examined in the context of America's more general "culture wars" (Gates, 1992), where policymakers and educators continue debate over who we have been, who we are, and who we are to become as a nation and a people. In this case, from the state of Georgia, policymakers have used coded language to erect what Foucault (1977) revealed to be a "positivist façade" over a language minority educational policy actually based in conservative discourses and folk linguistics. We analyze the ways in which anti-immigrant rhetoric and antibilingual/proassimilationist ideologies directed language policy development in Georgia from 1994 to 2000. The case study illustrates the ways in which students, teachers, and local educational professionals have been marginalized as Foucauldian "objects of policy." In the end, the study illustrates the ways in which the language ideology of a single elected state official and her senior appointees has been replicated and spread through an educational system with deleterious results for many Hispanic students across the state. The study also illustrates a few of the limited ways in which resistance to this ideology has thus far been able to find voice in the classrooms of Georgia.

We begin this case study by contextualizing it within the literature of language minority policy studies. Then we address the history of immigration and language minority education in the South and Georgia in particular. Next, we describe local newspaper[1] and national media representations of southerners' responses to the recent Latino[2] influx in the context of the rhetoric of U.S. English and other English-only initiatives. Then we analyze the influence of

anti-immigrant discourses at multiple levels (media, state politics, local actions) on Georgia policy regarding language minority education. Finally, we
describe how the Georgia Department of Education was "taken over" by U.S.
English sympathizers, and we outline ways in which this political change has
resulted in a continued lack of services for English language learning students
in Georgia schools.

TWO GAPS IN LANGUAGE MINORITY POLICY STUDIES

Two gaps in language minority policy studies are addressed in the following
case study: the rapidly increasing number of new incidence immigrant populations and the influence of language ideologies, or folk linguistics, in policy formation and implementation. Regarding the first, one can ask whether the
educational experiences of immigrant newcomers in locations only newly experiencing immigration are akin to the experiences of immigrants in sites that
have long received newcomers. Regarding the second, one can ask how the
salient beliefs of policymakers regarding language, identity, and language education diverge from current linguistic and educational research.

Language minority education policy studies have been preoccupied with the
ongoing search for "a single best method" to teach school-aged English language
learners.[3] This debate has tended to focus almost exclusively on areas with large,
long-established populations of immigrant and non-English speaking families.
States and urban localities such as California, Texas, Arizona, Colorado, Florida,
New York City, Chicago, and Washington, DC, have occupied researchers and
policymakers for the valid reason that these have been the places with the greatest numbers of English language learners. Numerous models for instruction have
been developed in locales with large immigrant populations. However, research
on how to apply these models in new incidence regions of the "New Latino Diaspora" (Villenas and Hamann, 1997) such as the Southeast has been scant (for
exceptions, see Villenas, Deyhle, and Parker, 1999; Center for Applied Linguistics, 1999; Carnuccio, 2000).

Arguments and research regarding the various instructional models—bilingual
education versus English for speakers of other languages (ESOL) versus sink-or-
swim submersion—have raged across academic journals, op-ed pages, and voter
proposition ballots for many years. Despite the appearance that these arguments
are about classroom practice, the debate has not been a research-based discussion
over pedagogy (Freeman, 2000). Donaldo Macedo writes, "The present attack on
bilingual education should not be understood as a simple critique of methodolo-
gies. First, and foremost, the present assault on bilingual education is fundamentally political" (2000, 16) and a manifestation of a colonial ideology toward
language minorities in the United States (Diwan, 1999; Memmi, 1967). Under-

standing the political nature of the debate is crucial, for as René Galindo (1997) asserts, we need a better understanding of how language ideology or "folk models" of linguistics (Niedzielski and Preston, 1999) influence language minority education policy.

A recent, widely publicized example of a politicized argument affecting policy is the success of Ron Unz's Proposition 227 in dismantling bilingual instruction across California. In the campaign leading up to the vote, many of Unz's assertions appealed to the general public because they were based in "folk models" of language and linguistics.[4] Unz maneuvered to counter research-oriented challenges to his political agenda by writing of education research in the *New York Times* that "it's all garbage" (Greene, 1998). Still, his antibilingual rhetoric was greatly persuasive to a voting public that shared his folk linguistics. The opposing discourse from bilingual education advocates appeared counterintuitive to the monolingual majority (Crawford, 1997, 14).

THEORETICAL FRAMES AND RESEARCHER ORIENTATIONS

We invoke a sociocultural approach to the study of educational policy, as advocated by Levinson and Sutton (2001). In order to examine the political dynamics of Georgia's language minority education policy process, we have found the concept of "symbolic violence" to be useful (Shannon and Escamilla, 1999). Shannon and Escamilla base their theoretical framework in the work of both Pierre Bourdieu (1991) and Rudolfo Acuña (1995). Bourdieu's "symbolic power" is exemplified by colonial domination, wherein the colonizer imposes its language and culture on the colonized through "coercion and condescension, although both the colonizer and the colonized do not recognize it as such" (Shannon and Escamilla, 1999, 348). Acuña's coded language "is a part of the ideological strategy of Euroamerican elites, serving to justify their domination of communities of color while disguising openly racist sentiments" (1995, xix). Together, with coded language masking symbolic power, these concepts explain symbolic violence as "the symbolic power that use of language can wield when positions of power are dramatically asymmetrical . . . [especially] forms of language that appear benign or neutral when in fact they are offensive and target specific people" (Shannon and Escamilla, 1999, 349).

In the following case study, we link analyses of media and political symbolic violence toward immigrants with analyses of symbolic power and violence in Georgia Department of Education staff rhetoric. This linkage demonstrates how a critical sociocultural analysis can provide educators with tools for challenging and reconceptualizing problematic policy. This understanding, when combined with a recognition of the ways in which local educators can use federal civil rights legislation to reassert democratic principals of inclusion, participation, and autonomy, can offer a road map to others as educators negotiate educational policy terrain.

Coauthor Scott Beck has had extensive opportunities for participant-observation and the development of an "insider's perspective" regarding Georgia's language minority educational policy. During the five years from 1994 to 1999, Scott worked as an outreach worker and curriculum coordinator for a federally funded, Georgia Department of Education-administered, regional migrant education agency. His work entailed facilitating communication between migrant parents and students, local schoolteachers and administrators, and regional and state educational bureaucracies. He made hundreds of visits to schools and thousands of visits to migrant farmworkers' homes, trailers, work camps, and shacks. Because his work for Migrant Education spanned the change in state superintendents of education and the attendant shifts in personnel and ideology, he witnessed firsthand the entrance of English-only sympathizers at the highest levels of the Georgia state educational establishment. He attended dozens of official and unofficial meetings between state, regional, and local school administrators. He left his full-time work in the migrant education program in 1999, when his job and the jobs of others were targeted by top administrators in the state Department of Education, as is described later in this chapter. Beck's field notes from specific meetings, work experiences in general, and correspondence and informal interviews with Georgia educators served as data sources for our analysis. In addition, oral history interviews that coauthor Beck has conducted with some of the first Mexican-American migrants to settle in rural south Georgia (Beck, 1999) have also informed this case study.

The second author, Martha Allexsaht-Snider, has worked in the field of bilingual education and ESOL in states with significant Latino populations (Arizona, California, and Colorado) for 25 years. She continues to conduct ethnographic research with administrators, teachers, and parents in school districts in southern California and Arizona that serve large populations of Latino students. Her move to a university college of education in Georgia in 1991 coincided with the rise of Hispanic populations in the Southeast. Allexsaht-Snider's role in Georgia has been that of concerned citizen and researcher, as programs for new immigrants have developed at the state and local level. At the university level, she has helped establish a cross-national teacher-training program that brings Georgia teachers and education students to Mexico and Mexican educators to Georgia each year. Through this work she has developed a perspective on Georgia educators' attempts to understand, appropriate, and resist state and local policies regarding the education of English language learners.

It is important to note that neither of us is a native Georgian or southerner. In fact, we both trace our roots to upstate New York. Thus, although we have extensive insider knowledge to help inform this study, we are not complete insiders. We have attempted to stay within our data, experiences, sources, and references. Nonetheless, we have little doubt that our perspectives as transplants to Georgia have influenced our interpretation and that native Georgians would offer different perspectives.

ARRIVAL IN *"EL NUEVO SUR"*[5]

In seeking to understand what has happened as the New Latino Diaspora came to Georgia, it is important to note the historical context of the South. The southeastern region of the United States did not receive the Great Immigration of the late 1800s and early 1900s that changed the face of many other regions of the United States.[6] In fact, the population of the South was, from the expulsion of Native Americans via the Trail of Tears in the 1830s until very recently, nearly exclusively defined by two English-speaking groups: Northern-European-descent whites and African American blacks.

Thus, Georgia had minimal prior experience with immigrants and immigrant education to help prepare for the sudden increase in immigrant population that has occurred since the 1970s. From 1970 to 1990, the percentage of foreign-born Georgians nearly tripled to 2.7 percent and is growing at an accelerating pace (U.S. Census Bureau, 1999). Particularly noteworthy was the sudden increase in Mexican immigrants. Mexican immigrants were not even among the top 10 foreign-born groups in Georgia in 1980. But in 1990, after a one-decade population increase of approximately 1,300 percent (U.S. Census Bureau, 1990), they were by far the state's largest immigrant group and comprised the majority of Hispanic immigrants.

Georgia's dramatic increase in immigration, especially Mexican-American immigration, did not stop in 1990. According to the anti-immigrant group Federation for American Immigration Reform (FAIR), "Census Bureau reports show that Georgia had the highest rate of growth (93.5%) in immigrant population of any state between 1990 and 1994" (FAIR, 2000). As during the 1980s, the better portion of growth in the 1990s is attributable to Latino, especially Mexican, immigration (Capelouto, 2000; Badie, 1999a).[7]

GEORGIA: *"HABLAN ESPAÑOL, Y'ALL?"*

This influx of immigrants has largely been driven by economic and social changes. Industrialization, urbanization, the Civil Rights movement, and governmental social programs have allowed many poor southern whites and blacks to leave low-paying, difficult jobs in fields, factories, and construction (Griffith, 1995). For example, by the 1970s southern farmers found that it was increasingly difficult to find enough hands to bring in the harvest (Hutcheson, 1995).

Contemporary white and black Americans have been reluctant "to do farm labor, even if it means unemployment. The jobs require backbreaking work and hundreds of miles of travel and the pay is low" (Anderson, 1998, 5C).

Thus, farmers in the Southeast, out of necessity, began to look to Mexican-Americans from the Southwest to fill their labor needs (Hamann, 1999; Griffith, Kissam, and Camposeco, 1995). Recruitment of Mexicans and Mexican-Americans, especially from the Rio Grande valley, brought entire families to work in the fields and packing sheds. This practice of hiring families followed patterns from both historical sharecropping in the South and Mexican-American migrancy in the southwestern, midwest and western regions of the United States (Donato, 1997). Thus, many school-aged, Mexican-heritage, English language learners suddenly arrived in the rural South and began to attend school. Tentatively at first, and then with enthusiasm, Georgia's farmers hired migrant crew leaders to bring in Hispanic crews. As the farmers realized that the Mexican-heritage migrants would work long, hard hours for minimal pay, they began to find year-round work for a few of them in the barn or with other field crops.

With time, non–farm employers in the region also employed large numbers of Latinos. For example, as of 1998, 32 to 40 percent of all poultry processing workers in Georgia, depending on the particular plant, were Latino (Townley, Demedeiros, and Rundell, 1998). The construction industry of Greater Atlanta has become similarly dependent on Mexican and Mexican-American labor. "Without Latinos, construction would grind to a halt" in the Atlanta metro region, according to National Public Radio's Susanna Capelouto (2000). The attractiveness of Latinos to southern agricultural, construction and industrial employers was explained by Paul Cuadros (2000): "The labor is cheap and pliable because many Hispanic immigrants are undocumented. Companies take advantage of that legal status with low wages, little or no benefits, and the knowledge that they will not complain of harsh treatment. . . . A new South is rising indeed, but it is being built with Latino hands."

The face of the South has changed permanently. *Taquerías* and *bailes* are here to stay in the heart of Dixie. As a cover story in the *Atlanta Journal-Constitution*'s Business Section put it, "*Hablan Español*, Y'all? The South Is Acquiring a New Accent" (*Atlanta Journal-Constitution*, 1998, P1) The relatively insular, historically black and white communities of the South, especially of rural Georgia, have never experienced an influx of outsiders like that of the Mexican-Americans. "Georgia is experiencing a wave of immigration unlike anything since the colonial era. . . . [This is] the most significant social and cultural upheaval in Georgia since the early days of racial desegregation" (*Athens Daily News*, 1999). Leah Totten, a sociologist with economic analysts MDC, Inc. comments: "In the South, we're in the situation where what is basically a biracial community that was still dealing with issues of prejudice has now become a multiracial community. . . . The problem this presents socially is that the black and white communities at least know each other. We've been working with these problems for hundreds of years. . . . Now there is a new group that does not speak the same language, and the social tensions have increased" (Pressley, 2000).

"SHE'S NOT BLACK. SHE'S NOT WHITE. WHAT IS SHE?"

Clear examples of the social uncertainty and mental dissonance created among locals by the presence of Hispanics can be found in Mexican-American children's reminiscences of arrival:

When [we first came,] I went and got my shots at the clinic, the little slip there said that I was Black. But then, here at the school, they put me as White. . . . One time, in my homeroom they were trying to select the homecoming queen [nominees]. They have a Black [queen] and a White [queen] here. One of the Black girls nominated me. The homeroom teacher said, "She's not Black." A boy asked "Well, she's not Black, she's not White, what is she?" She said "Spanish." "Where does that fall?" I don't think that she exactly knew the answer to that. (Alvarez,[8] 1999)

In Southern society where *race*, defined as either *black or white*, had for centuries been the primary determinant of the possibilities and limits of one's life; in a place where centuries of forced enslavement were followed by decades of Jim Crow; in school systems that, less than ten years earlier, had finally (and usually reluctantly) implemented the edicts of *Brown v. Board of Education*—in such a context, the introduction of a *brown* child whose language and culture were unknown was highly disruptive. "A biracial system of etiquette has no provision for a third race" (Loewen, 1971, 73).

THE SOUTH, ANTI-IMMIGRANT HOSTILITY, AND OFFICIAL ENGLISH

Challenges to a long-established social order are usually greeted with skepticism, at best, even when proposed by insiders to that social order. Challenges presented by outsiders are often rejected with great anger and hostility. It is important to note, however, that this discomfort with difference and change is not limited to the contemporary South—"immigrants have rarely been welcome in U.S. society" (Shannon and Escamilla, 1999, 35). The presence of immigrants has frequently inspired angry and xenophobic responses from local natives across the United States during our nation's history (Zinn, 1980). "Presently, Mexican immigration is the target of worries for a nationalistic ideology" (Shannon and

Escamilla, 1999, 35). This historical pattern has been repeated in the South's streets, restaurants, and schools as Mexican American migration to the region has exploded during the past twenty years.

[The teachers] would make fun of me. There was a coach here and we were in class. I asked him a question. . . . He repeated the same thing I said, with a thicker accent. Everybody started laughing. You just don't do that. I got upset. All the time I saw him, I hated his guts. (Alvarez, 1999)

"Official English" laws reflect contemporary xenophobic responses to immigrants, especially Mexican Americans. With increasing numbers of Mexican Americans settling in the South, appeals to tradition and heritage have been employed to enact such laws. As of 1996, 19 states had "official English" laws in effect. Of these 19, 11 were in the South, forming a contiguous region nearly identical to the old Confederacy, with Kentucky substituting for Texas (Intercultural Development Research Association, 1996). Clearly, in the South many people have chosen a "language-as-problem" disposition toward language policy (Ruiz, 1984) and have put this disposition into law.[9]

Galindo (1997) and Dicker (2000) both observe that, for English language learning immigrants, language is used as a surrogate for race, taking on the form of Skutnabb-Kangas' "linguicism" (1988). The ideology underlying symbolic "linguicist" attacks on other languages is discussed by Galindo (1997):

English is equated with "America" as if other languages did not have a historical presence in the United States before English and as if any language other than English was "un-American". Never in the colonial or national history of the United States has there been a time when only English was spoken within its territory. Nevertheless, for many, the English language is a symbolic marker of "Americanism" rather than the social and political ideas behind democracy.

Thus, for many Americans, concerns over democracy, equality, liberty, and civil and human rights are subordinate when it comes to the issue of language.

Pierre Bourdieu and cultural and social theorists who have applied his ideas have made frighteningly clear the links between symbolic violence such as English-only laws and real violence directed at real people (Bourdieu, 1991; Shannon and Escamilla, 1999). In opposing Georgia's official English law (Georgia Section 50-3-100, passed in 1986), the *Atlanta Constitution* editorial page made explicit the connection between symbolic and physical violence toward Latinos in Georgia:

There is nothing innocuous about [Georgia state legislator] Bill Cummings' attempt to have English designated as the state's official language. It is such an obvious slap at dozens of Mexicans who came to Cummings' Northwest Georgia district to work in a local meat-packing plant, only to find themselves targets of intense hatred and violence by local yahoos, that one wonders at the short span of some lawmakers' memories. Two employees of the plant, accused by locals of "taking jobs away" from the natives, were slain in separate roadside incidents in the last five years. Construction workers were tried and acquitted, in courtrooms packed with Ku Klux Klansmen. Many other Mexicans have been beaten and harassed. And the Ku Klux Klan has greatly stepped up its activities in the area since the plant began hiring Mexicans in the 1970s. . . . [Passage of the official English bill] could only have one purpose, and that is to focus attention on newcomers who already have reason to fear for their safety and the safety of their families. (*Atlanta Constitution*, 1986)

Not surprisingly, both the symbolic and physical violence against Latino immigrants have not stopped since the passage of English-only laws in the South. In metropolitan Atlanta, Mexican American business owners in three cities have fought the selective enforcement of ordinances "requiring that at least 75% of the words on commercial signs be in English" (Lezin, 1999; Glanton, 1999). Although French and Italian restaurants with non-English signs were left unharrassed, a Norcross, Georgia, *Supermercado* and four other Mexican-owned businesses were fined $115 each by officials claiming concerns about "public safety." Mexican American Legal Defense and Education Fund attorney María Valdéz commented, "the general reaction of the municipalities [to influxes of Latino immigrants] is, 'Let us find some way we think is lawful to make these people feel unwanted'" (Glanton, 1999). Such is the nature of symbolic violence. The intolerance has, inevitably, found its way into the schools. The entire 1999 printing of a high school yearbook in Suwanee, Georgia, was recalled when a student was identified in print as "Spic Rodriguez" (Puckett, 1999a).

Most recently, David Duke, one-time grand dragon of the Ku Klux Klan and founder of the National Organization for European American Rights (NOFEAR) (Pressley, 2000), was the keynote speaker at a February 2000 "anti-Hispanic-immigrant rally" in the rural, poultry-processing town of Siler City, North Carolina, where the elementary school is more that 40 percent Hispanic (Cuadros, 2000). Duke supporters, carrying signs proclaiming slogans such as "To Hell with the Wretched Refuse," attended the rally. A few local Latinos staged a counterprotest, but most stayed away. The rally passed without violent confrontation, but it did intimidate some Hispanics into leaving town (Pressley, 2000; Yeoman, 2000).

These hostilities cannot be fully understood if dismissed as the rantings of a vocal minority, for the consequences of these hostilities are much more pervasive than any small minority could effect. Georgia's U.S. Representative Cynthia McKinney agrees that racism should not be seen as limited to a few people, but instead it is an "atmosphere of intolerance [that] lurks just beneath the surface of the New South"—"a certain intolerance for people who are different" (Glanton, 1999)—especially along the dimensions of race and language. "The politics of racism and division do not belong solely to extremist hate groups, but are an unacknowledged and potent part of mainstream American ideology, thought and, action" (Bartolomé and Macedo, 1997, 222). Official English laws are symbolically violent manifestations of this general intolerance of linguistic difference.

GEORGIA STATE SUPERINTENDENT SCHRENKO AND ENGLISH-ONLY

In a national and regional climate of symbolic and real violence toward immigrants and non-English speakers, the rhetoric of U.S. English and English First-led attacks on bilingual education finds fertile ground. The atmosphere of intolerance in Georgia supports "overt hostility to immigration by many Georgia political leaders" (Hamann, 1999). For example, during much of the 1990s, Georgia's most prominent politician was Newt Gingrich. James Crawford noted that Gingrich "took a special interest in" the "English Language Empowerment Act of 1996" (H.R. 123), an attempt to declare English as the official language of the government of the United States, "asserting that English was 'at the heart of our civilization,' whereas language diversity could lead to its 'decay'" (1997, 11). Gingrich was a strong supporter of a 1996 House initiative to "allow states to deny schooling for children of illegal aliens and to block federal welfare benefits for American-born children of illegal aliens" (Reuter News Service, 1996).

Anti-immigrant hostility among Georgia politicians has also been particularly apparent within the Georgia State Department of Education. In 1994, as part of the national Republican landslide that brought Gingrich to the speakership, Linda Schrenko, a virtually unknown conservative supported by the Christian Coalition (Taxel, 1997, 421) became Georgia's first elected State Superintendent of Schools.[10] Hamann (1999) describes the resultant Schrenko-led State Department of Education as driven by a "seemingly hostile or, at best, facile understanding of the challenges and needs of immigrant, language minority, and Hispanic students." Since 1994 Georgia has had a state school bureaucracy filled with intolerance for, and short on research-based understandings of, one of the fastest-growing segments of the state student population.

Schrenko, running as a "stealth" candidate,[11] did not speak much of her attitudes or policies regarding English language learners during her 1994 campaign. Later, and likely in response to its reception among many in the Georgia electorate, Schrenko provided some of her clearest public statements regarding language education policy while successfully running for reelection in 1998. She publicly embraced "Official English" policies on her reelection Web site, noting that "this was one of the major ways her agenda is distinguished from the Democratic platform" (Hamann, 1997, 13). Moreover, she stated, "There are two different issues here. . . . I absolutely think all children should have the opportunity to study another language, especially considering the international nature of the business world. But for students who do not speak English as their native language, our No. 1 focus has to be on teaching them English" (Surpuriya, 1998a). This statement makes clear Schrenko's adherence to the common colonial distinction between elite and folk bilingualism wherein, "while [folk] bilingualism may not be officially valued within the educational system for Latinos who speak Spanish as their native language, [elite bilingualism] is recognized as an accomplishment for native English speakers" (Gaarder, 1976; Galindo, 1997; Macedo, 2000). Within the logic of Schrenko's rhetoric, English language learners are to be excluded from the multilingual business world, whereas native English speakers should have that "opportunity." As we will see, this ideology has been implemented into policy by the Schrenko administration during her tenure.

TRANSLATING IDEOLOGY INTO PERSONNEL AND POLICY: SNAFUS AND QUESTIONABLE CURRICULA

During her first year in office, Linda Schrenko's administration barred State Department of Education employees "from speaking to reporters without the superintendent's permission," ostensibly on the "rationale of ensuring that the superintendent's agenda not be undercut" (Hamann, 1997, 12). With this gag order in place, Schrenko set about purging the Georgia Department of Education of people who did not agree with her agenda.

For the longtime ESOL and migrant education director, an advocate for multiculturalism and bilingualism, this meant being placed under the tight supervision of the new director of federal programs, a Schrenko appointee who stated on one occasion that the Schrenko "administration does not support multicultural education and it does not celebrate diversity" (Hamann, 1997, 13). Due in large part to this philosophical conflict, this director and a number of her staff chose to leave the DOE. Once vacated, many of these positions were left unfilled for months.

In slowly refilling these positions, a crucial decision the Schrenko staff made was the hiring of a conservative Cuban American educational statistician, in early fall 1997, to be the new state Title I director and supervisor for all ESOL (Title VII) and Migrant Education (Title Ic) programs. His hiring was not without troubling ironies. His résumé was distinguished by time spent as part of the Reagan administration's effort to dissolve the federal Department of Education (Garcia-Quintana, 1999) and "devolve" control over schooling entirely back to the states (Spring, 1997). Under Schrenko, he was given responsibility for a number of federally funded programs that he had sought the destruction of only a few years earlier.

A second irony was to be found in this selection of a Latino as an "ideological role model" (Galindo, 1997). He was to be used by the Department of Education "to present the image that the administration was not entirely composed of non-minority persons and to consequently show that its perspectives are not held exclusively by non-minority people" (Galindo, 1997). Thus, his ethnicity helped shield Schrenko and her administration's language minority education policies from attacks.

Nonetheless, his ethnicity could not disguise his mismanagement, as revealed in an investigative report by the *Atlanta Journal-Constitution*:

School systems across Georgia may have to struggle to teach English to immigrant children next year because of a $1.7 million *mistake* by the state Department of Education. State funding for English for Speakers of Other Languages program was cut by $1.7 million for fiscal 1999 because the state ESOL office gave the wrong numbers to the state budget office. The incorrect numbers indicated that fewer children were using ESOL programs, so funding was cut accordingly. In fact, the number of ESOL students in the state is increasing dramatically, state School Superintendent Linda Schrenko said . . . "It's a mistake on our part." . . . Schrenko's staff had turned in a head count, rather than a more complex formula the state uses to calculate ESOL funding. (Kurylo, 1998a, italics added)[12]

Eight days later, Schrenko was forced to admit that the mistake was even larger. In the end, a grand total of $4.3 million was needed during fiscal 1999 to cover underfunding due to the mishandling of numbers by the state Title I director (Kurylo, 1998b).

Trained as an educational statistician, the state Title I director's lack of understanding of ESOL research and pedagogy was not surprising. Nonetheless, his repeated proposals of unorthodox pedagogical strategies, seemingly based in folk models of linguistics rather than educational research, brought his qualifications to manage the ESOL and migrant education programs into doubt. For example, during state migrant education program meetings, he:

- Proposed the use of the U.S. military's high-cost "intensive instruction" model of second language teaching to teach public school English language learners fluent English in six months.
- Claimed the ability to teach children to read in just six weeks of daily 20-minute sessions using the commercial "Failure-Free Reading Program" (from Field Notes by Beck from Georgia State Migrant Education Program Retreats, March 18–20, 1998 and October 14–16, 1998).

Beyond these suggestions, a more worrisome pattern emerged. At a metro Atlanta ESOL program coordinators meeting at the Fulton County Center, in the spring of 1998, the Title I director "horrified" the audience by publicly stating that it was the "patriotic duty" of ESOL administrators and teachers to turn over any suspected illegal alien students to the Immigration and Naturalization Service (Petrie, 2000). Such actions by administrators or teachers would be clearly unconstitutional under the Supreme Court's 1982 *Plyler v. Doe* ruling that schools may not implement policies that have a chilling effect upon the enrollment of Hispanic migrants or undocumented alien children. This was one of the clearest indications as to how hostile elements in the Schrenko administration were toward immigrant children in the state.

During the October 1998 Migrant Education Retreat, the state Title I director repeatedly denied the assertion that some Georgia school systems were violating Federal civil rights protections of *Lau v. Nichols* by not providing any specialized instruction for English language learners. This was despite the fact that Georgia State Department of Education data indicated that 32 school districts in Georgia had English language learning students, but no ESOL program (Cumming, 1999, C10). The state Title I director further rejected the assertion that if the school districts with large English language learning populations lacked both ESOL and bilingual education, such school districts could run afoul of the U.S. Department of Education's Office of Civil Rights (Field Notes by Beck from Georgia State Migrant Education Program Retreat, October 15, 1998).[13]

The Schrenko administration had great difficulty finding and retaining staff to help administer the programs under the control of the Title I director. In recounting his experiences interviewing at the Georgia DOE, a one-time applicant for the state ESOL consultant position provides some insight into the staffing priorities of the Title I director: "Basically his only concern was my opinion about bilingual education. . . . He asked my views based on his political viewpoints rather than his pedagogical ones. I responded according to what I saw best pedagogically. He proceeded on with a political diatribe. We had no discussion as to the pro/con of what was best to accelerate learning or integrate students. I followed up our interview with an e-mail the next day saying I wasn't interested in the position" (Johnson, 2000).

Given this procedure for selecting employees, it should be no surprise that some staff positions in the federal programs division of the DOE remained unfilled for extended periods. The problem of finding, hiring, and retaining competent staff led to "chaos" and a failure by Schrenko's Department of Education "to provide minimum services to local systems" (Shipp, 1996a). Georgia's premiere political commentator Bill Shipp noted at the time, "organizations of teachers and school administrators have complained that they can't get answers from Schrenko's department and that project deadlines are constantly ignored or missed" (Shipp, 1996b).

TRANSLATING IDEOLOGY INTO PERSONNEL AND POLICY: ANTIBILINGUALISM

The Georgia Department of Education's ESOL consultant position was filled after a long vacancy in March 1998, when the Schrenko administration found a former ESOL teacher with a congruent language education ideology. Willing to support Schrenko's pro-Americanization ideology, the new state ESOL consultant has consistently worked to purge and prohibit bilingual education from Georgia's schools.

Her choice of a featured presenter for a statewide Federal Education Programs "Mega-Conference" in Macon, Georgia, in 1999 revealed her agenda. All ESOL programs in the state were encouraged to attend that conference. Nonetheless, the ESOL consultant provided but one session regarding language minority education. That session, the only one scheduled in that time slot so as to encourage attendance (Baker and Heyer, 1999), was lead by Keith Baker, an antibilingual education speaker whose work has been frequently challenged (Greene, 1997).[14] In her introduction of Baker, the state ESOL consultant stated that his work "fits beautifully, hand-in-glove, with the philosophy of the Georgia Department of Education" in that he advocates for "English-only methods" (Baker and Heyer, 1999).

Most recently, during the Georgia TESOL conference in May 2000, the same ESOL consultant stopped by a presentation by coauthor Beck on raising children bilingually. The session was titled "Cultivating Gringo Bilingualism with Limited Resources" (Beck and Manning, 2000). Upon reading the title for the session, the consultant immediately and unjokingly remarked, "You used the 'b' word Scott. You know I don't like the 'b' word" (Field Notes by Beck from Georgia TESOL Conference, May 12, 2000).

The hostility to bilingual education and to immigrant bilingualism by the Schrenko administration and its staff has extended beyond conferences and presentations. The 1999 revision of the *Georgia ESOL Resource Guide*, compiled by the state ESOL consultant, stated "we do not have bilingual education in Georgia" (Georgia Department of Education, 1999, 4), ignoring the existence of bilingual programs in metropolitan Atlanta and northwest Georgia. In fact, the term bilingual education was entirely excluded from the guide's glossary (7–9)—a glossary that included definitions for numerous other English language learner instructional methods.[15] The same guide attempted to justify uncompromising advocacy for English-only methods with an anecdotal question that overlooks dozens of research-based factors that influence second language acquisition: "Why does it seem that students coming from low-incidence-first languages (e.g. Farsi, Twi, Punjab [*sic*]) seem to learn English faster than students who share the same first language as many school peers, staff and community members?" (2). Later, the guide's chapter on *Accommodations for ESOL Students in Regular Education Classrooms*, states: "Label items in the classroom **in English-only**. The student's [*sic*] already know their own language and would ignore the English if you displayed their first language in addition to English. Leave foreign language education of your American students to the foreign language class" (60, bold in original). This passage demonstrates the ESOL consultant's attitudes regarding English language learners in general. She ignored the difficulties of semantic scope in second language learning (i.e., Does a label on a brown wooden chair say "brown," "wood," or "chair"?). She also implied that English language learners are lazy and will not read in English unless forced. Finally, she excluded English language learning children from the category "American." This illustrates how the Schrenko DOE has conceived of Georgia's immigrants as objects of policy—who are seen, but do not see; who are the objects of information, but never subjects in communication (Foucault, 1977; Shore and Wright, 1997). Within this conception, immigrants are policy recipients to be acted upon, but never consulted in the processes of policy formation and implementation.

Mexican American author Gloria Anzaldúa has written, "If you really want to hurt me, talk badly about my language" (Anzaldúa, 1987, 81). Understood from this perspective, the rhetoric of the Schrenko administration has repeatedly demonstrated hostility toward the large, diverse, and growing populations of immigrant students in Georgia. Moreover, the Schrenko Department of Education staff has moved beyond rhetoric in this area by systematically denying funding for any language minority education proposals that support bilingualism.

In 1998, a grant proposal by the Hall County school system seeking federal funding to implement a dual-language immersion program was recommended for denial, during the federally mandated Georgia Department of Education's review process. The official memorandum stated that the project was "not recommended for further development" due to "inconsistency with policies" (Georgia Office of Planning and Budget, 1998) in the Georgia Department of Education. The accompanying explanatory comment from the Georgia Department of Education stated: "The expeditious acquisition of the English language will ensure the effective functioning of students in American society. . . . It is our belief that a strong English to Speakers of Other Languages program with effective methodology and materials will result in quicker proficiency of English language skills" (Georgia Office of Planning and Budget, 1998).

Two years later, a different line of reasoning was used by the Georgia Department of Education staff to deny continued funding to the highly innovative and successful bilingual/binational project in northwest Georgia. This time the Georgia DOE's explanatory comment stated: "This notice is not consistent with the goals, plans, policies, or fiscal resources with which this organization is concerned" (Georgia Office of Planning and Budget, 2000, underline in original). Keeping in mind that both of these proposals would have brought additional federal resources to Georgia schools, without increasing Georgia Department of Education obligations, these two examples clearly demonstrate the consistent efforts by DOE staff to limit and shape local program implementation on the basis of political ideology. This appropriation of the policy process is transparently political when one examines the justifications and explanations provided by the DOE staff.

TRANSLATING IDEOLOGY INTO PERSONNEL AND POLICY: AMERICANIZATION

In 1999, the state ESOL consultant lobbied the Georgia legislature for expansion of ESOL funding and services in the state (Cumming, 1999). And, in fact, the 1999–2000 school year saw significant, if still insufficient, growth in the number of ESOL programs in Georgia (Field Notes by Beck from Georgia TESOL Conference, May 12, 2000). However, this move by the Georgia DOE in the direction of supporting English language learners in the state must be examined within the context of two issues. First, in 1999, the U.S. Department of Education Office of Civil Rights (OCR) began a compliance review regarding the Georgia DOE's failure to enforce *Lau v. Nichols* requirements for English language learner services (U.S. Department of Education, 1999).[16] This investigation created a legal necessity for the DOE to enlarge the state's program. Second, the state ESOL consultant's advocacy for the expansion of ESOL programs must be understood in the context of her ideological position that the purpose of English language learner education is rapid "Americanization" of the immigrant children of Georgia. In other words, growth of ESOL per se does not change the vulnerability of ESOL to an ideological and methodological narrowing consistent with a cultural replacement–oriented, instructional program.

This heavy-handed focus on Americanization of language minority students was made apparent in the artwork of the new ESOL consultant's revision of the *Georgia ESOL Resource Guide* (Georgia Department of Education, 1999), and is especially transparent when contrasted with the artwork of the previous edition. The earlier guide (Georgia Department of Education, 1995) was developed by the pre-Schrenko ESOL director in the early 1990s and distributed before Schrenko's consolidation of power. This earlier edition was decorated with crayon-style drawings of four smiling children of various ethnicities, clearly evoking the "We Are the World" idealism of liberal multicultural education (Nieto, 2000; Spring, 2000; Ovando and McLaren, 2000; Sleeter and Grant, 1996, 150).

In contrast, the Schrenko-era revision includes nationalistic clip-art, an American eagle clothed in a red, white, and blue hat waving a Georgia flag.[17] Other images implicitly equating English with a monoculturalist American patriotism include Independence Hall, pilgrims, the U.S. flag, and the Liberty Bell (Georgia Department of Education, 1999). In comparison with the previous edition of the guide, this new edition graphically asserted that English language learning students must be quickly and firmly immersed in "the singular, great American culture." This imagery is remarkably consistent in its evocation of a "deficiency orientation" (Sleeter and Grant, 1996, 40) toward the education of language minority students. In this case, their presumed double deficiency is a lack of "American culture" as well as a lack of English.

In August 1998, the Schrenko DOE staff used many of the same images to decorate the agenda booklet for a Statewide ESOL and Migrant Education Workshop in Atlanta in August 1998. The theme for that workshop was, unsurprisingly, "English: The Language That Unifies U.S." (Georgia Department of Education, 1998). Within the agenda booklet were two quotes:

> There is no room in this country for hyphenated Americanism.
> —Theodore Roosevelt, October 12, 1915

> ... If a man is going to be an American at all let him be so without any qualifying adjectives; and if he is going to be something else, let him drop the word American from his personal description.
> —Henry Cabot Lodge, December 21, 1888

Tellingly, Dicker's study of official English movements revealed that the Roosevelt quote recently appeared in a membership recruitment letter from U.S. English (2000, 51).

The welcoming message by State Superintendent of Schools Schrenko in the same agenda booklet revealed another example of colonial ideology couched in patriotic discourse:

> America has always been a nation of immigrants. Nevertheless, in the United States, we have an American culture that is made up of the many beautiful heritages that these immigrants have brought with them. Furthermore, English has been the language that has enabled all Americans, regardless of heritage, to communicate with one another. For the past several years the population of limited English proficient students in Georgia has experienced a tremendous increase. . . . We must also teach them about our great culture and our great country so they will feel that they are Americans. (Georgia Department of Education, 1998)

Here we see the most powerful education official in Georgia performing a number of rhetorical back flips as she tries to hold a consistent position regarding immigrant education without revealing her bias. She was concerned, first and foremost, with the Americanization of immigrant students, not their academic success. Schrenko, in keeping with the rhetoric of U.S. English, made it clear that it is the teacher's responsibility to Americanize the immigrants. The English language is viewed as essential and instrumental in this process. Reminiscent of the "No English, No Hope" anti-Latino stereotype (Barrera, 1993, 211), according to Schrenko, learning English allows immigrants to set aside their "heritage" and Americanize "so that they will feel that they are Americans."

Schrenko's rhetoric supported the American monoculturalist assertion of a dichotomy between multiple immigrant "heritages" and a singular "American culture" (or "our great culture") and repeats the folk linguistic belief that existing languages and identities must be shed for the acquisition of English to proceed expeditiously. For Schrenko, immigrants lack true, broad-based cultures when they come to our country. Instead they must give up their interesting heritages to join the American "melting pot." Although she might momentarily regret the loss of home heritages, she has been unwilling to question the desirability of full assimilation by immigrants. The comparatively benign argument for teaching English obscures a more aggressive and symbolically violent agenda of cultural erasure. If the goal were strictly to teach English, then the research about how best to promote the language acquisition of non-native speakers of English would not be so stridently resisted. Macedo critiques this notion of linguistic assimilation as a symptom of a colonial ideology that "overcelebrate[s] the dominant group's language to a level of mystification" (Macedo, 2000, 16) and leads to systematic miseducation (Woodson, 1933/1990).

GEORGIA'S REGIONAL MIGRANT EDUCATION AGENCIES: THE PARTY LINE COMES DOWN

As the policies of Schrenko and her staff became apparent over the mid-1990s, the four state regional migrant education agencies (MEAs) began to feel their stifling effects. As Hamann (1997) noted, these offices are a significant part of Georgia's "statewide infrastructure that provides specific support to Latino students" (11). As Schrenko consolidated her control over the DOE, her staff began to probe the four MEA offices for employees unwilling to conform to the new agenda.

This process became explicit at the first statewide Migrant Education Retreat organized by the Schrenko team in March 1998.[18] The state Title I director verbally attacked the previous administration, and then asked if anyone present wanted to defend his predecessors or admit to recent unofficial contact with them (Field Notes by Beck from Georgia State Migrant Education Retreat, March 18, 1998). After that introduction to the new order, the regional offices faced a slow, steady erosion of their autonomy, especially in curricular matters and issues of information distribution.

With regard to curriculum, for the four- to six-week migrant summer school programs the state Title I director insisted upon a shift to a back-to-the-basics remediation approach to replace the established thematic, interdisciplinary model. He also forced the implementation of a standardized, *English-language* pretest and posttest to quantify the effectiveness of the program, despite the fact that the majority of the test-takers would be English language learners. The regional curriculum coordinators[19] resisted these changes. The success of the existing curriculum, doubts regarding instructional time lost to testing, concerns about testing English language learners in English, and assertions of the unreliability of testing data produced after such a short instructional program were all presented by the curriculum coordinators as counterarguments to the new migrant summer curriculum. Nonetheless, they were forced to implement the new approach.

The resulting tension reached a climax during the summer of 1999, when the state Title I director effectively fired all seven migrant education curriculum coordinators by defunding their positions. This action was likely retaliation against the curriculum coordinators for their resistance to the Schrenko administration's English language learner policies.

One regional migrant education curriculum coordinator had, for example, contacted the U.S. Department of Education Office of Civil Rights in Atlanta with a question about an English language-learning student in a rural southwest Georgia school district (*Atlanta Journal-Constitution*, 1999). Like many others, the district was not providing any ESOL classes, nor any other English language learner services, in disregard of federal civil rights law. As noted earlier, the state Title I director had publicly denied that there were any civil rights violations regarding English language learning students in Georgia. Thus, the Schrenko administration was opposed to any contact between Migrant Education staff and OCR regarding this issue.

After her firing, the curriculum coordinator pursued a lawsuit, described in the *Atlanta Journal-Constitution*'s Law and Order column:

MACON COUNTY: Dismissed Educator Sues State Officials

A state employee who says her job was eliminated after she raised questions about discrimination against a Macon County Hispanic student sued the Georgia Department of Education State School Superintendent Linda Schrenko and several others [including the state Title I director] August 9th. [The curriculum coordinator], a state migrant education worker, says she angered school officials by reporting concerns about a Hispanic kindergartner who she says was not taught English and then not promoted to the first grade to the office of Civil Rights of the U.S. Department of Education. (1999, D7)

This wrongful-dismissal suit forced the Georgia DOE to back down on defunding of the curriculum positions. Nonetheless, at least five longtime employees of Georgia's Migrant Education Program, including coauthor Beck, left in the wake of the attack on the agencies. As of summer 2000, the suit is still unresolved, and the curriculum coordinator who contacted OCR has found work elsewhere. Within the migrant education agencies, the attempted defunding of migrant education curriculum coordinators reinforced a reluctance to report illegal educational practices observed in the schools, and it has denied Georgia's migrant children the voices of many potentially strong advocates.

LACK OF ENGLISH LANGUAGE LEARNER SERVICES

A crucial question remains for English language learning children and their teachers in Georgia: How has the Schrenko administration's adherence to an English-only ideology impacted the schooling of immigrant children? The consequences have extended beyond the stifling of educators' critiques. The symbols, rhetoric, and functioning of the Georgia Department of Education have created a climate in which the continued denial of English language learner services to English language learning students is rarely questioned or addressed.

The "Assimilation via English-only" ideology at the highest levels of the Georgia Department of Education has influenced various levels of the state education bureaucracy. It has made permissible hostile attitudes and crippled the state's ability to accommodate the needs of English language learners. The analysis developed by Shannon and Escamilla (1999) is helpful here in demonstrating how the use of coded language by authorities creates space for school and classroom practitioners to maintain discriminatory policies and practices: "The code gives tacit permission for . . . teachers to continue the practice of symbolic violence" (365). This is because "the reproduction of society's values and beliefs about Mexican immigrants in schools allows educators to act in these negative ways with impunity" (366).

It should be no surprise that many Georgia school systems—all areas of the New Latino Diaspora that have been generally unfamiliar with the research and terms of the debate regarding language minority education[20]—have implemented the assimilationist and English-only policies that logically follow from their unchallenged "folk models" of language learning. Without the needed information, resources, and enforcement from state DOE officials to both spur and guide local program development and implementation, all too often local language minority education policies have amounted to near total neglect.[21]

The Georgia Department of Education estimated in 1999 that at least 32 school districts in the state had English language learners, but no ESOL or bilingual education program (Cumming, 1999, C10). Most of those school districts were located in the rural southern half of the state (Georgia Department of Education, 2000). In five years of working in the schools of rural south Georgia, coauthor Beck saw very few examples of school or district-led assistance to English language learners that reflected research in language minority education (i.e., that reflected Cummins, 1981; Thomas and Collier, 1997; Center for Applied Linguistics, 1999; Krashen, 1999a).

In these school districts, English language learners have often been provided with what research tells us is the worst possible pedagogy—sink-or-swim submersion—a strategy that is likely to delay English-language acquisition, as well as inhibit academic progress in other areas (Shannon and Escamilla, 1999). Some of these school districts have failed to start ESOL services and have offered only paraprofessional tutors to assist their students. English language learning students in these situations are often ignored in their regular classrooms, placed in the corner of the room with a busy-work handout or coloring sheet.

There are no bilingual education programs in south Georgia, a fact at least partially attributable to the absolute opposition to such programs expressed by the Georgia Department of Education. Moreover, many ESOL programs in the region have only been started under threat of federal civil rights action. As the OCR investigation of the Georgia DOE started in 1999 suggests, state-level enforcement has been nearly nonexistent. So very few of the school districts have voluntarily dipped into their general fund to cover the startup costs of ESOL instruction.[22] The issue of English language learner assistance has often been pushed aside by local school administrators as someone else's responsibility.

CARING AS APPROPRIATION AND RESISTANCE

For these reasons, as Hamann states,

Latino students and parents in Georgia are dependent at practically all levels on the compassion of Anglo and African American educators and administrators and, more importantly, on these individuals' comprehension of Latinos' needs and circumstance. (1997, 15)

There have been a number of educators who have made an extra effort on behalf of their language minority students. Consistent with Levinson and Sutton's (2001) assertion that policy can be produced at the local, even the classroom, level, these teachers have chosen to resist the policies of neglect and hostility. Their expression of goodwill and caring has been welcomed by English language learning students.

I had some teachers that really wanted to help me. . . . Here at the high school there was my homeroom teacher. . . . Somebody that would try to talk to you and say hi. Not just be your teacher, but also be your friend. . . . I guess she felt sorry for me. She is a very nice person. . . . Before school started, I could go to her classroom and talk with her. She gave me a sign that says, "I am not afraid to face tomorrow, for I have seen today." . . . She was a friend and a person who tried to help me succeed. She would talk to the other teachers good about me, and that makes a lot of difference. She tutored me when I was in college. She still talks about me to the other migrants. (Alvarez, 1999)

[The former high school counselor] was very important in my life. I always thought that she actually could understand. . . . So I always went there to talk with her on lunch break or recess. She always talked about dreams, important stuff, college. I liked that stuff. She always encouraged me to go to college. When things were really, really bad, she said that it was going to change. She always encouraged us to keep going. . . . She's always been interested in helping less fortunate people. She does not like lazy people and she saw that we struggled. . . . I would spend all my [free] time in the counselor's office. (Fuentes, 1999)

Beck (1999) found that for each informant who had found academic and professional success, the efforts of at least one concerned and empathic local southerner was an essential support during their struggles to find their place. As Peña described in her oral history of Mexican American educators, "the common theme that made these teachers special was simply the fact that they cared" (1998, 9). In the context of a lack of language minority education services and attacks on immigrants, the caring attitudes of school administrators and teachers have played an important role in establishing a space for resistance (Noddings, 1992). The effort of a single teacher to either ignore or redefine the rhetoric of the state DOE and thereby appropriate a new, more progressive local policy in his or her classroom has often determined the success or failure of immigrant students.

Nonetheless, it should not have to be this way. The educational fates of thousands of English language learners in Georgia's New Latino Diaspora should not be left to the luck of the draw and the energies, abilities, and spirits of caring teachers who, at some professional risk, resist problematic policy mandates from above. Teachers' and other educators' efforts to develop effective programs, grounded in their experiences with immigrant students and their families and supported by current research in language minority education, should not be undermined by state education officials' efforts to impose an ideologically based policy agenda.

CONCLUSION: RESPONSE AND RESISTANCE

This study has demonstrated how national English-only, antimulticulturalist rhetoric is being heard loudly and clearly across Georgia. The conservative agenda of nativism and English-only has found many receptive ears in this New Latino Diaspora region. Meanwhile, other opposing discourses have been quieted by threats, the frustrated departure of informed professionals, and scant opportunities to organize. The unbalanced, partial connection between the national debate regarding language minority education policy and local decision making has given advantage to rhetoric that excludes the voices of immigrant students and many of their teachers and advocates. Because Schrenko administration's agenda has defined the terms of the language minority policy debate in Georgia, any alternative has been forced to struggle against vociferous assault. Thus, the Schrenko English-only agenda has continued to impede the development of sensible local responses to the rapid increase in English language learner populations.

Only recently have the outlines of a sustained challenge to the Schrenko regime formed. These include the pending labor law–based wrongful termination lawsuit by a former migrant education curriculum coordinator, the compliance review of the Georgia Department of Education started in 1999 by the U.S. Department of Education Office of Civil Rights, and a sweeping education reform plan currently being implemented by Georgia's Democratic Governor Roy Barnes.

Federal power, especially in the realm of education, has often served a highly democratic function in policy making during the second half of the twentieth century. Nonetheless, at the same time as conservatives have focused much of their energy for the past two decades on "devolving control" back from the federal level to the states and localities, their political and pedagogical opponents have not always been adequately conscious of the importance of federal power for the protection of disadvantaged groups. The protection of laws and court decisions such as Title I, Title VII, *Brown v. Board*, *Lau v. Nichols*, and *Plyler v. Doe* is essential in forming anything more than small-scale (e.g., classroom-level) resistance to policies, such as the Schrenko agenda for education. It is only behind such strong and long-established defenses that an organized resistance can form. Caring teachers and educators can appropriate federal civil rights law and use it to assert democracy and inclusion over prejudice and exclusion. Educators who seek to resist problematic policies must learn about, protect, and invoke the power of federal law and law enforcement if they are to find common cause and to make their voices heard. We hope that this chapter can help inform such efforts to resist conservative discourses regarding English language learner education in the New Latino Diaspora.

NOTES

1. We rely heavily on Georgia's largest newspaper and the state newspaper of record, the *Atlanta Journal-Constitution*. For the past two decades, as immigration has increased in Georgia, the *Journal-Constitution* has included reports on the issues of immigration and prejudice.

2. We use the identity labels "Latino" and "Hispanic" nearly interchangeably in this chapter. Because we rely on U.S. Census Bureau and Georgia Department of Education statistics using the category "Hispanic," we present that term for the sake of simple accuracy. Second, in a previous study (1999), coauthor Beck conducted extensive oral history interviews with Mexican Americans of rural southeast Georgia and encountered a consensus among them in favor of the label Hispanic over Latino.

3. Lilia Bartolomé (1996) and Maria de la Luz Reyes (1992) have both articulated sharp critiques of this search for "'one size fits all' instructional recipes" (Bartolomé, 231).

4. Some of these misleading assertions and assumptions include:

- "Children can master a second language in a single year"—a myth no knowledgeable student of second language development would accept given that the research consensus that full academic fluency requires approximately four to eight years to develop (Thomas and Collier, 1997).

- "Bilingualism is without value"—a myth disproven by a recent study that demonstrated that bilingual English/Spanish Latinos earn, on average, $7,000 more per year than monolingual English-only

Latinos (Fradd and Boswell, 2000) and by the fact that "bilingual children perform better than monolingual speakers on measures of analytical ability, concept formation, and cognitive flexibility" (Bredekamp and Copple, 1997, 152; Hakuta, Ferdman, and Diaz, 1987).

• "Second language literacy is not supported by first language literacy"—a myth destroyed by nearly two decades of research supporting Cummins's Developmental Interdependence Hypothesis (1981; Macedo, 2000).

5. Cuadros, 2000.

6. According to census data, from 1870 to 1920, the historical peak years of immigration to the United States, the foreign-born percentage of our national population varied between 13.2 percent and 14.7 percent. During that same time period, the foreign-born population in the southern Atlantic states never exceeded 2.9 percent. Moreover, the foreign-born populace of Georgia was even lower, actually declining from 0.9 percent in 1870 to 0.6 percent in 1920 (U.S. Census Bureau, 1999). From 1850 to 1970, the percentage of foreign-born Georgians never exceeded 1.1 percent.

7. U.S. Census Bureau estimates are likely to be low due to the officially acknowledged undercounting of poor, illegal, and minority resident immigrants in the state during the 1990 census (Irvine, 2000; Gurr, 1999).

8. All informant names are pseudonyms.

9. A recent *Atlanta Journal-Constitution* poll found that 72 percent of respondents in a heavily immigrant-populated metro Atlanta county believe that "immigrants should receive government services—such as driver's license tests and classroom instruction—only in English" (Badie, 1999b).

10. The Schrenko administration's adherence to the political agenda of the conservative Christian Coalition (Spring, 1997) has been demonstrated on numerous issues beyond antimulticulturalism, English-only, and immigrant assimilation. Most recently, in defending the teaching of "respect for the creator" in a mandated character education program, the DOE legal director stated "this is a way to teach an understanding of America" (McClam, 2000)—thereby equating Americanism with a narrowly defined version of Christian religious faith. Previous examples include opposition to the teaching of an "anti-bias" Pre-K curriculum from the National Association for the Education of Young Children (*Augusta Chronicle*, 1996); attacking the National Parent Teacher Association (PTA) as "too liberal" and "prohomosexual" (*Augusta Chronicle*, 1997); and supporting the teaching of Bible history courses and creationism in public schools (Puckett, 1999b; Cumming, 1996).

11. During the late 1980s and early 1990s, Christian Coalition leader Ralph Reed encouraged conservatives to begin their political careers by "flying below radar" (Welch, 1997) during campaigns for elected positions. This strategy consisted of revealing as little as possible of their agenda during the campaign and then, upon election, implementing conservative policies that would often be surprising to the electorate (Schneiderman, 1993; *Washington Post*, 1998).

12. It is important to note that the "complex formula" for ESOL funding referred to in the article is little more than a standard FTE ("full time equivalent") count of student segments, a common formula used in funding nearly every level of education from kindergarten to the university. This misrepresentation helped Schrenko temporarily control the initial "negative spin" of the error.

13. This attitude would eventually be proven to be mistaken when OCR began a statewide ELL ("English language learner") service compliance review in the summer of 1999 (U.S. Department of Education, 1999).

14. Baker's work (1998) has been strongly refuted by researchers Stephen Krashen (1999a) and Nicholas Meier (1999). According to Krashen (1999b), "much of the research

Baker cited was unpublished and not available to readers, and in cases in which data was available, his report of this data was inaccurate."

15. Including "audio lingual method," "cognitive academic language learning approach," "English as a foreign language," "English as a second language," "English for speakers of other languages, and "total physical response."

16. In Georgia, there has been "no requirement that districts seek or accept special ESOL funding. . . . The federal mandate (from *Lau v. Nichols* Supreme Court ruling) that language minority students have equal access to an adequate education does apply in Georgia too, but there is little infrastructure or popular political sentiment to ensure that this guideline is adhered to" (Hamann, 1997, 11). This is in part the result of many years of poor enforcement by the Office of Civil Rights across the country (Figueroa and Gutiérrez, 2000; Ricento, 1998).

17. This list includes the controversial Confederate stars and bars.

18. Though Schrenko won office in 1994, Georgia's Migrant Education Program was run by a coordinator hired under the previous superintendent until August 1997.

19. Migrant education curriculum coordinators, by dint of their job responsibilities and training, were the migrant education staff members most likely to run afoul of the Schrenko agenda for English language learner education. A central part of their work was to provide guidance, support, training, and materials to teachers and administrators in schools serving migrant children.

20. In rural school districts in Georgia, very few teachers and administrators have traveled widely or studied another language. Thus, there is very little knowledge among school administrators and teachers with regard to the struggles of dislocation, being an outsider, and learning a second language. The English-only rhetoric and Americanization curriculum of the state DOE does nothing to challenge this situation.

21. It is instructive to note that the situation in rural Georgia reflects the approach taken by U.S. English and its sympathizers in other states. As documented by Dicker, U.S. English officially insists that immigrants must learn English, but then fails to invest substantial resources in helping make that happen (2000, 49–50).

22. The Georgia Department of Education's long-standing funding structure has put the rural schools in southern Georgia at a disadvantage for ESOL funds. For years, statewide ESOL funding has been determined by a single student segment FTE count each October. Funds generated by this count had been distributed to the various school districts during the *subsequent* school year. Thus, small, poor, rural school districts have been forced to find local funding for the first year costs of ESOL services.

REFERENCES

Acuña, R. 1995. *Anything but Mexican*. London: Verso.

Alvarez, Nancy [pseud.]. 1999. Personal interview with Scott A.L. Beck. January 27, 1999.

Anderson, C. 1998. "More Pay Is One Key to Migrant Worker Compromise." *Savannah Morning News*. July 22, 1998, 5C.

Anzaldúa, Gloria. 1987. *Borderlands*/La Frontera: *The New* Mestiza. San Francisco: Spinsters/Aunt Lute.

Athens Daily News. 1999. "Georgians Can't Ignore Needs of Fast-Growing Hispanic Population." *Athens Daily News*. February 19, 1999. Available: *http://www.athensnewspapers.com*.

Atlanta Constitution. 1986. "Bill Pushes an Official State Prejudice." *Atlanta Constitution*. February 1, 1986.

Atlanta Journal-Constitution. 1998. "El Acento Nuevo del Sur: The South's New Accent." *Atlanta Journal-Constitution.* April 19, 1998, P1.

———. 1999. "Macon County: Dismissed Educator Sues State Officials." Law and Order column. *Atlanta Journal-Constitution.* August 20, 1999, D7.

Augusta Chronicle. 1996. "Pre-K Curriculum Garbage." *Augusta Chronicle.* February 4, 1996, A4.

———. 1997. "Henson vs. Schrenko: The Nat'l PTA Record." *Augusta Chronicle.* October 14, 1997, A4.

Badie, R. 1999a. "Republicans to Woo Hispanic Vote." *Atlanta Journal-Constitution.* August 11, 1999, 2E.

———. 1999b. "Controlling the Growth." *Atlanta Journal-Constitution.* November 7, 1999, 1JJ.

Baker, K. 1998. "Structured English Immersion: Breakthrough in Teaching Limited-English Proficient Students." *Phi Delta Kappan.* 80(3):199–204.

Baker, K. and M.B. Heyer. 1999. Presentation at the Georgia Department of Education Federal Programs Mega Conference, Macon, Georgia, November 1999.

Barrera, R. 1993. "Ideas a Literature Can Grow On: Key Insights for Enriching and Expanding Children's Literature about the Mexican-American Experience." In *Teaching Multicultural Literature in Grade K-8.* V. Harris, ed. Norwod, MA: Christopher-Gordon.

Bartolomé, L. 1996. "Beyond the Methods Fetish: Toward a Humanizing Pedagogy." In *Breaking Free: The Transformative Power of Critical Pedagogy.* Leistyna, A. Woodrum, and S.A. Sherblom, eds. Pp. 229–252. Cambridge: Harvard Educational Review.

Bartolomé, L. and D. Macedo. 1997. "Dancing with Bigotry: The Poisoning of Racial and Ethnic Identities." *Harvard Educational Review.* 67(2):222–246.

Beck, S.A.L. 1999. "'We Were the First . . .' An Oral History of the First Mexican-American Migrant Students in Southeast Georgia." Presented at the American Educational Research Association Annual Meeting. Montréal, Quebec, Canada, April, 1999.

Beck, S.A.L. and M. Manning. 2000. "Cultivating Gringo Bilingualism with Limited Resources." Presented at the Georgia Teachers of English to Speakers of Other Languages Annual Conference. Athens, Georgia, May 2000.

Beck, Scott A.L. 1998a. Field Notes Taken at Georgia State Migrant Education Program Retreat, Helen, GA, March 18–20, 1998.

———. 1998b. Field Notes Taken at Georgia State Migrant Education Program Retreat. Dawsonville, GA, October 14–16, 1998.

———. 2000. Field Notes Taken at Georgia TESOL Conference. Athens, GA, May 12, 2000.

Bourdieu, P. 1991. *Language and Symbolic Power.* Cambridge, MA: Harvard University Press.

Bredekamp, S. and C. Copple. 1997. *Developmentally Appropriate Practice in Early Childhood Programs.* Washington, DC: National Association for the Education of Young Children.

Capelouto, S. 2000. "Georgia Hispanics." *All Things Considered,* February 2, 2000. Washington, DC: National Public Radio. Available: *http://www.npr.org/ramfiles/atc/20000202.atc.07.ram.*

Carnuccio, L.M. 2000. "Small Numbers, Big Challenges." *TESOL Academy 2000* (brochure). Alexandria, VA: TESOL.

Center for Applied Linguistics. 1999. "ESL Standards in Low-Incidence Districts." *The CAL Reporter*. March 1999. Available: *http://www.cal.org/public/rptr/ CR12.htm#ESL STANDARDS*.

Crawford, J. 1997."California's Proposition 227: A Post Mortem." *Bilingual Research Journal*. 21(1): 1–29.

Cuadros, P. 2000. "Hispanics Targeted for Hate in New South." *Hispanic Link News Service*. April 4, 2000. Available: *http://www.latinolink.com*.

Cumming, D. 1996. "Professors Lobby against Creationism." *The Atlanta Journal-Constitution*. March 24, 1996, H1.

———. 1999. "State School Board Wants Classes for Immigrants to Expand." *The Atlanta Journal-Constitution*. March, 12, 1999, C10.

Cummins, J. 1981. "The Role of Primary Language Development in Promoting Educational Success for Language Minority Students." In *Schooling and Language Minority Students*. Pp. 3–50. Los Angeles: California State University.

Dicker, S. J. 2000. "Official English and Bilingual Education: The Controversy over Language Pluralism in U.S. Society." In *The Sociopolitics of English Language Teaching*. J.K. Hall and W. Eggington, eds. Clevedon, GB: Multilingual Matters.

Diwan, R. 1999. "Gandhian Economics." In *Encyclopedia of Political Economy*. A.P. O'Hara, ed. Pp. 387–388. New York: Routledge.

Donato, R. 1997. *The Other Struggle for Equal Schools: Mexican-Americans during the Civil Rights Era*. Albany: SUNY Press.

Federation for American Immigration Reform. 2000. "Georgia Resources." Available: *http://www.fairus.org/html/042ga702.htm*.

Figueroa, R. and D. Gutiérrez. 2000. "Testing and Assessment Issues for Migrant Education Students." Paper presented at the American Educational Research Association Annual Meeting. New Orleans, LA, April 2000.

Foucault, M. 1977. *Discipline and Punish*. Harmondsworth, U.K.: Penguin.

Fradd, S. and T. Boswell, T. 2000. *Creating Florida's Multilingual, Global Workforce*. Tallahassee: Florida Department of Education.

Freeman, R. 2000. "Contextual Challenges to Dual-Language Education: A Case Study of a Developing Middle School Program." *Anthropology and Education Quarterly*. 31(2): 202–229.

Fuentes, Ester [pseud.]. 1999. Personal interview with Scott A.L. Beck. January 2, 1999.

Galindo, R. 1997. "Language Wars: The Ideological Dimensions of the Debates on Bilingual Education." *Bilingual Research Journal*. 21(2, 3). Available: *http://brj.asu.edu/ archives/23v21/articles/ar5.html*.

Garcia-Quintana, R. 1999. "Testimony of Roan Garcia-Quintana, Title I Director, Georgia Department of Education." U.S. House of Representatives Committee on Education and the Workforce Hearings, June 10, 1999. Available: *http:// edworkforce.house.gov/hearings/106th/fc/esea61099/garcia-quintana.htm*.

Gates, H.L. 1992. *Loose Canons: Notes on the Culture Wars*. New York: Oxford University Press.

Georgia Department of Education. 1995. *English to Speakers of Other Languages Resource Guide*. 3rd edition. Atlanta: Georgia Department of Education.

———. 1998. *First Statewide ESOL and Migrant Education Workshop*. Agenda Booklet. Atlanta: Georgia Department of Education.

———. 1999. *English to Speakers of Other Languages Resource Guide*. 4th edition. Atlanta: Georgia Department of Education.

———. 2000. "1998–1999 Georgia Education Report Card." Atlanta: Georgia Department of Education. Available: *http://accountability.doe.k12.ga.us/Report99/*.

Georgia Office of Planning and Budget. 1998. Memo Regarding: GA980126005. February 19, 1998.

———. 2000. Memo Regarding: GA000124006. February 4, 2000.

Glanton, D. 1999. "Culture Clash of the New South." *Chicago Tribune*. Reprinted in *Athens Daily News*. May 12, 1999. Available: *http://www.onlineathens.com/stories/051299/*.

Greene, J. 1997. "A Meta-analysis of the Rossell and Baker Review of Bilingual Education Research." *Bilingual Research Journal*. 21(2, 3). Available: *http://brj.asu.edu/archives/23v21/articles/art1.html#intro*.

———. 1998. "Rescuing Education Research: A Rule of Thumb for Fending Off the 'Nihilism' of Competing Claims." *Education Week*. April 29, 1998, 52.

Griffith, D. 1995. "*Hay Trabajo*: Poultry Processing, Rural Industrialization, and the Latinization of Low-Wage Labor." In *Any Way You Cut It: Meat-Processing and Small-Town America*. D.D. Stull, M.J. Broadway, and D. Griffith, eds. Pp. 129–151. Lawrence: University Press of Kansas.

Griffith, D., E. Kissam, and J. Camposeco. 1995. *Working Poor: Farmworkers in the United States*. Philadelphia: Temple University Press.

Gurr, S. 1999. "Accurate Count of Hispanics Crucial in Upcoming Census." *Athens Daily News*. September, 1, 1999. Available: *http://www.onlineathens.com/stories/090199/new_0901990007.shtml*.

Hakuta, K., B.M. Ferdman, and R.M. Diaz. 1987. "Bilingualism and Cognitive Development: Three Perspectives." In *Advances in Applied Psycholinguistics. Volume II: Reading, Writing and Language Learning*. S. Rosenberg, ed. Pp. 284–319. Cambridge: Cambridge University Press.

Hamann, E.T. 1997. "The Future Is Now: Latino Education in Georgia." Paper presented at the American Anthropological Association Annual Meeting, Washington, DC. November 22, 1997.

———. 1999. "The Georgia Project: A Binational Attempt to Reinvent a School District in Response to Latino Newcomers." Doctoral dissertation, University of Pennsylvania. Ann Arbor: University Microfilms.

Hutcheson, R. 1995. "Migrant Workers Provide Good Supply of Hard-Working Agricultural Labor." *Statesboro Herald*. Special Section: Agriculture Pride 1995, February 5, 1995, 7.

Intercultural Development Research Association. 1996. Did You Know?" *IDRA Newsletter*. (XXIII) 1, 12. January 1996. San Antonio: Intercultural Development Research Association.

Irvine. M. 2000. "Illegal Immigrants Shouldn't Fear Census Bureau." *Associated Press/ Athens Daily News*. February, 4, 2000. Available: *http://www.onlineathens.com/stories/020400/new_0204000004.shtml*.

Johnson, H. [pseud]. 2000. Personal e-mail correspondence with Scott A.L. Beck. May 3, 2000.

Krashen, S. 1999a. "What the Research Really Says about Structured English Immersion: A Response to Keith Baker." *Phi Delta Kappan*. 80(9):705–706.

———. 1999b. Another response to Keith Baker. Available: *http://ourworld.compuserve.com/homepages/JWCRAWFORD/Krashen6.htm*.

Kurylo, E. 1998a. "Error Leads to School Funding Cut." *Atlanta Journal-Constitution*. March 19, 1998, C4.

————. 1998b. "Schrenko Will Seek to Repair Slip-up." *Atlanta Journal-Constitution.* March 28, 1998, D2.

Levinson, B. and M. Sutton. 2001. "Policy as Practice: A Sociocultural Approach to the Study of Educational Policy." In *Policy as Practice: Toward a Comparative Sociocultural Analysis of Educational Policy.* M. Sutton and B. Levinson, eds. Westport, CT: Ablex.

Lezin, S. 1999. "Stores Fined for Spanish-Language Signs." *Atlanta Journal-Constitution.* March 7, 1999. Available: *http://www.accessatlanta.com/ajc/newsatlanta/signs.html.*

Loewen, J. 1971. *Mississippi Chinese.* Cambridge, MA: Harvard University Press.

Macedo, D. 2000. "The Colonialism of the English-Only Movement." *Educational Researcher.* 29(2):15–24. Available: *http://www.aera.net/pubs/er/arts/29–03/macedo01. htm.*

McClam, E. 2000. "'Respect for the Creator' Clause Causing State Educators Confusion." *Athens Daily News.* July 28, 2000.

Meier, N. 1999. "A Fabric of Half-Truths: A Response to Keith Baker on Structured English Immersion." *Phi Delta Kappan.* 80(9):704, 706.

Memmi, A. 1967. *Colonizer and the Colonized.* Boston: Beacon Press.

Niedzielski, N. and D.R. Preston. 1999. *Folk Linguistics.* The Hague: Mouton de Gruyter.

Nieto, Sonia. 2000. *Affirming Diversity.* New York: Addison Wesley Longman.

Noddings, N. 1992. *The Challenge to Care in Schools: An Alternative Approach to Education.* New York: Teachers College Press.

Ovando, C. and P. McLaren. 2000. *The Politics of Multiculturalism and Bilingual Education.* New York: McGraw-Hill.

Peña, D.C. 1998. "Three Teachers' Stories: The Construction of Self-identity." Paper presented at the American Educational Research Association Annual Meeting. San Diego, CA, April 1998.

Petrie, H. [pseud]. 2000. Personal e-mail correspondence with Scott A.L. Beck. September 12 and 13, 2000.

Pressley, S.A. 2000. "Hispanic Immigration Boom Rattles South." *Washington Post.* March 6, 2000, A3.

Puckett, P. 1999a. Gwinnett Letter Aims at Recalling Yearbooks." *Atlanta Journal-Constitution.* June 5, 1999, 3F.

————. 1999b. "School Board Fears Plague of Suits over Bible Classes." *Atlanta Journal-Constitution.* August 6, 1999, 1A.

Reuter News Service. 1996. "US Steps-up the Criminalization of Non-citizens: House Aims at Kids in Immigration Bill Debate." March 20, 1996. Available: *http:// mojo.calyx.net/~refuse/imm/3_96laws.html.*

Reyes, M. de la Luz. 1992. "Challenging Venerable Assumptions: Literacy Instruction for Linguistically Different Students." *Harvard Education Review.* 62, 427–446.

Ricento, T. 1998. "National Language Policy in the United States." In *Language and Politics in the United States and Canada.* T. Ricento and B. Burnaby, eds. Pp. 85–112. Mahwah, NJ: Lawrence Erlbaum Associates.

Ruiz, R. 1984. "Orientations in Language Planning." *National Association for Bilingual Education Journal.* 8, 15–34.

Schneiderman, E. 1993. "Let's Keep Political Coercion Out of Religion: Reed's Stealth Agenda." *New York Times.* August 29, 1993, §4, 14.

Shannon, S. M. and K. Escamilla. 1999. "Mexican Immigrants in U.S. Schools: Targets of Symbolic Violence." *Educational Policy.* 13(3):347–370.

Shipp, B. 1996a. "Next Governor Will Inherit a Very Full Plate." *Athens Daily News.* September 11, 1996. Available: *http://www.athensnewspapers.com/.*

———. 1996b. "Silly Turf Wars Sending Education Out of Control." *Athens Daily News.* September 18, 1996. Available: *http://www.athensnewspapers.com/.*

Shore, C. and S. Wright. 1997. "Policy: A New Field of Anthropology." In *Anthropology of Policy: Critical Perspectives on Governance and Power.* C. Shore and S. Wright, eds. Pp. 3–39. New York: Routledge.

Skutnabb-Kangas, T. 1988. "Multilingualism and the Education of Minority Children." In *Minority Education: From Shame to Struggle.* T. Skutnabb-Kangas and J. Cummins, eds. Pp. 9–44. Philadelphia: Multilingual Matters.

Sleeter C. and C. Grant. 1996. *Making Choices for Multicultural Education: Five Approaches to Race, Class, and Gender.* Columbus, OH: Merrill.

Spring, J. 1997. *Political Agendas for Education.* Mahwah, NJ: Lawrence Erlbaum.

———. 2000. *The Intersection of Cultures.* New York: McGraw-Hill.

Taxel, J. 1997. "Multicultural Literature and the Politics of Reaction." *Teachers College Record.* 98(3):417–448.

Thomas, W.P. and V.P. Collier. 1997. "School Effectiveness for Language Minority Students." In *Directions in Language and Education.* Washington, DC: George Washington University.

Townley, J., A. Demedeiros, and A. Rundell. 1998. "Identification and Recruitment Issues in Poultry Processing." Presentation at Georgia State Migrant Education Program Retreat. Dawsonville, GA, October 15, 1998.

U.S. Census Bureau. 1990. "Census 1990." Washington, DC: U.S. Department of Commerce. Available: *http://www.census.gov/.*

———. 1999. "Nativity of the Population, for Regions, Divisions, and States: 1850 to 1990." Washington, DC: U.S. Department of Commerce. Available: *http://www.census.gov/population/www/documentation/twps0029/tab13.html.*

U.S. Department of Education. 1999. "Letter Regarding: Compliance Review #04-99-5007." Office for Civil Rights, Atlanta Office, Southern Division. June 1, 1999.

Villenas, S. and E. Hamann. 1997. "The Schooling Implications of the New Latino Diaspora: Is It the Same Old Story?" Paper session at the American Anthropological Association Annual Meeting, Washington, DC. November 22, 1997.

Villenas, S., D. Deyhle, and L. Parker. 1999. Critical Race Theory and Praxis: Chicano(a)/Latino(a) and Navajo Struggles for Dignity, Educational Equity, and Social Justice." In *Race Is . . . Race Isn't: Critical Race Theory and Qualitative Studies in Education.* L. Parker, D. Deyhle, and S Villenas, eds. Boulder: Westview Press.

Washington Post. 1998. "Direct Access: Ralph Reed." *Washington Post.* December 8, 1998. Available: *http://www.washingtonpost.com/wp-srv/politics/talk/zforum/reed120898.htm.*

Welch, B. 1997. "Christ in Politics." *Hermes.* April, 1997. Available: *http://www.wesleyan.edu/hermes/prev/ap97/3A4_97.htm.*

Woodson, C. 1933/1990. *The Mis-Education of the Negro.* Trenton: Africa World Press.

Yeoman, B. 2000. "Hispanic Diaspora." *Mother Jones.* July/August 2000.

Zinn, H. 1980. *A People's History of the United States.* New York: Perennial.

4

¿*Un Paso Adelante?* The Politics of Bilingual Education, Latino Student Accommodation, and School District Management in Southern Appalachia

Edmund T. Hamann

Responding to the call that anthropological inquiry should be directed at the formation, enactment, and effects of policy (Shore and Wright, 1997), this chapter examines a Georgia school district's official and de facto policies for responding to Latino newcomers and the understandings that compelled their making of Latino educational policy. More specifically, it describes how a broad but vague consensus regarding the goals of a novel binational partnership hid the differences in various partners' interests and understandings. Looking at both a Georgia superintendent's initial letter to his prospective partners at a Mexican university and then at the experiences of a Mexican university-affiliated bilingual education coordinator, the chapter highlights the interface between culture, policy, and power, illuminating how and why only certain portions of the formal binational accord were enacted and then only in certain ways. The chapter describes the political posturing, advocacy, and maneuvering that shaped the curriculum that Latino newcomer students encountered at school.

INTRODUCTION

Whether students in U.S. schools who are not native speakers of English should go to school to be assimilated, or whether schooling for such students should acknowledge and celebrate their differences, is a central and unresolved debate in contemporary U.S. society (Wong Fillmore and Meyer, 1992) and elsewhere (Hornberger, 2000). This debate revolves around core issues of who we are, how and by what criteria we group ourselves (Barth, 1969), and who we propose to be. Because schools are a proposed vehicle for the realization of either of these contrasting ends, they are, in this regard, instruments of cultural policy. Yet because of the historic role of schools in relation to the society that has created them, schools are not equally well suited to the two prospective courses outlined earlier. As Hornberger (2000, 173) explains, there is an ideological "paradox wherein a traditionally standardizing education is increasingly called on to make room for and promote diversity."

In looking at a case of how a Georgia school district—Conasauga Public Schools (CPS)—and a Mexican university partner responded recently to dramatic demographic changes in Conasauga, this ethnography of education policy considers how contrasting cultural goals were articulated and enacted as policies and, as a further component of the policy process, how they were resisted and/or appropriated. To illuminate the interwoven nature of power, of culturally defined roles and statuses, of the comprehension of need and circumstance, of policymaking, and of policy enactment as all of these pertain to schooling in the New Latino Diaspora, this study focuses on the evolving understanding of several Mexico and Georgia–based leaders of a binational, K–12/university partnership. Two of the leaders noted here—the superintendent and the curriculum coordinator—were from CPS; another was from the Mexican university; a fourth individual had ties to the Mexican university, but mainly led a trilingual private school in the same city where the Mexican university was located. Finally, two private sector Conasauga community leaders—an eminent, community-oriented attorney, who lacked formal ties to either the university or the school district, and an equally eminent business executive—were also key instigators of the partnership.

In accordance with the other contributors to this volume, with this case study I seek to describe and analyze an example of educational policymaking in the New Latino Diaspora. In so doing, my focus is not directly on the Latino newcomers who were, as Foucault (1977, 200) would note, the "objects of information, but [almost] never the subjects of communication." That Conasauga leaders sought help from more than 1,000 miles away to find out who now lived down the street and what should be done for/with/about them epitomizes this pattern of objectification.

Taking advantage of my position as a partial insider in the Georgia/Mexico partnership's initial creation and implementation, I look at the contested and emerging ways that the needs of the newcomers were understood and responded to by host community leaders and the Mexican scholars they invited to assist them. Consistent with the framework of Shore and Wright (1997), such an analysis seeks to peel back the typical pseudo-objective veneer of policymaking to reveal the micropolitics of how policies responding to demographic change became linked to various leaders' attempts to gain or protect their power and decision-making prerogatives. Their efforts at both prerogative protection and vision articulation had consequences for the other leaders and the Latino newcomers.

Because my initial entrée to Conasauga was as the contracted grant writer for a *Title VII: Systemwide Bilingual Education* proposal, my first and best contacts there were the leaders of the school district. Because chronicling local need was a starting point for our relationship, the generally optimistic leaders not only shared rosy scenarios with me but also acknowledged at least some of the struggles they confronted. Thus my conversations with Conasauga partnership planners effectively highlighted their evolving understanding of the challenges brought forward by the new presence of Latinos. A related starting point for our relationship was my need to understand the still sketchy structure and purported intent of the binational partnership they were creating so that I could write convincingly about how that partnership responded to local challenges and merited funding. My relationships with these educational leaders have persisted up to the time of this writing in the summer of 2000.[1]

Levinson and Sutton (2001, 17) write, "In the processes of policy formation, problems are constructed for solution and thus the needs of individuals and society become subject to authoritative definition." In Conasauga I was privy to the tentative problem constructions engaged in by leaders. In my capacity as grant writer, I helped them articulate an authoritative, "official" policy in response. The Georgia/Mexico partnership that I wrote about in the Title VII proposal was their primary educational policy response to demographic change and to its related challenges to identity and community, though an alternative response—the broad introduction of a fully scripted, monolingual, phonetics-oriented Direct Instruction program—later became a rival policy response as the coalition that created the binational partnership began to fracture.

I first met the Mexican partners before the $500,000 Title VII grant was approved and before a local attorney prevailed on the Conasauga City Council to contribute $750,000 to the new partnership. My ability to speak Spanish (albeit as a second language), my background of having worked and studied in rural Mexico and with Mexican transmigrants in the United States (which meant I was more versed in their area of scholarly expertise than anyone else they encountered in Conasauga), my residence in Georgia (and relevant awareness of statewide currents of educational politics), and my shared status as an outsider to Conasauga (though one familiar with all the insiders) made me a useful sounding board for the Mexican partners. When I visited their university in Mexico for four days in 1998, my visit became an occasion for them to highlight their Georgia work within their university community—as I was asked to make a formal presentation. In turn, I was invited to stay at the home of one of the Mexican partnership leaders, and I was given open access to all of the files the Mexican leaders kept regarding the partnership (except for individual evaluations of teacher candidates sent to Georgia). I had an arranged interview with their university's president, and I had a chance to spend a day with the woman who later became the bilingual coordinator in Conasauga, at the private trilingual primary school she directed in Mexico. I also met with the Mexican leaders during most of their visits to Georgia.

In keeping with Shore and Wright's recommendation that the ethnography of policy should do more than study up, my research methodology was also consistent with Reinhold's notion of "studying through" (cited in Shore and Wright [1997, 14])—i.e., tracing the ways in which power creates webs and relations between actors, institutions, and discourses across time and space. Studying through entails multisite ethnography, as the actors in the "policy community" frequently operate in and are informed by different geographic spaces. In conducting this research, I visited administrative offices and classrooms in Georgia and Mexico. I sat in on the majority of the face-to-face encounters between Georgia and Mexico partners, and I collected documentation (e.g., faxes, letters) of much of their communication that was not face-to-face. To better understand the Conasauga context, I visited the workplaces of Latino newcomers and the corporate offices of their employers. I drew from previous experience living and working in Mexican sending communities and teaching in bilingual adult immigrant education programs in U.S. receiving communities (in Kansas and Georgia). I also spent a lot of time in Conasauga classrooms interviewing educators and observing instruction.

Because of what I found through this range of inquiry, in this chapter I also seek to broaden or counter any assumptions that locate policymaking, implementation, and appropriation as occurring at different hierarchical tiers (i.e., made at only one level and resisted/appropriated only at another). Although hierarchy and status are pertinent to this case study, they are not reliable means for predicting who was an enactor and who was a resister. This may be because, at least initially, the differently situated leaders came to the binational partnership as equals. However, it also reflects the perhaps not-so-surprising revelation that, in the jockeying to influence policy formation and the equally important interpretive tasks that guide policy implementation, the same individual could simultaneously be a policy enactor and a resister.

CULTURE, POLICY, AND THEORIES OF ACTION

Levinson and Sutton define policy "as a complex social practice, an ongoing process of normative cultural production constituted by diverse actors across diverse social and institutional contexts" (2001, 1). Among the norms produced and reproduced are those related to status, role, and decision-making prerogative. As an example of the inescapable embeddedness of culture in formal policymaking, consider that cultural guidelines about roles underlie the decisions regarding who is to make policy, who can formally adapt it, and who should implement it. In the case here, a 72-year-old attorney who had spent his entire professional life in public affairs presumed that it was his prerogative to monitor whether the schools in his community were being suitably responsive to their growing numbers of Latino newcomer students. Because he found no suitable plan, he presumed that it was appropriate that he be a key developer of such a plan. Because of his stature in Conasauga, others there agreed with his presumptions. His initial bid for a formal role in policymaking was broadly accepted. Moreover, his original problem diagnosis or "problem construction" (Levinson and Sutton, in press, 17)—that a "communication gap" was the reason for struggles of English monolingual teachers to teach Spanish monolingual students—became the most broadly accepted understanding of the challenge at hand. Redress meant bridging the gap, which was broadly assumed to be a language education task.

The excitement and the challenge for an ethnography of educational policy is to make sure that the detailed, on-the-ground ethnographic lens reveals underlying cultural beliefs as they favor certain policies and types of policymaking over others, and/or as they compel the resistance to an articulated policy. Argyris and Schön (1978), as understood by Hatch (1998), offer a useful heuristic—their model of theories of action—that helps reveal the cultural roots and cultural processes that are tacitly but powerfully a part of educational policymaking and enactment. Argyris and Schön (1978) differentiate between espoused theory and theory in-use. Both describe theories of action—that is, problem diagnoses, rationales and strategies of response, and posited outcomes. According to Hatch's (1998, 28) synthesis, "[O]fficial pronouncements and presentations reflect *espoused theories* . . . and the actions of program staff or individuals within an organization reflect *theories in-use*."

Describing one highly accessible source of espoused theory data, Shore and Wright (1997, 15) emphasize that an anthropology of policy needs systematically to collect new types of data, particularly "policy documents," and to interpret them as "cultural texts." "They can be treated as classificatory devices, as narratives that serve to justify or condemn the present, or as rhetorical devices and discursive formations that function to empower some and silence others." This chapter later focuses on one such document—a letter of introduction sent by the CPS superintendent to his soon-to-be collaborators at the Mexican university in September 1996, which proposed several possible arenas for collaboration and that, in retrospect, generated confusion at the Mexican end about what CPS leaders wanted and were willing to do. (See Figure 4.1 in the next section.)

In relation to a particular proposed action, both espoused and in-use theories of action can be in significant congruence, but they can also differ substantially. For example, a school district administrator might espouse that the rationale for a program such as the Georgia/Mexico partnership was to improve the way newcomer students were served at school, while the more salient theory in-use could be that, to maintain middle-class (non-Latino) support of the schools, the district needs to look like it has a strategy for responding to the newcomers. In this example, according to the espoused theory, newcomer students are the policy target, but according to the theory in-use, middle-class, Anglo families are the actual priority. Evidence of this theory in-use might be inferred by examining communication networks—Whom does the administrator call? Whose input do they seek for problem diagnosis and proposed remedies? Evidence of the theory in-use might also emerge from listening to the administrator's frequently stated hopes and fears, such as consistently decrying the steady trickle of white students leaving the public school system. In this instance, understanding the administrator's theory in-use would be much more useful for describing the administrator's view of the tasks at hand and his/her sensibility regarding appropriate responses.

Referring back to the concepts of espoused theory and theories in-use, the remainder of the chapter explores why conflicts arose in the enactment of the partnership, why the partnership in practice looked different than it did on paper, and why one of the four components of the project—the bilingual curriculum component—was resisted and then unilaterally terminated. The next section looks at the initial problem diagnosis and mobilization that created the Georgia/Mexico partnership. The subsequent section focuses on the resistance by some CPS partners to the proposed bilingual education component, which ultimately led to that component's uncomfortable termination and to a formal change in the complexion of the partnership. The final part describes how in trying to establish the educational policies that were to be operative in Conasauga, the various leaders described here were simultaneously engaged both in making those policies and resisting at least some of their collaborators' interpretations of that policy.

It should be acknowledged that this chapter describes at greatest length the most contentious and least successful element of the partnership—the bilingual curriculum component—and, in so doing, risks painting the partnership as a failure when, in other lights, the partnership can be held up as a more favorable model of responsiveness to the presence of Latino newcomers (e.g., Zúñiga et al., this volume). Focusing on the unsuccessful component makes sense because it clearly demonstrates the consequences of unacknowledged differences in theories of action, but it risks giving an unjustly negative assessment tone. In other reports that look cumulatively at all four components of the partnership (e.g., Hamann, 1999a), I offer a more balanced assessment.

AN ANATOMY OF POLICY DEVELOPMENT: REACTING TO NEWCOMERS

In the spring of 1996, in Conasauga, a small city north of Atlanta, a senior attorney began an informal inquiry into the quality of education available at local schools for the growing number of Mexican newcomer students.[2] For this inquiry and for the subsequent pursuit of the Georgia/Mexico partnership, the attorney's strategy was in keeping with the type of political decision making that Hunter (1963) found characterized the de facto governing process by the elite in southern cities—the highlighting of interpersonal ties, meeting often behind closed doors, and exchanging personalized correspondence.

When the attorney began to look at how the local schools were responding to demographic change, CPS enrolled 1,243 Hispanic students, about 28 percent of the district's total enrollment. This represented a dramatic change from the 151 Hispanic students (less than 4 percent of the total enrollment) who were enrolled in September 1989, and it also differed from the September 1999 tally of 2,280 Hispanic students (slightly more than 45 percent of enrollment).[3] The ongoing and dramatic changes in student enrollment were the main factors leading to the creation of the binational, four component, K–12/university partnership. The demographic changes were a consequence of changes in the employment patterns of the carpet and poultry industries in the late 1980s and 1990s, and of the related maturation of the migration streams that linked Conasauga to several Mexican sending communities.[4]

The septuagenerian attorney who initiated the Georgia/Mexico partnership was no ordinary individual—having represented Conasauga decades earlier in both the U.S. Congress and the state senate—and his interest in the schools' problems was both civic and personal. According to his frequent public explanations, he was compelled to act by his daughter's complaints. She, working as a monolingual paraprofessional in a suddenly majority–Hispanic elementary school, had complained about her and her colleagues' lack of knowledge regarding how to communicate with most of the students at her school. She added that those students and their parents appeared similarly frustrated in their attempts to communicate with her and her colleagues. Given this language gap, productive teaching was becoming difficult.

Visiting his daughter's school, the attorney was surprised by the frustration and confusion he encountered among instructors. He was further disconcerted when he asked school district leaders how they were responding to the presence of so many Spanish-speaking students with little or no English language skills.[5] The retiring superintendent admitted that they had no real plan. The attorney became convinced that the CPS status quo was inadequate and that he needed to make sure that the district did something quickly to respond to its changing demography. This decision to take action personally was consistent with a long-standing local pattern. Flamming (1992) notes that, in and near Conasauga, industrial leaders and other elite private citizens had personally intervened in schools and other civic institutions since the area's industrialization began in the late 1800s.

The attorney found that the district he was critiquing agreed with his call to action. Although they had no comprehensive plan of their own, district leaders were not opposed to accommodating the growing numbers of Hispanic newcomer students. Akin to the teachers that Heath (1983) worked with in the 1970s, who had broad latitude to shape curriculum because their districts were unsure how to negotiate the sudden changes of desegregation, the attorney initially had broad latitude to help shape Conasauga schools' first response to its new demographic reality. As with the teachers in Heath's study, the attorney's window of opportunity to innovate and improvise was eventually challenged by the district as it tried to reassert a more traditional protocol for policymaking, but that challenge did not emerge until later. At first the attorney did not always act with the district personnel's explicit awareness, but he always acted with their blessing.

Knowing that he was not an educational expert, the attorney wrote dozens of letters and initiated dozens of conversations with Georgia university personnel, political contacts, and bureaucrats at the state department of education, in all cases seeking advice and support for an initiative that would help the district. Early on he determined that attracting bilingual educators to the schools was crucial. Only bilingual personnel could bridge between groups that were monolingual in different languages.

As an indicator of the attorney's eminence and the regional appropriateness of his "campaign" style, the chancellor of the Georgia Board of Regents felt compelled to write back to the attorney, conceding apologetically that the Georgia public universities had no bilingual teacher training programs, endorsement protocols, or even strategies to attract bi/multilingual persons into teaching. The chancellor further acknowledged that the Board of Regents was slowly waking up to the need for such programs, but that they would be some time in coming.

Also among the people the attorney communicated with in 1996 was his client, longtime family friend, and neighbor—the wealthy CEO of one of Conasauga's large manufacturers. The attorney explained the schools' dilemma as he understood it—as a communication gap. The CEO responded by mentioning that he knew someone whom he thought could help, a Mexican business partner who had ties to a private Mexican university.

According to sources I interviewed at that private Mexican university, the Georgia CEO three times called his powerful business partner, asking that partner how Conasauga could be assisted in its efforts to accommodate its influx of Mexicans. After the third call, the Mexican business leader was convinced of the Conasauga CEO's seriousness, and he agreed to contact the university's rector to discuss creating a partnership between CPS and the Mexican university.

The chain of communication had quickly become quite extended—an attorney, acting somewhat on behalf of a school district, talking to a local industrialist, who contacted a Mexican industrialist, who contacted a Mexican university leader—and in September 1996, only four months after his original school visits, the attorney received the name of a sociology professor at the Mexican university. That professor had been approached by his university's rector to lead that university's still nebulously defined participation in a possible binational partnership. Ever impatient and feeling stymied by the insufficient response from Georgia institutions to his inquiries, the attorney called the Mexican professor to explain Conasauga's challenges and to ascertain how the professor's university could help. The first conversation was choppy. It was humorously recalled by both as hampered by a low-quality international connection, the attorney's complete lack of Spanish proficiency, and the professor's limited English proficiency, complicated by the attorney's unfamiliar southern accent. Nonetheless, the nascent partnership now had a leader in Georgia and a leader in Mexico.

Shortly thereafter, with a quick orientation from the attorney and a few others, CPS's new superintendent agreed to participate in the partnership. Although his initial understanding of what was being arranged was vague, the new superintendent had a well-honed political instinct reflecting his previous experience winning two elections for the superintendent role in a different Georgia jurisdiction.[6] Moreover he was familiar and comfortable with the personalized politicking (Hunter, 1963) in which the attorney, the CEO, and other local supporters of the nascent partnership engaged. As CPS's first superintendent with no previous experience in CPS, he knew that appearing responsive to local leaders was important. Thus he said "yes" when the Georgia attorney asked him to send a letter (Figure 4.1) to the Mexican professor that clarified how the Mexican university could help Conasauga schools. The "clarity" the letter generated, however, was both minimal and ephemeral. The Mexican partners were enthused by the letter, but also misled.

The letter marked the first substantive communication between CPS and the Mexican university. Thus it was disproportionately important to the Mexican partners' conceptualizations of CPS's wishes, understandings, and expectations. The analysis that follows considers how the letter led the Mexican partners to misunderstand both the modus operandi of CPS and the desired outcomes of its leaders. Notably, the letter suggested a greater familiarity with and support for bilingual education than was actually the case and it suggested a less hierarchic, more inclusive decision-making structure than actually prevailed in CPS.

Several facets of this letter merit specific attention. Levinson and Sutton (2001) emphasize policy's role in the production and reproduction of norms, and there were a number of norms embedded in the superintendent's text. For example, the superintendent explicitly refers to his Georgia experience with K–12/university partnerships to suggest that the Georgia template can be a model for the binational partnership they were creating. Within that template the superintendent initially envisioned Conasauga as a hosting site for preservice teachers (and administrators) engaging in their student teaching.

On the other side, because systematic consultation between instructors and administrators was a normal practice in the regular professional lives of the Mex-

Figure 4.1
The First Letter from Conasauga Public Schools to Mexico

Dear [Mexican partner],

As the Superintendent of the Conasauga Public Schools, I send you greetings on behalf of our students, faculty and Board of Education. I truly look forward to this excellent opportunity to work with you to provide the needed educational opportunity our students deserve.

You have already received information regarding our eight schools. I am extremely proud of these schools and the work being done to provide an outstanding education for our students.

I have now met with our eight school principals on two occasions to discuss the possibilities of assistance from [your university]. They are very excited about the assistance you may offer.

We have discussed many strategies which could assist us. We have a high percent of Spanish speaking students at three of our schools and this number increases each year. All of us agree that adult bilingual assistance in the classes would be of great benefit to all concerned.

By providing instruction in the native language, these students could increase their skill levels in academic subjects. Also, we could provide intensive English instruction with the ultimate goal being that of a literate bilingual student.

I am unclear of the training your teachers receive. In the University System of Georgia, a student in training to be a teacher must spend three months in a school in an experience called "student teaching." This person is under the supervision of the University and the classroom teacher. If you have such an experience for those in training to be a teacher, we could provide this experience in our schools. If your teacher training does not contain this requirement, perhaps the "Georgia Experience" with Conasauga Schools could serve in the place of some of your courses in education training.

Additionally, if there is training for school administrators, we would welcome these students. I am certain there are many positive experiences anyone would receive by working in our schools.

Also, if nurses or school counselors are available or in training, we would certainly welcome them.

Perhaps this program could lead to an exchange of educators. We could possibly send some of our teachers for training in Mexico. Other ideas include: instructing our teachers in the Spanish language, creating Saturday classes for children and adults (families), summer school, obtaining textbooks in Spanish and many others.

It is my desire and I have the approval of our Board of Education to hire someone to coordinate all these activities. I am certain this person should be extremely organized and willing to work hard to implement this program.

I have listed the schools below and the number of your teachers/students they have requested. I asked the principals to state their needs, perhaps these numbers are too high, but I believe they confirm our needs.

Signal Hill—13, Oakwood—2, Town Park—2, Hamilton—20, Guthrie—10,
West Glen—4, Conasauga Jr. High School—5, Conasauga High School—12.

This is a total of sixty-eight (68) people! Perhaps an unrealistic number at the beginning of this project. But please remember, I did ask for the needs. One-half of the number would be wonderful. As you analyze our needs it will be obvious that we will appreciate any assistance you provide.

We would do all we could to provide housing and substance [*sic*] for these individuals. I am certain our community would welcome your students/faculty with open arms.

Please consider this proposal and contact [the attorney] with your thoughts regarding this request.

Again, I truly look forward to working with you as we develop this program.

Sincerely,

CONASAUGA PUBLIC SCHOOLS SUPERINTENDENT

cc: [the attorney]

ican partners, they inferred from the superintendent's reference to consultation with building principals that such consultation was the norm in Conasauga instead of an anomalous example. This "misread" meant that later suggestions by the Mexican bilingual curriculum coordinator for CPS officials to consult with school site practitioners were heard differently than had been intended.

The letter misled the Mexican partners in another way. As I confirmed in several conversations with the Mexican partners, they presumed from the letter's overt expression of need for bilingual teachers, from its mention of the importance of native language instruction, and its support of the goal of bilingualism that there was enthusiasm in Conasauga for bilingual education and the assistance of Mexican instructors. (My Title VII grant application which the Mexican partners read six months later also made Conasauga educational leaders seem conversant with the main principles, strategies, and options of bilingual education.) The Mexican leaders inferred that the concept of bilingual education was broadly familiar in CPS and that bilingual education was to be an ongoing mechanism for developing all students' bilingualism rather than just a transitional vehicle for Latino newcomer students who had not yet sufficiently mastered English.

Because of the superintendent's seeming familiarity with bilingual education, it was easy to overlook the fact that though he promised to hire an "extremely organized and willing to work hard" partnership coordinator he did not promise to hire a coordinator with pertinent content knowledge. As it happened, after no external searching, the superintendent's executive secretary was designated to be the CPS coordinator, but none of her other duties were reduced. Clearly committed to the Project's success, the executive secretary supported the partnership's development by working extra hours and during weekends. This laudable dedication, however, permitted CPS to avoid any administrative reconfiguration to support the Georgia/Mexico partnership. As of the spring of 2000, CPS's execution of partnership-related administrative tasks still depended on the extra energy and goodwill of a monolingual employee who had many other responsibilities and no formal expertise in bilingual/multicultural education or with immigration issues.

Before writing the letter, the superintendent consulted with principals in each CPS school to discover their wishes and needs. However, after these meetings the principals (and other school-based personnel) were not systematically included in the Georgia/Mexico partnership planning process that led to and guided the partnership's formal enactment. During the 1997–1998 school year, the principals were consulted regarding the performance of the visiting instructors from Mexico, and there appeared to be open channels of communication between the schools and the superintendent, but the point remains that from this letter Mexican partners could surmise more site-based input than subsequently occurred and could presume more site-based knowledge of and support for the partnership than actually existed. This presumption of a collaborative relationship between CPS school sites and central administration later complicated the efforts of the Mexican university's designated bilingual curriculum coordinator.

Although the superintendent never subsequently lobbied for the number of Mexican instructors that he noted in the letter, and the principals initially claimed they needed, it is easy to see how the Mexican partners (and the attorney) inferred from his letter that he enthusiastically supported the visiting instructor component. Given the figure in his letter and the success of the initial 14 visiting instructors who came in October 1997, it is striking that the CPS superintendent successfully reduced the proposed number of visiting instructors for 1998–1999 from 25, the figure suggested by the attorney to the Mexican university officials, to the 16 that were ultimately agreed upon. When the Georgia/Mexico partnership seemed like an abstract wish list, the superintendent was willing both to echo the attorney's emphasis on the recruitment of bilingual instructors and to repeat the CPS principals' declarations of need. However, two years later the superintendent's sense of the cost and logistical complications of managing the visiting instructors from Mexico led him to request a much smaller number. He was not willing to argue for the substantial reallocation of resources and logistical adjustments that the principals' original request would have required. He was willing to ask for help from an unorthodox source, but only in a supplemental rather than transformative way.

In his letter the superintendent asked the Mexican partners to direct further questions and communication to the Georgia/Mexico partnership's instigating attorney. In hindsight this contributed to the Mexican partners' uncertainty regarding who at the Conasauga end was actually in charge of the Georgia/Mexico partnership. Was it the school district's chief executive or the private attorney? Referring to the partnership's ambiguous leadership in Conasauga, the Mexican professors subsequently recounted, "We were never sure who to send the faxes to."

Moreover, beyond this ambiguity, the superintendent's letter gave no indication of the important role the CPS curriculum coordinator would play in shaping CPS's actual participation in the partnership. Although it would have been awkward in a letter such as this to note that the curriculum coordinator, with 25 years of work for CPS to her credit, had been a finalist for the CPS superintendency (and would have been the first woman to ever occupy that position), failure to mention her while mentioning the principals could, by reasonable interpretation on the part of Mexican readers, suggest that the principals' input would be substantial and that no substantive (let alone discordant) role on the part of central administrators needed to be anticipated.

Toward the end of the letter, the superintendent asserted that he was "certain" the community would welcome the Mexican university's assistance with open arms. It is unclear how this welcome was to be made manifest and who was supposed to be included in the term "community." I assume the superintendent was not referring to the relatively small but obviously vocal group whose anti-immigrant letters-to-the-editor had compelled Conasauga's local newspaper to temporarily suspend printing such texts in 1995. Presumably many of the citizens who had successfully petitioned for the opening of a local Immigration and Naturalization Service office were also not included. It is true that, as a newcomer to town, the superintendent may well not have been aware of this recent local political history.

As it turned out, however, CPS educational administrators ended up heeding community voices that narrowly defined an acceptable welcome for newcomers. In promising the welcome of the host community, the letter left unacknowledged that the welcome available might not match the welcome that Mexican project leaders anticipated. In fact, as I have written elsewhere (Hamann, 1999b), Suárez-Orozco's (1998) "pro-immigration script" adeptly describes the allegedly pro-newcomer orientation of many Conasauga citizens, particularly those in professional positions. According to that script, newcomers are welcome because they are religious, familial, devoted, hardworking, and willing to take jobs no one else will. In Conasauga, the newcomers' presence was constructed as supporting the up-by-the-bootstraps model of social advancement and thereby proving Conasauga was an essentially fair place for all. This script, however, idealizes and bounds newcomers, simultaneously claiming that newcomers must want to be assimilated and that they are virtuous in part because of their willingness to tolerate hazardous, low-paying jobs. The script both rationalizes assimilative schooling and the presence and perpetuation of newcomer Latinos' marginal economic status. To quote David Spener (1988, 146), what the host society offers is "assimilation at the bottom." Ultimately it was only supplemental and assimilative portions of the Georgia/Mexico partnership that CPS leaders were willing to implement with any vigor.

As the Georgia/Mexico partnership was getting started, CPS officials were unsure of all that was potentially being offered—hence the superintendent's questions about bilingual nurses, administrators, and so forth and his reference to familiar models (e.g., the offerings of the University System of Georgia). Although officials acknowledged this uncertainty, they nonetheless remained certain about their responsibility and prerogative to be at the table as decision makers. Conasauga leaders were willing to ask for help, but because of their lack of expertise they were not well positioned to scrutinize whether what was being offered was really what they wanted. Thus they set up a scenario where, regarding some educational policy for Conasauga's Latino newcomer students, Mexican partners could say "you said this was what you wanted" and Conasauga leaders could say "yes, but we did not mean it." Of course, neither at that time nor since has such a frank interchange occurred.

Mexican participants in the first face-to-face meeting between Conasauga and Mexican leaders in December 1996 distinctly remember that, on the first day of the meeting, those on the Conasauga side only presented the attorney's wish for help finding bilingual instructors. Although their notes from that meeting indicate that they also received a one-page "curriculum goals" sheet from the CPS curriculum coordinator, none of the Mexican meeting participants remembered the sheet or any discussion of its contents.[7] Although she was technically "at the table" and "on record" in favor of bilingual education, in many ways the curriculum coordinator's input and prerogative regarding the partnership was downplayed at this early meeting. Direct Instruction, a tightly scripted, monolingual, phonetics curriculum that was later strongly championed by the curriculum coordinator (at the expense of some partnership initiatives), was not mentioned at the December 1996 meeting.

According to Mexican university-based partnership leaders, three-fourths of the four-component structure of the partnership initially agreed upon reflected items added to the partnership agenda by the Mexican collaborators and agreed to by the Conasauga contingent. In March 1997, the four-component structure of the Georgia/Mexico partnership was formally signed into being at a ceremony at Conasauga High School. Following the original vision of the Conasauga attorney, the agreement specifically promised the recruitment, specialized orientation, and placement of bilingual graduates of the Mexican university into Conasauga classrooms. It also promised the organization of a summer training institute for Georgia teachers at the university in Mexico. It outlined a multifaceted research, needs assessment, and community leadership development initiative that would have the Mexican researchers work with Conasauga's Latino newcomer community. And it promised that the Mexican university would help CPS to adapt the Georgia-mandated Quality Core Curriculum (QCC) into a bilingual, more culturally responsive format. In turn, this adapted curriculum was to be implemented, at least in part, by the Mexico-trained visiting instructors.

AN ANATOMY OF POLICY RESISTANCE

Space constraints do not permit a review of all the components of the Georgia/Mexico partnership's implementation through 1999. But highlighting the demise of the bilingual component illustrates how, beneath a superficial consensus favoring the partnership, there were competing ideas about what the partnership should accomplish and how it should be governed.

In June 1997 Mexican university personnel assured the attorney that the bilingual curriculum revisions were essentially complete. But in October 1997, when the first group of Mexican visiting instructors finally arrived, the revised curriculum had not yet been accepted by the district. This made the immediate tasks of the visiting instructors unsure and ambiguous. In fact, the revised curriculum was never accepted by CPS. Even in April 2000, the CPS curriculum coordinator maintained that it was never received, while Mexican university partners claimed that such an explanation was misleading. CPS seemed to have unilaterally changed its expectations regarding what the curriculum was to be, and then they avoided several Mexican efforts to clarify what was being sought.

In the summer of 1998, with neither the Mexican university's nor the attorney's assent, CPS indicated that it no longer had any interest in the bilingual component (though it would push ahead with a nonpartnership-related initiative to add Spanish as a foreign language classes four days a week at all elementary and middle schools). Rejecting the partnership's bilingual component did not indicate, however, that bilingual education per se was being abandoned. A CPS principal interviewed on National Public Radio's *All Things Considered* insisted as recently as March 1999 that her school embraced bilingual education. What seems then to have been in dispute was who would get to define bilingual education in Conasauga and what that definition would encompass. One hundred sixty minutes per week of Spanish as a foreign language classes and the acceptance of the use of Spanish by paraprofessionals tutoring Spanish speakers were de facto what CPS was characterizing as bilingual education.

In contrast, the Mexican sociologists who had first suggested the bilingual component had done so as part of a more complex maneuver related to whether and under what terms they were willing to join the partnership. Although the prospect of even limited links to CPS would have had some attraction to the Mexican university, leaders there remembered that they had rejected the initially proposed stand-alone package of sending Mexican teachers to be bilingual paraprofessionals in Georgia classrooms. They had agreed to provide such support only if they were also allowed to engage in a community study, to examine adult education opportunities for Latino newcomers, to identify potential Conasauga-based Latino leaders, and so on. To the Mexican partners, the bilingual component was an element in a multifaceted initiative that recognized, affirmed, and built on the cultural knowledge and frameworks that Latino newcomers brought with them to Conasauga.

Thus there were unreconciled differences in theories of action regarding both who was to make decisions and what was in the best interest of Hispanic newcomer students and the district at large. One administrative change in Mexico obscured the immediate recognition of difference in theories. Because the Mexican university's main Georgia/Mexico partnership leaders were applied sociologists (and supporters of but not experts in bilingual education), the Mexican team initially relied on one of its graduates to serve as a bilingual education consultant. When that consultant indicated he could no longer continue with the partnership in the fall of 1997, Mexican leaders turned to another alumna as their new bilingual education consultant. She made her first visit to Conasauga in January 1998, and returned for a second visit at the end of April.

When the new Mexican bilingual component coordinator visited Conasauga and CPS for the first time in January 1998, she brought several operating assumptions with her. First, she thought her main task was curriculum development and therefore that she needed to clarify what kind of curriculum CPS would want. She did not anticipate this would be problematic, because it was in line with the superintendent's original September 1996 letter and with the partnership agreement brokered in December 1996 and signed in March 1997. Second, she thought the curriculum would be implemented by the visiting instructors and perhaps others. According to the orientation she had received from the Mexican partnership leaders, the bilingual component and the visiting instructor component were linked. It followed that primary activities of her visit were observing how the visiting instructors were being used and listening to what CPS administrators thought of the instructors' performances to that point. Her final assumption reflected both her upbringing and her job. Because of her experience growing up in both the United States and Mexico and because of her job leading a combined, private, trilingual *primaria* and *secundaria* (elementary and secondary school) in a Mexican city, she thought of bilingualism and bilingual education as sensible and straightforward and as a permanent rather than a transitional strategy.[8]

During her three-day January 1998 visit, she met the attorney, the superintendent, and the curriculum coordinator, each of whom had been part of the Conasauga delegation that visited Mexico in December 1996. The new bilingual coordinator saw all 13 visiting Mexican instructors, watched many of them teach, and stopped at all eight schools in the system, even the two that since Christmas break were no longer hosting a visiting instructor.[9] She talked to principals, assistant principals, educational instructional specialists (EISs), and others who oversaw the visiting instructor's duties at the schools. In conversations with administrators, she recommended the bilingual education research of Jim Cummins, and she promoted the total quality management approach (TQM) to administration. She saw Direct Instruction for the first time and commented to several people that she was intrigued by it.[10] She did not say and perhaps did not see that Direct Instruction was inconsistent with the decentralization of decision making that is a core tenet of TQM and that it challenged several of the Georgia/Mexico partnership's four components.

Direct Instruction is a strictly scripted phonetics-oriented curriculum that CPS leaders, listening to consultants not involved with the Georgia/Mexico partnership, were implementing at the same time as the Georgia/Mexico partnership. Championed by the CPS curriculum coordinator in particular (who was one of the few people in the district authorized to approve the substantial investment required for the importation of Direct Instruction), Direct Instruction became the new curriculum adopted by CPS partially in lieu of the bilingual component that the partnership agreement had specified. Direct Instruction was adopted without consulting the Mexican university. Nonetheless, the visiting instructors from Mexico were centrally involved in the classroom delivery of Direct Instruction, which created the irony of Mexican nationals who spoke deeply accented English teaching English phonetics to Latino newcomers.

On February 19, 1998, the Mexican bilingual coordinator and the university's partnership leader faxed a report they had cowritten about the bilingual coordinator's visit to the CPS superintendent. The bilingual coordinator was the report's lead author, though the name of the partnership leader at the Mexican university was also attached, implying his review and endorsement of its contents. Reflecting both courtesy and the ongoing lack of clarity as to who in Conasauga was in charge of the Georgia/Mexico partnership, additional copies of the report were directed to the attorney and to the CPS curriculum coordinator. The presumption at the Mexican end was that the report would remain a private working document. In fact, because of political considerations in Conasauga, it did not.

In early February 1998, after the bilingual coordinator's visit but before the preparation of her report, there was a public meeting of the ad hoc Georgia/Mexico partnership committee, the loosely structured body headed by the attorney that was composed mainly of prominent local business leaders. For this occasion, there was a long list of invitees, including all the Mexican visiting instructors, a representative from a local junior college, the chair of the Conasauga City Council's Finance Committee, a bilingual priest, a social worker with the Migrant Education program, and four representatives from a neighboring school district that had participated modestly in the Georgia/Mexico partnership, as well as various business leaders, the attorney and his assistant, and four representatives from the CPS Central Office (including the superintendent and the curriculum coordinator). In all, there were 29 present, including me.

The meeting's official agenda was surprisingly brief. There were five items listed, including the fifth entitled, "Other matters for consideration." The CPS curriculum coordinator was supposed to speak second, giving an update on the Georgia/Mexico partnership's "curriculum design." I knew an hour ahead of time, however, that the printed agenda was to be changed. I was to present a "deliverables report" that I had prepared for the superintendent and dropped off just that morning. The deliverables report was not on the official agenda. It was a five-page summary of what the Georgia/Mexico partnership had accomplished to date that I had prepared as a favor to the superintendent. A local business leader had promised that his company would support the Georgia/Mexico partnership if only he could see proof of its "deliverables." I had made the report relatively short, but it was not organized to support an oral presentation.

The attorney presided over the meeting. He decided to insert me into the agenda second, ahead of the curriculum coordinator's curriculum report. In the packet assembled under the attorney's supervision and distributed to all attendees, the outline that the curriculum coordinator had prepared to support her presentation was enclosed last, after the new Mexican bilingual curriculum coordinator's résumé, after articles from *Time*, the *Atlanta Journal-Constitution*, and *The Kiplinger Washington Letter* regarding Hispanic education and national demographic trends, after sheets of statistics breaking down enrollment at CPS's two secondary schools and three Title 1 elementary schools by race and ethnicity, after a one-page Georgia/Mexico partnership budget, after several letters about the partnership written by an immigration lawyer who had assisted with the visiting instructors' visas, and after a recent local newspaper story that labeled the Georgia/Mexico partnership as a "bilingual education program." I do not know whether the agenda-bumping and placing the outline last in the packet were intentional slights, but the curriculum coordinator's role and report were deemphasized by these actions.

When the curriculum coordinator finally did speak, she introduced the "Bilingual Transitional Plan." The plan was described as not having been "formally presented or adopted," but it was based on the input of "many [unspecified] people, much reading, and some experience." The Mexican university was not mentioned, and no Mexican partners remembered having reviewed the document. The stated goal of the plan was to have "all students achieving at grade level in English while developing skill in a second language."

The first four points all related to non-native speakers of English and varied in their specificity. The plans for instruction in English were all much clearer than for instruction in Spanish, but there was acknowledged intent to include the latter. According to the second item of the two-page plan, "All research indicates the stronger one is in his/her first language the easier the transition to a second language." Based on this research, the plan recommended beginning Spanish instruction in kindergarten, offering Spanish for Spanish-speakers, and having bilingual staff and language learning related technology. This portion of the plan and all others notably excluded the idea of any academic content instruction in Spanish, apart from language arts. One line in the plan did promise that "primary instruction would be in English with the students' native language (Spanish) utilized to facilitate language and academic growth." Her report generated no public questions.

As the meeting ended, eight people lingered for an unannounced executive planning session. All were business leaders except the attorney, the CPS superintendent, and me (who, sensing a research opportunity, asked if I could stay). The CPS curriculum coordinator's presentation of the Bilingual Transition Plan was lost in the shuffle. No one asked about the recent visit of the bilingual curriculum coordinator from Mexico, nor whether any of the Mexican partners had endorsed the CPS curriculum coordinator's proposal. Despite the lack of attention that the curriculum plan received at the end of the meeting, it resurfaced in two separate and significant ways during the following month.

The February 19 report faxed by the Mexican partners clearly, if unwittingly, reasserted their assumption that they were still leading the bilingual curriculum development initiative. It made no reference to the CPS curriculum coordinator's outline or presentation at the early February meeting. Although all of the visiting Mexican instructors had attended that meeting (excluding the executive session), they had not reported back to partnership leaders in Mexico that the CPS curriculum coordinator had presented an alternative curriculum action plan.

The Mexican partners' report did make several pointed comments and a few subtle ones. For example, the report criticized the frequent casting of the visiting instructors as assistants or paraprofessionals, saying in the recommendations section: "The [name of the university] teachers are not U.S. certified, but they have been certified in Mexico. They are not at the level of paraprofessionals and they are not student teachers. In fact, most of them have had important experience as teachers in Mexican private, bilingual schools. [Name of the university] teachers could and should take a more pro-active role."

Although acknowledging that the visiting instructors were happy and had been treated well by the superintendent and his assistants and by the principals and teachers at the schools, the report complained about the Consasauga teachers' regular failure to pass along lesson plans and other preparatory materials to visiting Mexican instructors ahead of time. The Mexican teachers frequently first viewed a lesson plan at the moment they were supposed to be enacting it. The report also complained about the marginal spaces—hallways, cafeterias, supply closets, etc.—where the Mexican instructors (and newcomer students) were frequently expected to work.[11] Additionally, it criticized the lack of clarity regarding what the instructors' task was to be. (At the Mexican end, the assumption had been that they would implement the bilingual curriculum created as part of the partnership, but in the absence of that curriculum, Conasauga educators initially were quite uncertain about how to collaborate with the visitors.)

That so much of the report was devoted to detailing the experience of the visiting instructors reiterates that those on the Mexican end viewed the visiting instructor component and the bilingual curriculum component as closely intertwined. There was also much in the report about the still promised bilingual curriculum itself, but mostly questions. In a section entitled "The Conasauga Model for Bilingual Education," the Mexican authors proposed an April 1998 summit (which was never held) to hasten the development of the curriculum CPS was seeking. At the proposed conference, four questions were to be answered:

- "What do Conasauga teachers, principals, superintendent want?" [*sic*]
  (Note how they propose to consult with several groups. Note too that the CPS curriculum coordinator was not included in the list, though that did not necessarily mean she was to be excluded from the process.)
- "What do Conasauga students need?"
  (Note that the possible answers to this question could include much that was not part of Georgia's Quality Core curriculum or the Direct Instruction curriculum.)
- "How will all Conasauga students, Anglos and Hispanics, reach the goal of graduating at 12th-grade reading level?"
- "Will the 'Transitional Bilingual' model be used?"
  (Note that the reference to transitional bilingual models was a question. Though they had their own ideas regarding what was most appropriate, Mexican partners were still unsure as to what bilingual curriculum format CPS was seeking.)

This segment of the report ended with a final tie-in between curriculum development and the role of the visiting instructors: "These [answers to the questions] are issues which must be carefully defined by all. Once the model is clarified, the role for the [visiting Mexican] teachers should also be easier to clarify with respect to the difference between their roles and that of the U.S. teachers, the ESOL teachers, the paraprofessionals, etc."

Although blunt and perhaps critical of CPS's failure to recognize the visiting instructors' status as credentialed educators, the report was neither dismissive nor inappropriate. Assuming that it would be read only by those leading the Georgia/Mexico partnership and/or CPS, the authors' straightforwardness was intended constructively. These were questions that needed to be answered so that the Georgia/Mexico partnership could move forward and achieve the objectives that Mexican leaders thought were desired at the Conasauga end. Embedded in the report were assumptions and questions about policy—assumptions that the Mexican university was still supposed to contribute to curriculum policy development and questions about the hows and whats of detailing that policy.

What was desired at the Conasauga end varied, however. On February 27, in a maneuver that reasserted his own power, the attorney mailed copies of the Mexican partners' February 19 report to everyone on his Georgia/Mexico partnership mailing list (i.e., to more than 100 people). By mailing the bilingual curriculum coordinator's report, the attorney was inviting thought, feedback, and participation from many beyond the CPS Central Office regarding how the identified obstacles could be addressed. But he had also converted constructive private criticism between partners into public criticism of CPS.

On March 5, at a luncheon meeting with partnership leaders from both countries that included the superintendent, several other CPS Central Office figures, the attorney, his assistant, and four administrators from Mexico, the CPS curriculum coordinator again shared her Bilingual Transitional Plan. There were no adjustments in response to the February 19 report from Mexican partners, nor even an acknowledgment of it in the barely revised document, though she did refer to this report orally.

Early in the meeting, through the intervention of the superintendent's executive secretary (who had a large administrative role coordinating CPS's portion of the partnership), the curriculum coordinator was invited to present her comments regarding the bilingual curriculum component. The secretary had intervened because she knew the curriculum coordinator was trying to keep another appointment. The curriculum coordinator distributed the Bilingual Transitional Plan she had presented in early February and said that the model recommended in the Mexican bilingual coordinator's February report was not the one that CPS was seeking. This misrepresented the Mexican partners' February report, as it had not recommended a particular model—but rather had asked if transitional bilingual education (TBE) was what CPS was seeking. Although a departure from the spirit of what the Mexican university had initially suggested, TBE seemed like the closest match to what the Mexican bilingual coordinator thought was being asked for. Still, though the Mexican partnership coordinator had been named as coauthor of the February report, neither he nor anyone else present at this March meeting was enough of a curriculum expert to question the CPS curriculum coordinator's interpretation of the February report. Nor did anyone challenge her own plan as vague and contradictory.

The curriculum coordinator's presentation was not long, nor did it draw many questions. She did say that she had not yet had the chance to share her own plan with the bilingual component coordinator in Mexico (who was not present). She also said that the School Board had not yet seen it, and she asked the present Mexican partners to convey the message to their bilingual component coordinator that during the coordinator's next visit she was not to meet with CPS principals; rather her role was to act more as a private consultant to the superintendent and the curriculum coordinator. Honoring that request, when the Mexican bilingual coordinator did return in early May, she did not meet with CPS principals.

Later in the March 5 meeting, after the curriculum coordinator had left, when the Mexican university's budget for the partnership was reviewed, no one noticed the contradiction between the budget's inclusion of the bilingual component and the unilateral curriculum decision made by the curriculum coordinator. The budget text claimed that the curriculum design needed to be accepted by the principals and assumed that the curriculum would be put together by the Mexican bilingual coordinator.

After the meeting, on March 18, perhaps displaying frustration at the CPS curriculum coordinator's exclusion of the Mexican partners in her preparation of the Bilingual Transitional Plan, the attorney again tried to outflank the CPS coordinator (though again not overtly). In a letter to the partnership's amorphously defined "committee and friends" announcing a substantial gathering being planned for March 27, the attorney enclosed a copy of a letter written by a former Georgia State Department of Education administrator that praised the insight of the Mexican partners' February 19 report. The former state administrator wrote, "From an instructional point of view, I was most interested in Professor [bilingual coordinator]'s report. Her comments indicate that she has a solid foundation in how students learn within the context of multilingual, multicultural environments." The attorney was not enough of an education expert to convincingly intervene directly in a curriculum methodology debate, but, as he had before, he tried to be convincing by quoting someone whose expertise was clearer.

The Mexican bilingual coordinator made a return visit to CPS in early May 1998. According to a Mexican colleague who accompanied her, during that visit the CPS curriculum coordinator directly asked the bilingual component coordinator to send all future correspondence regarding the Georgia/Mexico partnership exclusively and directly to her. It was unclear whether the superintendent was also supposed to be excluded from the direct chain of communication.

In the summer of 1998, CPS moved to freeze the bilingual curriculum component (while continuing with other facets of the Georgia/Mexico partnership). Because the attorney did not concur with this decision, he disregarded it in his communication with the Mexican university. As late as the fall of 1998, the university was including a category for bilingual curriculum consulting in its budget submissions to CPS. As recently as the spring of 1999 (and perhaps since then), the Mexican leaders of the Georgia/Mexico partnership were still centrally involving the bilingual coordinator in their portion of the partnership's administration, as they still sought to clarify the curricular tasks of the visiting instructors. In April 2000, a Mexican partner still characterized the bilingual component as inactive rather than terminated.

In one light then, the conflict stemmed from the CPS curriculum coordinator acting out her belief that curriculum decision making for the district was centrally her prerogative, not a shared task of the partnership, whereas the Mexican collaborators continued to follow the March 1997 partnership accord (which stated that they would develop a bilingual curriculum). The partnership-founding attorney sided with the Mexican collaborators. In the months and years that followed the establishment of the partnership, the CPS curriculum coordinator became an increasingly outspoken champion and promoter of Direct Instruction—a curriculum that was completely scripted and monolingual and, as importantly, that was centrally managed and independent from the partnership agreement. No doubt, part of the CPS curriculum coordinator's theory of action for embracing Direct Instruction reflected her understanding of what would work best for Latino newcomer children. But she was also relying on theories in-use about her own power, responsibility, prerogative, and position. The curricular policy she proposed supported the cultural reproduction of a hierarchical management structure, a structure that formally offered her much authority.

Meanwhile, though initially intrigued by Direct Instruction, the Mexican partners quickly began to doubt the value of that curricular strategy, at least to the extent that it meant a major responsibility of the visiting instructors was to deliver a fully scripted, fully phonics–based curriculum in English. Whatever its virtues, Direct Instruction forfeited taking advantage of the visiting instructors' familiarity with Mexican schooling, cultural mores, and language. Direct Instruction was inconsistent with the cultural affirmation orientation that the Mexican partners thought had been built into the design of the partnership.

PARTNERSHIP POLITICS AND SCHOOLING THE NEW LATINO DIASPORA

The Georgia/Mexico partnership's existence increased Conasauga's capacity to accommodate Latino newcomers. However, remembering the partnership's origin outside the school system, as a program initiated by a savvy attorney and substantially developed by a Mexican university, the partnership's existence did not indicate CPS's unqualified embrace. Various CPS instructors consistently questioned the district's receptiveness to change, suggesting their own frustration with the administrators above them. Many times I heard predictions by CPS administrators that the influx of Hispanics to the district was finally topping off, as the availability of low-cost housing within the city limits was allegedly tapped out. These predictions may have reflected wishful thinking, but they did not indicate a district ready to consider what would happen if the demography continued to change. At the administrative tier, during the full course of my inquiry, there were few indicators of dissatisfaction with the existing educational program. Title VII funding was sought as a means to obtain extra resources. Later, Direct Instruction was portrayed as the solution to problems that otherwise might have emerged. Sarason (1990) has identified dissatisfaction as requisite for a willingness to change. Those leading CPS showed little overt dissatisfaction.

From the CPS leaders' point of view, the problem with the bilingual education component was not just that the idea was politically unpopular in many circles, but also that it depended on someone else's expertise. Accepting the Mexican bilingual coordinator's suggestion for a roundtable in April 1998 to discuss CPS future curriculum needs and desires would have helped the district anticipate and thoughtfully respond to ongoing change. That this invitation from the Mexican partners was declined is telling. In 1996 CPS had admitted that it was not sure how to move forward, but it was disinclined to make the same admission in 1998.

One reading of the curriculum coordinator's ultimate resistance to the bilingual curriculum component (resistance that was not challenged by the superintendent or CPS School Board) was that she was defending the status quo decision-making hierarchy, resisting an alternative form of governance and a concomitant loss of power for her role. Although initially unsure of how to respond to the dramatic change in student and parent demographics, and thus initially receptive to the involvement of the attorney and the Mexican university, CPS leaders became increasingly doubtful about the partnership, and particularly the politically controversial bilingual curriculum component, as they realized how vulnerable they had made themselves not only to broadsides by the attorney but also to the more vague challenges of the community. Without a good grasp of the hows and whys of bilingual education and the broader topic of culturally responsive pedagogy, CPS leaders were uncomfortable facing any doubts raised by the Anglo public about the new educational course promised by the partnership. As noted earlier, I have written elsewhere (Hamann 1999b) about how the Conasauga public was largely willing to welcome or at least accept the presence of newcomers, as long as the newcomers seemed willing to take work no one else wanted and seemed receptive to assimilation. Though the bilingual curriculum and other partnership efforts initiated by the Mexican university promised Conasauga assistance with the newcomers, they did not promise assimilation.

One assumption of formal policymaking is that policy should be made by experts, and for leaders to admit their lack of expertise would suggest that they should not be making the policies. One could say that the Georgia/Mexico partnership was enacted as a "political technology" (Foucault, 1977) that converted the political problem of how to accommodate the presence of Latino newcomers at school into a "neutral" social science question regarding best pedagogical and curricular practice. As Shore and Wright note (1997, 9) central to political technology is the deployment of "expert knowledge," and the partnership's struggle regarding bilingual education was sometimes contested around issues of expertise.

The curriculum coordinator was the one educator in this study for whom the binational partnership was not readily a means for displaying her educational expertise or advancing her theories of action regarding how CPS should operate and what it should seek to accomplish. Through its new curriculum and the (re)deployment of expert visiting instructors and Summer Institute–trained CPS educators, the Georgia/Mexico partnership promised a reconfiguration of power away from the Central Office and to site-based personnel. It seemed to confirm the bypassing of her that had been routine in the enactment of the partnership, be it at the December 1996 meeting in Mexico, the February 1998 meeting of the ad hoc oversight committee, and at other times. Within the partnership, the curriculum coordinator found her attempted contributions to be overlooked or ignored.

Reacting in part to the superintendent's original consultation with the CPS principals in September 1996, the Mexican partners assumed that site-based personnel had decision-making input within CPS and, unwittingly, further challenged the curriculum coordinator's role when they made claims and requests to that effect. These dynamics all jeopardized the status that the curriculum coordinator had obtained by diligently climbing the traditional hierarchy that had prevailed in CPS. Sarason (1990, 55) notes that "Those who wield power do not look kindly on any possible dilution of that power. I do not say this critically but rather as a statement of empirical fact. To gloss over that fact is to reduce mightily the chances that any significant proposal to alter power relationships will be successful, even in part."

The curriculum coordinator's traditional authority came from her control over curriculum decision making and her authority over a substantial curriculum and staff training budget. The Georgia/Mexico partnership sought to intervene in these two arenas, extending more curriculum authority directly to instructors and site-based administrators and designating portions of the staff-training budget to underwrite the substantial expenses of Summer Institute participation.

Nonetheless, despite being implicated by the attorney's original critique of the status quo in CPS, the curriculum coordinator initially sought Title VII funding and otherwise supported the nascent Georgia/Mexico partnership. However, as the new partnership's implications for her own status became clearer, she stopped supporting it. Instead she substituted the heavily scripted, expensive Direct Instruction model.

Contrary to the espoused theories of the superintendent (as expressed in the September 1996 letter), but perhaps not contrary to his theories in-use (as he apparently did not try to limit her maneuvers), in 1998 the curriculum coordinator moved to limit the communication channels available to the Mexican bilingual coordinator and failed to coordinate her own curricular ideas with that partner. In fact, she tried to recharacterize the Mexican coordinator's role as more akin to a consultant than a partner. Ultimately, she advocated the abandonment of the bilingual curriculum component. Each of these steps reasserted her authority. Although rejecting the inputs of the attorney and the Mexican partners, none of these actions presumed authority beyond that which had been traditionally associated with her position. As I finished my research, the partnership faced a crucial challenge of trying to win back the favor of the curriculum coordinator. Doing so would be difficult and would require attention to her professional status and to her theories regarding her role and the larger interests of CPS.

Yet reviewing the political maneuverings of partnership leaders hardly finishes this story. It was still the case that the diagnosis of the attorney was accurate regarding the need to reform practice and policy in CPS, if Latino newcomers were to be sufficiently accommodated. Dentler and Hafner (1997) found that site-level autonomy, practitioner accountability, and expert professional support seemed important for districts struggling with the arrival of large numbers of immigrant students. However personally sensible, the machinations that restricted communication between Mexican partners and school site personnel, that tied up large quantities of instructional time delivering a scripted (and monolingual) curriculum, and that resisted reallocation of resources (i.e., moving existing funds and changing existing structures rather than just adding on programs with new external resources) all kept CPS from adopting the practices noted by Dentler and Hafner.

The machinations also restricted the input of the local Latino community and left intact local Latinos' status as "objects of policy" rather than contributors to it. This was accomplished through the obvious mechanism of challenging the input of the Mexican university and the less obvious mechanism of reasserting the traditional arrangements regarding which community members should have input on educational and community policymaking decisions. Traditionally there were no local Latinos, so traditional local decision making did not incorporate them.

The Mexican partners' efforts did challenge the local Latinos' status as only objects of policy. They engaged in a substantive community case study and generated several reports with pointed suggestions about how CPS and the larger Conasauga community could be more responsive to the newcomers. CPS leaders' failure to engage with those reports (by circulating them to site-based educators, for example) limited their consequence. Similarly, restricting the direct contact between the Mexican partners and CPS educators restricted the exchange of the Mexican experts' expertise. CPS did not restrict contact between local educators and the visiting instructors, but the visiting instructors' local status as paraprofessionals (which reflected Georgia educational law rather than local maneuvering) and the failure to exploit the instructors' expertise (by asking them to spend much of their time teaching a fully scripted curriculum in marginal spaces) diminished their input on CPS Latino education policy.

Thus it seems accurate to say that, at least during the duration of my study, attempts to be more responsive to local Latinos still largely excluded local Latinos from shaping what that response would look like. Maneuvers of informed proxies (i.e., those from the Mexican university) and vigorous advocates (e.g., the attorney) were parried, reducing the indirect voice of local Latinos, as well as the contribution of external experts. To say, however, that Latino education in Conasauga was inappropriate or unimproved seems like a question of perspective. The local capacity to teach newcomers English clearly improved. If, as Wong Fillmore and Meyer (1992) asked, the task of schooling is an assimilative one, then the CPS schools improved. If, however, the goal of schooling should be democratic self-determination, with greater student, parent, and teacher input, and with the promotion of multiple and diverse views, then the picture is more mixed. Often one step forward seems to have been countered with a forced step back. The extant Latino educational policy in CPS seems to have been the product of a host community orientation for assimilation mixed with accommodation of Latinos when forced to by agents outside of CPS, like the attorney and the Mexican university, or when educators at levels below the district leadership who had attended Summer Institutes or who had gained professional respect for the visiting instructors appropriated the official policies. The accommodations to difference that did happen seemed often to be begrudging compromises rather than part of an inclusive, multicultural vision. As Shore and Wright note (1997, 7), "Not only do policies codify social norms and values, and articulate fundamental organizing principles of society, they also contain implicit (and sometimes explicit) models of society." The norms in Conasauga were a traditional hierarchical organization for the school district and a skepticism of multiculturalism framed in the not-as-welcoming-as-it-first-appears "proimmigration" script (Suárez-Orozco, 1998; Hamann, 1999b).

NOTES

1. Concerned perhaps that in writing a critical educational ethnography I risk angering the administrators who permit access to school district research (Levinson and Holland, 1996, 19), readers might wonder about the ethical standards that I am following. Readers might also worry that I am betraying confidences gained through my grant writer role. These concerns are fair, but I justify this writing in several ways. First, from the moment I initially came to Conasauga as a grant writer I was explicit about my research intentions, and informants spoke with me knowing I was documenting what they were saying and doing. Second, like Deyhle (Deyhle, Hess, and LeCompte, 1992), who felt that successful grant writing for Anglo education administrators on a Navajo reservation gave her license to scrutinize and critique the implementation of the program she helped fund, I too feel a right and responsibility to see how my work has been followed up. Like her, I agreed to be a grant writer because I believed I could help bring needed resources that would benefit newcomers who otherwise would continue to confront problematic educational circumstances. Third, though I never made or implied any promises of anonymity (except in specific instances when I was asked to keep, for example, a specific comment "off the record"), I have consciously used pseudonyms here because I think the specific identities of place and people matter less than the larger lessons that can be derived from this case study. Although I believe that public figures are fair foci of public scrutiny, in this instance I feel that "naming names" is gratuitous and would offer little assistance to readers' comprehension of my thesis. Fourth, though I have not shared this particular manuscript with all the individuals who centrally figure in this account, I have shared with all of them copies of my dissertation from which this is derived. In what amounts to a verification of the interpretive validity of this qualitative research (Maxwell, 1992), informants in Conasauga and at the Mexican university have told me that they found my dissertation fair, insightful, and on target. Finally, I do not believe that anyone described here acted with deliberate malice and I have similarly sought to avoid any malice in my account.

2. The use of the term Hispanic reflects both local practice by Anglos and many Latinos in Conasauga. The terms Latino and Mexican are also used locally, but somewhat less frequently. I use the term when reflecting local usage and/or, as here, trying to portray an emic perspective.

3. All these statistics come from Conasauga Public Schools (CPS) records.

4. For a good discussion of employment changes in Georgia's poultry industry and their social contexts and consequences, see Griffith (1995). For general discussions of how Hispanic immigrants are transforming many rural towns and small cities, see Stull, Broadway, and Griffith (1995) and the introductions and sections on the Changing Relations Project in Garden City, Kansas, in Lamphere (1992) and Lamphere, Stepick, and Grenier (1994). Massey, Alarcon, Durand, and Gonzalez (1987) and Tienda (1989) describe how migration streams mature. Put briefly, the longer a community hosts immigrant newcomer workers, the more likely some workers will establish roots in their new community and be able to support the reunification of their families. Economic factors become less important over time for the sustenance of migration streams, and single workers or workers apart from their families make up a declining portion of the newcomer population. This means, among other things, that the indirect costs of corporations employing newcomer workers grow over time as, for example, the number of immigrant children in the schools increases.

5. Although the attorney's initial construction of the challenge faced by the schools was simplistic—identifying the challenge faced by newcomer families as strictly linguistic—it was accurate as far as it went. At the time that the attorney visited the school where his daughter worked, two-thirds of its enrollment was Hispanic, 41% of the Hispanic students there had been born outside of the United States, and nearly all lived in Spanish-speaking households with parents who had been born in Latin America. Across the district, the majority of Hispanic students in CPS were foreign-born—59 percent in 1996–1997 (Conasauga Public Schools, 1997; Hamann, 1999a). Moreover, almost half were identified as limited English proficient, and nearly all came from Spanish-speaking households (Conasauga Public Schools, 1997).

6. In Conasauga the superintendent is appointed by the School Board.

7. That sheet described a mix of quite specific English language–phonetics instruction strategies with very vague notions of including Spanish across the curriculum.

8. In the Mexican city where the partnering university is located, bilingual education (with rare exception) means dual instruction in Spanish and English. Although at the university level in Mexico the association of English with the imperiousness of the United States sometimes means that English is viewed ambivalently (Francis and Ryan, 1998), both languages are taught because both are deemed useful. This contrasts with much bilingual education in the United States, where cultivation of the first language is often supported only as a bridging step for the process of teaching English (i.e., transitional bilingual education). Foreign language instruction in U.S. schools is not usually thought of as bilingual education. See Rippberger (1993) for more about the different assumptions about bilingual education in the United States and Mexico.

9. One of the original 14 visiting instructors did not return to Conasauga after going home to Mexico for Christmas 1997. Because of the way catchment zones were divided in Conasauga, the two elementary schools that dropped their visiting instructor support each had about 12 percent Latino enrollment, whereas the Latino enrollment at the elementary schools on the poorer side of town averaged about 70 percent.

10. She apparently was unaware that Cummins (1996, 201–203) opposed the use of Direct Instruction with LEP (limited English proficient) students because empirical data showed that the method helped such students only minimally with sustained academic gains and that it was significantly less effective than a properly implemented bilingual program. See Adams and Engelmann (1997) for a description of the Direct Instruction

model and Heshusius (1991) and Allington and Woodside-Jiron (1999) for a useful critique of it.

11. During the 1990s, largely because of the influx of Latino students, the CPS student population grew by 25 percent, making most school buildings overcrowded and necessitating the use within them of some marginal spaces. Perhaps because they arrived after the start of the school year, the Mexican instructors were disproportionately overrepresented as users of such spaces, though Grey (1991) notes that frequently language minority students and their educators are forced to work in the most marginal spaces. Wortham (this volume) describes a similar pattern.

REFERENCES

Adams, Gary L. and Siegfried Engelmann. 1997. *Research on Direct Instruction: 25 Years beyond DISTAR.* Eugene, OR: Association for Direct Instruction.

Allington, Richard L. and Haley Woodside-Jiron. 1999. "The Politics of Literacy Teaching: How 'Research' Shaped Educational Policy." *Educational Researcher.* 28(8):4–13.

Argyris, Chris and Donald A. Schön. 1978. *Organizational Learning: A Theory of Action Perspective.* Reading, MA: Addison-Wesley.

Barth, Fredrik. 1969. "Introduction." In *Ethnic Groups and Boundaries: The Social Organization of Cultural Difference.* Fredrik Barth, ed. Pp. 9–38. Boston: Little, Brown and Company.

Conasauga Public Schools. 1997. Systemwide Bilingual Education Program: Conasauga Public Schools Commitment to a Changing Population. Title VII Bilingual Education: Systemwide Improvement Grants, (Catalog of Federal Domestic Assistance number: 84–291R). Grant application. Conasauga, GA: Conasauga Public Schools.

Cummins, Jim. 1996. *Negotiating Identities: Education for Empowerment in a Diverse Society.* Ontario, CA: California Association for Bilingual Education.

Dentler, Robert A. and Anne L. Hafner. 1997. *Hosting Newcomers: Structuring Educational Opportunities for Immigrant Children.* New York: Teachers College Press.

Deyhle, Donna L., G. Alfred Hess Jr., and Margaret D. LeCompte. 1992. "Approaching Ethical Issues for Qualitative Researchers in Education." In *The Handbook of Qualitative Research in Education.* Margaret D. LeCompte, Wendy L. Millroy, and Judith Preissle, eds. Pp. 597–641. San Diego, CA: Academic Press, Inc.

Flamming, Douglas. 1992. *Creating the Modern South: Millhands and Managers in Georgia, 1884–1984.* Chapel Hill: University of North Carolina Press.

Foucault, Michel. 1977. *Discipline and Punish: The Birth of the Prison.* Alan Sheridan, trans. New York: Vintage Books.

Francis, Norbert and Phyllis M. Ryan. 1998. "English as an International Language of Prestige." *Anthropology and Education Quarterly.* 29(1):25–43.

Grey, Mark A. 1991. "The Context for Marginal Secondary ESL Programs: Contributing Factors and the Need for Further Research." *The Journal of Educational Issues of Language Minority Students.* 9:75–89.

Griego-Jones, Toni. 1995. "Implementing Bilingual Programs Is Everybody's Business. NCBE Focus Occasional Papers in Bilingual Education, 11." Washington, DC: National Clearinghouse for Bilingual Education. Available: *http://www.ncbe.gwu.edu/ncbepubs/focus/focus11.html.*

Griffith, David. 1995. "*Hay Trabajo*: Poultry Processing, Rural Industrialization, and the Latinization of Low-Wage Labor." In *Any Way You Cut It: Meat-Processing and Small-Town America*. Donald D. Stull, Michael J. Broadway, and David Griffith, eds. Pp. 129–151. Lawrence: University Press of Kansas.

Hamann, Edmund T. 1999a. "The Georgia Project: A Binational Attempt to Create a School District in Response to Latino Newcomers." Doctoral dissertation, University of Pennsylvania. Ann Arbor, MI: University Microfilms.

———. 1999b. "Anglo (Mis)Understandings of Latino Newcomers: A North Georgia Case Study." In *Negotiating Power and Place at the Margins: Selected Papers on Refugees and Immigrants*, 7. Juliene Lipson and Lucia Ann McSpadden, eds. Pp. 156–197. Arlington, VA: American Anthropological Association.

Hatch, Thomas. 1998. "The Differences in Theory That Matter in the Practice of School Improvement." *American Educational Research Journal*. 35(1):3–31.

Heath, Shirley Brice. 1983. *Ways with Words: Language, Life, and Work in Communities and Classrooms*. Cambridge: Cambridge University Press.

Heshusius, Lous. 1991. "Curriculum-Based Assessment and Direct Instruction: Critical Reflections on Fundamental Assumptions." *Exceptional Children*. 57(4): 315–328.

Hornberger, Nancy H. 2000. "Bilingual Education Policy and Practice in the Andes: Ideological Paradox and Intercultural Possibility." *Anthropology and Education Quarterly*. 31(2), 173–201.

Hunter, Floyd. 1963. *Community Power Structure: A Study of Decision Makers*. Garden City, NY: Anchor Books.

Lamphere, Louise, ed. 1992. *Structuring Diversity: Ethnographic Perspectives on the New Immigration*. Chicago: University of Chicago Press.

Lamphere, Louise, Alex Stepick, and Guillermo Grenier, eds. 1994. *Newcomers in the Workplace: Immigrants and the Restructuring of the U.S. Economy*. Philadelphia: Temple University Press.

Levinson, Bradley A. and Dorothy Holland. 1996. "The Cultural Production of the Educated Person: An Introduction." In *The Cultural Production of the Educated Person: Critical Ethnographies of Schooling and Local Practice*. Pp. 1–54. Albany: State University of New York Press.

Levinson, Bradley A. and Margaret Sutton. 2001. "Policy as/in Practice: Developing a Sociocultural Approach to the Study of Educational Policy." In *Policy as Practice: Toward a Comparative Sociocultural Analysis of Educational Policy*. Westport, CT: Ablex Press.

Massey, Douglas S., Rafael Alarcón, Jorge Durand, and Humberto González. 1987. *Return to Aztlán: The Social Process of International Migration from Western Mexico*. Berkeley: University of California Press.

Maxwell, Joseph A. 1992. "Understanding and Validity in Qualitative Research." *Harvard Educational Review*. 62(3):279–300.

McDermott, Ray and Frederick Erickson. 2000. "A Life with Anthropology and Education: Interviews with George and Louise Spindler." In *Fifty Years of Anthropology and Education 1950–2000: A Spindler Anthology*. George Spindler, ed. Pp. 1–23. Mahwah, NJ: Lawrence Erlbaum Associates.

Miramontes, Ofelia B., Adel Nadeau, and Nancy L. Commins. 1997. *Restructuring Schools for Linguistic Diversity: Linking Decision Making to Effective Programs*. New York: Teachers College Press.

Nader, Laura. 1972. "Up the Anthropologist—Perspectives Gained from Studying Up." In *Reinventing Anthropology*. Dell Hymes, ed. Pp. 284–311. New York: Pantheon Books.

Rippberger, Susan J. 1993. "Ideological Shifts in Bilingual Education: Mexico and the United States." *Comparative Education Review*. 37(1):50–61.

Sarason, Seymour B. 1990. *The Predictable Failure of Educational Reform: Can We Change Course before It Is Too Late?* San Francisco: Jossey-Bass Publishers.

Shore, Cris and Susan Wright. 1997. "Policy: A New Field of Anthropology." In *Anthropology of Policy: Critical Perspectives on Governance and Power*. Cris Shore and Susan Wright, eds. Pp. 3–39. London: Routledge.

Spener, David. 1988. "Transitional Bilingual Education and the Socialization of Immigrants." *Harvard Educational Review*. 58(2):133–153.

Spindler, George. 1982. "Self-Appraisals: Concerns and Strategies." In *Doing the Ethnography of Schooling: Educational Anthropology in Action*. George Spindler, ed. Pp. 14–18. New York: Holt, Rinehart and Winston.

Stull, Donald D., Michael J. Broadway, and David Griffith, eds. 1995. *Any Way You Cut It: Meat-Processing and Small-Town America*. Lawrence: University Press of Kansas.

Suárez-Orozco, Marcelo M. 1998. "State Terrors: Immigrants and Refugees in the Post-National Space." In *Ethnic Identity and Power: Cultural Contexts of Political Action in School and Society*. Yali Zou and Enrique T. Trueba, eds. Pp. 283–319. Albany: State University of New York Press.

Tienda, Marta. 1989. "Looking to the 1990s: Mexican Immigration in Sociological Perspective." In *Mexican Migration to the United States: Origins, Consequences, and Policy Options*. Wayne A. Cornelius and Jorge A. Bustamante, eds. Pp. 109–147. San Diego: Center for U.S./Mexican Studies, University of California.

Wong Fillmore, Lily and Lois M. Meyer. 1992. "The Curriculum and Linguistic Minorities." In *The Handbook of Research on Curriculum*. Philip W. Jackson, ed. Pp. 626–658. New York: Macmillan.

5

The New Paths of Mexican Immigrants in the United States: Challenges for Education and the Role of Mexican Universities

Víctor Zúñiga, Rubén Hernández-León, Janna L. Shadduck-Hernández, and María Olivia Villarreal

The Mexican Diaspora in the United States, in spite of its more than one hundred years of history, still produces novel changes. Since 1986, Mexican migration has stopped being a principally male, seasonal, circular, undocumented process with California, Texas, or Illinois as primary destinations. At the start of this new century, the Mexican exodus to the United States includes (a) whole families (extended as well as nuclear), (b) new strategies of integration into the labor force (especially in urban areas and in secondary and tertiary levels of the economy), and (c) new social and linguistic characteristics because of the increasingly varied cultural and geographic origins of the newcomers, including more Mexicans from indigenous backgrounds, more from the large metropolitan cities, and more from central and southern regions of the country. New migrants are also showing a major interest in establishing their lives in the United States. Of course, this post-1986 migration has not completely lost characteristics of the previous immigration, from the beginning of the *Bracero* program in 1942 to the adoption of the Immigration Reform and Control Act (IRCA) in 1986. Changes in U.S. immigration policy—notably IRCA—the economic transformations in Mexico during the last 20 years, the continuing accumulation of immigration experience among Mexicans, and the consolidation of familial networks have supported the appearance of these aforementioned novelties.

This chapter focuses on one of the main surprises that appeared in the decade of the 1990s: the new geography of Mexican-origin communities in the United States and its institutional and symbolic repercussions. For this purpose, this chapter focuses attention on the case of Conasauga, Georgia and the institutional intervention enacted by the Universidad de Monterrey since 1996 under the title of "The Georgia Project." All four of us work or have worked for the Universidad de Monterrey, and all four of us are or have been deeply involved with the project. Because this project was still ongoing at the time of our writing (in April 2000), we have frequently chosen to use the present tense in our descriptions.

We are not writing this paper as observers, but as participants. All four of us have had specific responsibilities designing, organizing, negotiating, and evaluating the different components of The Georgia Project's "Mexican side." We have made multiple trips—more than 20—to Conasauga and the surrounding county in a very short time (three years), "living" in Conasauga for more than 120 days. We have conducted and continue to conduct a large variety of tasks in order to achieve the objectives of The Georgia Project. For example, while one of us was planning the Latino community leaders' seminar, others were initiating contacts with Mexican and Mexican American businessmen. While one of us was selecting and training the Mexican bilingual teachers for the Conasauga schools, others were visiting the local factories and Mexican *barrios* and talking with Mexican and other Latino workers. While one of us was trying to start adult and community educational programs in Conasauga, others were educating university authorities in Monterrey about our Georgia learning. While some of us were conducting survey research in the schools, others were organizing the intensive immersion Summer Institutes in Monterrey for more than 50 Georgia teachers. Meanwhile, our everyday lives in Monterrey have been transformed as we have received letters, e-mail messages, phone calls, and reports and been visited by civil and school authorities (including both Mexican and American teachers, principals, and district administrators) and researchers, journalists, and others interested in Conasauga. Our participation in The Georgia Project built a bridge, making possible an everyday communication with our partners in Georgia. In some senses, we were/are living, at the same time, both in Conasauga and Monterrey.

We are a multidisciplinary and binational team (three Mexicans and an American) who have tried to work together combining our professional backgrounds—adult education, binational labor markets, sociology of education and culture, and sociology of Mexican females in the United States. We have written other reports and articles describing our observations and methods (see especially Hernández-León, Shadduck, Zúñiga, and Villarreal, 1997). This chapter represents a reflective opportunity for us to freeze our roles as participants in The Georgia Project and Conasauga's demographic transition in order to respond to three personal and professional questions: What have we been doing as members of a Mexican university in Georgia? What were/are our (possible) contributions to the Conasauga community? And, in keeping with this volume's emphasis on the Latino Diaspora across the United States, in what sense is it possible to reproduce The Georgia Project in other U.S. regions, or at least have other regions gain from our learning and experience? We respond to these questions as scholars, as well as individuals engaged in Conasauga's future.

We expect our approach differs substantially from that of other chapters of this book. Unlike many of the other studies, which are about policy making done by others, we have written reflections on our own participation in a local changing process. Our goal is to describe our current concerns and provisional conclusions. Like the other scholars in this book, we are interested in the new geography of the Mexican Diaspora in the United States and its social and cultural impacts. In this chapter, however, all four of us are trying to link our particular academic fields with our personal participation in the difficult process of creating a new institution, as well as the process of challenging and/or supporting existing institutions.

The new geography of the Mexican Diaspora in the United States has recently been documented by various authors (Durand, Massey, and Charvet, 2000; Saenz and Cready, 1999; Hernández-León and Zúñiga, 2000), but it appears to be such a new phenomenon that, without explanation, it was ignored by the Mexico–United States Binational Migration Study (1998). The new Diaspora includes the presence of Mexican laborers and their families in such vastly different and distant states and regions as Maine, Utah, Oregon, Florida, Minnesota, Nebraska, Tennessee, Iowa, both Carolinas, and Georgia. Although we name these states, they are not the only ones. In reality, what has happened in this past decade affirms, to paraphrase Durand, Massey, and Charvet (2000), that "Mexicans reside within the entire territory of the United States," although their presence is felt with different intensities from place to place.

Within this new process, we find a dynamic of marked interest: the sudden formation of Mexican communities in small to midsize towns and nonmetropolitan areas of distinct states and regions. This means that Mexicans have been abandoning both the older Diaspora destinations of the large metropolitan zones such as Los Angeles, Houston, Chicago, as well as the more recent destinations, such as New York and Dallas, where they enjoyed at least three benefits:

- social networks with high levels of organization
- settlements with high ethnic homogeneity, and
- by consequence, high levels of invisibility in the eyes of the dominant society.

This means that in the new locales where many Mexican migrants have chosen to resettle throughout this last decade, the Mexican communities are reinventing forms of community organization, interethnic relations, and public presentation etiquette.

In these new, often nonmetropolitan areas where new immigrants have settled, there has been a major shift not only in ethnic composition, but also in the way society sees itself. Indeed, the recreation centers, the streets, the shopping malls, the schools, the churches, the factories, the banks, the restaurants, etc.—in short, all public spaces—have acquired a visibly new configuration. The coordination of institutions, existing power relations, and sociodemographic trends are initiating movements that, up to a few years ago, were unimaginable. In other words, small to midsize towns in the United States are beginning to resemble the border towns of the Southwest.

Allow us to quote, in this introduction, a citation from the field observations of Edmund Hamann (1999, 26), in Conasauga, Georgia, which clearly illustrates what we are suggesting:

At a January 1997 dinner party that was organized to celebrate the first visit of Universidad de Monterrey scholars to Conasauga, the attorney who instigated The Georgia Project declared, during an after-dinner toast, that Conasauga had become a "border city" and had a responsibility to act inclusively in regard to this new status. From his perspective there were enough Mexicans in Conasauga at that point whose reference point and identity were intertwined with Mexico and not just the U.S., that characterizing Conasauga's population as American was an incomplete gesture.

This speaks to the "borderization" of small and midsize locales not directly located on the U.S.–Mexican border.

The novel changes that we refer to should not be measured in terms of absolute quantities. Indeed, the number of Mexicans in Los Angeles is, and undoubtedly will continue to be, higher than any other place inside the United States. Thus the changes we are describing are best measured in relative terms. Mexican communities composed of 10, 20, or 30 thousand people compose just a small proportion of the total of Mexican migration, but they have very important economic, political, and symbolic repercussions in the locales and regions to which they are moving.

THE CONASAUGA CASE: MIGRATION DYNAMICS, IMPACT, AND COMMUNITY CHALLENGES

Conasauga is an industrial city situated in the northwest of Georgia, 30 miles south of Chattanooga, Tennessee, and 90 miles north of Atlanta. Conasauga and the surrounding county were populated according to the 1990 census by 72,462 residents of the following racial/ethnic backgrounds: 93 percent white, 4 percent African American, .05 percent Asian, and the remaining 2 percent Other. Among the "Others" were 1,847 residents who declared themselves to be of Mexican origin. In contrast, according to recent estimates by the Center for Applied Research in Anthropology (CARA, 1998) of Georgia State University, approximately 45,000 Latinos were residing in the city and county, of which, according to our own 1998 survey (Zúñiga and Hernández-León, 2001), at least 90 percent were Mexican or of Mexican origin. According to these data, a city and county, which in 1990 were predominantly Anglo American and typically southern, have in one decade been transformed into a locale inhabited by Mexican men, women, and children who compose more than one-third of the total population.

The city's school registry is compellingly illustrative. In the 1989–1990 academic year, 4 percent of students registered were identified as Latino, in contrast to 81 percent white. In the 1999–2000 academic year, Conasauga public school statistics indicate a 44 percent Latino student population in contrast to a 45 percent white student population. According to the ethnic composition of the public schools, there are as many children of Mexican newcomers as of local southerners.[1]

Conasauga's Mexican immigrants, according to our 1998 survey (Hernández-León and Zúñiga, 2000), can be categorized into two main divisions—those who moved to Conasauga from California, Texas, Florida and other U.S. states, and those who arrived in Conasauga directly from Mexico. The first group represented more than half of the actual Mexican residents in Conasauga (56 percent), and was predominantly male and of western Mexican origin. Many in this group have a long personal history of migration and are experts in the urban life of large North American metropolitan areas. The second group was mostly made up of women and younger men, many of whom had come to the United States as part of the process of family reunification facilitated by the 1986 IRCA amnesty (Durand, 1998).

As a direct consequence of this migratory process, the Conasauga society was still confronting (at the time of our writing) numerous challenges and changes, all of which have been accompanied by the public debate that seems inherent to the arrival of the newcomers. Among these major changes we would like to emphasize five:

The Redefinition of the Imaginary Present and Future of This Typical Industrial Community Located in the Valleys of the Appalachian Foothills

The surprising growth of western Mexican Catholicism within a society that was predominantly Presbyterian, Southern Baptist, and Methodist and historically antipapal, the sudden emergence of soccer leagues (echoing the passionate love of the sport by western Mexicans) in a region that has overtly prioritized football and baseball, the spatial and culinary impact of Mexican restaurants and cuisine competing alongside U.S. fast food chains (the largest restaurant in town, which boasts several murals depicting various Mexican national symbols, is owned by a naturalized U.S. citizen from San Luis Potosí, Mexico), and, above all, the substantial presence of the Spanish language everywhere (in factories, churches, schools, banks, television and radio, etc.) are events that undoubtedly create a crisis in the local imaginary of the host community.

The Redefinition of the Interethnic Relations in a Traditional Context Dominated Not Just by the American Way of Life but the More Particular Bible Belt Strand of the American Way of Life

In a local society still branded by the raw imprints of the Civil War—General Sherman's scorched-earth march to the sea came through Conasauga—and ashamed by its slaveholding past, yet, at the same time proudly religious, traditional racial/ethnic marking was until recently divided into two colors: white and black. The pre-Mexican migration ethnic orchestration was defined by the social contracts of the end of the nineteenth century, first, and also by the social reforms of the 1960s and 1970s (i.e., the end of "legal" segregation). These contracts were based on extant social concepts of wage, debt, shame, forgiveness, reconciliation, and equality of opportunity. The arrival of Mexican newcomers has complicated the local definition of interethnic space. In a region where interracial contact was limited, the large-scale arrival of Mexicans has produced unprecedented new local forms of intergroup contact: interracial gangs composed of Mexicans, African Americans, and whites; interracial marriages of Mexican men with white women of rural heritage (Kelley, 1996); interracial public spaces like Mexican dances attended by black and white youths; and, of extreme importance, enduring interracial public spaces such as schools and workplaces, where Mexicans and other Latinos have become a major presence.

The arrival of Mexicans was not a product of forced migration, but the result of economic globalization—more specifically, the global economic triumph of the United States. In the regional space of North America, this triumph has manifested itself through the economic integration of Mexico with the United States. Although this process has traveled from the border southward, incorporating Mexicans into the ups and downs of the U.S. economy, through immigration the Mexican Diaspora has also moved the border northward into new locations; hence, the borderization of places such as Conasauga, Georgia.

The Dislocation of the Relations among the Social Classes at the Level of the Local Society

For nearly a century, Conasauga succeeded in constructing an interethnic "consensus" which established that manufacturing work be exclusively destined for whites (cf. Flamming, 1992). This consensus allowed the white workers and the white managers and supervisors to identify with each other, despite class differences and their spatial manifestation in the citywide division into two large areas: poorer east and wealthier west. In the 1990s, the consensus was dislocated. Managers promoted the hiring of Latinos and supervisors praised the work of the Mexicans in their plants. Employers advertised their job announcements in Spanish as the industrial labor force became multiethnic.[2] The traditional working class in the city reacted negatively to the influx of Mexicans into the plants and were further distressed as merchants cast their eyes toward an inescapable growing Latino market. Meanwhile the traditional institutions characterized by social class (such as the Chamber of Commerce) opened their doors with awkwardness but little reluctance to members of the rising Mexican-origin middle class.

This emerging Mexican-origin middle class is composed of (a) the most successful small business owners of the immigrant community, (b) the Mexican employees who have filled needed high-skilled and administrative positions in the plants, and (c) the children of pioneer Mexican migrants to Conasauga (i.e., children of the several hundred Mexicans that came to Conasauga in the 1970s and 1980s). The latter are members of the first local generation of Mexican Americans and are characterized by their bilingualism, their higher educational attainment, and their "tertiary sector" (Omi and Winant, 1994) intermediary roles between Anglo locals and the immigrant community. In sum, Conasauga's interclass and intraclass relations have been dislocated because the working class and, to a lesser degree, the middle class have become multiethnic and because the local merchants appear to have accepted (and promoted) this phenomenon.

The Redefinition of the Roles of the Institutions

Principally the schools, but also the churches, banks, and the local governing and judicial bodies, have been the object of a redefinition. The local debates over the characteristics and functions of the police, the role of local businesses, and the presence of Spanish-language insertions in the main local newspaper reflect the controversial crossroads in which the city and county school districts find themselves. This redefinition of institutional roles and responsibilities has many faces, but one of the most important is that all of these institutions have become mediators in the process of incorporation of Mexican immigrants into the local society. This function simply did not exist 10 or 15 years ago when the Mexican community included only a few hundred *pioneros*.

The response of these institutions to the arrival of immigrants and their families depends, in part, on embedded ideas regarding immigrant incorporation. Not surprisingly, as they respond to the presence of thousands of newcomers, these institutions, their structures and dynamics, also change. The case of schools is paradigmatic and central to the experience of locals and newcomers. A city proud of its school system, convinced that their plans and programs satisfy the highest of national standards, has become obligated to establish school functions totally unknown to them a decade ago—e.g., accommodating bilingualism, multiculturalism, parallel curricula, and intercultural exchange. These issues were not only recently unknown to school administrators, but are also still perceived as harmful and dangerous by many of them.

Local migratory dynamics have brought challenges for educational policy making. It is not merely negotiating the presence of Spanish-speaking children in the classrooms, the changing relations in the schools, and the troubles of the teachers facing novel forms of cultural diversity that matter. Rather, the new demography has brought crucial challenges for how curriculum and instruction are and should be defined. This has challenged educational policy makers' imagination and raised key questions about who should be the policy makers. Hence, the arrival of the New Mexican Diaspora has compelled public and private debate on the social and political role of the schools, at least in Conasauga. Migration means changes both for local people and newcomers. Because of their role in defining and reproducing community, the schools are undoubtedly the most sensitive institutions to these changes, and educational policy makers are the most centrally involved in this matter. These policy issues are intertwined with the past, the present, and the future of a local society defining itself in both a national context and a borderland/binational context.

The Redefinition of Local Politics

This is a redefinition that cannot be postponed for long. Inasmuch as the Mexican residents organize themselves, seek representation, establish alliances with traditional governing bodies, strengthen their economic power, and frame ad hoc discourses regarding the new community circumstances, they convert themselves into a factor in local and regional power relations. At first one might hesitate before seeing Conasauga Latinos as possible significant actors in the short term, in regard to statewide and national politics, because the numbers of Latinos statewide are still comparatively small. However, Georgia's fine balance between Republicans and Democrats means the needed swing vote in statewide elections is slim. Thus there are emergent efforts by both parties to assert their Latino-responsive credentials. In Conasauga, the Mexican American youth and the naturalized members of the emergent Mexican middle class are beginning to be wooed by local civic leaders and by representatives of the political parties. In turn, a new Latino leadership organization that the Universidad de Monterrey helped initiate is presently pondering whether it seeks to become a traditional not-for-profit community-based organization or whether taking on the role of political advocacy organization would be more expedient.

In sum, the case of Conasauga, Georgia, illustrates how local societies enact and respond to the series of transformations and challenges that result from the rapid and massive arrival of Mexican and Latino immigrants. Immigration studies in the United States have traditionally concerned themselves with showing how immigrants change in their process of resettlement into a new country. Topics such as assimilation, adaption, and incorporation play a central concern in this process (cf. DeWind, Hirschman, and Kasinitz, 1997). However, only a handful of researchers have concerned themselves with indicating and studying how destination-societies change as a result of immigration (cf. Rodríguez, 1993). The preceding paragraphs sought to redress some of that imbalance, and the next section, describing the birth of The Georgia Project and our involvement in Conasauga, should further that effort. In December 1996, The Georgia Project was born in response to the fives changes and the related challenges and debates just noted.

THE GEORGIA PROJECT:
THE ROLE OF MEXICAN UNIVERSITIES

Without holding back on the circumstances that gave birth to a project whose distinct characteristics are simultaneously its binational character and its local legitimacy—characteristics that we elaborate later—we start our explanation of the birth of The Georgia Project by paraphrasing Hamann (1999). He described the project as born by the coincidence of diverse events: the insistent wish of Conasauga business and educational leaders to safeguard the reputation and the leadership of the city school system, and, on the other hand, the long-shared sentiment by business leaders that they have the authority and prerogative to direct changes in schools (cf. Flamming, 1992). As these contextual elements converged, local school administrators were confronting the scarcity of credentialed bilingual teachers, a dilemma shared with other regions in the United States (American Association for Employment in Education, 1997), and were finding unsatisfactory the responses to requests for help from both Georgia and other regional state universities. The project was born as well, according to Hamann, because it placed at the disposition of diverse local actors a popular discourse: the best way to confront the academic challenges was to welcome the children of the immigrant workers, many with low English proficiency, in exchange for their presumed commitment and loyalty to the hosting society. Finally, the project was born because our Mexican university recognized the multiple opportunities that a collaboration of this nature offered. Among these opportunities were the offering of an international professional development experience for our graduates, development of innovative extension programs with great potential for growth, and an opportunity for our professors to research a social phenomenon—service to the Mexican communities residing in the United States—that was new and not yet much explored by either public or private Mexican universities.

Although every one of these factors merits a deliberate analysis, we propose solely to describe the last of these, including a brief explanation of some of the project characteristics. The fact that our private Mexican university accepted the invitation to be not just the evaluator or observer of a process, but also an active external participant and enactor of change in response to a dynamic developing 1,000 miles away, was particularly unusual. But it has been the unusual step of having an entity like us participate that has produced the most contributions in Conasauga.

Under a pact, signed by city and county school district leaders, by private industry representatives, and by our university's rector in March 1997, we, the Universidad de Monterrey, promised (a) to provide Universidad de Monterrey–educated bilingual instructors to the school system and to supervise, evaluate, and further train them periodically; (b) to offer programs of community development to Mexican and other Latino adult residents in the city and county; (c) to offer in Mexico and Georgia professional development in bilingual education, the history and culture of Mexico, and academic Spanish for teachers and administrators of both educational systems; (d) to become acquainted with the characteristics and needs of Conasauga's Mexican/Latino community; and (e) to assess the suitability of each school's curriculum for Latino students.

Our partnership has been broadly publicized locally, regionally, and across the United States by the written media, as well as by the electronic media since the project's commencement (e.g., in the *Los Angeles Times*, the *Washington Post*, the *Atlanta Journal-Constitution*, and on National Public Radio). More recently, the partnership has been the object of various public, semipublic, and private debates, between supporters and opponents of the project. In the crossroads of these discourses, and in our capacity as external actors, we acknowledge that the challenges that confront the local society are extraordinarily complex. The arrival of immigrants of Mexican origin is stirring old fears, resentments, and conflicts, as well as creating new ones. No one in Conasauga can claim to be indifferent.

From this context we ask, What has an institution of higher education from the same country of origin as most of the migrants realistically been able to offer? In our judgment, there are four basic promises, distinct but interrelated. Their practice has not been free of contradictions.

Institutional Legitimacy

The issue of institutional legitimacy permeates many of the initiatives that are promoted by local actors in Conasauga, sometimes fomenting change and sometimes resisting it. The fact that a foreign university issues reports, opinions, evaluations, suggestions, observations, or simply data, with the formality of a "university," under the rights of a bilateral agreement, gives legitimacy or stature to what we say and do that is superior to what we could offer individually as researchers and professors. One illustrative manifestation of this dynamic is the defense of Spanish in schools and in the workplace that the university has sustained over three years, using technical-pedagogical arguments and direct testimonies of bilingual teachers from Monterrey. The discussion over the use of Spanish in Conasauga, like in many other places in the United States, is undoubtedly political in nature. However, speaking in the name of a foreign university depoliticizes the arguments (at least partially) and converts the discussion to the technical issues of pedagogy, which allows progress in the controversial debate.

The Cultural Know-How

The Georgia Project is fundamentally an association between a community and a university, in this case a binational association. Associations between universities and communities have a long history in the United States, where they have been promoted at least since the beginning of the twentieth century by such educational scholars as John Dewey as a means to reestablish the role of these institutions as social actors in the definition of politics and educational strategies. However, the projects that bind universities and communities have encountered all types of obstacles, one of which is a Euro-centric educational perspective that ignores the culture and experiences of non-European immigrant communities. This perspective is often produced and reproduced by institutions of higher education and K–12 entities. The Georgia Project overcomes this obstacle because in our case, the community-university association has included an institution from the non-European country of origin of the large majority of the immigrants in Conasauga, Georgia.

In this way, among the things that our institution has had to offer is a "cultural know-how" from the place of origin of the migrants. Our prerogative to introduce this know-how to non-Latinos in Conasauga has been aided by the technical legitimacy we have because of our university affiliation. In other words, we are recognized conveyors of cultural knowledge (e.g., through our teacher training) not just because of our personal Mexican cultural know-how (which others in Conasauga also have), but also because we are operating with institutional sanction, adding status and legitimacy to our personal and scholarly expertise. The importance of this contribution consists in integrating cultural elements of the immigrant community into the schools of the receiving community where they can be used to support the process of the learning among the children of the newcomers. The presence of a large contingent of Mexican teachers (cultural experts) who bring with them Spanish fluency and a "Mexican way" of relating

with the children is one of the Universidad de Monterrey's mechanisms for op-
erationalizing and legitimizing this know-how within the schools. Thus, what
our Mexican university has been able to offer is the cultural integration and affirmation of the immigrant community's place of origin in the educational
process in the migratory destination site. It is not easy to picture how such a contribution could have been furnished by an American university.

The Interlocutory Dialogue

The presence of professors, students, and researchers from a Mexican university in Conasauga has converted the modes and patterns of interethnic dialogue.
Before the arrival of the university, two religious ministers were key intermediaries between Mexican newcomers and the host community. One, a bilingual
Anglo, "affirmed" to fellow Anglos that "there were no people more ignorant
than farmworkers from Michoacán" and that "the worst enemy of the Mexican is
another Mexican." Another intermediary, an Evangelist of Puerto Rican origin,
had also made himself into a spokesperson, mediator, and representative of the
Latino community, speaking in their name, interpreting their needs, explaining
their presence to local authorities and business leaders. The Georgia Project
changed this interlocutory dialogue. By collecting information from the newcomer community and facilitating the creation of a Latino community organization, the actions of the project have set up and then facilitated the direct dialogue
of the school officials and local civic leaders with Mexican and Latino parents,
youth, and merchants. This direct contact is allowing numerous immigrants to be
acknowledged by local institutional players as real partners in dialogue regarding
how community change can be achieved. This communication and related
recognition of newcomers is necessary to establish mutual trust and frames of
understanding from which a multiethnic vision for Conasauga can be generated
and realized.

The Mediation

The presence of external university actors has allowed the creation of mediating spaces among the different players. As external actors from the same
country of origin as the majority of immigrants, both the bilingual teachers who
work in the Conasauga schools and the university researchers and evaluators
(i.e., us and some colleagues) have facilitated the intercultural comprehension of
diverse viewpoints. This process operates due to the trust and stature embedded
in the formality of the university, and it allows the intermediary "to explain" to
the members of the Mexican community the "institutional reasoning" and/or
the local traditions of Conasauga. It also allows intermediaries to explain to the

school, religious, economic, judicial, and political officials the "reasoning of the migrants" and the "expectations of the Mexican community." These spaces of mediation on occasion are the fruit of program efforts, but more often are the result of spontaneous exchange. In the first case, we can point out the Summer Institute that allows American educators from the Conasauga school district to experience Mexican society and thereby to become mediators themselves within their own schools. In the second case, at the numerous planning meetings with diverse objectives that the Mexican university personnel have had with local authorities and also in formal project documents, we have shared narratives and new discourses about the lives and aspirations of the newcomers, narratives that we have collected through our fieldwork in the newcomer community, but that we have formatted in accordance with the expectations of the host community (i.e., as part of technical reports or as our "informed" opinion as scholars).

DISCUSSION AND CONCLUSION

Can the experience of The Georgia Project be reproduced in other destination sites of the Mexican and Latino Diaspora in the United States? Can a project with similar characteristics be reproduced in traditional destination sites of this migration such as the metropolitan zones of the Southwest and Chicago, or even in the new metropolitan destinations such as New York and Atlanta? Do Mexican institutions of higher education have the capacity to contribute to the developments of new and old Mexican and Latino communities in the United States?

Setting aside the specific local circumstances that facilitated the creation of The Georgia Project, the authors of this chapter believe it is feasible to reproduce a project with these characteristics in other nontraditional destinations of Mexican and Latino migration in the United States. In fact, the effort and work of institutional intervention and subsequent research in Conasauga has been designed, in certain aspects, from previous models and existing projects between university and community partners (Arches et al., 1997). We can say, inclusively, that if other new destination sites are experiencing these same transforming experiences as Conasauga, projects of this type should be adopted in such localities. We state this, not because we believe that this or other projects benefit immigrants or host communities (in an either/or sense), but because we think that The Georgia Project offers a space and mechanism of interlocutory dialogue and mediation for newcomers and the local community and institutions. The multiple channels of dialogue that have opened and that are multilaterally perceived as legitimate (because they have the cachet of an academic institution) have made it possible for newcomers to begin to participate in the local construction of educational and social policy. In contrast, newcomers previously were excluded—although, as Foucault (1977, 200) and Shore and Wright (1997, 5) would note, they sometimes were the object of others' policymaking. This does not mean that immigrants and their representatives are routinely or consistently included yet in the formulation of policy that affects them, but rather that a long and winding process has been initiated in that direction. In this manner, one of the lessons from The Georgia Project is that in the efforts for social and political inclusion of those traditionally excluded such as Mexicans and Latinos, much can be accomplished by relatively small–scale local and regional initiatives like ours.

For a project of similar characteristics such as The Georgia Project to be reproduced in other places requires at least a few of the dynamics noted in Conasauga to be present—in particular, one of the local established partners (e.g., school officials, civic leaders) must acknowledge the need for intervention by an external partner (cf. Hamann, 1999). In our case, this acknowledgment and invited entreé facilitated to a great degree the actualization of the project and diminished the mistrust and resistance with which the local traditional interests often react to the intervention of external players.

As much as our reflections are derived from new destination sites and non-metropolitan areas where immigrants have surprisingly and massively arrived since the 1990s, we believe that Georgia Project–like programs are also viable in the traditional metropolitan destinations such as Los Angeles, Houston, or Chicago. There are parallels between our Conasauga experience and these metropolitan centers. These cities have received waves of Mexican and Latino immigration, spreading into new neighborhoods and suburban zones. In these sites, the discourses and newcomer needs are novel and/or transplanted from elsewhere. The controversies of bilingualism and multiculturalism, the need for bilingual school and social service staff and personnel familiar with the culture of the country of origin of the newcomers, and the difficulties of incorporating immigrant parents into a dialogue with school officials exist in these communities too. Likewise, these places can also use what Mexican universities have to offer (institution-derived legitimacy, cultural know-how, interlocutory dialogue, and mediation) to promote the dialogue with newcomers.

Nevertheless, there are also important differences. In these cities, a long historical experience has been accumulated with respect to the presence of Latin American immigrant communities. In many cases, the very children of immigrants fill important positions of power in school districts, town boards, and universities. Moreover, in these cities one encounters prolonged traditions of struggle among immigrant and ethnic-minority advocacy organizations. Discussions over multiculturalism and bilingualism are not novel, although they never cease to spark debate and disagreement. Also, there often exists in these places a larger technical capacity among nearby institutions of higher education to initiate projects such as The Georgia Project (although the prospects of such institutions creating programs from a Euro-centric world view seems likely, as previously noted). It seems likely that in the large cities the institutional and group interests are more complex and difficult to mobilize than in smaller sites. In these contexts, the political and ideological negotiations to undertake programs of this type can be more prolonged and winding, but the viability and promise of Georgia Project–like initiatives remains.

In contrast to all this, Conasauga's inhabitants and institutions could not draw from long-term experience with Latino migration, nor could they rely on their local and regional university infrastructure to decipher what had been happening at the local level. When Conasauga civic leaders requested the support of nearby universities and other educational institutions in Georgia, those entities responded only slowly and with varying degrees of apology for what little they could offer.[3]

Although this is an area where public and private Mexican universities alike have scarcely ventured, the experience of The Georgia Project demonstrates that Mexican universities have an important contribution to make to the development of Mexican and Latino communities in the United States. The Mexican Diaspora in its nonmetropolitan destinations offers a unique historical opportunity, although more established loci of immigration also could benefit from the partnership with Mexican universities. Mexican institutions of higher education can provide the technical knowledge, cultural know-how, and institutional legitimacy. This, as other chapters in this volume point out, is typically absent in destination sites without a significant or suitably skilled university infrastructure and with little experience with permanent Latino immigration. Mexican universities' other major form of contribution can be communicative, with respect to the interlocutory dialogue and mediation. The possibility arises that Mexican universities can spearhead the construction of binational social policy in response to binational social realities. Immigration is just one of these realities, albeit perhaps the most obvious one (cf. Ward, 1999).

To take advantage of these opportunities, Mexican institutions confront two challenges. One of them is their limited knowledge of American social reality. Mexican specialists have produced a wealth of knowledge about immigration to the United States and about Mexican communities there, but have produced much less about American society and its multiple local and regional variations. The other challenge is clearly structural and has to do with an inequality of development. Traditionally it has been the American institutions of higher education, and its researchers, that have descended upon Mexico (and the rest of the developing nations) to assess, guide, and develop "legitimate" academic knowledge. In fact, Mexican educational authorities often reproduce this form of cultural colonialism by ignoring the technical and scientific capacity of their very own specialists, while seeking to obtain the authoritative opinions of international consulting firms and of American scholars. Mexican universities interested in contributing to the development of Mexican communities in the United States will have to confront the impact of these practices and structures. In exchange for facing these challenges, the Mexican institutions of higher education will have the opportunity to internationalize themselves through activities "north of the border." They will offer compelling, alternative professional development experiences for their students and alumni. They will develop extension programs for teachers in American schools with the significant presence of children of immigrants and, in a special way, participate like pioneers in the construction of binational social policy that contributes to the development and well-being of the Mexican communities in the United States.

In sum, we believe that as Mexican and other Latino immigrants have traveled across the border to the north to join networks and to bring their languages, customs, funds of knowledge, symbols and needs to countless new destination sites, Mexican institutions of higher education have a rich opportunity and a moral obligation to follow closely in their footsteps.

NOTES

This chapter was written in Spanish and translated by Enrique Murillo Jr., with assistance from Ted Hamann. The authors corrected the translation. The editors have chosen to use the pseudonym selected by Hamann (this volume) to disguise the identity of the town involved.

During the first two and a half years in the life of The Georgia Project, Rubén Hernández-León was an associate professor in the Humanities Department at the Universidad de Monterrey and Janna Shadduck-Hernández was an adjunct professor in the Education Department at the Universidad de Monterrey.

1. Although there has not been a massive white exodus from public schools, there has been some white flight to private schools; this has contributed modestly to the recent parity in Latino and white enrollment percentages. The inflow of Mexican newcomers to these traditional and new urban receiving sites is growing, so the net Mexican-origin population in these cities continues to grow even as the exodus from them also grows.

2. With the end of "Jim Crow" segregation laws in the 1960s and the decreasing resistance to hiring African Americans for manufacturing, Conasauga's industries were not strictly white when the Mexican influx began, but the long local history of African American exclusion and the related history of a regional African American exodus meant that there were not large numbers of African Americans taking industrial jobs in Conasauga simply because there were not large numbers of African Americans left in the region.

3. As the chapter by Allexsaht-Snider in this volume indicates, at least one institution of high education in Georgia—the University of Georgia—has begun to improve its own responsiveness to the needs of Latino newcomers and the Georgia districts where many attend school. In 1999, the University of Georgia in partnership with the

public Universidad Veracruzana began a Mexico summer training program in Xalapa for both preservice and in-service Georgia teachers. This welcome new partnership does not contradict our original point about slow local responsiveness, however. In fact, Georgia leaders of that new partnership credit The Georgia Project with highlighting both the need for action and for laying strategies of responsiveness (i.e., our Summer Institute for Conasauga teachers) which they have been able to build on. This allocation of credit supports our point about the portability and relevance of The Georgia Project in other locales.

REFERENCES

American Association for Employment in Education. 1997. *Teacher Supply and Demand in the United States: 1996 Report.* Evanston, IL: American Association for Employment in Education.

Arches, Joan et al. 1997. "New Voices in University-Community Transformation." *Change.* 29(1):36–41.

Center for Applied Research in Anthropology. 1998. *Cultural Diversity and Education: Focus on Latino Students in Georgia.* Program Handouts. Georgia State University. Atlanta, Georgia.

DeWind, Josh, Charles Hirschman, and Philip Kasinitz, eds. 1997. "Special Issue: Immigrant Adaptation and Native-Born Responses in the Making of Americans." *International Migration Review.* 31(120).

Durand, Jorge. 1998. *Politica, modelo y patron migratorios.* San Luis Potosí, Mexico: El Colegio de San Luis.

Durand, Jorge, Douglas S. Massey, and Fernando Charvet. 2000. "The Changing Geography of Mexican Immigration to the United States: 1910–1996." *Social Science Quarterly.* 81(1):1–15.

Flamming, Douglas. 1992. *Creating the Modern South: Millhands and Managers in Dalton, Georgia, 1884–1894.* Capel Hill: University of North Carolina Press.

Foucault, Michel. 1977. *Discipline and Punish: The Birth of the Prison.* Alan Sheridan, trans. New York: Vintage Books.

Hamann, Edmund T. 1999. "The Georgia Project: A Binational Attempt to Reinvent a School District in Response to Latino Newcomers." Ph.D. dissertation, University of Pennsylvania.

Harkavy, Ira. 1999. "School-Community-University Partnerships." *University and Community Schools.* 6(1–2):3–24.

Hernández-León, Rubén, Janna L. Shadduck, Víctor Zúñiga, and María Olivia Villarreal. 1997. "Hispanic Community Needs Assessment." University of Monterrey and the Georgia Project. Unpublished manuscript.

Hernández-León, Rubén and Víctor Zúñiga. 2000. "'Making Carpet by the Mile': The Emergence of a Mexican Immigrant Community in an Industrial Region of the U.S. Historic South." *Social Science Quarterly.* 81(1):49–66.

Kelley, Kathryn A. (Kitty). 1996. "On Their Own: American Working Class Women Married to Mexican Immigrant Men in the Rural South." Master's thesis, Georgia State University.

Mexican Ministry of Foreign Affairs and U.S. Commission on Immigration Reform. 1998. "Migration between Mexico and the United States. Mexico–United States Binational Migration Study." Mexico City and Washington, DC.

Mitchell, Bonnie L. and Joe R. Feagin. 1995. "Americas's Racial-Ethnic Cultures: Opposition within the Mythical Melting Pot." In *Toward the Multicultural University*. B.P. Bowser, T. Jones, and G.A. Young, eds. Westport: Praeger.

Omi, Michael and Howard Winant. 1994. *Racial Formation in the United States: From the 1960s to the 1990s*. 2d edition. New York: Routledge.

Rodriguez, Néstor P. 1993. "Economic Restructuring and Latino Growth in Houston." In *In The Barrios: Latinos and the Underclass Debate*. Joan Moore and Raquel Pinderhughes, eds. Pp. 101–127. New York: Russell Sage.

Saenz, Rogelio and Cynthia M. Cready. 1999. "Adios Aztlan: Mexican-American Outmigration from the Southwest." Unpublished.

Shadduck, Janna, Rubén Hernández-León, Víctor Zúñiga, and María Olivia Villarreal. 1997. "Hispanic Community Needs Assessment." University de Monterrey and The Georgia Project. Unpublished manuscript.

Shore, Cris and Susan Wright. 1997. "Policy: A New Field of Anthropology." In *Anthropology of Policy: Critical Perspectives on Governance and Power*. Cris Shore and Susan Wright, eds. Pp. 3–39. London: Routledge.

Ward, Peter M., ed. 1999. *Reducing Vulnerability among Families in the Mexico and US Border Region*. Austin: The University of Texas System and DIF Nacional, México.

Zúñiga, Víctor and Rubén Hernández-León. 2001. "A New Destination of an Old eMigration: Origins, Trajectories and Labor Market of Hispanics in Dalton, Georgia." In *Latino Workers in the Contemporary South*. Arthur D. Murphy, Collen Blanchard, and Jennifer A. Hill, eds. Southern Anthropological Society Proceedings Series, No. 34. Athens: University of Georgia Press.

6

Gender and School Success in the Latino Diaspora

Stanton Wortham

More and more Latinos are moving to areas of the United States where few Latinos have settled before—a migration that has been called "the new Latino diaspora" (Hamann, 1999; Villenas, 1997). This chapter describes an isolated community of about 200 Latinos, located in a small rural northern New England town that I call Havertown.[1] When I knew them in the mid-1990s, almost all community members were Mexican immigrants or Mexican Americans who had lived in or passed through south Texas, whose families had at some recent point been involved in migrant agricultural labor, and who came from rural working-class backgrounds. Over the prior ten years, they had been recruited to Havertown to work at a local meat-processing plant.

Based on fieldwork conducted between 1995 and 1997, this chapter explores the social identities that Havertown Latino adolescents adopted in school and at home. All Havertown Latinos found themselves in a culturally alien setting. They lived many hours away from any sizable Latino population, and only a few had access to Spanish language media. Latino adolescents in Havertown experienced cultural isolation and cultural conflict particularly acutely, because they spent substantial time in school with Anglo teachers and students. At their stage of life, as adolescents, they were also confronting questions of identity. This chapter describes how they struggled to identify themselves, and to deal with others' identifications of them, in a culturally alien setting.

Havertown Latino adolescents seemed to face a choice between adapting to the mainstream Anglo values embodied in school practices and maintaining their identities as Mexicans. Some important theories of cultural identity and school success might describe this as an either/or choice—either the Latino adolescents in Havertown would "act white" and conform to mainstream Anglo expectations or they would maintain their minority cultural identities and resist the schools' mainstream expectations (e.g., Fordham and Ogbu, 1986). Others, however, have described how some minority adolescents manage "accommodation without assimilation," where students conform to mainstream expectations enough to do well in school but also preserve their own cultural identities (Gibson, 1988, 1997; Hall, 1995). In Havertown, different Latino adolescents fit each of these patterns. The adolescent males mostly identified with working-class Mexican role models and rejected the mainstream Anglo expectations of the school. But most adolescent females adopted some of the mainstream Anglo values they encountered at school and managed to accommodate without assimilating.

This chapter first describes, and then tries to explain, the gender difference among Havertown Latino adolescents. My analysis follows the lead of Mahler (1998), Mehan (e.g., Mehan, Hubbard and Villanueva, 1994), Suárez-Orozco (e.g., Suárez-Orozco, 1998; Suárez-Orozco and Suárez-Orozco, 1995), and Trueba (e.g., Trueba, Rodriguez, Zou and Cintrón, 1993), who argue that, although social forces limit many U.S. Latinos' options, anthropologists must not deny them agency. Instead of describing life as it happens to U.S. Latinos, these authors recommend that we explore the adaptive strategies many Latinos use to negotiate social barriers. This chapter follows their lead by exploring the divergent adaptive strategies that male and female Latino adolescents adopted in Havertown.

The divergence between male and female strategies shows the need for more complex theories of cultural identification and school success. Some accounts (e.g., Ogbu and Simon, 1998) try to predict minority adolescents' responses to school with reference to structural variables such as the "voluntary" or "involuntary" nature of the minority group's incorporation into the nation. Others have recently reported, however, that particular groups of minority adolescents often adopt identities contrary to Ogbu's predictions, due to local contextual factors (cf. Gibson, 1997). Mehan, Hubbard, and Villanueva (1994), for example, describe how a special school program allowed many "involuntary" Latino and African American minority adolescents to accommodate without assimilating and succeed in school. Levinson (2001) describes how some marginalized adolescents with indigenous ancestry became integrated into groups of successful students at a Mexican secondary school. The Latino adolescents in Havertown also challenged Ogbu's predictions, because males and females from the same social and ethnic background (and often from the same families) adopted strategies that he predicts should characterize different minority groups. This chapter shows how these divergent strategies emerge in the context of a particular configuration of social, cultural, and economic conditions in Havertown.

I argue that we need to develop more complex accounts of minority adolescents' cultural identification and school success if we want to explain the complex dynamics of schooling and cultural identity in Latino diaspora communities such as Havertown. All adolescents make decisions about identity, school, and their futures based on partial knowledge, while remaining constrained by larger cultural and social forces. This process can be particularly challenging for adolescents in the Latino diaspora.

The first section provides ethnographic background on the Havertown Latino community. The second section describes the differences between a typical Latino and a typical Latina adolescent, focusing on their reactions to school. The third section offers provisional explanations for why male and female Latino adolescents use different strategies to adapt to school in Havertown. The conclusion stresses the need for more complex configurations of individual, cultural, and social variables in our theories of cultural identification and school success.

ETHNOGRAPHIC BACKGROUND

In conducting our study of Havertown Latino adolescents, three Latino research assistants and I observed classes and bilingual tutoring sessions at four Havertown schools over two academic years. We interviewed both teachers and students, and we visited Spanish-speaking families in their homes. My assistants also socialized informally with Latino adolescents on a regular basis. Our research took place in a small rural northern New England town several hours from any sizable Latino community. About 200 Latinos, mostly from Mexico or southern Texas, lived in Havertown in the mid-1990s. A few residents came from Guatemala, El Salvador, or Puerto Rico, but the majority were Mexican or Mexican American. Virtually all of the Latino adults in Havertown had come to work at a local meat-processing plant. Turnover was very high, as families regularly left town for other jobs or to return south. Because of the constant arrival of new Spanish-dominant workers (cf. Solé, 1975, 1987), the primary language of almost all the adults and most of the children remained Spanish. At any given time during our study period, about 50 Latino children were enrolled in the local schools—comprising about 3% of the total school population. On average there were four or five Latinos, out of about 150 students, in each grade. All Latino students attended mainstream classes, but many were pulled out of one or two classes a day in order to work in the ESL room. Each of the four local schools had an ESL room with a permanent staff member.

All Latinos experienced some culture shock at being transplanted into a community so devoid of Latinos. One newly arrived adolescent Latina refused to leave the ESL room at the high school for over a week, because she could not face the unfamiliar Anglo world of the school. Several adolescents and adults told me that they would only go into town in a group of Latinos, for fear of the alien Anglo world. Even Latino adolescents who had lived in Havertown a while, and spoke excellent English, worked to blend into the Anglo town—as illustrated by the following fieldnote.

Levania [one of my research assistants] has (finally) earned the trust of Esperanza, it seems. She has been invited to Esperanza's house for dinner twice now, and Esperanza asks for her when she's not in Peggy's room [the ESL pullout room at the high school]. Today Levania described a recent attempt to reinforce Esperanza's ethnic pride. After school they were driving into town, listening and moving to loud Mexican music on the stereo. As soon as they came within earshot of town, Esperanza hurriedly turned off the music and remarked that she hated to have people see her listening to Mexican music like that. (LandGnts.596.P3)

Unfortunately, this adolescent's desire to downplay her Latino identity makes sense in light of some Anglos' attitudes. I interviewed Havertown Anglos, and many of them held inaccurate stereotypes of Latinos—as exotic, as dirty, as violent, as having huge families, or as all being illegal immigrants. In the schools and the town, I heard occasional mutterings about how "Proposition 187 had the right idea." One Latina adolescent, who was known for dressing and grooming herself very carefully, told us about an event in which Anglo boys behind her in class whispered, "Sure does smell like cow shit around here"—apparently alluding to the smell of the meatpacking plant. In addition to these sorts of degrading stereotypes and comments, Havertown Latinos occasionally endured physical threats as well. Two Latinos were once driving through a nearby town (one known as the KKK capital of northern New England), where they were harassed while buying something in a convenience store, chased in a car, and threatened with a gun just because they looked "ethnic" (a term used by some local, working-class whites for anyone nonwhite, including Jews—who are known to have curly hair and big noses). Police, unfortunately, more often contributed to the problem than helped with it. One of my research assistants, who fits Anglo stereotypes about what Latinos look like, was stopped more than once by Havertown police in a spot where I never had any trouble.

More common than this sort of overtly hostile act, however, were thoughtless ones. For instance, once in an elementary school unit about Hawaii we observed an Anglo student say, "I could be a Hawaiian." The teacher responded by pointing to the one Latino and one black student in the class and saying, "No, you're too white, these are the only two who could be Hawaiians." One day another teacher decided to go around the class and have each student say what his or her parents did. We could see the Latino students squirming uncomfortably long before their turns, because they were ashamed to compare their parents' occupations with the others'. Although such incidents were in our experience uncommon in Havertown schools, they could nonetheless have serious effects.

In general, Havertown Latinos were marked as different, and they did suffer for it. But Latino adults and children overwhelmingly reported less discrimination in Havertown than they had experienced elsewhere in the United States. In areas of the United States densely populated by Latinos, Anglo resentment of Latinos can be strong (Trujillo, 1996). One can see this in recent initiatives such as Propositions 187 and 227 in California and in the national English-only movement. In less Latino-dense areas, however, Anglos often feel less threatened. Stull, Broadway, and Erickson (1992) describe a Latino diaspora community similar to Havertown, where Anglos do not see Latinos as serious competition for resources. In such communities Latinos do what local Anglos see as dirty but necessary work, which local Anglos would not do themselves. Meier and Stewart (1991) also report that Latinos face less discrimination in schools where they do not stand out as the primary minority or working-class group, and there were too few Latinos in Havertown for them to become the main target of stereotyping. On the whole, despite some racism and thoughtlessness, Havertown Anglos saw the Latinos as hard-working and had some sympathy for the difficult conditions they worked under.

In fact, Anglo sympathy sometimes reached such proportions that it was a problem. When Anglos' good intentions become patronizing, as they sometimes did in Havertown, Villenas (2001) describes it as "benevolent racism." By the end of our fieldwork, Havertown Latinos had become a "charity magnet," as one local Anglo described it, with many Anglo groups vying to do things for them—from health care to food and clothing donations to tutoring to legal assistance. Some Latinos appreciated this help. They appreciated outsiders' willingness to help expose the unsafe working conditions at the plant, and many Latinos joined with Anglo lawyers to sue the plant over wages unfairly withheld. Anglo charity made most of the Latinos uncomfortable, however, and they wanted to be left alone. A few Latinos, especially male adolescents, openly resented the implication that they needed charity.

Today the issue of unwanted charity boiled over. Yesterday Gerardo [one of my research assistants] had reported the boys' unhappiness about the recent article [the local paper had run another "exposé" on the plant, describing poor working conditions and housing for the Latinos]. Paco worried: "what do people think of us?" Then today, while we were at school, someone piled boxes of used clothes at the entrance to the trailer park [where Latino families live]. Jesús was furious, kicking the boxes and yelling that this was not a Goodwill collection site. He got Paco to borrow his father's car, and they drove the boxes to the Salvation Army—without ever looking at what was inside. (GandRnts.497.P2)

Besides having to confront hurtful Anglo attitudes, Havertown Latinos' isolation and their precarious economic position also caused everyday difficulties. Life in their Havertown neighborhood was relatively sterile for the adolescents, especially for the Latinas. They reported that, in Texas and Mexico, they had many Spanish-speaking friends and easy access to Mexican television, restaurants, and radio. In Havertown, they did not even have easy access to the few activities available in town, because their neighborhood was miles out in the woods. Many male and female adolescents spent substantial time watching TV, both in English and (for those with satellite dishes) in Spanish. The male adolescents did spend substantial time outside their houses, tinkering with cars or playing basketball. Almost all the female adolescents stayed close to home and rarely went outside after dinner. This difference in gender roles is characteristic of working-class Mexican families (Levinson, 2000; Rothenberg, 1995).

The absence of extended family took a particular toll on Havertown Latinos, because their former, rural Mexican (and/or south Texan) lives centered so much around extended family activities (Rothenberg, 1995; Valdés, 1996). Many families had one younger relative living with them, working at the plant, and a few had a brother's or sister's entire nuclear family nearby. But the vast majority had no relatives outside their own nuclear family, this side of Texas. Furthermore, in many of these families one parent and some siblings would be gone for several months out of the year—either to migrant labor sites or back to Texas or Mexico to deal with family responsibilities. Few of the families had overcome the loss of proximate family networks by reaching out to other Latino families in the neighborhood. Most said that the family cannot be replaced, and in any case, most adults spent almost all their time and energy working. There was, in addition, considerable fragmentation and even some mutual suspicion in the community, especially over attitudes toward the plant's owner (some saw the plant as providing steady work, and others resented the working conditions and wanted to unionize). Among the adolescents, individuals usually had one or two good Latino friends—but these friends could not fill the void left by an extended family and a supportive Latino community.

The transience of Latino families also took a toll on both adolescents and others. Stull, Broadway, and Erickson (1992) report that the turnover of workers in this sort of meatpacking job can be 6 to 8 percent a month, and turnover in Havertown approached that at times—especially during the recurring financial and regulatory crises at the plant. Even children from families that had stayed for several years often speculated that they would be leaving soon, and this expectation disrupted their commitments to school and friends. As Anderson (1991) and Chavez (1994) would put it, even these more settled Latino families often did not "imagine" Havertown as their "community." Many families also left temporarily, often during the school year, in order to visit relatives or explore job opportunities elsewhere. In the spring, when the migrant agricultural jobs had begun in Texas, many families moved south temporarily. This disrupted children's schooling, because even a child who had been successful from September to April could not complete a grade without the last six weeks of school. In some years this spring migration so reduced numbers that the ESL staff feared that the superintendent might visit their rooms and get the impression that they were overstaffed.

Another result of Latino families' transience was that the adolescents (and probably others as well) seemed particularly sensitive to loss and were sometimes suspicious of others' commitment to them. Although they felt that they could rely on members of their family, some Latino adolescents hesitated to develop friendships with other families, because they expected that these others might leave soon. For instance, after an auspicious beginning to our work in Havertown, when the Latino adolescent males had begun to accept one of my male research assistants, this assistant overslept one morning and was fifteen minutes late for school. According to the ESL teacher, the Latino students concluded right away that he was "ditching" them, and it took quite a while to restore their confidence in him. On another occasion, my female research assistant had promised to accompany a Latina to the school fashion show one evening, but she could not get a ride and missed the appointment. This Latina adolescent literally never forgave her, having concluded that she was unreliable.

All Latinos that we spoke with sometimes felt alien, stereotyped, and transient in Havertown. The situation was particularly hard for the adolescents. Unlike their parents, Havertown Latino adolescents confronted mainstream American culture daily in school. In addition, their identities as Mexicans were in most cases not as firmly established as their parents', and as adolescents they worried about their identities on a regular basis. Thus, the adolescents faced even more than the (substantial) difficulties of being economically marginal and culturally alien in an otherwise homogeneous town. They also faced the problem of establishing their own identities in a context that too often offered fragmented models of Mexicanness and alluring but sometimes hostile models of mainstream Americanness. Others have described this difficult situation, in which many U.S. Latino adolescents find that they *no son de aquí ni de allá* (Goldfarb, 1996)—in which they no longer feel fully Mexican, but are still marginal in mainstream Anglo society (Griffith and Kissam, 1995; Rothenberg, 1995; Suárez-Orozco and Suárez-Orozco, 1995; Valdés, 1996).

Given the difficulties and the unfamiliarity of life in Havertown, one might expect that Latino adolescents would have faced the either/or choice described: either rejecting the Anglo values of the school and community as "acting white," or assimilating to those Anglo values and rejecting their Latino identities. It turns out that the adolescent male Latinos did primarily adopt the first of these options, but the adolescent females managed to accommodate without assimilating—they adopted Anglo values enough to succeed in school, but they also maintained their identities as Latinas. The next sections describe this gender difference, first quantitatively and then with case studies of two typical adolescents. Then I offer a provisional explanation for the gender difference.

GENDER DIFFERENCES

To establish that this gender difference did in fact exist, I collected and analyzed quantitative data on the 57 Latino students who were enrolled at Havertown High for at least two semesters between 1992–1997. Because of school rules about privacy, outside researchers do not have access to individual student records, so two ESL teachers generated these data, after removing all identifying information. First, they compiled a list of the 57 Latino students and checked their records on these students. Then they met and came to consensus, assigning each student a score on eleven variables. They gave me the resulting data matrix, without student names. Table 6.1 presents the variables.

Table 6.2 presents the results of a multiple regression analysis on the resulting matrix, using the ten other variables to predict school success.[2] In these data, only three variables were independently[3] related to school success: females were more likely to succeed than males; students with good attitudes toward school were more likely to succeed; and students whose families did not move them around during the school year were more likely to succeed (with "success," of course, defined using the school's criteria).

The correlations between attitude and success and migrancy and success make sense. Attitude might be either a cause or a consequence of school success, but either way one would expect the two variables to be related. The correlation between family migrancy and school success also makes sense. These data do not distinguish between several possible explanations: it could be that students who often leave school during the academic year decide school is not worth the effort and so do not work hard; it could be that pulling children out of school during the year causes them to miss important school lessons, which makes failure more likely; it could be that teachers have stereotypes of more migrant children and more often fail them; or it could be that parents of failing children notice their lack of success and decide that it makes no difference if they pull their children out during the year. The first two of these explanations seem the most plausible, but it would require more data to make firm conclusions.

These quantitative results also confirm our ethnographic observations of a gender difference. The Latinas valued school more and succeeded more, according to the school's standards. Unlike the other two significant results, however, this one does not have an obvious explanation. The next two sections describe the gender difference in more detail, by presenting two typical Havertown

Table 6.1
Definition of Variables

Number	Variable Name	Potential Values
1	Gender	1: male 2: female
2	Age at arrival	1: in elementary school 2: in seventh grade or above
3	Length of stay	1: one year or less 2: two years or less 3: more than two years
4	Attitude to school	1: school not valued at all 2: values school rarely 3: values school sometimes 4: values school often 5: fully committed to school
5	Success in school	1: dropped out 2: multiple failing grades 3: C's and D's 4: B's and C's 5: A's and B's
6	Family migrancy	1: move constantly 2: move some during school year 3: do not move during school year
7	Family literacy	1: parents illiterate 2: read basics only if necessary 3: read occasionally 4: read sometimes for pleasure 5: print-rich environment
8	Family aspirations	1: expect no school success 2: expect attendance 3: hope for high school graduation 4: expect some college 5: expect college degree
9	Generation in United States	1: student was born in Mexico 2: student was born in US
10	English on arrival	1: Spanish monolingual 2: some conversational English 3: verbally close to fluent 4: some English literacy 5: fully literate in English
11	English on departure	1: Spanish monolingual 2: some conversational English 3: verbally close to fluent 4: some English literacy 5: fully literate in English

Table 6.2
Multiple Regression Coefficients, Using Ten Variables to Predict School Success

Independent Variable	Coefficient (Standard Error)
gender (female)	.514**
	(.160)
attitude to school	.690**
	(.087)
family migrancy	.316*
	(.129)
family literacy	.056
	(.068)
family aspirations	−.132
	(.110)
generation in United States	.028
	(.208)
English on arrival	−.090
	(.084)
English on departure	.023
	(.104)
age at arrival	−.317
	(.175)
length of stay	.118
	(.129)

$^*p \leq .05,\,^{**}p \leq .01$

Latino adolescents and the strategies that they adopted for establishing their identities in Havertown.

Jesús

Jesús Villalobos was a 17-year-old Latino adolescent in Havertown. The Villalobos family tried to uphold the traditions of rural, working-class Mexico. Mrs. Villalobos arranged for all of her children to spend a couple of months a year back in Mexico, even if it meant missing school, in order to maintain connections with their traditions and their family. All four Villalobos children were born in Mexico, although the two youngest had lived most of their lives in the United States when we knew them. All the children showed great respect for their parents. My assistants and I once observed Jesús, who at the time had a cast on his broken arm, leap up to take out the garbage for his mother when he saw her about to do it. The following field note describes another such incident. "Today don José worked a sixteen-hour shift at the plant. During dinner word came down from the plant that they needed him back to work another shift. Everyone knew that he would go back, but no one said anything. The kids looked at their food and shuffled their feet. Then Jesús jumped up, said he would take the shift, and insisted that José stay home and sleep. He'll be up all night, shoveling feces, but he did not hesitate. Don José accepted the offer and fell into bed right after dinner" (Rnts.997.P2).

Jesús also encouraged his younger siblings to retain their connection to Mexican traditions. He regularly insisted, for instance, that everyone speak only Spanish in the house. Almost all Latino Havertown families spoke Spanish at home, though a fair number of children spoke better English than Spanish. Jesús was in the middle of the continuum—his Spanish was fluent and he spoke good conversational English, but he had not mastered academic English. Among the Havertown adolescents, Jesús was unusually adamant about speaking English only when necessary.

To a mainstream American, the most telling evidence of the Villalobos' Mexican values was their attitude toward money. The older children gave every dollar they earned (which sometimes came to a couple of hundred dollars a week) directly to their mother, for the maintenance of the family. If they wanted money to go out, they asked her for some. The whole family worked toward the goal of saving enough to buy a house in Mexico. Jesús's more Americanized friends thought he was crazy for giving all "his" money away, but to him the family was without hesitation the highest priority.

When asked why they came to Havertown, Jesús' parents cited, for one thing, the lack of drugs and gang violence. In south Texas, Jesús and his friends were in a gang. Jesús himself reported that he smoked and drank in Texas, but he engaged in these practices much less often in Havertown. Both children and adolescents reported that they felt safer in Havertown than in other U.S. locations, and parents worried less about gangs and other bad influences their children might have fallen under. The primary reason for the Villalobos family to be in Havertown, however, was work. As described comprehensively by Griffith and Kissam (1995), recent changes in farm mechanization and a partial breakdown in job-finding networks have disrupted the migration patterns of many agricultural workers. These workers value a steady job above all else, because they have too often experienced jobs where the work dries up and they get paid for only a few hours in a week. José Villalobos once told me, when I asked whether the jobs at the Havertown plant were good: "Well, they're not good jobs, but there are lots of hours." From a mainstream American point of view, the Havertown jobs were exhausting, dirty, low paying, and exploitative. Havertown Latinos recognized these problems, and they would have changed them if they could have done so without jeopardizing their income. But workers got steady work and ample over-time year-round, and these were most important to them.

José Villalobos was by training a mechanic, and Jesús was himself skilled at auto repair. They always had old cars in various states of repair in the trailer park, which served as sites of social interaction among the men and boys who came by to tinker with them. Jesús enthusiastically recounted stories of cars that he had fixed and automobile races in Mexico that he had participated in. He did not talk much about his aspirations, but he did confide to one of my assistants that he would like to be a mechanic like his father. His best friend had a cousin in Texas who completed a course in refrigeration and subsequently made good money as a technician. Jesús cited this as a precedent for how he might succeed using his mechanical skills.

In more imaginative moments, when asked about their aspirations, Jesús and his friends hoped to emulate a former plant employee who had been embellished into a legend: a Latino who came to the meatpacking plant and worked seven days a week, 18 hours a day, spending no money on himself at all; after seven years, he had accumulated half a million dollars (this must be an exaggeration, al-though I know of one attested case of a family that saved about $100,000 over several years in Havertown); with this money he bought two pickup trucks, re-turned to northern Mexico, bought a ranch, and lived happily ever after.

Because of his blue-collar aspirations, Jesús did not see school as important to his future. He attended tenth grade (for the second time) on a somewhat regular basis, but he would often skip school when an open shift at the plant came up. When he was in school, Jesús participated socially but not often academically. He was smart, and his work at the plant showed how diligent and reliable he could be. On one occasion, when challenged by one of my assistants, Jesús showed that he could do surprisingly well on English grammar worksheets for someone who failed most of his classes. But he did not apply himself in school. He said that the classes were "useless" and boring, and he felt that they had noth-ing to do with him. One can understand this boredom in some cases, as he had been forced to take the same classes over because of failing grades. Until high school he was able to pass his classes through a combination of resourcefulness and charm, but by high school he had fallen so far behind his classmates in aca-demic English literacy skills and various types of content knowledge that teach-ers could no longer pass him through.

Both teachers and students nonetheless liked Jesús. Teachers liked him for his liveliness and good humor. Several told me that he would make an excellent politician or salesman, because of his interpersonal skills. Jesús also displayed a genuinely good spirit. We saw this especially in his actions toward the disabled special education students, whose room was next door to the ESL room. Most of us smiled and walked quickly past the special education students, feeling pity—

or simply being self-conscious as they stared at us. But Jesús always had a minute to joke with them. With the ESL teacher's help, he regularly arranged to get out of study hall and play basketball in the gym with the special education students. One day I saw him positively ebullient, because he was so looking forward to line dancing with them later in the day. I do not believe this emotion came from any particular love of dancing, but instead from the opportunity to do something different and the opportunity to help. Perhaps Jesús's greatest success with these students was the day he taught several of the disabled boys to burp at will. I have rarely seen anyone look so proud as he made those boys on that day.

Jesús also got along well with most of his classmates. Almost everyone knew him and appreciated his good humor. Despite his popularity, however, Jesús confided in private that he had no "real friends" among Anglos and that he did not feel popular. He spent most of his time in class daydreaming or fooling around, or in the ESL room with his few good Latino male friends. He did occasionally get into fights with Anglo boys—especially the "poor white trash" who, he claimed, hated Latinos. On one occasion Jesús instigated a fight at school with an Anglo boy who had said, "When I grow up I'm going to help out you Latinos." Before starting the fight, Jesús' response was: "I don't need your help; I make more in a week at the plant than you make in a month flipping burgers."

We can sum up Jesús' attitude toward school with two anecdotes. On one occasion I was sitting in the ESL room, talking with the teacher. We heard some giggles among the special education students, and then Jesús suddenly appeared at the door, somewhat out of breath—and much to the teacher's surprise. He had been in a closed, teacher-supervised room. He said: "Paco didn't make it out." Note the presupposition that school is a place, like jail, to be escaped. Jesús also had a trademark exit: whenever he left a room, he flicked the lights on and off. In the ESL room, the flick lasted long enough that the teacher often had time to glare at him. I once observed him leave the main office after a disciplinary meeting with the vice principal. Even there he dared to flick the lights, but very quickly. He was gone before anyone else looked up.

In assessing Jesús' attitude toward school, we must be careful not to adopt the perspective of the school uncritically. He did not lack ability, nor was he a wayward, rebellious adolescent. He chose not to apply himself in school because he believed school success would not help him reach his goals, and perhaps because he could not imagine the school conferring success on someone like him. He chose instead to make money for his family, and he hoped someday to get a better blue-collar job and to become the head of his own Mexican family. The school, however, provided only one model of a successful student—one who works hard on academic tasks for the sake of his or her own individual achievement. When we knew him, Jesús made no effort to fit this model. The school responded by labeling him as unsuccessful. Jesús responded in turn by adopting what the school considered mildly oppositional behavior. In this way Jesús made it clear that, instead of being a "failure," he did not aspire to the mainstream model. At home Jesús showed where his real values were, by contributing to his family and spending time with his Latino friends.

Teresa

Like Jesús, Teresa Fuentes was the oldest in a family of four children. Teresa's family had been in Havertown for eight years, and she had spent most of her life in the United States. Like the Villalobos family, the Fuentes family moved to Havertown for the work. They remained, however, partly for the schools—which they found superior to those in south Texas or rural Mexico. Teresa's father had heard of opportunities for work elsewhere in the United States, but he remained at a difficult job largely so that his children could finish school in Havertown. Mr. Fuentes was Mexican, and he came to Havertown after spending a few years in California and south Texas. He worked many hours at the plant, but when at home he expected a Mexican household. Teresa's mother was born in the United States and was fully bilingual. She played an important role for many others in the community, occasionally serving as an intermediary between the Latinos and governmental or legal institutions.

Perhaps because of Mrs. Fuentes's American background, Teresa's family was not as committed to preserving Mexican traditions as Jesús's. (It was not generally the case, however, that adolescent Latinas came from more Americanized families than adolescent males.) Teresa and her siblings did not work outside the home, but if they did they would likely have kept at least some of the money for themselves. Teresa's siblings sometimes demanded and got expensive pairs of sneakers and relatively expensive clothes. Note that these differences in values cannot explain the difference between Jesús and Teresa, however, because Teresa's brother, Tomás, behaved much like Jesús. Like Jesús, Tomás did not work hard in school and identified most closely with his Latino family and friends.

In her loyalty to the family, however, Teresa was more clearly Mexican. She almost always stayed home in the evenings and helped her mother with household tasks. On one occasion that we observed, she had the opportunity to participate in a fashion show at school. She was normally shy, but she was looking forward to this activity. One of the teachers told me that it was her "one opportunity to shine" publicly at school. That evening, before the show was to start, Teresa received word that her mother had been slightly injured at the plant and had gone to the hospital. Without hesitation, she left the show to care for her siblings. And, despite her normally scrupulous attendance, she willingly missed school the following two days in order to continue helping her mother.

In school and out, Teresa was quiet and diligent. She rarely spoke to new people, and even with my younger, Latina assistant she did not initiate conversation, for many months. At home, she spent most of her time in her room doing schoolwork or in the kitchen helping her mother. In school, she behaved as if she did not want to be noticed. Until our last year in Havertown she did not come to the ESL room at all, and she did not interact much with the other Latino students at school. The following field note illustrates how she was perceived in school by other Latino students: "Today was María's second day in school after arriving from Mexico last week. Peggy [the bilingual aide] has been with her all day, translating forms and introducing her to students and teachers. She can carry on rudimentary conversations in English, but not much more. She seems to think that Teresa is an assimilated Latina, however. When Teresa entered Peggy's room today, María tried to talk to her in English. She can see that Teresa's Latina, and I think she heard Teresa speaking Spanish yesterday. But she's already decided that Teresa would rather speak English in school" (GandRnts.297.P5).

Despite her preference for English in school, Teresa did not seem embarrassed at being Mexican. In fact, when a new ESL teacher created a more welcoming climate in the ESL room, she began to appear there and offered to help tutor some of her compatriots. On one occasion we also observed Teresa in the ESL room, deeply involved in a discussion with another Latina about life in the United States with a strict Mexican father. They shared frustrations about the constraints this imposed, but they also agreed that they would likely marry Mexican or Mexican American men and that they would teach their children Spanish. So Teresa thought of herself as Latina, and she was not a pariah among her classmates. There was one Latina in the high school whom the Latino boys accused of "acting white" and abandoning her people. This girl wore expensive catalog clothes, had bought herself a new car with money she made working, and dated Anglo boys. Teresa did none of these things, and she was not actively ostracized. Others were suspicious of her academic success to some extent, but her isolation resulted more from her position as a daughter in a Mexican home torn from its context and from her choice to devote herself to school.

In our last year of observations, Teresa began applying to colleges. She had a very good academic record, and both parents and teachers expected her to attend college. I had the opportunity to accompany her and several other Latino students from Havertown on a college tour that one of my assistants and the ESL teacher arranged. All these students would be the first in their families to go to college, and they seemed overwhelmed by the college environment. They were strikingly quiet and wide-eyed during all the tours. At one institution we had lunch in the cafeteria. Teresa seemed awed by the diversity of food choices and the atmosphere. She said, "This is very different from lunch at Havertown

High." This was the only thing I heard her say the entire day. When back in Havertown the next day, however, she did tell my assistant that she had been particularly impressed with one of the schools we had visited and that she now wanted to go there. Before this visit, she had planned to apply only to nearby junior colleges, but she ended up applying to this more prestigious school. I am happy to report that Teresa was accepted and now attends this college.

In the degree of her academic success, Teresa was unusual. But most adolescent Havertown Latinas, unlike their brothers, adopted the mainstream model of academic success in school. Most did not aspire to be mainstream Americans in all aspects of their lives. Like the immigrants described by Gibson (1988, 1997), Mehan, Hubbard and Villanueva (1994) and others, Havertown Latinas worked to maintain dual identities—as Latinas at home and as successful students in school. Most of the girls managed to balance these two identities. But why did the male and female Latino adolescents choose such different strategies? The next section sketches a provisional answer to this question.

A MULTIPLE-FACTOR ACCOUNT

Why did the Latinas value school more? I have searched the literature, and discussed this finding with various ethnographers of U.S. Latinos, without hearing of such a striking gender difference in school success as this—although Pugach (1998) does report the same gender difference in less extreme form. An adequate explanation for this pattern must cite the particular configuration of factors that came together in Havertown. Influences from the home culture, the particular community context, and the economic situation all influenced Latino adolescents' aspirations and attitudes toward school. This section describes these factors and how they fit together.

In general, gender roles are more differentiated among rural Mexicans than among mainstream Anglos (Rothenberg, 1995). Male Mexican adolescents also enjoy considerably more freedom than their sisters (Levinson, 2000). The separation between male and female adolescents in Havertown was very sharp: male and female ethnographers spent months building close relationships with same-gender Latinos but hardly knew members of the opposite gender. Siblings of opposite genders sometimes had relatively close relationships within the house, but most often they ignored each other in public. In Havertown, male adolescents congregated outside the house and had few responsibilities until they were old enough to earn money. Females mostly stayed inside the house and were responsible for many household chores. Virtually all the Latina adolescents went inside in the late afternoon to help prepare dinner, and even the adventurous generally went in at the first sign of their fathers coming home. This sharp differentiation in gender roles that they inherited from rural, working-class Mexican culture makes possible, but does not in itself explain, the gender difference in adaptive strategies among Havertown Latino adolescents.

Levinson (2000) reports that adolescent females in Mexico often take on more responsibility in school and sometimes take school more seriously than adolescent males, and Pugach (1998) found a similar difference in her work on the U.S.-Mexican border. Because of gender segregation in working-class Mexican culture, girls and boys face different choices: Girls choose between school and early marriage, whereas boys more often choose between school and early employment. Levinson (2001) reports that working-class Mexican fathers often discourage their daughters from interacting with boys and that mothers often encourage their daughters to pursue school success as a way to earn some independence from domestic relations. On the other hand, working-class Mexican parents sometimes encourage or allow their sons to work and help support the family. Thus Levinson does sometimes observe a gender difference in attitudes toward school and school success among working-class Mexican adolescents—although it is not as extreme as the one I observed in Havertown. Nonetheless, the gender segregation and different life options that underlie this gender difference in Mexico may also have played a role among Havertown Latinos.

These factors cannot fully explain the gender difference among Havertown adolescents, however. Levinson (2001) reports that many of the male adolescents he spoke with in Mexico valued school, worked for school success, and aspired to the sorts of nonmanual labor that an education would make possible for them. These male students looked down on other boys who dropped out of school to work. So—although the segregated gender roles that Havertown Latinos brought from working-class Mexican culture, and the fact that adolescent Latinas often face a choice between school and early marriage, may help explain the Havertown Latinas' commitment to and success in school—these cultural gender roles do not explain the rejection of school among adolescent males in Havertown. For that we must consider other factors, such as their socioeconomic position as working-class immigrants and the role models they observed in Havertown.

Levinson (2001) does report that, when the Mexican economic crisis hit in the mid-1990s, some male adolescents in Mexico stopped aspiring to school success because they saw fewer and fewer white-collar jobs available. This introduces a second factor, in addition to cultural gender roles, which helps explain the gender difference in school success among Havertown Latino adolescents. Students' appraisal of economic opportunities can affect their decisions about whether it makes sense to work hard in school. In Havertown, male Latino adolescents did often talk as if it would be unrealistic for them to aspire to white-collar jobs. They sounded in some ways like the working-class "lads" described by Willis (1981). Like Willis' lads, some Havertown Latino adolescent males participated in "antischool cultures"—sets of values and practices opposed to mainstream society and its schools. Both the English working-class boys and the working-class Latino adolescents in Havertown disparaged nonphysical work as unmasculine and aspired to jobs that involve physical exertion and some danger. They also engaged in activities, such as "having a laugh," that reinforced group solidarity and rejected school authority, activities that Willis argues can make a life of physical labor bearable. Male Havertown Latinos often had values similar to those Willis describes: loyalty to family and the need to help support the family took precedence over individual success; and work was considered a way to make money, not a calling (cf. also Rothenberg, 1995; Valdés, 1996). I am suggesting, then, that the male Latino adolescents did not work hard in school partly for the same reasons as other working-class adolescent males—they decided that people like themselves would likely not be allowed to succeed in middle-class institutions, and they found the option of life as a working-class male more attractive.

Why would adolescent males and females from the same Latino families in Havertown develop different expectations about their economic prospects? At least two different factors play a role here, one involving socioeconomic structure and the other involving the Anglo role models available in the particular context of Havertown. At the level of social structure, Tienda (1989) describes how some jobs in the U.S. economy have become "reserved" for Mexicans. That is, both Mexicans and others in the workforce come to think of certain manual jobs as Mexican work, and Mexicans have come to dominate the labor pool for those jobs. Tienda describes how the stereotypical Mexican jobs are manual labor most often done by men. Mexican women do some manual labor, but they also do clerical, sales, and service-sector work much more often than Mexican men. In Havertown, then, the male adolescents in particular might have decided that they were unlikely to get white-collar work because of social stereotypes that portray Mexican men as manual laborers. Like Willis' (1981) lads, of course, the male Latinos in Havertown did not see manual labor as undesirable. On the contrary, they denigrated nonphysical labor as effeminate. But male Latino adolescents in Havertown perceived their upward mobility as limited, and did not see school as a viable vehicle for advancement.

So cultural gender roles and perceived economic opportunities both play a role in explaining the gender difference among Havertown Latino adolescents. But even these two factors together do not suffice as an explanation. Mehan, Hubbard and Villanueva (1994), among others, describe groups of Latino adolescents in the United States that share similar working-class Mexican culture and that face the same stereotypical expectations for Mexican men that Tienda (1989) describes, but who do not show the same gender differences in school success.[4] We need one more factor, particular to the Havertown context, to give a more complete explanation for the gender difference there. Latinos in Havertown entered schools where Anglo students also showed a striking gender difference in school success. Anglo adolescents in Havertown had different attitudes toward school and different rates of school success, depending on their gender. Teachers at Havertown High often complained that upper-track classes were overwhelmingly female, and they worried about how to reach the boys. In one recent year, all top ten students at the high school were female. This was not considered particularly unusual, although the administration was sufficiently disturbed that they moved student number eleven, a boy, into a "tie" for tenth. In high school classrooms, girls were much more often attentive and conscientious, and even upper-middle-class boys showed less interest in school. Teachers explained this male tendency partly as a pragmatic issue: Boys imagined that in the future they would do physical labor, or take over their father's business, and they did not need to go to college for this; girls, on the other hand, realized that even secretaries and medical assistants need some educational credentials. I agree with the teachers that perceived economic opportunities did seem to play a role in the Anglo gender difference, although the gender difference in these schools was more extreme than I have seen elsewhere.

Adolescent Latinas in Havertown, then, saw Anglo females working hard, succeeding in school, and expecting to succeed in life after school. They observed the surrounding Anglo society, in which women had greater chances for advancement through education than they do in Mexico. And because they faced less discrimination in Havertown than in other parts of the United States, many were able to see school as a route to escape from the constraints of their current lives. With a peer model of Anglo females who worked hard and hoped to succeed through education, they could see themselves doing the same. Like Latino adolescents elsewhere in the United States (Griffith and Kissam, 1995; Suárez-Orozco and Suárez-Orozco, 1995), and in Mexico (Levinson, 2001), these girls and their families hoped that they would not have to do the same sorts of difficult labor as their parents. Because of lowered discrimination and positive female models, Havertown Latinas often saw school as a way to accomplish this. Most of them managed to do so by becoming Americanized to some degree, but without breaking their connection to their parents and their Mexican culture.

Male Latino adolescents, however, did not have the same positive Anglo model available as their sisters. Local Anglo males were more often concerned with toughness than school success. Suárez-Orozco and Suárez-Orozco (1995) describe how Anglo adolescents' ambivalence toward school sometimes rubs off on second-generation Latinos. In Havertown we might have observed a similar pattern, but only among adolescent males. Like their Anglo counterparts, the Latino males saw opportunities for making substantial money in the near term through physical labor. They were drawn both to the idea of having their own money and a car (or, ideally, a pickup truck) and to the idea of making money to help their family. So most of the adolescent males rejected the school's values and affiliated with "oppositional" U.S. adolescent practices or with traditional Mexican working-class ones.

Several factors, then, predisposed male and female Latino adolescents in Havertown toward different strategies with respect to school. Sharply differentiated cultural gender roles, perceived and actual economic opportunities, and the availability of gender-specific Anglo role models all contributed to the gender difference among Havertown Latino adolescents. As described by MacLeod (1987), these more structural factors were mediated through the adolescents' aspirations. That is, based on their perceptions of and experiences with these more structural factors, Havertown Latino adolescents adjusted their aspirations and their life strategies. Thus we observed that, like Jesús, Latino adolescent males in Havertown generally did not work hard in school. Those few that did hid their good grades, and bragged about their occasional failures, to avoid being stigmatized as a "schoolboy." We observed no similar peer pressure among the girls. Some girls, in fact, enjoyed lording their academic success over their brothers. (Teresa and her sisters once had a pool going over how many classes their brother would fail that term. Teresa's parents allowed this, and even concurred occasionally when the girls called their brother "the dumb one." Her brother responded by trying to be "cool"—drinking, acquiring relatively tame gang paraphernalia, etc.).

The gender difference in attitudes toward school and in school success is related to the groups that adolescents identify with. As described earlier, the girls identified with successful Anglo role models in school and identified with Mexican role models at home. Many of the boys were instead drawn to "oppositional" identities, like those described by Fordham and Ogbu (1986). These involved gang signs and paraphernalia, even though the boys rarely participated in dangerous gang activity. Insofar as these boys adopted "oppositional" identities, they rejected the mainstream Anglo values represented by the school. As described in the case of Jesús, they did this partly to show that they freely chose not to live up to mainstream expectations in school and thus that their "failure" did not result from incompetence. Like Jesús, most adolescent males remained integrated in their families and planned to pursue the kind of work their fathers did. This aspect of their behavior might have appeared "oppositional" from an Anglo perspective, insofar as it led them to ignore school activities. But in fact they were simply identifying themselves as working-class Latinos. Jesús took pride in his family, and in being a man as defined by traditional Mexican culture. He aspired to be like other working-class Mexican heads-of-household that he saw around him. He did not have to succeed in secondary school to reach this goal.[5]

On the other hand, most of the female Latina adolescents were like Teresa in that they partly identified with mainstream Anglo values. Many of them aspired to success in school and a career. This involved some rejection of their parents' values, as the Latinas imagined themselves learning about and succeeding in the Anglo world (Suárez-Orozco and Suárez-Orozco, 1995). This could lead to isolation, both within and outside the Latino community, for Latinas like Teresa. Most girls nonetheless still identified as Latinas. They planned to remain close to their families, and they expected to marry Latinos themselves. Teresa and others also reported that they planned to succeed primarily so that they could help their families.

CONCLUSIONS

Male and female Latino adolescents in Havertown adopted different strategies for adjusting to a culturally alien environment. Both groups were caught between two cultures, but they reacted in different ways. Most of the male adolescents reacted to mainstream Anglo stereotypes by celebrating their difference, much like the working-class African American adolescents described by Fordham and Ogbu (1986) and the English "lads" described by Willis (1981). These Latinos identified primarily with working-class Mexican men and not with the mainstream Anglo values practiced in school. They aspired to hard work and to become the heads of their own Mexican families. Most of the female adolescents, on the other hand, adopted more Anglo identities in school. They mingled more readily with Anglo teachers and students and focused on their own academic success. But these Latinas were not fully assimilated. At home they maintained Mexican identities. So they had dual identities, acting partly Anglo in school and largely Mexican at home—a phenomenon also described by Gibson (1988, 1997), Hall (1995) and others.

Both genders' strategies helped Latino adolescents adapt to Havertown. The males both experienced and presented themselves as different from the mainstream Anglo norm—even though their strategy resembled working-class Anglo males in some ways. Many boys enjoyed opposing the mainstream institution of school—although for some their opposition created unpleasant conflict with parents or teachers, and for a few it created internal conflict because of competing desires to assimilate or succeed professionally. They nonetheless retained a positive sense of what they wanted to be: Mexican or Mexican American men who preserved important aspects of their culture. The female adolescents adapted by conforming to mainstream values and practices while in school and to Mexican values at home. They hoped to retain this dual identity throughout their lives in the United States—to succeed in the mainstream world, but to maintain their cultural traditions at home.

Each of these strategies has costs and benefits. The Latino adolescent males will likely forego academic success and thus will not be able to compete for most high-status jobs. I do not mean to blame the Latinos for this choice, in two respects. First, their choices are constrained by ideologies and economic discrimination (Smith and Guarnizo, 1998). Second, because they will retain a strong connection to their cultural tradition, their choice makes sense. In contemporary U.S. society, with the disintegration of families and the resulting pathologies, there is much to be said for a tradition that preserves family and community. Most of the Latinas, on the other hand, will attain academic success, which will give them greater professional opportunities. But if they pursue opportunities that require more mainstream lifestyles, they will risk losing more of their cultural tradition. We will have to wait another generation to see whether these girls will be able to maintain dual identities and pass them on to their children.

I have tried to show how this gender difference in attitudes toward school and school success results from a configuration of factors, a configuration that is in part specific to the Havertown context and that ties both to the heritage Latino newcomers bring with them and to the way they are received by the host community. If this sort of more complex, contextualized account turns out to be generally required to explain minority students' cultural identification and school success, we will have to replace more decontextualized single-factor accounts. As Erickson (1987) argues, both cultural (e.g., Cazden, John, and Hymes, 1972) and sociohistorical (e.g., Ogbu and Simon, 1998) factors play an important role in explaining minority adolescents' behavior in school. And as Mehan, Hubbard and Villanueva (1994) argue, both sociocultural structures and student aspirations (MacLeod, 1987) play a role. The Havertown example illustrates how we must identify particular configurations of these factors to account for particular cases.

In planning educational policies to meet the challenges of schooling in the new Latino diaspora, then, we must not homogenize Latino needs, aspirations, and beliefs. Students from similar structural positions may have different needs, depending on particular aspects of the context. In order to identify promising policies, we must first explore the particular configuration of factors in each context within which Latino adolescents make decisions. Because ethnography is often required to understand such contextualized configurations, in many cases ethnography should precede policy.

NOTES

I would like to thank Roger Andersen, Ted Hamann, Enrique Murillo, Kathy Schultz, Enrique Trueba, and Sofia Villenas for critical comments on earlier versions of this chapter. I would like to thank my research assistants—Levania Davis, Gerardo Joven, and Robert Chavira—whose help has been indispensable. And I would like to thank the National Academy of Education and the Spencer Foundation for their financial support of this project.

1. All names and many identifying details have been changed, to hide participants' identities. For the same reason, some of the people and events described are composites of several actual people or events.

2. For the overall regression, $F = 20.5436$ ($p \leq .0000$) and $R^2 = .7933$.

3. In other words, the analysis controls for other correlations that might confound the results. For instance, it is not the case that girls in this sample more often succeed in school because most of these girls happen to come from less migrant families. The correlation between gender and school success is independent of the other variables.

4. The case described by Mehan et al. also contains one other important difference— an educational program that helps Latinos of both genders succeed in school. Innovative educational policies appear to make a difference in some contexts.

5. I do not mean to imply that working-class Latinos in general do not value education. Most studies report that they do (e.g., Griffith and Kissam, 1995; Suárez-Orozco and Suárez-Orozco, 1995; Valdés, 1996), and most Havertown parents did as well. We observed two types of exceptions: Families that needed their adolescent children to make money (most of these families hoped that in the next generation children would have more opportunities for education); and a few parents who genuinely did not see the use of more advanced schooling. But even when parents valued education, they could not always convince their male adolescent children of its importance. I am trying to articulate why, under the circumstances, these adolescent males' attitudes might make sense.

REFERENCES

Anderson, Benedict. 1991. *Imagined Communities: Reflections on the Origin and Spread of Nationalism*. Rev. ed. London: Verso.

Cazden, Courtney, Vera John, and Dell Hymes, eds. 1972. *Functions of Language in the Classroom*. New York: Teachers College.

Chavez, Leo. 1994. "The Power of the Imagined Community: The Settlement of Undocumented Mexicans and Central Americans in the United States." *American Anthropologist*. 96(1):52–73.

Erickson, Frederick. 1987. "Transformation and School Success: The Politics and Culture of Educational Achievement." *Anthropology and Education Quarterly*. 18(4):335–356.

Fordham, Signithia and John Ogbu. 1986. "Black Students' School Success." *Urban Review*. 18:176–206.

Gibson, Margaret. 1997. "Complicating the Immigrant/Involuntary Minority Typology." *Anthropology and Education Quarterly*. 28(3):431–454.

———. 1988. *Accommodation without Assimilation*. Ithaca: Cornell University.

Goldfarb, Katia. 1996. "No Soy de Aquí ni Soy de Allá." Paper Presented at the American Educational Research Association Annual Meeting. New York, April 1996.

Griffith, David and Ed Kissam. 1995. *Working Poor*. Philadelphia: Temple University.

Hall, Kathleen. 1995. "There's a Time to Act English and a Time to Act Indian: The Politics of Identity among British-Sikh Teenagers." In *Children and the Politics of Culture*. Sharon Stephens ed. Princeton, NJ: Princeton University Press.

Hamann, Edmund. 1998. "Anglo (Mis)Understandings of Latino Newcomers: A North Georgia Case Study." In *Negotiating Power and Place at the Margins: Selected Papers on Refugees and Immigrants*, 7. Juliene Lipson and Lucia Ann McSpadden, eds. Pp. 156–197. Washington, DC: American Anthropological Association.

————. 1999. "The Georgia Project." Ph.D. dissertation. University of Pennsylvania Graduate School of Education.

Levinson, Bradley. 2000. "Contradictions of Gender and the (Dis)Empowerment of Women at a Mexican Secondary School." In *Género y Cultura en América Latina*, (Col. 2, Literatura y Educación). Maria Luisa Torrés, ed. Mexico City: ICES (Center for Sociological Studies) and PEM (Program on Women's Studies) of El Colegio de México.

————. 2001. *We Are All Equal*. Durham, NC: Duke University.

MacLeod, Jay. 1987. *Ain't No Makin' It*. Boulder, CO: Westview.

Mahler, Sarah. 1998. "Theoretical and Empirical Contributions toward a Research Agenda for Transnationalism." In *Transnationalism from Below*. Michael Peter Smith and Luis Eduardo Guarnizo, eds. Pp. 64–100. New Brunswick, NJ: Transaction Publishers.

Mehan, Hugh, Lea Hubbard, and Irene Villanueva. 1994. "Forming Academic Identities." *Anthropology and Education Quarterly*. 25:91–117.

Meier, Kenneth and Joseph Stewart. 1991. *The Politics of Hispanic Education*. Albany, NY: SUNY.

Ogbu, John and Simon, Herbert. 1998. "Voluntary and Involuntary Minorities." *Anthropology and Education Quarterly*. 29:155–188.

Pugach, Marleen. 1998. *On the Border of Opportunity: Education, Community, and Language in the U.S.–Mexico Line*. Mahwah, NJ: Lawrence Erlbaum Associates.

Rothenberg, B. Annye. 1995. *Understanding and Working with Parents and Children from Rural Mexico*. Menlo Park, CA: The CHC Center for Child and Family Development.

Smith, Michael Peter and Luis Eduardo Guarnizo, eds. 1998. *Transnationalism from Below*. New Brunswick, NJ: Transaction Publishers.

Solé, Yolanda. 1975. "Language Maintenance and Language Shift among Mexican-American College Students." *Journal of the Linguistic Association of the Southwest*. 1:22–48.

————. 1987. "La Difusión del Español entre Mexicano-Americanos, Puertorriqueños, y Cubano-Americanos en los Estados Unidos." In *Language and Language Use*. T. Morgan, J. Lee, and B. Van Patten, eds. Pp. 161–174. New York: University Press of America.

Stull, Donald, Michael Broadway, and Ken Erickson. 1992. "The Price of a Good Steak." In *Structuring Diversity*. L. Lamphere, ed. Pp. 35–64. Chicago: University of Chicago.

Suárez-Orozco, Carola and Marcelo Suárez-Orozco. 1995. *Transformations*. Stanford: Stanford University.

Suárez-Orozco, Marcelo. 1998. "Terrors: Immigrants and Refugees in the Post-National Space." In *Ethnic Identity and Power: Cultural Contexts of Political Action in School and Society*. Yali Zou and Enrique Trueba, eds. Pp. 283–319. Albany: State University of New York Press.

Tienda, Marta. 1989. "Looking to the 1990's." In *Mexican Migration to the United States*. Wayne Cornelius and Jorge Bustamante, eds. Pp. 109–147. San Diego: Center for U.S.–Mexican Studies.

Trueba, Henry, Cirenio Rodriguez, Yali Zou, and Jose Cintrón. 1993. *Healing Multicultural America*. London: Falmer.

Trujillo, Armando. 1996. "Bilingual/Bicultural Education and Politics in Crystal City, Texas: 1969–1989." In *Chicanas and Chicanos in Contemporary Society*. R. De Anda, ed. Pp.157–177. Boston: Allyn and Bacon.

Valdés, Guadalupe. 1996. *Con Respeto*. New York: Teachers College.

Villenas, Sofia. 1997. "Una Buena Educación." Paper Presented at the American Anthropological Association Annual Meeting. Washington, DC, November, 1997.

———. 2001. "Latina Mothers and Small-Town Racism." *Anthropology and Education Quarterly*. 32:3–28.

Willis, Paul. 1981. *Learning to Labour*. New York: Columbia University.

7

Fragmented Community, Fragmented Schools: The Implementation of Educational Policy for Latino Immigrants

Elias Martinez

This chapter describes a community at the end of the twentieth century that is experiencing rapid "Latinization" of its workforce and school system. I focus on school policies designed to cope with an influx of Spanish-speaking children for whom teachers and school staff were unprepared. Educators responded with a piecemeal approach to education for Latino students, an approach that further marginalized Latino immigrants and retarded the development of a coherent community. I examine the conflict between the cultural expectations of long-term Anglo and Chicano[1] residents and those of newcomers—Latino immigrant families and their children from Mexico, El Salvador, and other Central American countries—and how these divergent cultural expectations created a heterogeneous set of available identities for Latino immigrants. The study is based on five years of ethnographic fieldwork and applied practice in this community and its schools. I begin by describing the disruptions of community life caused by economic and population growth in the area, and then I move to a specific discussion of the school district's attempts to cope with change and crisis.

This study focuses on the notion that the development of educational policy is tied to, and reflects, the cultural, contextual, and political dimensions of the community in which it is embedded. As Levinson and Sutton (2001) note, "Authorized policy is a form of governance, to be sure, but one that is constantly negotiated and reorganized in the ongoing flow of institutional life." By establishing the larger context of educational policymaking for Latinos in La Sierra County, and then by describing the implementation of a federal Title VII grant proposal there, I show how policy was negotiated and reorganized in the ongoing flow of the community culture as well.

This chapter comes from an ethnographic study (Martinez, 1998) of educational policies and practices at Snow Mountain Elementary school, located in La Sierra County in the Rocky Mountains.[2] In 1991, I was hired to develop and implement a Title VII–funded Transitional Bilingual Education (TBE) program for the La Sierra County School District. In this capacity I worked with school district administrators, local school personnel, and members of the local community. Through this experience I came to understand the ideas and attitudes that governed the development of educational policy for Latino students. Later I worked as a teaching assistant and lived with the Latino newcomer community. This experience helped me understand how educational policies and community attitudes affected the lives of Latino students and their families. From 1991 to 1996, I participated in community events, and I was able to witness the changes in the community that were caused by population growth. Interviews with local residents, analysis of newspaper accounts, and personal experiences trying to find my own affordable housing, all gave me firsthand experience of what it meant to live in a rapidly changing community. Further data sources employed for this study were participant observation in the schools, interviews with school district personnel and students, and observations at parent and community meetings. I also used a 1993 demographic analysis which I conducted for the BUENO Center at the University of Colorado at Boulder (Martinez, 1993).

The original purpose of this study was to explore what happened when a community experiencing a high influx of immigrants decided to implement a TBE program to meet the needs of Latino immigrant children. The program was to be a "bellwether" site (LeCompte and Preissle, 1993), one which I felt would be an excellent site in which to explore effective instruction for language minority students. However, in my research, I came to discover how external conditions conspired against the implementation of a well-conceived program and transformed it instead into a program that further disempowered and marginalized Latino students. The program that was actually implemented—a pull-out instructional program for limited English proficient children—marginalized students through rituals which reflected conventional school practice, rather than empowering them as the original design had envisioned. This chapter tells the story of how various factors combined to generate unanticipated outcomes for the Latino immigrant students.

CHANGES AND FRAGMENTATION IN THE COMMUNITY

At the beginning of the 1990s, the "world class" ski resort towns of Christiana and Ajax began to negotiate the effects of a burgeoning immigrant population that spoke little or no English and brought their own cultural traditions. Health care providers, educators, state and local government personnel, as well as long-term residents and business owners, sought ways to better understand and inter-act with the immigrants. However, the growing Latino immigrant population, along with an explosive population growth in the general population, created in-creasing concern for many long-term community residents. Their idyllic moun-tain resort towns were being transformed dramatically.

La Sierra County, the site for this study, is located in the heart of the Rocky Mountain region. The majority of its communities lie in the long and narrow east/west La Sierra valley. At the easternmost end of the valley is the Christiana ski resort, the economic engine and the largest employer for the valley. A scant seven miles west of Christiana is the community of Agua Fria and the entrance to the exclusive gated community, El Encanto Resort, home of a former presi-dent of the United States and other multimillionaires. The town of Snow Moun-tain, the specific site for this research project, is another six miles west and lies at the foot of the La Montana Resort.

La Sierra County has a resort economy that is based on the ski industry and related support businesses. Employment is seasonal, and in the 1990s Latino im-migrants and Hispanic residents filled the majority of the manual labor posi-tions. The economy prior to the ski boom was based on the mining, railroad, and cattle industries which attracted many of the county's original Hispanic[3] resi-dents. White college students and "ski bums" once filled most of the service in-dustry jobs associated with the ski industry, but as the work increased, housing became more expensive, and white college students began leaving the area. Latino immigrants, primarily from Mexico and Central America, began to take the service jobs.

As the valley's economy grew, so too did the number of people wanting to live in "paradise"—thus increasing the demand for affordable housing. The mayor of Trackville, a mining and railroad community behind Christiana Mountain, complained that the increasing wealth of the valley was creating problems for long-term residents of his town. He commented that although the demand for new housing forced the town to build new condos and town houses, these homes were too expensive for the local workforce and were quickly bought up by out-of-towners.

What happens is that property is assessed at a higher rate by the county, causing property taxes to increase. This forces long-time residents to sell their homes and move to a more affordable place. Many of the long-time Hispanic residents in this town are selling be-cause they cannot afford the property taxes. People from California are moving in because they have sold their houses back there for inflated prices and now can afford to live here. (MR, interview, 1996)

As a result of these inflated housing prices, and the resulting rise in property taxes, affordable housing was increasingly hard to find. These changing conditions created tensions throughout the valley. Scenic small towns near Christiana soon began to take on the characteristics of a burgeoning suburb—expensive housing, crowded neighborhoods, and increased noise and traffic.

Latino newcomer workers faced even greater economic difficulty. The Latino workers of Christiana lived in crowded trailer parks in full view of the opulent El Encanto Resort, La Montana Resort, and the expensive Lone Pine subdivision. Their mobile homes did not appreciate; they remained valued between five and ten thousand dollars, even though the value of other kinds of housing was doubling and tripling. Also, as the areas surrounding Christiana became saturated with housing, escalating rental prices forced more people to move further downvalley. As one report noted, "[A worker] taking home $1,600 a month may have to pay $800 to $1,000 a month for rent in the resort areas" (*The Clarion*, August, 23, 1995). For the Latino population, the high cost of living made it extraordinarily difficult to save money, so most workers shared apartments or trailer homes with others.

"Affordable employee housing was a problem a few years ago. Today it's a state of emergency," commented one Christiana city official (Interview, 1996). As the problem became more widespread, white community residents began to look for ways to explain the problems they were facing. Some residents suggested that the quality of life in the valley was declining due to greedy landlords. As a result of high rents, workers were forced to share apartments, creating what some termed "parking problems, trash, and other problems throughout the valley" (*Christiana Tomorrow*, 1994). Although these "commentators" did not state it directly, I believe that their comments were aimed squarely at the Latino immigrant population.

Diversity and community dichotomization emerged as overlapping public issues. Participants in a community roundtable discussion noted that "It's more diverse than it used to be, but we are not communicating well with each other; we have the Hispanic population which is separate [from Whites and Latinos], rich vs poor, local vs. non-local; we label each other; we bring the 'us vs them' feeling with us when we come from other places in the country.... We are a community of haves and have-nots and in schools it shows up in student achievement" (*Christiana Tomorrow*, 1994, 18). Such comments indicated that many were concerned about the fracturing of their various communities because of class, cultural, and linguistic differences. One issue that most people did not discuss publicly was their belief that the problems were brought on by the rapid increase in the Latino newcomer population. In a later section, I present evidence that this was in fact a common view.

Expensive housing and tensions caused by an increasing population created a situation that impeded communication and integration across economic and cultural division. Class and ethnicity factored in the increased segregation of housing. As one respondent noted, "When the Mexicans started moving into the trailer courts, the Whites quickly moved out." As a result, Latino immigrants were concentrated in low-lying areas of the valley where most of the trailer courts were located, whereas white residents were segregated in gated communities or apartment enclaves across the valley and the hills. Long-term Hispanic residents lived in communities located in side valleys leading off of the larger valley.

Many of the workers were not able to live close to their places of employment. Longer commutes to the workplace and traffic congestion left little time for valley residents to develop a sense of community. As some residents noted, this situation diminished the quality of life for all residents: "You lose part of why you moved here if you have to commute; commutes affect our air quality. The farther you have to drive the less sense of community you have. Commuting adds lots of stress to lives, with speed and traffic. As we're getting more and more polarized and larger, there's an 'us versus them' feeling between communities, and that wall needs to be broken down" (*Christiana Tomorrow*, 1994, 47, 62). A local priest added, "The living conditions resort workers endure can destroy families and cause societal problems. . . . Having a decent place to live near work is the key to keeping families together" (Father J, St. Johns Church, *Mountain State News*, September 4, 1994).

TROUBLE IN PARADISE

In September 1994, a regional newspaper reported that the population of La Sierra County and surrounding counties had increased to 91,716 in 1993, up from 83,451 in 1990. The newspaper reported that the Catholic archdiocese located 100 miles away "is alarmed at the urban crisis overtaking the area and is leading the crusade for change." The archbishop commented that he knew of the devastation that can occur from unsuitable living conditions, having served as a priest in Baltimore's inner city. He stated, "The church is also raising the issue of 'a just wage' for workers, is making a moral issue of the pay service workers receive from the recreation industry" (*Mountain State News*, 1A).

The archbishop was concerned because La Sierra County's Latino newcomers could barely live on their wages earned, and they often had to work two jobs to make ends meet. Worse, very few of their jobs included health insurance (*Mountain State News*, 18A). As the bishop noted, "This urban pattern and commuting lifestyle has led to a litany of problems that once were the province of the metropolis area, not resort communities. . . . They include long hours on the road, neglected children and a lack of the sense of community that once was the hallmark of life in the west. . . . We are seeing a dramatic increase in the working poor throughout the rural resort community" (*Mountain State News*, 18A).

The report noted further that many of the working poor were legal and illegal immigrants from Mexico and Central America. A social services provider, quoted in the report, commented that the "harsh routine of working in the resort areas is taking its toll on people's lives. When you leave at 6 A.M. and come back at 7 P.M., and you've worked all day and driven over a mountain pass, parents don't really want to deal with kids" (*Mountain State News*, 18A). I heard this concern repeatedly from many Latino parents, during parent/teacher meetings at Snow Mountain Elementary.

HOSTILITY TOWARD THE LATINO COMMUNITY

The fear experienced by long-term residents, caused by the rapid changes happening in the communities of the valley, created a form of nativism that made whites and long-time residents question the legitimacy of the Latinos' presence. This led to hostility not only toward the new immigrant population but also toward the long-time Hispanic residents. Nativistic attitudes, manifested in letters-to-the-editor and community comment portions of the newspapers, communicated the message to most Latinos that they were not welcome. Latinos were aware of the disparaging comments made about them, and this made them feel like a marginal people. These feelings were exacerbated by the overt hostility many experienced. In a letter-to-the-editor, one resident wrote, "People all over the USA are getting more angry daily over being forced to pay for illegal immigrants." The writer elaborated with the following poem:

> LOVE AMERICA
> Come for visit, get treated regal.
> So I stay, who care I illegal?
> Cross the border poor and broke,
> Take the bus, see customs bloke.
> Nice man treat me good in there.
> Say I need welfare.
> Welfare say come down no more.
> We send you cash right to your door.
> Welfare checks, they make you wealthy.
> Medicare, it keeps you healthy.
> By and by, I got plenty money.
> Thanks, American working dummy.
> (Unpublished poem. See *The Clarion*, August 23, 1995, 8a)

Although not all residents felt this way, the poem represents how many felt, and it illustrates how antinewcomer sentiments were voiced in public. Callers to "the Phoneline" (*The Clarion*, July, 17, 1996), a newspaper column that polled and printed anonymous comments by residents of the area, listed a series of comments made on the topic of immigration:

Is it because so many Californians have moved here that La Sierra County believes it must cater to the illegal aliens, allow them to drain our welfare social services, burn our hospital for free care, and fill our jail and court system, just like in Southern California, and run us into the ground?

Why are the illegals allowed to have free babies? And also, why are they all driving new pickups in six months?

I have lived in the valley for 23 years, and I was just wondering why there are so many illegal aliens in this valley and nothing is being done about it, and why every time I go into City Market or Wal-Mart that there just seems to be more and more of them, and none of them speak English. So I was just wondering when they're going to clean up this valley?

Hi, I've lived in the valley for 15 years, and I wonder why there are so many illegal aliens in the valley taking our jobs. Who makes the decision to allow this to happen, and what should we be doing about it, as legal citizens of the United States?

Some white residents directly expressed their hostility. In a focus group interview conducted in July 1996, Latino and Hispanic High School students stated that they were often taunted in the workplace or as they walked down the street:

People in cars will often drive by and holler at us "go back to Mexico." Even throughout the community you hear bad remarks like that.

I work at Wal Mart and right now at Wal Mart everyone that's a cashier practically knows Spanish so everyone pretty much speaks it. And then there was a white guy that was in my line, and he goes to his wife, "I cannot believe all these mojados [wetbacks] that are working in here. I don't see why they all get jobs here, they should all go back to Mexico." I turned around and I closed my line. I swear. I didn't help him whatsoever.

I heard about many such experiences during my research. The editor of a local newspaper wrote that much misinformation and virulent anti-Latino feeling existed in the community. He added, "There's considerable misinformation. I don't think immigrants are draining our treasury by gaining welfare benefits. As for people soaking the system, I would sooner look at everybody around here who dodges paying their income taxes" (*The Clarion*, August 23, 1995).

TAKING ACTION TO REMOVE LATINOS

Some white residents were not content merely to express their sentiments in the newspapers and direct comments. Some took the serious action of pressuring politicians to call in the Immigration and Naturalization Service (INS). This was viewed as a solution to perceived social problems, but people acted without stopping to think what it would do to local businesses. As a result of this pressure, the INS conducted several raids during the research period, and many Latino residents were deported. One business owner, perplexed at losing a valued employee, said that finding help was extremely difficult. The owner added that he had tried recruiting in other mountain areas, and that recruiting college graduates didn't work—"they are here for the short term and I'm in business for the long haul" (*The Clarion*, December 13, 1995).

Local businesses suffered from the raids. Immigrant residents reported that they were afraid to go out of their homes, and, as a result, many of them stayed home from work for fear of being deported. Businesses were left short-handed. One restaurant owner commented in December 1995 that he had been forced to wash dishes during the rush hour because two of his workers had not come in. A dry cleaning business had to close until the owner could recruit new workers.

The INS raids created additional fear and turmoil in the Latino community. The fear of losing homes, plus the fear of being deported, created tense situations. Unfortunately, the children felt this tension. Latino children, traumatized by the fear of losing their parents to deportation, stayed away from playgrounds and school. One child, a second grader at Snow Mountain Elementary, was terrified that *la migra* was going to come into the school to take her and her friends away. The bilingual teachers and I explained to the students that they were safe in the school and that *la migra* could not come into her classroom. This offered some comfort, but the children were still worried about going to the park to play after school. Even if the students themselves were safe, they still worried that their parents would be picked up by *la migra*, and neither I nor the bilingual teacher could assure them that this would not be the case.

Along with INS raids, and the hostility expressed by individual Anglos, police agencies in the community also disproportionately targeted Latino immigrants for traffic violations and other rule infractions. As one Latino resident noted, "As soon as they see a Latino driving, there are the cops. They know full well that many of us don't carry insurance or that we might have something wrong with our cars. Right away they stop us. This thing about insurance is difficult because it is very expensive. Also, many of these young men drink and drive in Mexico and think they can do it here too." A review of the local newspapers verified this comment about increased police surveillance. Newspaper reports showed increased numbers of Spanish surnamed persons arrested for domestic violence, driving under the influence, driving without insurance, resisting arrest and fighting. These statistics indicated that the increase in Latino arrests was out of proportion to their numbers in the population. With a sense of frustration, some Latinos commented that they were only in the United States temporarily until they could amass sufficient funds to live more comfortably in Mexico. They did not understand why the community was so upset by their desire to make a living.

PRESSURES ON LOW INCOME HOUSING

As private property became more valuable and as the demand for housing increased, it became apparent that many trailer parks would be redeveloped to make more money for their owners. La Sierra River Trailer Park, home to many Snow Mountain Elementary students, opened in 1985 as affordable housing for employees of the Christiana ski industry with 150 mobile homes, but within a short period it grew to 270 units. This park quickly became the largest trailer park in the area, catering mainly to service industry workers and becoming a Latino enclave. One resident commented that as the Mexican workers began to move in to the park, the Anglos moved out (AT, personal communication, 1994).

On March 21, 1994, it was announced that the trailer court at nearby Agua Fria would close and that 200 people, mostly Latino, would have to vacate the area. The residents were expected to move to Snow Mountain trailer park or to other areas farther "down-valley." The Arbors trailer park in the center of the business district of Snow Mountain, and home to another 50 primarily Latino families, was slated to close in the spring of 1997 because the property was deemed too valuable to be "just" a mobile home park (PT, personal communication, 1995). Many of the Latino families with children at Snow Mountain elementary school expressed concern that their trailer park would be the next to close and that there would be no place to move. As one parent asked in September 1995,

¿Dónde vamos a vivir? No tenemos a donde llevar las trailas. Cuando se cerró el parcadero de Agua Fria, mucha gente tuvo que dejar el área porque no había donde llevar su traila.

(Where are we going to live? We have nowhere to take our trailers. When the trailer court at Agua Fria was closed, many people had to leave the area completely because there was no place to take their trailer.)

The Snow Mountain Elementary parent was referring to the additional stress created in 1994 with the closure of Agua Fria trailer park, after it was bought by Christiana Ski Associates. Fifty trailers were eliminated in order to make way for a parking lot. One school district respondent noted that the wealthy people of El Encanto hated to see the dilapidated trailer court at the entrance to a world-class ski resort (PT, personal communication, 1994).

The Latino parents of Snow Mountain Elementary lived with the constant fear of losing their homes. In 1995, rumors surfaced that even La Sierra trailer park would be closing. A white resident commented that the trailer park sat on prime real estate alongside the Sierra River and, as such, was too valuable to serve as a trailer park. A Latino parent noted, "We don't plan to be here very long, but I wish that we wouldn't have to move before then." The parent was referring to an oft-stated belief by many Mexican immigrants that they would only remain in the United States for a short period of time. A more philosophical parent commented that,

Muchos de nosotros decimos que vamos a regresar a Méjico pero la verdad es que ya tengo diez anos de vivir aquí y sería difícil dejar este lugar.

(Many of us say that we will return to Mexico but the truth is that I already have lived here 10 years, and it would be difficult to leave this place.)

Complicating the problem was the financial reality that many of the immigrant parents worked for low wages. The high cost of living, coupled with high housing costs, did not leave much money to save for a return to Mexico (CG, personal communication, 1994). In a discussion with parents at Snow Mountain Elementary, several commented that they did not desire to return to Mexico because they enjoyed a better standard of living here, but this higher standard of living also exacted a price. "This high cost of living," as one parent explained, "forces us to work long hours in Christiana, often having to leave our children in the care of a friend or a relative." Another mother made the observation that they often were not able to heed the school's recommendations because of their living situation.

La escuela nos dice que leamos a nuestros hijos y que le ayudemos con sus lecciones. Pues yo salgo de la casa antes de que los niños se levantan y regreso ya noche.

(The school tells us that we should read to our children and to help them with their schoolwork. Well, I leave the house before the children are up and return late in the evening.)

The high cost of living, coupled with the threat of losing their homes, created a climate of uncertainty and vulnerability. One respondent noted that in previous years they would travel as a family during the off season to visit family and friends in Mexico, but that now they had to make sure one parent stayed behind to safeguard the home. When asked what he meant by "safeguarding" the parent replied,

Pues uno nunca sabe que va pasar con esto de que van a quitar el parqueadero. También no podemos dejar el lugar y venir a encontrar otro lugar para vivir. No es fácil encontrar viviendas.

(Well, one never knows what is going to happen with these things being said about taking away the trailer park. Also, we cannot leave the house and come back to find another place to live. It is not easy to find housing.)

Thus, the high cost of living, coupled with low-paying wages and the threat of losing their homes, created a climate of tension for the immigrant parents and attenuated their ties with family and friends in Mexico.

THE DEVELOPMENT OF EDUCATIONAL POLICY IN A FRAGMENTED COMMUNITY

During the 1990s, Latino newcomers' increased nervousness and economic vulnerability, the host community's distrust of Latino immigrants, the loss of open space, the raids by the INS, and the increase in traffic all disrupted the once peaceful valley. White residents blamed the Latino immigrants. Increased arrests of Spanish-surnamed persons, along with INS raids, created a hostile living environment for Latinos. Long-term Hispanic residents were also targeted, along with new Latino immigrants. A tense social environment pitted Latinos against Hispanics, whites against Latinos, the rich against the working class, and new housing developers against established residents. All this influenced the educational policy that was developed and implemented for the Latino community. As school enrollments outstripped earlier projections, forcing principals and teachers to find new ways to educate non-English-speaking students, makeshift educational policy was made in the context of the larger community's increased disquiet. A hostile environment that marginalized Latino immigrant students was also created in the schools.

In the early stages of Latino population growth, roughly 1989–1991, community and school leaders did not envision the explosive growth of non-English-speaking students that was yet to come. Ski bums and college students did not affect the schools to the extent that new Latino immigrants would. Once the new wave of Latino immigrants came, their children needed specialized texts, Spanish language materials, and bilingual teachers.

Teachers and other community persons who spoke Spanish, but who had little or no formal training in second-language teaching, were drafted to help the non-English-speaking students. Latino immigrant students were given 30 minutes a day of "survival English" by a person who spoke Spanish but did not have training in second language acquisition. Throughout the area, teaching assistants who spoke Spanish were given the task of tutoring Latino immigrant students at schools.

The policy that was hastily put in place in the early 1990s mostly marginalized and failed to educate Latino students. Its makeshift curriculum reflected the lack of a coherent educational policy. Latino students received the bulk of their instruction in pullout classes, where the curriculum was often unrelated to the regular school curriculum. Regular classroom teachers did not have the training to teach limited English speaking students. They also lacked proper educational materials in Spanish. Teachers who did speak Spanish had to develop their teaching materials from magazines and books that they could "scrounge" in the community. The physical conditions for learning were not much better. One school administrator converted storage space behind the cafeteria into a classroom for Latino immigrant students. In another school, a broom closet was converted into an ESL classroom. The room was carpeted and made available to an itinerant ESL teacher who taught survival English to the students.

The Latinos' use of Spanish created tension in many classrooms. Because no formal policy was presented to the classroom teachers, many of them felt that Latino students were not their responsibility but belonged, instead, to the English tutors. Long-term resident Hispanics felt that immigrants were receiving an unfair advantage because a tutor would sit with Latino immigrants and translate what the teacher was saying.[4] This increased the tensions between Latino immigrants and long-term Hispanic residents. Overcrowding and a disorganized approach to educating Latino immigrant students created a situation that reflected the fragmented communities in which the schools were located.

REPLACING THE MAKESHIFT PROGRAM IN LA SIERRA COUNTY SCHOOL DISTRICT

Recognizing that the fragmented approach for educating Latino immigrants was having limited success, La Sierra County School District joined a neighboring school district in October 1991 to compete for a federal grant. With the help of a regional university, they authored a successful Title VII Transitional Bilingual Education (TBE) grant, acquiring funds from the U.S. Department of Education's Office of Bilingual Education and Minority Language Affairs (OBEMLA). This grant enabled the two districts to design a TBE program that could meet the educational needs of monolingual Spanish-speaking (MSS) and limited-English-proficient (LEP) students. The districts agreed to collaborate in applying for the grant because the number of LEP students in each of the districts alone was insufficient to compete effectively with urban districts that had larger numbers of LEP students.

The initial program design included diagnosis of the Latino students' "deficits" and recommendations for a prescriptive educational approach. If the child was found to have no English proficiency, the child would be provided with native language instruction in the core content areas—math, science, and language arts. If the child had limited English proficiency, native language instruction (NLI) and/or English as a second language (ESL) would be provided until such time as he/she was able to transition into an all-English program. NLI would be used on a diminishing basis for a three-year period. Additionally, "regular" classroom teachers were to be given training on how to make the curriculum comprehensible for Latino students. Inherent in the language of the proposal was the problematic idea that Latino immigrant students were deficient, but even this problematic program design would soon be sabotaged, and instruction of Latino immigrant students would once again revert to a fragmented approach.

The first alteration in the design came about because of the lack of qualified bilingual teachers. Rather than a true bilingual program, wherein students would acquire content in the native language until they could make the transition into an all-English classroom, nonbilingual teachers were reduced to tutoring Spanish-speaking children in "survival" English—on how to form English vowel sounds and basic vocabulary. Then, because the need for language services was so great, district administrators decided to spread the grant monies among three elementary schools instead of just two. They reasoned that the three elementary schools in the upper valley had the largest number of students and that the grant would have a greater impact if it were spread out. This resulted in fewer resources for each school.

Further complications surfaced once the grant was announced. Several of the Hispanic teachers were very doubtful about embarking on a Title VII Transitional Bilingual Education project, because of their previous experiences. The district had created a bilingual program in 1975, but discontinued the program in 1979 after only four years. Several of the skeptics had participated in that program and were bitter that the district had abandoned the program in favor of providing a "submersion" experience for Latino students.[5] The teachers felt that the district had betrayed their high hopes, and they were not willing to begin a new project until assurances were given that this program would be well designed and well implemented. To reassure them, the district director of curriculum, who was also new to the area, gave her word that the program would be continued— arguing that the school board would have to promise an ongoing program in order to receive the federal funds.

As the goals of the original grant were explained to the La Sierra principals, in the fall of 1992, one of the principals from the three selected schools commented that the goals, as written in the grant, were unrealistic and that they would either have to be rewritten or the program could not be implemented at her school. I (having recently come to La Sierra) explained that, according to information given to me by a state department of education official, most of the schools in the district were in substantial noncompliance with the *Lau Remedies* and that only by complying with the grant as written could they avoid punitive action by the U.S. Department of Education's Office of Civil Rights (OCR). My argument referred to the 1974 U.S. Supreme Court *Lau v. Nichols* ruling. In that case, Justice William O. Douglas stated, "There is no equality of treatment merely by providing students with the same facilities, textbooks, teachers, and curriculum; for students who do not understand English are effectively foreclosed from any meaningful education" (Crawford, 1995).

LACK OF COORDINATED AND INCLUSIVE PLANNING FOR THE TRANSITIONAL BILINGUAL PROGRAM

The principals in La Sierra County were correct that the objectives of the original Title VII program were not appropriate for their schools. The initial objectives for the grant proposal had been written by the assistant superintendent of the neighboring Mountain River School District, without input from any of the La Sierra County schools. Details of the program design did not surface until the award had been granted and schools had been notified of their selection in late August of 1992. Although many of the principals had expressed a need for help in educating the Latino immigrant students, they reasonably expected to participate in deciding how the program would work. Principals were now being asked to institute a program that would disrupt their already established plans for the school year on very short notice. Students had been scheduled into classes and parents had received notice of those schedules. Teachers had already organized their classrooms for the coming year, and they did not have the books, materials, or instructional strategies and teamwork plans necessary to teach Latino immigrant students as described in the grant proposal.

The timing of the award required the principals and staffs of the selected schools to lay aside established plans and reschedule their classes, to allow more time for students to attend native language instruction. Some teachers had to be reassigned to different classrooms. Regular classroom teachers who had volunteered for the bilingual program had to reschedule their classes to allow for in-class training with the bilingual resource specialist during their regular class time. Also, teachers and teaching assistants selected to work in the native language classrooms needed to find time in the already adopted—and crowded—school calendar to attend in-service training events and conferences.

The U.S. Department of Education insisted that the program had to be implemented immediately, or the district risked losing the second and third years of funding. This policy exacerbated the lack of preparation and planning at the local level. The second year of funding had to be requested by October 1992, barely three months after the inception of the grant. The request for second year funds had to be accompanied by a report documenting the progress made toward meeting the first year's goals and objectives—a report that would only cover two months at the beginning of a hectic school year. This new deadline increased the pressure to implement the program as quickly as possible. The U.S. Department of Education's demands made it impossible to implement a carefully thought out program. As a training consultant described it, "You are trying to build and fly the airplane at the same time. You are going to have problems because you don't have the time to overcome people's resistance to change and still meet the demands of the federal government" (AG, personal communication, 1992). Thus the district began developing a TBE program, even though the main players remained very skeptical about its prospects. The following section details the adaptations that were made in order to meet the principals' concerns in implementing a bilingual program in their schools.

Before receiving the Title VII grant many of the schools had decided that courses in ESL were all that were required to educate LEP students. However, research in bilingual education makes it clear that, without a content-based ESL approach and a well-designed NLI program, there is usually discontinuity between the ESL and the rest of the academic program. This, in turn, retards academic progress for the LEP student (Berman et al., 1992).

Shortly after the award of the Title VII grant was announced, in August 1992, some farsighted teachers and a principal decided to establish a model program using the Title VII funds, but going beyond the ESL and Spanish tutorial approach. This was the program I was hired to work with at Snow Mountain Elementary. The first program model proposed a form of dual language instruction that not only would help Latino students maintain their Spanish proficiency, while learning content subject matter and English, but would also provide immersion in Spanish for monolingual English students. However, concerns from the community sabotaged these attempts to create more effective educational programs for Latino immigrant students.

DESCRIPTION OF THE SPECIAL CHARACTERISTICS OF THE INITIAL SNOW MOUNTAIN PROGRAM

Recognizing that overcoming the Snow Mountain staff members' objections to the Title VII program would be difficult, I decided to invite the principal of Snow Mountain Elementary and several of her staff members, along with other principals, to attend the National Association for Bilingual Education Conference in January 1993. They returned filled with excitement and new ideas for creating a bilingual education program. Snow Mountain's program was to be different from the proposed TBE program, going beyond the initial Title VII program's diagnostic/prescriptive and deficit model of education. Snow Mountain Elementary proposed a program that incorporated native language instruction in the regular classroom, along with a restructuring of the total school environment. Regular classroom teachers would work with the Title VII bilingual resource specialist to minimize the effects of pullout instruction; the resource specialist would provide teaching techniques and model second-language acquisition

Table 7.1
Modifications to Initial Title VII Program (Martinez, 1998)

The Initial TBE Model	The Snow Mountain Model
1. Principals do not have experience with LEP students. They have little or no understanding of second-language acquisition (SLA) processes or of the issues affecting the education of LEP students.	1. Principal is committed to a two-way bilingual program where LEP students learn English and English-speaking children learn Spanish.
2. Students are supposed to transition into the mainstream classrooms after three years. Linguistic and cultural differences are not directly addressed in the school as part of policy.	2. Linguistic and cultural differences are valued and integrated in school programs and in the classroom.
3. Regular classroom teachers often do not speak the language. They send LEP students to ESL teachers for instruction or utilize tutors to work with LEP or MSS students outside the classroom.	3. Four regular classroom teachers are fluent Spanish speakers and form the core group of teachers for LEP students. Seven teachers attend school in Mexico in order to learn Spanish and participate in the bilingual program.
4. SLA in-services not provided for regular classroom staff. Many teachers are skeptical of or hostile to native language instruction for the LEP child. SLA teachers complain that regular classroom teachers do not accept responsibility for LEP students.	4. Regular in-services are provided for all staff members to acquaint them with techniques and methods for educating the LEP child. LEP children are the responsibility of all staff members.
5. Limited investment in Spanish language computer software.	5. Major investment in computer software for educating the LEP child.
6. Limited investment of building funds to provide Spanish language materials for the LEP student. State LEP education funds or Title VII money used to purchase supplies.	6. Building funds used to provide Spanish language versions of the regular curriculum.
7. Bilingualism and biliteracy not part of the regular curriculum. Students are there to learn English as quickly as possible.	7. Clear goals are set. Bilingualism and biliteracy form part of the curriculum for LEP students.
8. Students are pulled out for native language instruction or for tutorial help. In class instruction is limited to tutorial help by the bilingual aide or by peer tutor.	8. Students are taught in the regular classroom and pull-out instruction is limited.
9. ESL forms major part of the instruction for the LEP student.	9. ESL forms one part of the curriculum. The student's primary language is used for subject-matter instruction.

(continued)

Table 7.1 (*continued*)

The Initial TBE Model	The Snow Mountain Model
10. Team teaching not part of the original TBE proposal.	10. Regular classroom teachers team teach with bilingual teachers and bilingual teaching assistants.
11. Latino parents not visible in regular classrooms.	11. Major efforts made to involve Latino parents in the school.
12. Teachers work individually with the bilingual resource specialist to address needs of LEP students.	12. Collaborative groups of teachers meet regularly to evaluate and develop effective lesson plans for the LEP student.
13. Latino cultural artifacts not prominently displayed.	13. Spanish is spoken in all areas of the school. Cultural artifacts are displayed prominently in the building.
14. Assessment for academic proficiency done with Iowa Test of Basic Skills in English.	14. Academic reading and writing assessment done with Spanish language assessment scales and with the LAS in English along with portfolios.
15. No reading and writing assessment in the child's native language.	15. Academic proficiency done with Spanish language test and portfolios.
16. No specific curriculum developed for the LEP student.	16. Specific curriculum for the bilingual program is aligned with regular curriculum.

strategies for educating the LEP students, strategies such as cooperative grouping and sheltered English instruction.[6]

The enhanced program at Snow Mountain went beyond the deficit model, offering sheltered instruction in the regular classroom along with Spanish as a second language (SSL) instruction to all students in the school. The principal and the staff thought that this program would enhance LEP student proficiencies by enriching the educational experiences in the regular classroom, and it would create a school climate that valued students' ability to speak two languages. The approach resembled a two-way, maintenance bilingual program wherein Anglo children learned Spanish and Latino children learned English, but it was not a fully content-based ESL or SSL program.

The differences between the standard TBE Program that was initially proposed by the school districts and the enriched program that was proposed for Snow Mountain Elementary are described in Table 7.1.

CHANGES IN LEADERSHIP OF THE SCHOOL

However, shortly after the new program design was implemented, changes in leadership began to affect the school. The superintendent of schools, who had supported the Snow Mountain program, was fired in October 1994. The new superintendent decided to implement a new curriculum to more closely match state standards. The principal under whom the enhanced bilingual program had been initiated moved to another school district. The interim principal took over just in time to deal with a crowded school and a changing district curriculum. The school board had decided to adopt a new curriculum that would be in place by the spring of 1995, and this meant that many teachers would be involved in the design and implementation of the new standards-based curriculum. The new standards defined by the state legislature defined what a student should know or be able to do in ten content areas: reading, writing, mathematics, science, history, geography, art, music, and physical education. "When the state content standards are determined and each school district has adjusted its goals to meet or exceed those standards, teachers will know precisely what each student must achieve" (State Education Association, 1993). However, these standards included no mention of ways to teach LEP students, nor did they value the Spanish skills that Latino newcomers had.

To her credit, the new principal was committed to the Title VII bilingual program and wanted to strengthen it. She, along with the assistant principal and the bilingual resource specialist, visited an exemplary bilingual program at Washington Elementary in Boulder, Colorado, and she came back excited about developing a two-way bilingual program. The previous principal's vision of developing a "true TBE" program was upgraded to a two-way bilingual instructional program. But the idea of spreading LEP children throughout each classroom in the different grade levels became a guiding principle for the new principal. It was her belief that white children needed to be "exposed" to Latino children in order to begin building cross-cultural relationships and to alleviate the pressure on non-Spanish-speaking teachers. This meant that often there would only be one or two Latino students in a classroom. This, together with increasing numbers of LEP students, created an insurmountable barrier for the bilingual program staff who could not "float" to every classroom where LEP students were located. Hence, the enriched program ideas were never fully implemented.

Even these conditions did not stop the second-language acquisition program personnel from attempting to create a two-way bilingual program. They persevered, even though they had to contend with the increased numbers of LEP children and limited resources. Responding to my question of how the semester year was going, the new principal stated, "We have some growing to do yet.

We are currently working on developing a more adequate second-language curriculum and that is affecting the implementation of the Title VII program. We have one less teacher and 15 more kids on top of what we already had. We need to go two-way bilingual but we really need staff" (NR, Personal communication, October 1994). Once again, the airplane metaphor was appropriate: they were trying to build an airplane and fly it at the same time, only this time with fewer resources.

During the spring of 1995, the new principal asked to be moved to a neighboring school. She reasoned that it was closer to her home and would enable her to participate more fully in school programs. So another principal change took effect during the summer of 1995. At the district level, two other new changes also were taking place. The director of curriculum and personnel, a major supporter and key administrator of the ESL and Bilingual Programs, announced that she would be resigning at the end of 1994/1995 school year. She had been hired as superintendent of a neighboring school district. With a new district administration and a new principal at Snow Mountain Elementary, plus the end of the grant monies, the prospect of developing and implementing an exemplary bilingual program dimmed.

This prospect even further dimmed one week before the start of the 1995–1996 school year, when a much beloved bilingual teacher drowned in a diving accident in Mexico. "La Maestra," one of the two mainstays of the bilingual program at Snow Mountain, had been in Mexico to learn more about the culture and also to indulge her passion for scuba diving. This tragedy cast a pall over the entire opening day of school.

In a touching moment during the memorial service, La Maestra's students performed a song learned in class. Another student dedicated the following poem to her:

Para mi maestra
Maestra
Nunca olvidaremos
Momentos felices
Vivimos contigo

Tus enseñanzas
Nunca olvidaremos
Siempre en nuestras mentes Las recordaremos.

Viva!
JE, 3rd grade.

For my teacher
Teacher
We shall never forget

Happy moments
We live with you

Your teachings
We shall never forget
Always in our minds We remember them.

Viva!
JE, 3rd grade.

Soon after the funeral and memorial service, counselors from the area met separately with the staff and students to discuss their feelings. In the session with
Spanish-speaking students, the counselor would speak in English, and the translator would translate. The translator would then ask the students what they were
feeling, and this would be translated back to the counselor. The school counselor,
who did not speak Spanish, later stated that it was very difficult to provide grief
counseling this way and that Latino students did not receive as much grief counseling as the counselor would have wanted to provide (SW, personal communication, October 1995).

FROM A FRAGMENTED EDUCATIONAL POLICY TO
A MISEDUCATIVE EXPERIENCE

In order to better understand how the educational policy came to be implemented at Snow Mountain Elementary school, it is important to understand first
the various contexts in which the learning task is embedded. Various obstacles
prevented an effective educational experience for Latino immigrant students.

One of the biggest initial obstacles was the U.S. Department of Education's
insistence that substantive progress be shown for the first year of funding just a
few months after the announcement of the grant. This forced district educators
to hastily develop and implement a less-than-ideal TBE program. It also made
coordinated and coherent planning for the project impossible.

The development of the program was further complicated by the lack of well-
trained and certified bilingual education teachers. Recruitment of such personnel
was almost impossible on such short notice. Also, although books and other educational materials had been ordered at the start of the grant period, these took
time to arrive. This meant that teachers had to continue scrounging for bilingual
books to use in the newly formed native language classrooms.

Increasing enrollments made it difficult to find space for the Title VII NLI
classrooms. As mentioned earlier, the population around Snow Mountain was
increasing rapidly, and one elementary school was not sufficient to meet the demand. Snow Mountain Elementary attempted to alleviate these conditions first
by using every available closet—however inappropriate—as a classroom for
Latino students, and then by setting up portable classroom buildings on the play-

ground. However, this soon created new problems for the district and the school. Wealthy residents complained that their view corridors were being obstructed or negatively affected by "those ugly buildings." They demanded that the portable buildings be removed and that art, music, and other so-called nonessential classrooms be converted into regular classrooms. These demands put the principal and teachers under increased stress and tension.

Along with these various obstacles to the development and implementation of a high-quality bilingual education program, the La Sierra community also expressed negative attitudes toward the educational system and its new clients. The hostility experienced by Latino immigrants was also directed at those who tried to help the Latino immigrant students, as well as toward those who tried to change the educational system. Between 1992 and 1996, educational leaders who tried to bring change to the educational system came under attack. La Sierra County School District had four different superintendents in those four years. Three different principals served Snow Mountain Elementary, the site for this study. The director of curriculum and instruction, who had been the main advocate for the bilingual program, also left the district at the end of the 1995 school year. After the grant ended, I too left the district, as no appropriate positions for me remained. The teachers and principals who had struggled to devise new programs were forced to continue the program with little direction or support from the school district.

The larger context in which the bilingual program was embedded thus played a major role in creating a "miseducative" experience for Latino immigrant children.[7] The lack of a coherent educational policy for Latino students in the school district meant that the instructional program reverted to pull-out instruction.

OF PULL-OUTS, UNEQUAL CURRICULA, AND MISEDUCATION

Being pulled out from the regular classroom meant that Latino children were placed in smaller classrooms with limited supplies where they received instruction in reading, vocabulary, and grammar, while English-speaking students received an enriched curriculum. It was extremely difficult to coordinate the content taught in the native language and ESL classes with what occurred in regular classrooms, so Latino immigrant children fell behind in content knowledge.

One poignant incident occurred while I was a teaching assistant in the program. On this day, Latino children were hesitant to leave their first grade classroom for the LEP bilingual classroom because the teacher had promised that the class would be creating a dinosaur village. The non-LEP students were going to learn to write by writing a dinosaur newspaper. The children would read richly illustrated books on dinosaurs and create a village out of painted cardboard. The

Latino children asked if they could do that in the bilingual classroom, but they were told that there was neither room nor sufficient supplies to support such a project. The Latino children had to content themselves with learning vowel sounds. One regular classroom teacher noted that the pull-out program was unfair to the Latinos, because the non-LEP students could then enjoy smaller class sizes during the language arts and science periods, and because teachers had more time and space to develop creative projects for their students. Latino children, on the other hand, learned only grammar and vocabulary in Spanish and English, while missing science and social studies, as well as any special activities that the regular classroom teacher might have planned.

Thus Latino children received what Hudak (1995) terms a "truncated curriculum." With a truncated curriculum, the student is left to memorize isolated fragments of information rather than developing comprehensive conceptualizations of the content. Thinking and verbalization become more context-specific, rather than an expansion of ideas that connect to the student's prior knowledge and experiences. Responses are dependent on teacher questioning, rather than on a more independent ability to express one's own ideas and opinions.

Formation of identity in the La Sierra Latino Diaspora, given the conditions prevailing in the schools and the community of La Sierra, was difficult. Latino children found it difficult to fit in or to define themselves. Hostility in the community, and the resulting internalized message that they were deficient/ undeserving, left many of the children in a position of liminality, "betwixt and between" two unknown cultures (LeCompte and Dworkin, 1991)—the natal culture of Mexico or Central America and that of the school and the dominant culture it represented. In situations such as these, Suárez-Orozco's (1991) notion of a "dual frame of reference," or the ability to contrast and differentiate ongoing experiences in the host country with experiences in the home country, does not apply. The Latino immigrant children in La Sierra County could neither identify with the home cultures of Mexico and Central America nor could they fully participate in the Anglo or Hispanic cultures of La Sierra County. Latino immigrant children felt out of place when parents took them to visit relatives in Mexico. The children explained that they had no friends in the home country, nor could they speak Spanish properly, which caused the neighborhood children to make fun of the way they spoke.

When they returned to La Sierra County, they felt equally out of place, even though their homes and friends were there, because they were unable to speak English well and unable to participate fully in the institutions that were available to white and Hispanic children in the community. They were further alienated from school because teachers could not or would not make use of the knowledge Latino children gained in the home and in other social settings—as they did with the ideas and skills of the more familiar culture that white students brought to school. Rather, Latino students were pulled out of regular classrooms to learn vowel sounds in Spanish and to learn new vocabulary in English. This situation, coupled with the marginality experienced outside of the school, alienated the Latino students.

Over time these students became less and less able to interact in either the culture of the home or the culture of the school. Many of the students, attempting to fit in, had begun to reject the speaking of Spanish, even though they were still far from being competent in English. However, long-term established Hispanics and whites rejected their efforts to "act white" (Fordham and Ogbu, 1986). Hispanics did not accept Latino immigrant students, nor did the Latinos have the language skills to interact effectively with their Anglo peers. Even at the elementary school level, children had begun to develop an oppositional identity. As they realized that they were not wanted, fights began to occur regularly between the Hispanics and the Latinos. At an intervention I moderated at one area high school, the pain and frustration that these students experienced was apparent. I realized then that a fragmented educational policy had not only failed these students academically but had also inflicted deep pain. This pain happened in part because the community provided no legitimate identities for them to grow up into. What most community members really wanted them to do was to disappear, to go back to Mexico. But this option was impossible.

A lack of educational resources does not justify our denial of a high quality educational experience to Latino immigrant students. A fragmented educational policy creates a fragmented learning experience for children. And that, in turn, contributes to fragmented identities in communities that make no legitimate or appropriate roles available to immigrant children. My research also shows that a miseducative experience creates psychic and emotional pain in the lives of children who have to live and learn in such a situation.

I also believe that the larger society suffers from this same pain, though the La Sierra community has yet to recognize the price it is paying. My subsequent research in the high school demonstrated that the learning experience for all students was affected by the violence in the hallways and the classrooms. The frustrations experienced by Latino immigrant students in the early years of their education are starting to be felt by all students—Hispanics, whites, and Latinos—in middle and high schools. At this moment, Latino children in La Sierra are left without a coherent educational policy, and until the community itself recognizes the problems and injustices in its midst, the social problems created by such educational inadequacies will continue to grow. As someone once noted, "A hole in the ship is a hole in the whole ship." The educational ship of La Sierra cannot sail well until the community rallies to the support of its new Latino residents.

NOTES

1. Chicano is a self-identifying term used by Hispanic middle and high school students. These were students that had been born and raised in the United States who used the term to differentiate themselves from new Latino immigrants.

2. A pseudonym. The names of the school, the county, the towns, and the regional newspapers have been changed to protect the identity of the respondents.

3. Hispanic is another term of self-identification. It is used in La Sierra County for purposes of differentiating oneself from new Latino immigrants.

4. This type of assistance, while common, is educationally abysmal. "[Such] an ESL program does not consider the affective nor cognitive development of the students" (Crawford, 1995, 46).

5. Submersion is the practice where a non–English-speaking student is placed in an all-English classroom without any type of academic support, to "sink or swim."

6. A specially designed instructional model that provides comprehensible input wherein students learn English through content-based instruction.

7. Any experience is miseducative if it has the effect of arresting or distorting the growth of further experience. An educative experience, on the other hand, "rests upon a continuity of significant knowledge and to the degree that this knowledge modifies or modulates [in a positive direction] the learner's outlook, attitude, and skill" (Dewey, 1938).

REFERENCES

Berman, P., J. Chambers, P. Gándara, B. McLaughlin, C. Minicucci, B. Nelson, L. Olsen, and T. Parrish. 1992. *Meeting the Challenge of Language Diversity: An Evaluation of Programs for Pupils with Limited Proficiency in English*. Executive summary. Berkeley, CA: BW Associates.

Crawford, J. 1995. *Bilingual Education: History, Politics, Theory and Practice*. Trenton, NJ: Crane Publishing.

Dewey, J. 1938. *Experience and Education*. New York: Macmillan.

Fordham, S. and J.U. Ogbu. 1986. "Black Students' School Success: Coping with the Burden of 'Acting White.'" *The Urban Review*. 18, 176–206.

Hudak, G. 1995. "Popular Media, Socialization and Speech Codes in Education: The Media-School Couplet." In *Knowledge and Pedagogy: The Sociology of Basil Bernstein*. A. Sadovnik, ed. Pp. 259–282. Norwood, NJ: Ablex.

LeCompte, M.D. and A.G. Dworkin. 1991. *Giving Up on School: Student Dropouts and Teacher Burnouts*. Newbury Park, CA: Corwin Press, Inc.

LeCompte, M.D. and J. Preissle. 1993. *Ethnography and Qualitative Design in Educational Research*. 2d ed. San Diego: Academic Press.

Levinson, B.A.U. and M. Sutton. 2001. *Policy as Practice: Toward a Comparative Sociocultural Analysis of Educational Policy*. Westport, CT: Ablex.

Martinez, E. 1993. "Population Characteristics of Latino Immigrant Population in the Roaring Fork Valley." Technical report for the University of Colorado, Boulder and the BUENO Center for Multicultural Education, School of Education, University of Colorado.

Martinez, E.L. 1990. "Study of the Roaring Fork." Research Funded by the University of Colorado, Boulder.

————. 1998. "Valuing Our Differences: Contextual Interaction Factors That Affect the Academic Achievement of Latino Immigrant Children in a K–5 Elementary School." Unpublished doctoral dissertation. School of Education, University of Colorado, Boulder.

Suárez-Orozco, M.M. 1991. "Migration, Minority Status, and Education." *Anthropology and Education Quarterly.* 22, 99–120.

8

Lowrider Art and Latino Students in the Rural Midwest

Karen Grady

This chapter describes how one high school interpreted the new presence of Latino students and the students' response to that interpretation. More specifically, it is the story of how a group of Latino students succeeded in expanding the curricular space available to them, by participating in the construction and circulation of a decidedly different discourse from that available in their classes. Over the course of the school year, through their drawing and distribution of lowrider art, the students resisted their marginalization and the stultifying, culturally unresponsive curriculum they faced on most school days. Through lowrider art, they constructed a visible Latino identity at school and created a social network around which particular social roles developed. According to Gee (1996, 1999) identity is a function of membership in a group, of being able to recognize oneself and be recognized by others as a particular kind of who. Group membership is maintained through participation in discourse practices. In this chapter I describe how some of the Latino students came to be members of a discourse group that centered around the expressive practice of lowrider art.

The data come from a yearlong ethnographic study, in which I examined the schooling experiences and literacy practices of a group of linguistically diverse adolescent newcomers to the town of Roseville, Indiana. Because I wanted my role as a researcher to be participatory, I volunteered to work as a classroom aide and tutor in the ESL "area" of the school library. I had been an ESL teacher in the California public schools for many years, and I was proficient in Spanish, which enabled me to communicate with most of the students in the ESL classes. I usually spent three days a week at the school, from August 1998 through May 1999.

LATINO STUDENTS IN ROSEVILLE

Before turning to the specifics of lowrider art as a discourse of identity, I briefly describe the circumstances that created a Latino presence at Roseville High and briefly summarize the school's response to new Latino students. Until the 1990s, Roseville, Indiana, had experienced a fairly steady decline in population and economic viability. When a major meat processor located there in 1995, Roseville did not have the population base to provide the necessary workers—at full production, the plant required two shifts of workers who would slaughter and process 14,000 hogs a day. In spite of initial promises that hiring would only occur locally, the company recruited heavily from the U.S. Southwest and Mexico, targeting Mexicans through a recruitment office in Mexico City and Latinos in general by placing advertisements in Spanish language publications in southern California and Texas. For the first time since the late 1800s, Roseville had significant numbers of people living in the town who spoke languages other than English and who did not trace their roots to Germany, Ireland, or Italy.

Under the auspices of a federally funded Title I Migrant Education grant, an English as a second language program was started in the Roseville schools in 1997 (see Figure 8.1). Even though the new workers in the slaughterhouse were not seasonal, their employment was related to the agricultural industry and, thus, the

Figure 8.1
Timeline

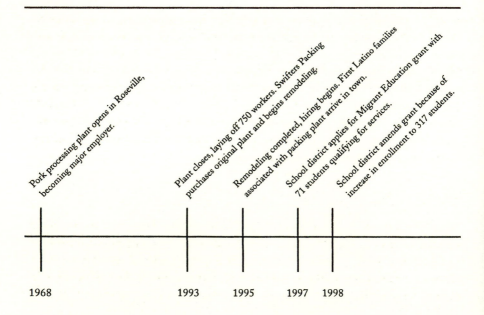

school district was eligible to apply for migrant education funding. The fall of 1998 was the first year the school district had a full-time teacher at the high school assigned to provide ESL instruction and content area tutoring to students who tested as limited English proficient on the Woodcock-Muñoz English language test.

Other than receiving migrant education funding, the school was relatively unprepared for the demographic change. ESL teachers were hired from existing staff in the district, teachers who had had temporary teaching assignments. Although dedicated to creating a quality program, none of the four ESL teachers who had been hired had any background in second language acquisition, nor were any of them bilingual. The state of Indiana offered an endorsement in teaching English as a second language, but at the time ESL teachers did not need any course work related to ESL or bilingual education in order to qualify for an ESL teaching assignment. The Indiana Department of Education's Office of Language Minority and Migrant Programs provided a one-day in-service for the four ESL teachers prior to the beginning of their new teaching assignment. The in-service covered initial language assessment and the legal requirements for providing equal access to the curriculum.

With little more than a testing kit and a few books in hand, Mrs. Morton, one of the ESL teachers, set out to convert a tiny conference room off of the high school library into a place where new immigrant students would be able to learn English and receive academic help in all of the content areas. The program included both new immigrants and students who had initially immigrated to more diverse cities, such as Los Angeles and Chicago, whose families had relocated to Roseville.

Through September and October, as the meatpacking plant continued to add workers to the second shift, new immigrant students arrived on a weekly basis. The number of students in the program had already outgrown the ESL room. The school was short of classroom space in several departments, with all of the less senior teachers having to teach in different rooms during various prep periods. The students in the migrant program were acutely aware that the ESL classes did not have a classroom at all. While the students joked about the close quarters, the principal promised Mrs. Morton that plans for remodeling in the next few years would alleviate the overcrowding.

SCHEDULING MIGRANT EDUCATION STUDENTS

In the fall of 1998, 33 students from the migrant education program were assigned to either Mrs. Morton's ESL 1 or ESL 2 class, that is, they had one period of ESL every other day (because of block scheduling, all core subjects met for an extended period every other day). For the rest of the school day, the students were scheduled into content area classes, based on their English proficiency score and previous school record—if they had come from another school in the United States or had brought school records from their countries of origin. The sole measure of English proficiency was the score on the widely used Woodcock-Muñoz Language Survey. Nevertheless, school personnel were following state guidelines (IDOE, 1989) and federal regulations (35 Fed. Reg. 11595, 1964) in determining educational needs based on English proficiency. The practice of placing students into courses based on their tested English proficiency was not only in keeping with policies that call for students to be "identified" for services based on standardized test scores in English, but was also based on a genuine concern that students not feel overwhelmed by the demands of an all English curriculum. Members of the counseling department wanted the students to experience success rather than failure and to be eased into the academic curriculum after they had some time to adjust to the school and the language. But government policy and staff concern led the school to weight English proficiency more heavily than the students' educational experiences, interests, and goals—thus essentializing students in terms of a single test score in English, a test score of questionable validity (Kao, 1998).[1]

The immigrant students, for the most part, had only the most marginal spaces in the school open to them (i.e., low-track courses and the tables that hugged the side walls of the cafeteria). As Mrs. Morton and I helped students complete stacks of unchallenging worksheets, which flowed from the content area classrooms to the ESL room, it was clear that school for the Latino students mostly involved endless seat work. This led immigrant and migrant students to focus on memorizing rather than on understanding and on individual rather than group work. In classrooms where teachers did not allow immigrant students to speak in their native language, they were effectively silenced and prevented from learning from bilingual peers.

Many of the immigrant and migrant students, nonetheless, dutifully went through the required sheets, memorizing how far from the edge of a table to place flatware (for a test in their foods class) or calculating how much polypropylene was needed to make a key fob in plastics class. Unlike the Anglo students enrolled in these low track classes, the students in the ESL classes had very little access to the actual meaning of the words they filled in, the definitions they copied, and the pieces of information they memorized for tests. The content of much of the curriculum was irrelevant to their own goals and aspirations and, for some students, was not related to their previous schooling experiences. For example, two students, who reported to me that they had been studying algebra in Mexico, had been placed into math problem solving 1, a course two years "below" algebra in the typical sequence of math courses.

Roseville High was implementing a block eight schedule for the first time in 1998–1999. This meant students took four 90-minute classes each day in a two-day block of eight classes. The schedules for the students in the migrant pro-gram, particularly those who were newcomers or who scored at a very limited level of English on the Woodcock-Muñoz, were usually completed with electives such as foods or sewing, basic art, crafts, and industrial arts classes, such as plas-tics or woodshop. Most were also enrolled in the lower track math and science classes (problem solving, prealgebra, and general science) because the language of the textbooks was thought to be less demanding linguistically. There was also a greater willingness on the part of the art department and one of the general sci-ence teachers to work with students not yet fluent in English.

With no bilingual support available on a daily basis (I was only there three days per week) beyond what the students themselves could provide each other, the counseling department was hard-pressed to find classes where students could successfully participate. As one counselor reported, she avoided placing students in classes where teachers had expressed resentment toward students who were not fluent in English. Scheduling the immigrant and migrant students into classes involved finding classrooms where they would not fail, rather than find-ing classrooms where they would learn. A counselor explained that students could always be moved up into higher track classes once they were successful in the lower track. Evidence from research, however, shows it is rare for students to leave the tracks into which they are originally placed (Oakes, 1985). During my year at Roseville High, only a few students were able to change tracks, most often because the change was initiated by Mrs. Morton or myself, not by coun-selors or content area teachers.

By the end of September, the "soft" electives were full. To deal with this crisis until the beginning of the new semester, the school created a noncredit course called ESL Audit in which students were assigned to the ESL room. (They also had ESL earlier in the day.) Seven Latino students had either one or two classes of ESL Audit. School personnel explained that no additional sections of existing classes could be added because of the constraints of the master schedule, con-straints that were very familiar from my days of being a high school teacher. That is, there were not enough students without a full schedule to form another sec-tion of an existing course, and, in any event, there was no teacher with an unas-signed period to teach an additional course.

Some students in the migrant program who were quite proficient in English enrolled too late in the semester to earn credit in a course, and were therefore also placed in ESL Audit. The official policy of a student not being able to earn credit in a course after missing so many days would apply to any student, re-gardless of proficiency in English or immigrant status or social class. But it would be unlikely for this policy to affect transfer students from other U.S. schools, whose records could be requested, or students whose parents were aware that school in Roseville started in mid-August rather than after Labor

Day. It was no coincidence that those without a full schedule of classes were Latino newcomers.

The students' only advocate at this point in the school year was Mrs. Morton. But her own marginal status at the school made it difficult for her to make significant changes. Although she had been a community resident for 20 years, after marrying a local man, she described herself as an outsider because she was not born and raised in the town. Within the school she had the doubly low status of being a new member of the school staff and being paid out of special migrant education funds, which led some other teachers to conclude that she was not a legitimate member of the school staff. One teacher commented to me that "it must be nice to be getting a teacher's salary without having to teach." Some staff members did not know what her teaching assignment was, and others did not realize that she worked at the school full time. Mrs. Morton's tenuous position was not unusual (Grey, 1991). Because of her association with the migrant education program and the ESL students, Mrs. Morton was not granted the rights that a citizen/teacher of the school would normally have, such as the same amount of preparation time, access to a computer for reporting and checking on attendance, and having her name and room listed on the master schedule. She, like the students, was invisible in many respects, and therefore her effectiveness as an advocate was limited. No administrator, not even the one overseeing the migrant education grant, stepped in to remedy the situation.

As I mentioned earlier, seven Latino students were assigned to ESL Audit in the ESL room, even though it was Mrs. Morton's preparation period every other day and a teaching period otherwise. The students dutifully sat every day, sometimes working on homework or looking at books or participating in activities that Mrs. Morton and I created for them. But I was not there every day, and Mrs. Morton had a class to teach every other day. It was not long before the students established their own routines, and my insistent attempts to engage them in reading and writing activities were politely rejected. They knew I was not their teacher and that structurally the time did not earn them credit toward any requirement. Instead, they worked on what held meaning for them: lowrider art.

LOWRIDER ART

As I worked with students during the fall, I noticed a few of the students in ESL Audit, and also in the larger ESL classes, passing around, talking about, and copying images from a magazine called *Lowrider Arte*. Although I was familiar with *Lowrider* magazine and some of the expressive forms of low riding, I had never seen this publication. To find out more, I contacted the editor, Armando Avila, in Los Angeles. He told me they began publication in 1992 in response to the large amount of artwork that was being submitted for publication in

Lowrider, which usually only included one or two pages of artwork. The editors of *Lowrider* decided they were receiving enough art to publish a separate magazine devoted entirely to the genre of lowrider art.[2] Mr. Avila reiterated the editorial policy written in the front of the magazine: artwork "must be free of gang slogans, violence, weapons, drugs and/or alcohol" (3). He mentioned that the theme of family togetherness was represented in a lot of the artwork. He also proudly described how the magazine had helped support the family of one of their award-winning artists, who had been paralyzed by a stray bullet in a drive-by shooting. As a distinctly Latino art form, lowrider art therefore had the potential to counter the local invisibility and subordination of Latinos. In addition to creating a particular bond between students, *Lowrider Arte* also created a connection to the larger Latino cultural community throughout the United States.[3]

Lowrider Arte has very little written text. The first page has instructions in English for submitting artwork, and occasionally a page or two of written text (also in English) provides background information about a featured artist. The magazine accepts submissions in any medium, but elaborate drawings in pencil or ink appear to be the most prevalent. In addition to renderings of classic lowrider cars such as the Impala and other Chevrolets, repeated themes in the imagery include Aztec and other pre-Columbian motifs, the Virgin of Guadalupe, zoot-suited *pachucos*, as well as contemporary Latinos often in romantic embrace.

In her article on signification in barrio art T-shirts, Goldman (1997) discusses the juxtaposing of contrasting icons, such as prison buildings with the Virgin of Guadalupe, to create a narrative montage. This layering of vernacular iconography by artists, called *rasquachismo* (Gaspar de Alba, 1998; Goldman, 1997), is easily seen in much of the art in *Lowrider Arte*. For example, in one drawing in the February/March 1998 issue, a deep royal blue lowrider Chevrolet with a license plate reading Azteca is parked in front of the Pyramid of the Sun of Teotihuacán.

In gathering together and repeating many of the same iconographic themes (pre-Colombian motifs, the Virgin of Guadalupe, the Mexican Revolution) over and over again in each issue, the magazine contributes to the construction and distribution of a visual imagery that celebrates Mexican heritage. Salvador, who was born in Michoacán, had lived in several cities in California, in Washington, back in Mexico, in Chicago, and now lived in Roseville, found an aesthetic continuity that was meaningful to him across state and national borders. He told me that the artwork showed that "Mexicans could do other things besides work in the fields" and that looking at the artwork would help me understand what it is to be Mexican. Lowrider art is a borderland discourse (Gee, 1996), literally and metaphorically. It developed in the border culture of the Southwest, and it embodies corrections between U.S.–born Latinos, immigrant Latinos, and Mexicans.

Over the course of the school year, a few copies of *Lowrider Arte* became an integral part of peer relations among several of the students, functioning not only as a resource for cultural pride and identity, but also as an archive of master artists from whom students could learn particular skills.

CULTURAL PRIDE

In all, 11 Latino youth seemed to find particular significance in *Lowrider Arte*. Ten of these self-identified as Mexicano, and one identified himself as Salvadoreño. Being immigrants, they are in many ways distinct from the Mexican American "inventors" of low riding practices. Michael Cutler Stone (1990) describes how the historical and socioeconomic roots of lowrider representational practices were "derived from the particularities of the Mexican-American urbanization and assimilation experience" (87), and he details the complex relationships in contemporary lowrider "tradition," which were widely diffused through the publication of *Lowrider* magazine in the 1970s and 1980s: "As an expressive subcultural genre, low riding contests stereotypes of Mexican-Americans. It evokes a self-consciously positive, stylized public representation of Mexican-American identity and pride, and insists upon recognition within American society" (87). As a distinctly Latino art form in its historical roots, lowrider art had the potential to counter the local invisibility and subordination of Latinos. The students were able to use *Lowrider Arte* as a means for putting forth a positive image of Mexican heritage and for resisting school practices which ignored or denied certain aspects of their Latino identity, such as prohibiting the use of Spanish in class. When I asked Xochitl in the journal we exchanged about the genesis of ideas for her artwork, she indicated the role of *Lowrider* in countering dominant images of Latinos: "How I got my ideas was when I started reading the *Lowrider* magazine. I like to read that magazine because it talks about my culture and I feel so proud when I read that my people are doing good things and not going out in the streets and sell drugs or getting into trouble."

Flores and Yudice (1990) describe language as one of the most obvious signaling systems for discrimination against Latinos. At Roseville High some staff members considered the students' use of Spanish a problem to be corrected, or even an act necessitating disciplinary action. Some teachers prohibited the use of Spanish in the classroom, even when students were trying to help each other with assigned work. One teacher told me that when the students spoke Spanish to each other, they were "building walls between themselves and everyone else in the class." She did not see that native English speakers or accepted school practices had any role to play in the isolation of the Latino students. According to student interviews, teachers often ignored without comment the demand from

English speaking peers, "Speak English!" Mrs. Morton told me that one of the bus drivers would not allow conversation in Spanish on the school bus because she did not want them "saying things she couldn't understand." Lowrider art, then, became a nonverbal declaration of Latino identity. It provided "the semiotic material around which identity [was] deployed in the 'public sphere'" of Roseville High (Flores and Yudice, 1990, 61).

The Latino students in Roseville did not own the highly stylized cars or adopt the distinctive dress often associated with lowriders. But some of the students, having lived in the United States for several years, were aware of these practices. In their reading of *Lowrider* and *Lowrider Arte,* they found an aesthetic discourse that valued Mexican cultural images and history, a discourse they reproduced in their own artwork and incorporated into the objects connected with school life—such as binders and notes given to friends.

The network of relations that developed around *Lowrider Arte* included five artists and several other Latino students performing other roles (see Figure 8.2). Of the artists, Victor and Xochitl were seniors with enough credits to graduate in May. Victor and his family, Zapotecans from Oaxaca, Mexico, moved to southern California in 1992 and then to Roseville in the fall of 1998. Xochitl moved from Nuevo León, Mexico, to Roseville in 1995. Her father had lived and worked as a migrant worker and in various other jobs in the United States for most of Xochitl's life. Juan's family were migrant workers who had traveled the harvest circuit from Texas to Michigan until they settled in Roseville when the meatpacking plant opened. Juan was a ninth grader and had come to the United States from Michoacán, Mexico, in the fourth grade. When he enrolled in school in Michigan, he was put back into second grade, ostensibly because he did not speak English. José, also a ninth grader, was born in Guanajuato, Mexico and had moved to California when he was five years old. From California, his family moved to Chicago. When his parents divorced, his mother moved with the children to Roseville in 1996. Miguel, a ninth grader, was born in El Salvador. Not able to feed their children, his parents went to California to look for work, and the children stayed behind with their grandparents. The parents divorced and Miguel's mother married a man from Mexico. After several years, they were able to bring Miguel to join them in California. They moved to Roseville in 1997. The students were diverse in their places of origin, their length of residence in the US, and in their immigrant status. Yet all shared an interest in *Lowrider Arte.*

Lowrider Arte could not be purchased in Roseville, but a few of the students brought this cultural artifact with them when they moved to the town. Victor brought about 10 copies with him when his family moved from southern California. Juan first saw the magazine in Michigan, but he also had experience with lowrider cultural practices in Texas as he and his family traveled back and forth

Figure 8.2
The Network of Relationships and Social Roles that Developed around
Lowrider Arte

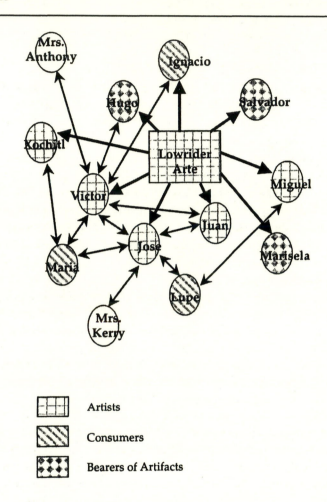

▦	Artists
▨	Consumers
▦	Bearers of Artifacts

to Texas every year. Like Victor, he also brought some copies to Roseville, and he brought the knowledge that the magazine could be purchased through the mail. José ordered his copies through the mail after Juan told him how to do it. Xochitl was introduced to *Lowrider* magazine by her boyfriend, who had lived in the United States for several years, and then to *Lowrider Arte* through Salvador, another member of the group. Ignacio, a newcomer from Vera Cruz, Mexico, became familiar with *Lowrider Arte* when Victor brought a few copies to school. Several more students in the ESL program were introduced to *Lowrider Arte* through these students. Among these students, Victor, Juan, José, Xochitl, and Miguel were the most active producers of lowrider art, even though other students from the ESL class would occasionally try their hand at drawing some of the images.

CULTURAL CAPITAL OF THE STUDENT ARTISTS

Reading, sharing, replicating, and carrying around lowrider art did more than allow students to bring significant cultural iconography into the school site. Among the ESL students themselves, those who could draw images similar to those in the magazine gained status within the group. By talking to and observing Victor during ESL Audit, I also began to understand *Lowrider Arte* in relationship to how the students used the unstructured time they had in school. Even though Victor had taken art classes in California, he was placed into basic art (a beginning art class) because of his test score on the language proficiency test and because the advanced art classes were full. Victor spent 90 minutes a day of unstructured time sitting in the ESL room. He often used both the art class and ESL Audit to work on drawings, sketching the images he saw in *Lowrider Arte*.

As some of the other students took note of his talent, they began to ask him to draw particular images for them. María usually requested roses or the quetzal bird that she would then give to different friends. Ignacio needed a picture for his Día de los Muertos poster assignment for Spanish 1, and Victor drew him a dancing skeleton in a serape (a picture very similar to one he had seen in *Lowrider Arte*). Some of the students who were enrolled in the crafts class would ask Victor to draw pictures for them to serve as a basis for whatever craft assignment they were working on.

I never saw Victor turn a request down. He did confide one day that María's constant requests were wearing on him, "She wants me to draw everything for her." But even when not fulfilling specific requests, he gave away most of his drawings. His work was much admired, and I was not able to get many drawings from him to photocopy before he had given them away. José also gave away most of the lowrider art he drew. José was not enrolled in ESL Audit because he had been an eighth grader in the district, but he did work on lowrider art during the study hall period that all students had. I never observed or heard of requests for artwork from Anglo students—all the exchange of art was among Latinos.

Xochitl, the only female student who produced lowrider art, also gave away much of her artwork. She gave drawings to María, her best friend, and to her boyfriend, among others. She too used spare minutes in class to work on her art. She said that in this, her senior year, she had much more schoolwork to do and did not have as much time to work on her drawings. School was actually the one place where she could find time to draw. At home she had many other responsi-

bilities—helping her mother with the cooking, cleaning, and shopping, and helping her sister with child care.

CULTURE MADE VISIBLE AND PRESERVED

Free access to the photocopy machine in the school library (where their ESL
class was located) also facilitated the distribution of lowrider art. All students
were allowed to use the photocopy machine for school-related reasons if they
asked permission of the librarian, but the English language learners spent so
much time in the library that the librarian gave them free rein. By December,
many students in the ESL program were carrying photocopies of the magazine
pictures or photocopies of the drawings made by Victor, Juan, José, Miguel, and
Xochitl in their binders. Francisco, a very organized and conscientious student,
who had divided his binder into sections with index tabs, had reserved one section for lowrider art. He had also purchased plastic sleeves in which he inserted
the magazine pictures and photocopies to preserve and protect them as he carried them from class to class. Similarly, Salvador protected his lowrider art in
plastic sleeves, although he had decided to create a separate binder of lowrider art
which he carried every day, along with his other binder for school subjects. By his
estimate, Salvador had approximately 150 pages torn from issues of *Lowrider
Arte* in his binder. It was thick and heavy, but he took it to most of his classes
every day. When he did not have any work to do or was bored with the class, he
would take out the binder and thumb through the pictures, just as Victor or
Xochitl or the other artists would take out a drawing to work on.

Salvador told me that Anglo students often commented on the pictures, saying how cool they were and asking about them. He also said that none of his
teachers had ever asked him to put the pictures away, and a few had even asked
about them. In carrying the binder of lowrider art, Salvador created conversational openings into images of "being Mexican." By engaging members of the
dominant culture in conversations about the drawings, Salvador found a way of
momentarily avoiding domination. But within the limiting and unresponsive
structures of the school, such moments were fleeting.

María, who dated Salvador's brother, described the walls of Salvador's room as
covered with photos from *Lowrider* and drawings from *Lowrider Arte*, drawings
of women portrayed as sexual objects—another prevalent theme in *Lowrider
Arte*. Illustrations of scantily clad women in provocative poses are common. In
his discussion of lowrider practices in their broader context, Stone (1990) describes how low riding reaffirms many of the values of the parent culture, such as
religious and family values. "More darkly, the ideology of patriarchal authority,
and the subordination and sexual objectification of women, persist as well in low
riding" (107). Yet Salvador chose for his school binder the pages that represented

scenes from the history of Mexico (of the Aztecs, of the Revolution), the family, lowrider cars, all of which might be considered more positive images for public display.

SOCIAL ROLES

Within the group of students who gave *Lowrider Arte* a place in their school lives, three particular roles developed (see Figure 8.2). Victor, Xochitl, Juan, José, and Miguel used the text as a source for ideas and images that would help them become artists. They referred to their art as lowrider art. They had the respect and admiration of their peers, as evidenced by the number of requests they received to photocopy their work.

Several other students acted as consumers in relationship to the five artists. They were an admiring audience and solicited the production of artwork for themselves. Some of it went into their binders, some was given to other friends. In addition to María, Xochitl's best friend Lupe was another student who made many requests for drawings.

Some students were what I call artifact bearers. They carried and displayed the art. Salvador and Francisco, for example, rarely requested drawings from the artists, but they did carry original magazine pages and photocopies of *Lowrider Arte* pages in their binders. Their "portfolios" gave them something to do during classes when nothing was going on, or after they had finished the assigned work. The pictures created opportunities for conversation among themselves and between them and other students in the class.

Some Latino students also wore lowrider T-shirts, thus making Latino cultural iconography visible at the school. The T-shirts displayed the same themes represented by the images published in the magazine, themes that scholars of Chicano history and art (Fregoso, 1993; Goldman, 1997) consider narratives of Chicano and Mexican American self-affirmation. Goldman argues "that wearing the shirts becomes an act of resistance against Euro-American dominance" (125). The Latino students I asked about the shirts responded in a similar way to those interviewed by Goldman, that wearing the T-shirts was a way to show they are proud of being Mexican. "In comparison to other clothing forms, the T-shirt 'talks' directly to its audience" (Symes, 1989, quoted by Goldman, 134). Male and female students, both students recently arrived from Mexico and Latino students who had more or less grown up in the United States, wore the oversized T-shirts with designs like the Virgin of Guadalupe above a lowrider car.

The roles of artist, consumer, and artifact bearer were not mutually exclusive. The artists and the consumers were, of course, also bearers of visual artifacts when they carried them in their binders and took them out to share with someone else. But the artists' primary interest in *Lowrider Arte* was using it in their own productions. The consumers were actively engaged in requesting particular images that they had seen in the magazine or that they had seen the artists produce from the magazine. Even though Salvador was a talented artist in his own right, it was an activity that he tended to keep to himself or at least did not display at school, choosing instead to carry from class to class the images that he might use in another space. He, like others in the group, certainly was a consumer in that he purchased copies of the magazine, but at school he did not position himself in this way in relationship to the other student artists and the text.

LEARNING FROM LOWRIDER ARTISTS

As I mentioned earlier, the magazine provided a discourse of cultural pride and positive identity for some of the Latino students at Roseville High. It was also at the heart of the students' learning to be members of the larger community of lowrider artists. In stark contrast to the irrelevance of the curriculum in many of their classes, the Latino student artists were engaged in an activity that had meaning. They decided what they wanted to learn. They critically analyzed what they needed to be able to do, and they evaluated which artists in the magazine could help them learn. Nespor (1997) points out that Moll, Tapia, and Whitmore (1993), in their discussion of how material and intellectual resources are distributed through the social relationships within a community, only considered the funds of knowledge from a network of households where predominantly adults communicate directly with each other.

They did not address the nature of communities that include inanimate or nonhuman elements, have kids as central participants, or are spread across time and space and link people through mass-distributed images or representational spaces. Yet it is this latter type of community that is becoming increasingly important in kids' lives. (169)

I believe this was the case with *Lowrider Arte*. To paraphrase Nespor, the students' use of the text as a cognitive resource was at the intersection of several networks. Their friendship allowed for the exchange of the magazine and also contributed to the formation of friendships. The librarian's laissez faire approach to the photocopy machine allowed for the ongoing duplication of the images at no expense. These relationships intersected with the various cultural and commercial networks that produce and distribute the magazine.

A COMMUNITY OF PRACTICE

Through mass distribution, the artists published in the magazine taught their skills and their worldviews to the Roseville students who worked to re-create a similar aesthetic effect in their own drawings. Each of the five student artists aspired to have their art published in *Lowrider Arte* some day. The students apprenticed themselves to the master artists in the text. As Victor noted, when we were discussing why he chose to copy certain images, "See, that's hard to do, that's why I'm doing it, to get better . . . it's hard to do the shadows that he does. So, like, I'm trying to do the same. But it is not the same, that's why I'm learning." Victor, Juan, and Miguel all noted that they were not yet at the point of being able to do original artwork, that is, to consider themselves masters of the genre.

Victor also chose to copy certain images based on the content or sociohistorical meaning (see Figure 8.3). When I asked him to tell me how he decided what to draw, he took the magazine I was holding and slowly turned each page. As he turned the pages, he said, "See, this one has meaning, this one doesn't." The drawings that had meaning for him were images portraying Mexico's indigenous heritage, pre-Columbian stone carvings, buffed Aztec warriors in positions of victory and strength, and other historical images that contested the conquest and colonization of Mexico.

Victor went on to describe how he was using his pencil now instead of his finger to blend and shade, something that Mrs. Anthony, one of the art teachers, had shown him how to do. Even though the artists in *Lowrider Arte* were most

Figure 8.3
Victor's Rendering of an Image from *Lowrider Arte*

central to his learning, Mrs. Anthony was part of the network of relationships when she addressed concepts and activities that he considered important for his own art. Mrs. Anthony had told me that, as much as she admired Victor's work, she found him to be quite stubborn and referred to him as "Do your own thing Victor." Another way of thinking about Victor and his artwork might be that he was very clear on what he needed to learn to become a full participant in the community of lowrider artists. Mrs. Anthony, like most teachers, myself included, wanted to objectify both the learning activities and Victor as a learner in terms of the content of the art curriculum (Lave and Wenger, 1991), and he would not accept this position.

José referred to Juan as "the father of our art." He described how Juan came to middle school with *Lowrider Arte* and some of his own drawings which he showed to José. José began drawing in middle school when he and Juan became friends. When Victor moved to Roseville, Juan and José and Miguel sought Victor's advice about how to improve their drawings. Lowrider art created one of the links between them at school. During the study hall period that all students had, Victor and José often joined each other to work on drawings.

José described the possibility of becoming an artist in terms of continued practice and attention to what he was able to learn from Victor and the artists in the text. Victor had shown him how to use his pencil (from the demonstrations and guidance he received from Mrs. Anthony) to create the desired shading on portraits. He also believed in the capacity for everyone to be a learner. "A lot of kids go, 'I'm not good at drawing.' Everybody is good at drawing, but you have to practice."

Xochitl was experimenting with drawing original images and liked one in particular that she had produced, a montage of female faces. Xochitl's nickname was Brown Tears, a name bestowed on her by a young adult Mexican who had lived in the United States for many years as a migrant worker. She often thumbed through *Lowrider Arte* looking for drawings that gave special attention to faces. It was a fitting moniker for the sensitive, brown-eyed 17-year-old.

LOWRIDER ART AS CURRICULUM

By spring semester, the discourse of lowrider art and the social relationships around it opened a space in the curriculum of Mrs. Kerry's basic art class, adding another adult from the dominant culture to the network and allowing her to participate in the funds of knowledge that the students were exchanging with each other. She too had noticed the binders and magazines that the Latino students carried. Juan, José, Salvador, Miguel, and several others were enrolled in her basic art classes for the spring semester. During one of our conversations she mentioned her interest in popular art and that she wanted to include a unit on lowrider art in her classes.

The basic art curriculum was arranged historically, mostly based on the canon of Western art, but with some inclusion of art from other regions and cultures. Students generally listened to an introductory lecture, and they produced a piece of art similar in style and symbolism to the art they were studying. Then they were assigned some textbook reading in order to learn more about the different artistic movements and the representative artists.

Mrs. Kerry began the unit in April. It is hard to imagine any more respectful position than the one Mrs. Kerry assumed, not only during this unit, but in her interactions with the Latino students in general. She had submitted their works throughout the year to the art shows in which the school participated, and she displayed many of their pieces in the school display case. Both she and Mrs. Anthony welcomed the opportunity to work with the students and sought advice from Mrs. Morton and myself on what they themselves could do differently in class to make the curriculum more accessible. They viewed accommodation as a two-way process, not holding the immigrant and migrant students as solely responsible for changing to fit into their new environment (Nieto, 1999).

José became Mrs. Kerry's main informant about the meanings and history of lowrider art. She had invited all of the Latino students in her classes to talk to her about what they knew, but José was the only one who came forward. When she introduced the unit, she invited all of the students to "look at the sketch books that some of the Hispanic students have. It is some of the most beautiful art I have ever seen." She insisted that the community of Latino students who created lowrider art were the best resources for others in the class to draw upon for understanding and appreciating "this contemporary art form." Mrs. Kerry decentered her own authority and repositioned herself as a learner in regard to lowrider art.

Mrs. Kerry handed out photocopies of several pages from *Lowrider Arte*, and she told the students they would have to memorize the meanings of the symbols as they had been explained to her by José. In announcing to students that they would be tested on the meanings of the symbols, Mrs. Kerry was enacting a view of lowrider art as curriculum that clearly was in keeping with the way curriculum (and learning) is conceptualized in most high schools. First and foremost, what is taught must be tested. Pencil and paper tests involving multiple choice and fill-in-the-blank options necessarily construct knowledge as static and fragmented, as pieces of information whose ultimate value is the extent to which they are memorized and then exchanged for grades. But by treating lowrider art in the same way she treated units on Greco-Roman art and Impressionism, for example, she was also giving the same curricular value to popular Latino art that she gave to "elite" art forms. Despite her own interest in the aesthetic qualities of lowrider art and her deep concern for affirming the Latino students in her class, this unique form of artistic expression was filtered through entrenched school practices. Thus, the peer culture of lowrider art was at least partially transformed into the dominant discourse of schooling. As I explain below, Salvador was the only Latino who spoke to me about this being problematic.

Mrs. Kerry did, however, ask the six Latino students in this class for help with the meanings in the various drawings. There was a long silence. Salvador, although quite fluent in English and sometimes a boisterous student in the ESL room, hesitantly narrated in a barely audible voice the legend represented by the eagle and the serpent in one drawing. After more silence, she pleaded for one of the other Latino students to continue and then finally turned to José. He described the art as having begun with prison inmates who wanted to communicate with their families on the outside. He added to Salvador's explanation that the eagle meant freedom and the snake, danger. He pointed out some other recurrent images such as the tragedy and comedy masks which are often drawn with the automobiles and found on lowrider T-shirts. José explained that "Smile now, cry later" meant you have to be happy because, inevitably, life is hard. The rose was a symbol of love and togetherness, the jaguar a symbol of strength, the dice, that life is about taking chances. He further recounted his understanding of the historical images in another drawing Mrs. Kerry had photocopied for the class— "This we call a charro, they were like the pioneers. The Aztecs were warriors, they sacrificed people by cutting out their hearts." A portrait of Benito Juarez was also part of the drawing, and José identified him as "the Robin Hood of Mexico, a man who stole from the rich to give to the poor." Even though I was a little confused by José's explanations, I did not say anything. The other students took notes on what the "symbols" meant according to José. Mrs. Kerry had listed the symbols to remember: the rose, the jaguar, the eagle and snake, the comedy and tragedy masks, and the dice.

Following José's explanation, Mrs. Kerry presented the art assignment: to choose one symbol to draw in three different media—colored pencil, pastels, and markers. For one representation of the symbol, they had to use the technique of pointillism—a bridge to the unit they were just completing on Impressionism. Mrs. Kerry's efforts went further than those of any other content area teacher toward valorizing the presence of Latinos in the school. At the same time, I thought these efforts produced problematic interpretations of Mexican and Chicano history and of the art form itself. The lesson reinforced one of the principles of traditional schooling, that meaning is fixed, singular, and predetermined in the text. José's explanations were taken as information rather than interpretation. Still, when I asked Nicolas, a Latino student not enrolled in ESL classes, what he thought about doing lowrider art in the basic art class, he reflected, "It was okay, we did something I liked. Before we always did something from Rome or other stuff. This was more interesting to me." Nicolas also said that since he didn't know the symbolism they had to memorize, he felt he had learned something.

Mrs. Kerry told the students she hoped they would produce drawings which could be submitted to the magazine. Most of the Anglo male students drew cars or trucks for the assignment, and most of the girls drew roses or masks. As students were completing their three renditions, I mentioned to Mrs. Kerry that, to my surprise, all the students I observed seemed to be working very seriously and with great effort toward creating a representation of lowrider art. She expressed her own astonishment at the lack of complaining and derogatory comments about the assignment. She had anticipated some resistance on the part of the Anglo students, given the limited interaction of the two groups of students, the pejorative comments sometimes heard in the halls, and the anti-immigrant sentiments among some members of the Roseville community.

I could always count on Salvador to theorize beyond my own incipient grasp of what was occurring in classrooms. When I asked him about the notion of lowrider art as part of the basic art class, he informed me that some students had said "lowrider art is dumb." Then he elaborated on why that perspective made sense to him: "You have to draw what you feel like drawing, not what someone tells you to draw. [Some say] it's cool, but they don't really know what it means [pausing] they don't care what it means. I don't agree with everything that José said. Some of the meanings are not what José said. People draw what it means for their life. They [the images] don't really have *one* meaning. Some don't even have *a* meaning. The drawings are stories, they tell something." Salvador had articulated a relationship between artistic expression, identity, and culture. The creation of a piece of art is not only an act of personal expression, but also an act embedded in larger cultural narratives. Without access to these narratives, in this case, the lived experiences of Latinos, the production can be devoid of significance. I also took Salvador's response to mean that because the expression of experience is still open to interpretation, it did not make sense to memorize one person's (José's) version of "what it means."

AN EXPANDING NETWORK

Mrs. Kerry was so pleased with the art the students created that she invited a reporter and photographer from the town's newspaper to visit her class and write a story about lowrider art. With only one high school in the town, what happened there was indeed news worth reporting. Not only was there often a school related story on the front page, but one of the reporters had also told me that the editor was determined to reach out to the "new members of the community." In December I had talked with one of the reporters about an article on the Spanish mass which celebrated Nuestra Virgen de Guadalupe. The reporter found a bilingual resident to translate the story into Spanish and both the English and Spanish versions appeared on the front page the next day.

A reporter and photographer came to Mrs. Kerry's third period class, and she introduced them to José. While the reporter interviewed him about the genre, the photographer took several pictures of students working on or holding up their finished art. The article appeared as a front page story in the Sunday paper in early May with the following headline: "Bridging the Culture Gap—Project Helps Basic Art Students at [RHS] Learn about Classmates' Heritage." The article quoted Mrs. Kerry, "the students are proud of their heritage and this is a way for them to teach us about that heritage," and it drew heavily from the interview with José: "A Mexican history buff, [José] said a lot of the stories in that history parallel those in American and European history. For example, Spanish explorer Hernando Cortes conquered the Aztec people much like the [Europeans] conquered American Indians. And Benito Juarez robbed from the rich and gave to the poor, just like Robin Hood" (2).

The next time I saw Victor, I asked him about the newspaper article. He said it was stupid. When I asked why, he shook his head and replied in a tone of condemnation that José was wrong and repeated several times, "Benito Juarez did not rob from the rich to give to the poor. He was the president of Mexico, he did not rob from the rich to give to the poor." I countered that José had lived in the United States for a long time and would not have taken any classes on Mexican history as long as he was in U.S. schools. But Victor refused to accept this as an explanation for what he considered a misinterpretation being publicly reported. He told me that he and José did not talk anymore and he ended our conversation with irritation in his voice. "He should have checked his information before talking to a reporter."

It was not only because of the newspaper article that the social relations around lowrider art began to change. The end of the school year was rapidly approaching. Victor and Xochitl had senior activities and concerns that took up many of the remaining days. Indeed, all of the students in the program were in the final press to complete work and pass their classes. Assemblies were being held, and students were meeting with counselors to arrange their schedule of classes for the next year. Karina, another senior in the program, was getting married, and many of the students were involved in one way or another in helping with preparations.

Xochitl and Victor graduated. Juan and his family moved back to Michigan over the summer. When I returned to Roseville in the fall of 1999, I asked Salvador about his binder of lowrider art. He told me that his mother had thrown away all of his magazines and drawings one day when she was angry with him. José said he draws very little now because he does not have time. But I did see the most recent issue of *Lowrider Arte* in Miguel's binder. He bought it at a store in another town about 30 miles from Roseville, which had recently started stocking the magazine. Mrs. Morton showed me a note from Mrs. Anthony about what a skillful artist Miguel was becoming, and Miguel was now receiving requests for his drawings. As I was talking to him during his math class, a new student who had just come from Mexico opened her binder and showed me Miguel's drawing that she kept at the front.

CONCLUSION

When Mrs. Kerry created an official space for lowrider art in the basic art curriculum, she was enacting one important aspect of multicultural education, that of curriculum integration. James Banks (1994) has pointed out four other dimensions of multicultural education which are equally important: "the knowledge construction process, prejudice reduction, an equity pedagogy, and an empowering school culture and social structure" (1). The art department was looking for ways to have their pedagogy based on equity by making changes in presentation, materials, and assignments to facilitate the achievement of the English language learners. Mrs. Morton worked through lunch periods and without preparation periods to promote academic achievement for students in all the classes where no pedagogical changes were being made. At the same time, she offered suggestions to teachers about changes in their classrooms which would be helpful to students. But prejudice reduction and an empowering school culture are schoolwide issues. Mrs. Kerry and Mrs. Morton would not have been able to address these issues alone, even though each of them did make numerous attempts to provide the administration with examples of policies and practices that were excluding the immigrant and migrant students.

The discourse of lowrider art enabled some of the Latino students to resist the practices that pushed them to the edges of the social world at Roseville High. When subjected to the truncated pedagogies, relegated to marginal physical and temporal spaces, and subjected to the racism and linguicism of some peers and school staff members, the students invested themselves in their art. When they were denied bilingual support and could not understand schoolwork, they brought to school a text they could understand and enjoy. They carried and displayed through the hallways and into classrooms (occupying the space as it were) an iconography that was noticeably different in this setting. They used a Chicano art form, itself an aesthetic of resistance to the assimilationist demands of mainstream art (Gaspar de Alba, 1998), as a bridge between their Mexican origins and their current U.S. residence. They demonstrated through their apprenticeship to the text and in their community of practice at school that Latino students are proficient and talented. They found a way to make visible their culture, their knowledge, and their skills, and indeed these were noticed. Unfortunately, the recognition was fleeting and was not supported by a critical reconsideration of the school's practices.

NOTES

I am grateful to Stanton Wortham and Edmund Hamann for their support-ive editorial comments and to Greg Lyons, Allen Koshewa, and Deryn Ver-ity for their suggestions on earlier versions of this chapter. I also wish to acknowledge the financial support of the John Edwards Dissertation Year Fellowship from Indiana University.

1. Kao (1998) in reviewing the Woodcock-Muñoz Lanuage Survey noted, "Informa-tion reported about the content validity is insufficient. . . . This reviewer wonders who would need a test that could classify subjects into CALP levels but could not provide sub-stantial validity evidence of the CALP cut-scores and inferences made concerning those scores" (1146–1147).

2. Dorie Goldman (1997) writes that *Lowrider*'s first art issue, "Chicano arte del var-rio" was published in 1979. I assume there was a lapse in publication and that *Lowrider Arte* may be a revamped version of the earlier publication.

3. According to Armando Avila, low riding itself has become a widely distributed practice with participants and subscribers to the magazine in many countries. When a friend told me she saw a Honda Civic lowrider, I protested that it wasn't a "real" lowrider. The arrest of a member of the white supremacist group Nazi Low Riders helped me see the extent to which any cultural practice can be co-opted and transformed to create mean-ings far removed from the historical material roots of the practice.

REFERENCES

Avila, A., ed. 1998. *Lowrider arte.* 7:(2).

Banks, J. 1994. *Multicultural Education: Theory and Practice.* 3d ed.. Needham Heights, MA: Allyn and Bacon.

Flores, J. and G. Yudice. 1990. "Living Borders/Buscando America: Languages of Latino Self-formation." *Social Text.* 24:57–84.

Fregoso, R.L. 1993. *The Bronze Screen.* Minneapolis: University of Minnesota Press.

Gaspar de Alba, A. 1998. *Chicano Art Inside/Outside the Master's House: Cultural Politics and the CARA Exhibition.* Austin: University of Texas Press.

Gee, J.P. 1995. *Social Linguistics and Literacies: Ideology in Discourses.* 2d ed. Bristol, PA: Falmer Press.

———. 1999. *An Introduction to Discourse Analysis: Theory and Method.* New York: Routledge.

Goldman, D. 1997. "'Down for La Raza': Barrio Art T-shirts, Chicano Pride, and Cul-tural Resistance." *Journal of Folklore Research.* 34(2):123–138.

Grey, M. 1991. "The Context for Marginal Secondary ESL Programs: Contributing Fac-tors and the Need for Further Research." *The Journal of Educational Issues of Lan-guage Minority Students.* 9(Fall):75–89.

Indiana Department of Education. 1989. *Legal Requirements and Funding Sources: Educa-tional Equity for Language Minority Students.* Indianapolis, IN.

Kao, C.-W. 1998. "Woodcock-Munoz Language Survey." In *The Thirteenth Mental Measurements Yearbook.* J.C. Impara and B.S. Plake, eds. Lincoln: University of Nebraska Press.

Lave, J. and E. Wenger. 1991. *Situated Learning.* Cambridge: Cambridge University Press.

Moll, L., J. Tapia, and K. Whitmore. 1993. "Living Knowledge: The Social Distribution of Cultural Resources for Thinking." In *Distributed Cognitions: Psychological and Educational Considerations*. G. Salomon, ed. Pp. 139–163. Cambridge: Cambridge University Press.

Nespor, J. 1997. *Tangled Up In School*. Mahwah, NJ: Lawrence Erlbaum Associates.

Nieto, S. 1999. *The Light in Their Eyes: Creating Multicultural Learning Communities*. New York: Teachers College Press.

Oakes, J. 1985. *Keeping Track: How Schools Structure Inequality*. New Haven: Yale University Press.

Stone, M.C. 1990. "Bajito y Sauvecito [Low and Slow]: Low Riding and the 'Class' of Class." *Studies in Latin American Popular Culture*. 9:85–126.

9

Policy Design as Practice: Changing the Prospects of Hispanic Voices

Michael Brunn

"When someone with the authority of a teacher, say, describes the world and you are not in it, there is a moment of psychic disequilibrium, as if you looked into the mirror and saw nothing."

(Rich, as cited in Rosaldo, 1989, ix)

The things said and the languages spoken in the communities we are born into are central to our identities, and they are a fundamental part of our socialization. Policies that regulate and otherwise control the languages we speak, where we may speak them, and the status given or ascribed to them, have the ability, among other things, to either affirm us as valuable members of our communities, or to marginalize our participation within the mainstream of the greater social milieu—i.e., they may define one as not part of a certain community, or at least not a welcome part. In schools, formal language policies prescribe at least part of the education language minority children receive. Moreover, language policies directed toward English language learners (ELLs) (1) fundamentally affect these students' levels of achievement, (2) influence their perceptions of self, and (3) either impede or promote these children's social acceptance within, and acculturation to, the school community. Within a Vygotskian paradigm, able and experienced adults should direct the learning and achievement of their students. In terms of policies that direct and govern the schooling of language minority students, teachers and administrators carry the responsibility for organizing the linguistic and the social contexts necessary for students' success in school.

In the fall of 1996, the Clayton Community Unit School District (CUSD), situated in rural Illinois, had nine Hispanic students out of the approximately

1,000 students in the district.[1] This number grew to over 120 by the fall of 1997 and neared 200 at the close of the 1999–2000 school year (approaching 20 percent of total enrollment). The purpose of my study was to investigate how teachers and administrators made and implemented policy that would affect the learning and the socialization of these recently arrived Hispanic students.[2]

To clarify the way in which "policy" is used here, I draw upon the recent work of Shore and Wright (1997) and of Sutton and Levinson (2001). Shore and Wright frame policies as directive forces that contribute to an individual's self-perception and characterization as the subject of the policy. They problematize policy in order to tease out and review the relationships between policy, policy making, policy makers, and individuals within societies. Sutton and Levinson bring to the fore a "[reconceptualiztion of] the notion of policy itself as a complex social practice, an ongoing process of normative cultural production constituted by diverse actors across diverse social and institutional contexts" (Levinson and Sutton, 2001, 1). Both sets of authors refer to Foucault's notion of "political technology" to frame the way formal policy obscures its central political nature by the use of neutral and/or shared terminology. However, they insist that policy's core functions of problem-definition and "solution" delineation are inherently political. Finally, both sets of authors distinguish "official policy" from their more inclusive definitions. Official policy includes formal articulations of problem and solution, whereas policy writ large adds originators' tacit cultural understandings and implementers' redefinition through interpretation.

Using this theoretical perspective, I employed ethnographic methodology to reveal how the teachers, the administrators, and the Hispanic parents and students negotiated their agendas and the official language policy for the Clayton schools. I focus on the central fact that the Anglo majority expected newly arrived Hispanics to change their ways in order to fit into the community. The stated goal of the official policy was to avoid marginalizing the new students by facilitating their acculturation to the Clayton schools and by organizing contexts where they could achieve both socially and academically. But, in fact, the policy expected Hispanics to adjust to the Anglo norm.

The major questions guiding this research were: How did a language policy function to separate, and how did it work to integrate, two disparate cultural groups? Did the policy, as formally conceived and de facto implemented, expect both sides to change and in what ways?

THE SITE AND THE METHODOLOGY

Clayton is sited in a rural and historically agrarian community in the west central portion of Illinois. Its approximate 1999 population of 4,000 persons was slightly less than several decades ago. However, the recent influx of the Hispanic workers has added considerably to the current population. The town is adjacent to a large river that has affected its growth and commercial activity since its founding. It is connected to other parts of the state by a bridge, and by two lane roads that transect the town from several directions. The population mostly relies on corn and soybeans for its economic support. Associated with the farming activities are an assortment of goods and services that are integral to their agricultural enterprises, including a meatpacking plant.

Until recently, Clayton was almost entirely Euro-American with only an occasional ethnic minority family among its population. The English language was the only one spoken, read, or heard on the streets and in the schools, except for a course in Spanish as a foreign language available to the high school students as an elective. The arrival of the Hispanic workers to take jobs in the packing plant, beginning in the fall of 1996, brought interesting responses from the residents, especially about the status and acceptance of Spanish. As a long-established, monolingual English speaking community, most voiced the belief that "this is America, and *they* (Hispanics) need to speak English." This attitude prevailed across all occupations, including school personnel, and was a part of conversations throughout the community. In the spring of 1998, there was a slight thawing of this attitude among some of the business professionals who saw Spanish/English bilingualism as an avenue to greater commerce. Two banks enrolled their employees in the Spanish language classes for teachers that were being taught by a university professor.

The meatpacking plant is on the fringe of the community, beyond the town limits, and had been in existence for more than 20 years at the time this study began. The packing plant was unionized for many years, before it was closed in the mid-1990s because it was unprofitable. A few months later it reopened as a nonunion business, and rehired many of the laid-off workers from the community, but not enough to fill all three shifts. Following this, in order to fulfill the need for additional inexpensive labor, the plant owners relocated a significant number of Hispanic laborers from another midwestern state where they had closed another packing plant.

The five schools that comprise the Clayton CUSD are typical small, rural schools. There are fewer students in each grade level than the national average; the school buildings are not all centrally located in the town; the schools have limited choices in the curricula they can offer to their students; and each school is primarily managed by a building administrator. Akin to the dynamics Peshkin (1994) documented 20 years ago, the schools' cultures can be characterized as having and producing a strong sense of community among the teachers, the administration, and the students that reflects the social ties within the community. Moreover, the teachers and most administrators were natives of the town, and they received their teaching and administration credentials from a nearby university (where I taught until recently). Most retired school personnel stay on in the community.

In 1999–2000 there were approximately 1,200 students in the pre-K–12 system. The kindergarten and preschool were in separate buildings from the 1–12 grade students, and were managed by one principal. The two buildings were located several blocks away from each other, and from the superintendent's office, which was in a small building across the street from the large, two-school, 1–12 complex. That complex, all under one roof, contained a 1–6 wing with a lunchroom, library, and its own principal. A gymnasium that was used by all the 1–12 students separated the elementary wing from the junior/senior high wing. This secondary-level wing also had its own lunchroom, library, and principal. Several miles out of town was a small, K-6 building that was also a part of the district.

The educators interviewed and observed in this study included 33 teachers (41 percent of the pre-K–12 faculty), two counselors, one administrative assistant, two librarians, four bilingual staff, and all six of the top administrators (four principals, the bilingual coordinator, and one superintendent). Except for one of the principals, all of the regular school personnel interviewed were originally from the Clayton community. The bilingual staff numbered 10 in all: the bilingual coordinator and five of the bilingual staff were from outside the country; three others were from outside the community; and one was a local. The grade levels of the teachers ranged from first grade through the twelfth, and included the bilingual teachers, as well as a wide range of subject specific teachers and resource personnel. In addition to the regular school personnel, interviews were conducted with three Hispanic students and three Hispanic parents who participated in the policymaking activities.

Each of the 54 semistructured interviews followed one of three protocols, but was conducted in a conversational framework, and was then recorded and transcribed, then coded using data management software for ethnographic research. In most instances, the interviews took place either before or after school. Interviews with the Hispanic students and parents were conducted privately, in their homes, in order to provide maximum confidentiality to the interviewee. On occasion, follow-up interviews were necessary to clarify and amplify certain points in the conversations.

Because none of the educators were new to the community, except for the bilingual coordinator, the initial research design excluded newcomer voices. In the summer of 1999, the research project added several new participants who were involved in the language policymaking processs. At that point, three Hispanic parents and three Hispanic students were incorporated into the research. Their participation extended throughout the many months of policy discussions. An interview protocol was developed specifically for the language policy process. The protocol was also written in Spanish to facilitate the inclusion of the Hispanics' voices.

An inductive approach to the analysis of the data was conducted. Among the central concerns of the informants was, first of all, the changes in their educational community. The demographic changes brought to the fore their thoughts about the current and future needs of the schools, and the need for an official policy directive concerning languages used in academic and social venues. Faculty also noted the major changes in their district and expressed concern for how those changes would affect their interactions with the Hispanic parents and students. Other concerns included how the district could afford new programs, both academic and social, which would provide for the inclusion of the new students. A final concern was informants' lack of knowledge about the Hispanic students matriculating in their schools.

It was apparent that the development of a document that addressed these concerns could become important to managing the pedagogical, cultural, social, and demographic changes within the Clayton CUSD. Several years into my inquiry, my research project became an applied one—as I took on the role of facilitating the development of a formal language policy for the school district.

THE LANGUAGE POLICY CASE STUDY

The pre-K–K principal, Mrs. Osmund, administered two schools: a pre-K facility and a kindergarten building. The pre-K facility, Granite School, was established in response to the rapid increase in the preschool-aged Hispanic children, and was operated primarily as a bilingual school. Her original building, Whitmore School, housed three kindergarten classes—one of them a Spanish-only room staffed by a bilingual teacher. In the fall of 1996, Mrs. Osmund began systematic research on bilingual education. She relied heavily on the position statement on language acquisition from the National Association of Early Childhood Education (NAECE). She used those materials to help her teachers and her Hispanic students' parents understand the necessity of bilingual education to design curricula and to institute effective instructional practices. Mrs. Osmund's beliefs were expressed in the following quote, "We need to respect and promote the primary language as we teach English. I also have a firm belief that we should be teaching in the primary language, and teaching English until English is proficient. And then they can switch over to English."

The Hispanic parents wanted their young children to immediately begin learning English, in order to gain access to education and to American society. Although there was not as yet an official position taken by the district, the undeclared language policy in the pre-K–K grades was that if their dominant language was Spanish, then their language of instruction would be Spanish. At first this was not an issue with most of the parents, but a few declared on their intake forms that their children were dominant English speakers. This caused some difficulties with the students' placements. Later on, the students' classroom work and subsequent testing revealed that these children's language was Spanish, not English. Subsequent agreements were reached between Mrs. Osmund and the Hispanic parents. These agreements placed the students in bilingual learning contexts that maximized their strengths and potential for achievement, but that sometimes contradicted parents' understanding of what should be.

Parent involvement became an immediate agenda item in the pre-K–K school and in the elementary wing, as the number of Hispanic students grew the first year after the plant had reopened. Mrs. Osmund and most of her faculty were very concerned with the acculturation of the young children and about the involvement of their parents in the educational process. She determined that a parents' program should be instituted that would help the new arrivals join the school and larger community. She believed that the program, delivered as "classes," would provide an avenue for the parents to access the social and academic resources of their children's school and of the local community. Because many of the parents worked the second shift at the packing plant, the classes were held in the late mornings to accommodate their work and home schedules. Topics of study ranged as widely as how to read to your child, where to go for assistance with housing and other social matters, and procedures for contacting and communicating with the school and the teachers.

In the elementary wing, however, most of the teachers made little or no effort to involve the Hispanic parents. Mrs. Osmund stated: "In [the elementary school] parents are not encouraged. There are teachers who say, "I don't want them in my classroom.' And then they'll have, just out of the blue, a science night and nobody comes. Well, no they don't come. They haven't felt welcome all year. Why are they going to come now? Then that feeds the faculty's negativism, well what's the point, why try. It's a cycle."

When Hispanic workers began coming to Clayton, there were no practices and programs that would integrate them into the schools and meet their educational needs. Without an understanding of the cultural and linguistic needs, and the interests of these new students, the teachers and the staff needed to begin their own "education" and devise novel responses. A few, like Mrs. Osmund, did so. But, although most of the teachers made significant efforts to engage the newcomers in the curriculum and the instructional flow of the classrooms, they had no clear understanding of what were the best practices for language minority students, nor could they communicate effectively with many of these students.

One response by the superintendent, in the spring of 1997, was to hire two bilingual teachers—one for the pre-K–K school and one for the elementary school. These were the grade levels that first experienced the greatest intake of Hispanic students. The new migrant workers were typically young men, some with families and young children. In the summer of 1997, other bilingual staff and faculty were hired as the number of Hispanic students grew, and as they were dispersed into other grade levels. That summer, the pre-K bilingual teacher became the bilingual coordinator for the district; a position she held for two years. One of her tasks was to secure funding from state and federal agencies, and another was to provide leadership and direction to the bilingual program. Her efforts to secure funding were successful, but her ability to formulate a language policy and to direct and develop instructional practices was limited.

She had no prior experience with, nor did she have formal knowledge about teaching methods and theories of second language acquisition. As she accumulated such information from state and national conferences, she instituted changes in the instructional practices of the bilingual teachers and in the regular education teachers who had ELLs (English language learners), in their classrooms. On average, every two months there would be a major overhaul of the goals and organization of the bilingual program. Students would be redirected to different teachers, and programs would be instituted, altered, or curtailed. For example, at the beginning of his tenure in 1997, the bilingual teacher in the elementary wing was given a particular set of goals and objectives by the bilingual coordinator. These were derived in part from her accumulated conference information and in part from the granting agencies' guidelines. The directives were at times unclear and in conflict with what he knew to be best practices for his students. Furthermore, the guidelines of various grants sometimes conflicted. In short, policies derived from the various funding agencies were not necessarily the policies and the practices the teachers and the administrators wanted, understood, or saw as beneficial for the students or the district. The end result was that there was little forward progress made in Hispanic students' education and language acquisition in either Spanish or English. Assessment measures indicated that that they were marginalized in the learning processes, while their Euro-American classmates continued to achieve.

There were, however, a few successes. One principal urged a vocal group of Hispanic parents to "demand" that they be heard and that their opinions be counted. These parents had acquired sufficient English to engage in discussions and conversations in effective ways, and they did open a conversation with school personnel. The bilingual teacher in the elementary wing instituted an after-school program for students of all grades. His actions helped integrate them into the school. Another bilingual teacher and a Hispanic aide developed a program which gave individual help to Hispanic students.

In 1997, the first summer following the initial influx of migrant students, the district sponsored and organized a summer school program for the Euro-American and the Hispanic students of all grade levels. Each group was separated from the other in their instructional practices and in their extracurricular activities. It was believed that pedagogically the two groups would be better served by this segregation. An unofficial language policy was the determining factor in this configuration. Teachers and other planning personnel believed that the challenges and difficulties of instructing children with such a wide range of abilities and knowledge would be compounded by the language differences. However, the next summer the two groups were integrated into one program. This proved to be the better paradigm. It afforded the Hispanic students opportunities to learn, and it revealed the cultural constructs and the social norms of both groups of students within the educational community.

The summer of 1999 saw an even stronger, more integrated educational program. That program included more emphasis on dual language learning, on activities that took the children into the community, and on cooperative and collaborative learning. The driving force behind the strong summer program was one of the bilingual teachers, Mrs. Hough, in the Junior/Senior High. She was very frustrated with the previous lack of direction in the bilingual program and with the lagging achievement of the Hispanic students. Throughout the spring of 1999, she took an unprecedented leadership role in structuring and organizing the summer program and in giving direction to the grant proposal that was to support it. She was adamant that positive changes would occur and that a redirected program could make a difference in the lives and the achievements of the Hispanic students. At the same time, the bilingual director had lost favor with the district administrators, and she was notified in the spring of 1999 that she would be terminated at the end of the academic year. That summer the district also began the yearlong process of developing a formal language policy that would delineate instructional practices, socialization processes, and language use for the entire school district, focusing on the Hispanic students and parents.

THE DEVELOPMENT OF A LANGUAGE POLICY THAT CHANGED THE PROSPECTS FOR THE HISPANIC STUDENTS

The principal from the elementary wing and the principal from the junior/senior high school met with me during the summer of 1999 to determine a long-range direction for the bilingual program. I proposed to seek input from three sources: teachers, Hispanic parents, and Hispanic students. We agreed that these three groups of stakeholders had valuable insights about the functioning of an effective bilingual program. The plan centered on the process of consensus building among these three major stakeholders, and involved a series of meetings leading to the ratification of the policy by the School Board. Three representatives from each group would meet to form a Steering Committee, charged with combining all the statements into one document in English and Spanish, using the process of consensus building. The "Statement of Principles and Beliefs," as the document was eventually called, would then be sent back to the general faculty, to the parents in the Hispanic community, and to the Hispanic students for their responses. At the same time, a committee of the School Board that dealt with official policies and planning would also be given a copy of the Statement. The final outcome was that, eight months after that initial meeting between me and the two principals, the statement was presented to the School Board for final ratification.

The project of developing a formal language policy was divided into three phases: program exploring, consensus building, and response and ratification. The objectives of program exploring were first to establish a common base of understanding among the participants in all three groups about the various available bilingual program models. The second goal was to begin dialogues about elements of an effective bilingual program for Clayton. Consensus building involved nine members of the Steering Committee whose task was to draft a document that combined the principles and belief statements submitted from each of the three groups during the program exploring phase. The function of response and ratification was to ensure that the faculty and administrators, the Hispanic parents, and the Hispanic students supported the Statement of Principles and Beliefs.

This procedure was designed by two of the four principals, along with myself, in the summer of 1999. The superintendent, Mr. Malloy, was apprised of the evolving plans. He was concerned only with the developments in general. He agreed to commit funds for release time for 12 teachers to participate in the program exploring phase, and he authorized the release of the Hispanic students from classes to attend the steering committee meetings. His attention was focused on the difficulties that he was having with the new bilingual director for the district, Mr. Brandeis. The superintendent was already receiving complaints from parents and from teachers about Mr. Brandeis' (non)performance of his duties and of his inability to make decisions regarding student placements, teaching assignments, and resource allocations.

Once the Statement of Principles and Beliefs was finalized by the Steering Committee, the superintendent met with the Policy and Planning Committee of the School Board to review the document with them, and to receive their initial responses. He took a more active role in the response and ratification phase, acting as the representative of the School Board and its committee. Analysis of his interviews and his interactions showed that he believed that the process would be therapeutic for those who were most concerned with the education of the Hispanic students. Yet he also intended the Statement of Principles and Beliefs not to be formal policy, but rather to have advisory significance only. He believed that the instruction of the bilingual students should be left to the direction of the bilingual director, who should retain ultimate control over the bilingual programs. In interviews he revealed that the district was out of compliance with their Migrant

Education and Title VII grants and with Illinois regulations for bilingual and LEP students' education. These issues were uppermost in his mind.

The driving force behind the process of developing a Statement of Principles and Beliefs was the junior/senior high principal, Mr. Karnesky. He was hired in the summer of 1998. He filled a vacancy when the then-principal, Mr. Malloy, moved up to become superintendent. This principal was the only administrator who was not from the local area. He was very concerned with the lagging success of the Hispanic students, with the resistance of many teachers to engage the ELL students, with the establishment of a long range plan for ELL instruction, with the need for qualified bilingual teachers, and with bilingual materials necessary for affective instruction. He took a strong leadership role in organizing faculty development programs for his staff to help them understand the issues of second language acquisition, working with diverse students, and developing cultural awareness and sensitivity toward the newcomers. He successfully requested after-school Spanish language classes for his staff, believing that they should attempt to communicate with their LEP students. The staff attended on a voluntary basis, and the school district paid their tuition. Mr. Karnesky was himself a student in those Spanish classes and actively used his new language skills in hallway communication with Hispanic students and bilingual staff. He actively participated in all three phases of the development of the Statement of Principles and Beliefs, and he lobbied aggressively for its approval and ratification. His active leadership, which emulated that of a strong superintendent, gave direction to the elementary wing, as well as his own junior/senior high. He reorganized his staff assignments to match Hispanic students with those teachers whose skills and abilities would benefit them most. Mr. Karnesky also attended several national conferences for teachers and administrators that centered on language and diversity issues and effective instructional practices.

Mrs. Osmund, the principal introduced earlier, was very active in procuring grants to fund her two buildings—tapping the resources of migrant education programs and the Title VII programs. She took a leadership role in designing parent involvement programs that would require all parents, Hispanic parents included, to make regular sustained visits to the classrooms on a weekly basis. She was a strong leader, committed to the success of her students, and to the continued advancement of her staff's knowledge. Because of her concerns and commitments to her two buildings, she often found herself at odds with the superintendent. Mrs. Osmund aggressively pursued programs and issues that she believed were advantageous not only for her buildings, but for the district as well, which made her somewhat of a maverick. The bulk of the young Hispanic students were in her two buildings, resulting in her feeling that she was responsible for the leadership in the lower grades. Throughout the development of the statement, she attended program exploring sessions and Steering Committee meetings when she could find the time in her busy schedule. She actively participated in the review and response activities, facilitated her teachers' input, and gave her opinions during the administrator meetings that reviewed the final Statement of Principles and Beliefs.

The teachers most involved in the discussions of bilingual education and instructional strategies were the bilingual staff. However, there were four (out of 19) teachers in George Elementary, and six (out of 39) teachers in the junior/senior high school who actively worked to develop effective instructional programs. Most of the regular elementary teachers taught a minimum of four ELL students each year, out of their usual 20 students in a classroom. I describe several teachers who participated in discussions during the program exploring phase, in order to illustrate the diversity of teacher views.

Mrs. Collier was an active participant in the program exploring phase, asking pointed questions and offering her thoughts about what the changes in the bilingual program meant for her students and for her. At times her remarks were cynical, casting this new process as just another attempt to force a program upon already overworked teachers. Her interviews later showed her to be very concerned that her Hispanic students were not making much academic progress. She revealed that whenever the bilingual director or a state official visited her classroom, she told them what she believed they wanted to hear about how she conducted her class. Left on her own, she taught her class in a manner that she deemed effective for her mixed language students. She concluded that the program exploring sessions confirmed some of her strategies and helped her improve other practices.

Mrs. Rothman was attentive, but she offered no opinions during the lively discussions. Analysis of her interviews showed that she came to the process with many questions about effective practices for instructing ELLs, including questions about the efficacy of Spanish for instruction. She had heard many differing views from her colleagues, and held a tentative belief that allowing Spanish in her classroom would delay her students' progress. Because she was not bilingual, she had doubts about her capacity to teach in a mixed language class. The program exploring sessions gave her insights into the difficulties the Hispanic students faced. Moreover, she came to understand that the ELL students should have Spanish-based instruction in certain instances, and that some students only needed Spanish to support their developing ability to formulate responses in English.

During the final session, though not an official teacher representative, Mrs. Maller chose to attend and become involved in the discussion. She was critical of the process and of the bilingual education models presented in the discussions. Her strong English-only views at times dominated the discussion, leaving little opportunity for others' perspectives. She resisted any attempts by others to engage her in an open discussion of her views. Analysis of her follow-up interviews revealed that the Hispanic students represented a threat to her sense of nationalism, to her security in her pedagogical beliefs, and to her way of life in that small, rural town. She often said that her ancestors came there from Europe not speaking English, and that they were able to assimilate and prosper. She believed that offering Spanish language to the Hispanic students would lead to the downfall of America. She saw English as the central vehicle for education, as the way to unify the country, and she believed that it would fracture the nation to have more than one language spoken.

Mr. Starsky, a non–Spanish-speaking high school teacher, engaged actively in the sessions, asking questions about many issues raised. Mr. Starsky brought insights, and offered his perspectives about the bilingual program models, based on his experiences as a multilingual speaker. He and his parents emigrated from Croatia when he was six years old, and began life in the United States without any English language skills. He strongly believed that ELL students needed first language support during all phases of their schooling, but also that their ultimate goal should be to learn English. At times he expressed dismay at the English-centric views adhered to by several of the other teachers in the sessions. He believed that their emphasis on English-only was detrimental to the Hispanic students in school and to the growth of the nation. He believed that his students not only struggled with English in general, but that they also had difficulties with the concepts in their subjects. He preferred that his students converse in whichever language was most productive for understanding the subject, but he encouraged them to respond in English when reporting their answers. His interviews showed further that he had tempered his approaches to other teachers in discussing the merits of bilingual education. He understood that the life changes he experienced as an immigrant gave him a different perspective compared with the insular lives of most of his colleagues.

The different factions among the teachers each selected one of their own to represent teacher viewpoints during the subsequent, consensus building phase. One of the elementary teachers was Mrs. Maller, the vocal English-only advocate. The faction of teachers she represented believed that she would serve to curb the policy development and direct it away from the use of Spanish in classroom instruction and toward an English immersion model that they believed would best serve Clayton. Ms. Crocker, one of the bilingual/biliterate teachers who acted as the "resource" teacher for Hispanic students and elementary wing teachers, was the other teacher representative from her school. She worked closely with the other elementary teachers and their Hispanic students, providing assistance in their classrooms, and conducting small classes in her own room for students who needed extra help with language and content. The elementary teachers she represented felt that she would advocate for a policy that was effective for their students and that would provide informed direction to their pedagogies. The junior/senior high teacher chosen as the third member was Ms. Hough. Her duties as one of the bilingual/biliterate teachers in the ESL program biased her against an English immersion stance. The majority of the 7–12 grade teachers believed that Hispanic newcomers needed support in their primary language and that Ms. Hough would work to ensure that.

During the time that the teachers were meeting in the program exploring phase in the early fall of 1999, the Hispanic parents and the Hispanic students were also meeting separately to learn about the models of bilingual education, and to discuss their principles and beliefs. Their sessions were conducted by the parent liaison, a man from El Salvador, who used the Spanish versions of the same materials used at the teachers' sessions. Most of the parents worked the second shift (3–11 P.M.) at the meatpacking plant, so the meetings were held in the late mornings. At first the parents were skeptical about the school's interest in their input. However, once the parent liaison, Sr. Chavez, convinced them that their ideas were truly valued, the parents participated very actively in the discussions. They were able to meet for longer periods of time than the teachers, which afforded the parents more time for questions. Their responses were characteristically more in-depth and more probing. Because they brought a different cultural conception of school-parent interaction, Sr. Chavez took longer to complete the program exploring phase with the parents' group. The Hispanic parents maintained a close interest in the language policymaking activities throughout the program exploring phase, and during the deliberations of the Steering Committee in the consensus building phase. Alliances were formed between the parents on the Steering Committee and the Hispanic community, where few had existed before. These social networks grew out of the parents' desire to maintain access to the information and the progress of the policy development. Sr. Chavez was instrumental in building the basic structure of the networks through his position as the liaison for the school.

In the parent sessions, three strong voices emerged who eventually became the parent representatives on the Steering Committee. Sra. Gonzalez had been an elementary teacher in Mexico and was quickly engaged in the process. She was able to provide examples from her own experiences that helped parents examine the three bilingual models that were being discussed. Her history as a teacher in Mexico and her position as a parent of young students at the elementary wing afforded her much respect within the predominantly male group. She spoke convincingly about parent involvement and advocated for a bilingual education that would ensure their children's academic success and social inclusion. Sr. Garcia spoke thoughtfully but quietly and provided another strong voice. He actively participated in the discussions, often bringing divided opinions together to form a united stance. Because of his background as a successful businessman in Mexico, he had skills and strategies for reaching consensus during negotiations. The third member to represent the parents on the Steering Committee was chosen because of his ability to succinctly focus the point of a discussion. Sr. Diaz did not speak often during the discussions, choosing instead to listen to the other parents as they posed questions and made statements, but throughout, if the argument wandered, he would refocus the discussion by concisely stating the point.

The Hispanic students met initially on a Saturday morning with Sr. Chavez to hear about the proposed language policy. Nearly 40 students attended that first informational meeting, consitituting about one-third of the Hispanic students in the junior/senior high. Sr. Chavez chose to invite only the older students, based on his perception that the younger students would not be able to understand the issues. The students were excited to learn that their concerns about their education were finally going to be addressed. The first portion of the meeting brought forth many negative statements about the school, the teachers, and the Euro-American students. Sr. Chavez allowed the students to vent their frustrations about their academic and social difficulties. Once those comments began to subside, he discussed the proposed language policy development process and the activities in which they were invited to participate. The students were more skeptical than the parents that they would be given a voice in developing such a document. Still, they listened to what he had to say, asked relevant questions, and offered their ideas and opinions. Sr. Chavez concentrated on the students' statements of principles and beliefs about bilingual education as they presently lived it. At the end of their first session, the students chose three peers to represent them on the Steering Committee. These three met twice more with Sr. Chavez to further discuss the three models, and to delineate their principles and beliefs. The large group of students did not meet further after that initial meeting. Many reported that they could not take the additional time away from their studies, that they had family responsibilities on the weekend, and that they believed that their representatives would communicate with them.

The three students chosen as representatives had differing backgrounds and experiences with education in the United States. Srta. Garcia was a junior in high school who had moved to Clayton as a sophomore. Although her facility with English was adequate for social conversations, she preferred Spanish for more complex subjects. Her grades were outstanding in Mexico, but she was not achieving very well in her new high school. She was chosen as one of the representatives to the Steering Committee because of her leadership abilities among the students. She was regarded as a serious student, someone who knew much about the bilingual program and the school, and one who would advocate for the students.

A second student, Srta. Gutierrez, volunteered to participate because of her interest in the policy-development process. She had a good command of oral and written English and Spanish, was a senior in the high school, and was one of the few American citizens among the Hispanic students. She felt strongly about the democratic ideal of student participation in the drafting of a language policy document for a diverse school district. Her experiences as a student in California were the experiential basis for her support of bilingual education.

The third student, Sr. Ramirez, was a sophomore in his first year in Clayton. He had attended a private school in Mexico, where he received a solid academic background. His command of English in social and academic situations was very limited. He was excited about the prospect of developing a policy that would ensure his and other students' access to the curriculum of the high school, and that would attempt to ameliorate the difficulties he and others were experiencing in the school.

With the program exploring phase completed, the Steering Committee took up the next step in the development of the language policy: consensus building. I facilitated the sessions by providing the necessary materials, updating documents from previous sessions, and keeping the task group focused on the objectives of policy making. It was the responsibility of the nine members to articulate their constituents' ideas, and to build consensus with their colleagues on the Steering Committee. This committee was composed of three teachers, three Hispanic parents, and three Hispanic students. Each was to have an equal voice in the meetings, and each was to respectfully discuss the perspectives of others, in addition to the designated members. Principal Karnesky attended these sessions. His main role was to act as an advisor for legal issues and to indicate when the proposed policy would comply or interfere with state and district policies already in place. He also wanted to stay current with developments because he was interested in the policy.

The initial meeting of the Consensus Building phase sketched the general procedures for reaching a final document. In general, the process was to combine statements generated by each of the three groups into one document representative of the ideas for bilingual education program in Clayton. Each of the three groups contributed their statements of principles and beliefs. The teachers submitted 16, the parents submitted 24, and the students submitted 10. Individually, they read the group of statements through once, then began asking questions. At that meeting, initial statements were translated into both languages. The process was slow because of the need for translations of comments—only two members of the Steering Committee were bilingual/biliterate. Moreover, the process of clarifying the precise meaning and intent of the statements required considerable discussion.

The next task was to generate a document that listed all of the statements in both languages. I reviewed the group of statements, then developed 14 general categories based on the topics presented. One wall in the bilingual education office was given over to a long strip of butcher paper that contained the 14 categories. At the next meeting, each member received a copy of the dual language document with instructions to independently place each statement into one of the categories. There was some discussion among the members about the meaning of certain statements, but for the most part each member made her/his own decisions about where to post each statement. Once this was completed, I collated the statements in each category, then prepared a new document listing the 14 categories, and the statements in each one, in both languages.

This next activity involved refining the statements and the language of each— that is, building consensus about the intent, the meaning, and the application of the language policy. The language differences presented significant challenges. At almost every turn, vocabulary and cultural constructs differed, yet needed to be mutually understood. The language of the document represented the intersection of the two sociocultural groups. It had to be correct—such that the intent of the document was agreed to and understood by both groups. To that end, the topics of the statements were reviewed and determinations were made as to the appropriateness and applicability of a statement to the Clayton context.

The final document contained 10 interrelated categories originating from the work in the program exploring phase: academic programs, cultural relations, language in the social context, implementation, after-school activities, programs for parents, faculty development, content of instructional materials, pedagogy, assessment, and placement. It should be noted that the listing here in no way implies or affirms priority of importance: it was simply the way they evolved. There were 52 statements. What was projected to take one month to accomplish instead involved six sessions conducted over a two-and-a-half-month period. The committee did not lose sight of the goal: a policy that teachers, parents, and students could agree to, for the most part, and that they could refer to for developing instructional programs and pedagogies for bilingual education at their schools.

When the Steering Committee finished their work, the document was sent to the teachers, the parents, the students, the principals, and the superintendent for their review and responses. Meetings were held formally and informally throughout the district to discuss the document. An immediate furor arose over the title, "Language Policy and Instructional Practices: Statements of Principles and Beliefs." Beyond those who served on the Steering Committee, the teachers did not want the document to be a "policy" that would direct how and what they would teach. The administrators did not want the document to convey any directives such as a policy would, preferring that it serve only in an advisory capacity to the school district. Yet the parents wanted the term policy because they felt it would ensure that their children would receive the academic and social support they desperately needed. The students concurred with the parents' position because they felt that the term policy carried more authority than any other term.

This basic difference in the use/nonuse of the term policy indicated the underlying beliefs of the two groups (Anglos and Hispanics; educators and educational clients). For most of the teachers and administrators, the term policy conveyed a sense of "have to." In several instances, teachers could not articulate any other response toward the document because they were so focused on that one term. In many instances, the teachers did not want to accept any part of the document because they did not believe that it was necessary to have such a document, let alone a policy that broached the language of instruction issue.

The term policy meant something different for the Hispanic parents and students. They wanted assurances that there would be regard for their heritage language, but at the same time that Spanish would not act as a barrier to their academic success. That is, they believed that the Spanish language carried traditions, beliefs, and values that they wanted to maintain. Simultaneously, they acknowledged that it was imperative for their children to learn English in order to succeed in school. Parents saw how their own Spanish monolingualism presented difficulties for their interactions with the school and for helping their children with schoolwork. For the students, English only without the support of Spanish meant that they would encounter barriers to information which would adversely affect their access to content knowledge. The parents and students believed that a policy that bound teachers and administrators to certain actions and instructional practices would work to dismantle the sociocultural and linguistic boundaries that limited their learning and that defined them as marginal. Together, they believed that the proposed policy would serve these ends.

In the formal meetings held throughout the district, two of the principals attempted to disavow the language policy. They perceived the process as squandered time which addressed two nonissues: language of instruction and social inclusion. They believed that if teachers would just be considerate of the newcomers, then all would be well. The elementary school principal's responses showed that his awareness of the policy's development was quite vague, even though he participated in the initial planning of the process. One result of his noninvolvement was that in the elementary wing, the teachers remained divided between advocates for bilingual education and advocates for an English only program.

During the review process in meetings with the principals and the superintendent together, there was strong opposition to the use of the term policy in the title and anywhere else in the document. The superintendent reported that the Policy and Procedures Committee of the School Board was also opposed to the use of the word policy. That committee took issue with the strength of the language contained in the document. In one particular session, the superintendent and two of the principals voiced strong opinions that terms such as "will," "must," and "shall" needed to be tempered and changed to less binding words such as "could," "can," and "should"—in order to fit with their beliefs that the document should carry advisory status only. As the superintendent put it, the words needed to be "softened."

Input was received from many individuals and groups over a two-week period in which any person could respond. Replies ranged from formally written pages to casual comments made by individuals. The teachers' responses were almost always typewritten, and usually represented a group rather than an individual opinion. Their responses typically began with what they did not like or agree with in the document, and concluded with a statement about one or two points they thought to be acceptable. The parents and the students mostly voiced their opinions orally in social contexts. They agreed with the statements in the document, and they continued to express some skepticism that it would be ratified. The parent liaison was pessimistic about the chances of the document being approved by the School Board. He had held this belief since the beginning of the process. However, he moderated his view when he saw that the proposed changes were only in the degree of forcefulness of the words, and not in the topic or content of the statements.

The final version of the policy was ratified by the Clayton School Board in July 2000. It was titled, "Language Learning and Instructional Practices: Statements of Principles and Beliefs" and was a seven-page, dual-language document. The document initially conceived in August 1999 and sent out for review and response in March 2000 was put into practice in September 2000. I cannot assess its impact here, because this chapter was completed that same month.

CONCLUSION

The environment in which teachers work is becoming increasingly diverse. Language issues and instructional practices for language minority populations will continue as contested areas and will continue to spawn policy making. The schools in Clayton are a clear example of a community undergoing change and of the political turmoil surrounding language issues and instructional paradigms. How schools respond to these shifting linguistic, political, and instructional issues, and to changing demographics, is critical to the development of our schools as effective learning communities for all children.

I have analyzed the Clayton schools as an institution engaged in the ongoing process of organizing itself into new structures to accommodate changing demographics (Shore and Wright, 1997). I have used ethnographic methods to disclose "the lived experience of people in everyday life" as they went about their tasks of policy making (Levinson and Sutton, 2001, 5). In Clayton, Hispanic students and parents succeeded in being not just "objects of policy" (Foucault, 1977), but in being cocreators of it as well—at least officially. Whether this progressive change in policy formulation is accompanied by a turnabout in how the policy is actually practiced remains to be seen.

This work has illustrated how language policy influences the acculturation and the socialization of Hispanic children. As the children were socialized through talk in the schools, they experienced discontinuities, and attempted to resolve those to achieve a fit with their notions of self in their new sociocultural context. The children were caught between efforts to maintain their heritage and their language, their need to express their evolving identities, their need to learn English, and the belief systems of the teachers. Few of the teachers and administrators worked to develop new socialization contexts that would assist the students to succeed in the school and in the community, though the Statement of Principles and Beliefs directly confronted this disposition. According to Ruiz (1981), teachers can either acknowledge language as a difference and as a problem, thereby erecting barriers to the language minority students, or they can delimit the obstacles through their own efforts to bridge the boundaries of language differences, recognizing language as a resource.

Many Clayton teachers' resistance to dealing with language differences severely affected many of the Hispanic students. Before the adoption of the statement, only in the pre-K–K buildings were there substantial efforts to ameliorate the differences. Moreover, the unsuccessful actions of the first two bilingual coordinators exacerbated the isolation of the Hispanic students and limited their engagement with the curricula. The separation went beyond just the regular classrooms—it was evident in the lunchroom, where the Hispanic and the Euro-American students gathered in separate groups, and in the fact that many monolingual Spanish speakers never left the self-contained homogenous ESL classroom. Prior to the creation of the statement, the unofficial policies and programs were unable to address the social and academic needs of the Hispanic students.

In the process of policymaking in Clayton CUSD, educators approached the process of reform from varying perspectives—some from a position of openness to new ideas, and some from an adherence to their beliefs in "one country, one language." Those who were receptive to new pedagogical approaches were regarded as "progressive" by some colleagues and administrators. Those who were resistant to the changes were characterized as "traditional" teachers, teachers unwilling to alter their instructional practices to accommodate the diversity in their classrooms. The reform efforts illuminated the belief systems of the teachers, highlighting their differences. A fundamental part of the policy making unveiled the different philosophies toward bilingual education, thereby indicating the possibilities and limits for policy implementation once developed.

In reform efforts by schools, especially those with rapidly diversifying demographics, the challenge is to involve as many groups as possible in the change process so as to reduce marginalizing stakeholders (Burnaby, 1996; Freeman, 2000; Genesee, 1994). When instructional program decisions are approached through a paradigm of informed, shared responsibilities, they have a greater chance of support by students, parents, teachers, and administrators. Furthermore, when the resulting instructional practices are supported by grounded research, students and teachers can experience a greater degree of achievement. Clayton's efforts to engage both teachers and administrators in the program design were, in some instances, highly successful. The teachers in the program exploring phase gained expertise about instructional programs for language minority students. Furthermore, the inclusion of Hispanics as equal voices in policy development was deemed extraordinary by many of the participants, and this generated a whole new dynamic of sociopolitical inclusion. On the other hand, formal policymaking activities were not fully successful, as many teachers and administrators refused to afford the statement policy status.

In the final analysis, an innovative language policy, formulated locally and specifically for the Clayton School District's unique situation, was established through a process that included the perspectives of teachers, Hispanic parents, and Hispanic students. The emergent document was grounded in the beliefs and the perspectives of these disparate stakeholders. The redesign of the bilingual program was not left to "recognized experts" recommending top-down policies from afar (Freeman, 1998). The teachers, administrators, parents, and students who participated in the policy development shared responsibility for it, but not in the typical hierarchical or provider-client relationships that usually characterize educational policymaking. This small, rural school district offers a glimpse at what can be possible. Yet that glimpse was of the prospective, not the realized. The process of responding effectively to Clayton's small segment of the students and parents in the New Latino Diaspora was often but not always encouraging. The work of following through on the statement's promise lies ahead.

Of the 19 elementary and 39 junior/senior high teachers at the close of the 1999–2000 school year, 23 were not there to open school in August 2000. Most left the district for work in other schools. One of the 23 was a bilingual teacher in the elementary wing. One principal retired, and one took another position out of state. The school district has an opportunity for a new beginning, with 21 new teachers, two new principals, and a new document to guide the education of the growing number of ELL students who continue to come with their families to this midwestern community. Of course, with so many new teachers who played no role in the drafting of the statement of Principles and Beliefs, and with that document's role as "requiring" versus "advising" not yet clear, the prospect of improved Hispanic education in Clayton is real, but not yet a foregone conclusion.

NOTES

1. Clayton is a pseudonym, as are all the names of teachers and administrators referred to later in this chapter.

2. In the community and schools studied, the terms "migrant" and "Mexican" were used interchangeably by almost all non-Hispanics when referring to Hispanic newcomers. The majority of newcomer families were immigrants from Mexico, whereas other Hispanic families had migrated from elsewhere in the United States. There was a continual arrival and departure of Hispanic immigrants and "in-migrants." When I use the term "migrant" in the text, I am referring to agricultural endeavors or to the specific Title I Migrant Education program for which many Hispanic students in Clayton were eligible.

REFERENCES

Burnaby, B. 1996. "Aboriginal Language Maintenance, Development, and Enhancement: A Review of the Literature." In *Stabilizing Indigenous Languages. 3rd.* G. Cantoni, ed. *Annual Symposium on Stabilizing Indigenous Languages.* Flagstaff: Northern Arizona University, Center for Excellence in Education.

Foucault, M. 1977. *Discipline and Punish.* Harmondsworth: Penguin.

Freeman, R. 1998. *Bilingual Education and Social Change.* Philadelphia: Multilingual Matters.

———. 2000. "Contextual Challenges to Dual-Language Education: A Case Study of a Developing Middle School Program." *Anthropology and Education Quarterly.* 31(2):202–229.

Genesee, F., ed. 1994. *Educating Second Language Children: The Whole Child, the Whole Curriculum, the Whole Community.* Cambridge: Cambridge University Press.

Hornberger, N. 1997. "Language Policy, Language Education, and Language Rights: Indigenous, Immigrant, and International Perspectives." *Working Papers in Educational Linguistics.* 13(2):1–22.

Jimenez, R.T., G.E. Garcia, and E.P. Pearson. 1996. "The Reading Strategies of Bilingual Latina/o Students Who Are Successful English Readers: Opportunities and Obstacles." *Reading Research Quarterly.* 31:90–112.

Levinson, B. and Sutton, M. 2001. "Policy as/in Practice: Developing a Sociocultural Approach to the Study of Educational Policy." In *Policy as Practice: Toward a Comparative Sociocultural Analysis of Educational Policy.* M. Sutton and B. Levinson, eds. Pp. 1–37. Westport, CT: Ablex Press.

Peshkin, A. 1994[1978]. *Growing Up American : Schooling and the Survival of Community.* Prospect Heights, IL: Waveland Press.

Rosaldo, R. 1989. *Culture and Truth.* Boston: Beacon Press.

Ruiz, R. 1981. "World View Studies: A Synthetic Review and Appraisal." Unpublished manuscript. The University of Arizona.

Shore, C. and S. Wright. 1997. "Policy: A New Field of Anthropology." In *Anthropology of Policy.* C. Shore and S. Wright, eds. Pp. 3–39. New York: Routledge.

Sutton, M. and B. Levinson, eds. 2001. *Policy as Practice: Toward a Comparative Sociocultural Analysis of Educational Policy.* Westport, CT: Ablex Publishing.

10

How Does It Feel to Be a *Problem*?: "Disciplining" the Transnational Subject in the American South

Enrique G. Murillo Jr.

Latinos in Diaspora are changing the face of U.S. regions, cities, and towns, in response to the demands of a global economy. The American[1] South is no exception, particularly North Carolina, with a Latino population that has burgeoned 110 percent from 1990 to 1998, the most dramatic demographic shift among all the southern states (Census Bureau estimates, *Washington Post*, March 6, 2000).[2] The new global economy centrally involves the hypermobility of capital, plus deindustrialization, the emergence of new centers of finance and information industries, new regional economic specializations in cultural commodities (e.g., tourism), and the privatization and devolution of government programs to local levels. In terms of economic growth, the American South, including North Carolina, has been one of the regions benefiting most from these processes (Applebome, 1996).

Due to new technologies of production, communication, transport and changes in the markets of capital and labor, citizens of former "colonizers" (like the United States) have been forced to respond to increased diversity from reconfigurations in local economies and work forces (Lamphere, Stepick and Grenier, 1994). At the same time, there are increased popular anxieties about economic security and the allocation of public resources among contesting groups (Suárez-Orozco, 1998). Under these conditions, people in the South and elsewhere enact new "dramas" (Turner, 1974) about social division and entitlement to public goods (NCPS, 1997).

These dramas often claim that some groups or categories of persons are entitled, whereas others are not entitled either to participate in the debate over the distribution of goods to receive their "fair" share of them. These new dramas have partially shifted the focus on "racial problems" away from those groups most commonly "racialized" and toward examining whites as racial subjects themselves. In this light, this chapter paints a complex localized portrait of the cultural and demographic shifts that have accompanied economic restructuring and globalization in North Carolina.[3] In turn this will illuminate the "public sphere" context within which the educational policy-making accounts that appear in this chapter (and in this volume) occur. In short, I describe how demographic and cultural change challenges educational policy at the local level.

In the western section of Rodham County, concentrated in the small town of Sunder Crossings, significant demographic change took place in the 1990s.[4] Immigrants from Mexico, El Salvador, and Guatemala, tired of migration and the difficulties of farmwork, began moving to Sunder Crossings to work at year-round jobs offered by the chicken plants. The number of Latino poultry workers increased steadily as relatives of workers and other Latinos began moving to the area when they learned there was work available.

In 1997, Latino workers comprised an estimated 43 percent of the workforce at the two local poultry plants, which together employ more than 500 workers.[5] However, as many previous researchers have argued, we must not identify the arrival of immigrant workers as the precipitating factor. Instead, it is the processes of national and global restructuring that have transformed occupational structures and that encourage and sustain immigration (Hondagneu-Sotelo, 1997, cites Cornelius, 1986). In this light, this chapter moves beyond the large literature that researches the effects of immigrant workers on the labor market to consider how the arrival of year-round residents in the new Latino diaspora has influenced the public sphere construction of newcomers and long-term residents, and their respective socially constructed rights to various social services and supports.

In Sunder Crossings, the settlement and/or intermediate relocation of entire families has placed particular unforeseen stresses on the social services, housing, legal, health, and educational facilities of the town. The local poultry plants have actively recruited and lured workers, but the local infrastructure has not kept up with the growth.[6] There has been a lack of affordable housing and crowded, unhealthy living conditions. There has been a high incidence of tuberculosis, occupational injuries, and illnesses, and a lack of appropriate instruction in local schools for the children of the new laborers. In the face of these inadequacies, nonetheless, the strength of the local economy has been due in part to the contributions of the Latino immigrant community, both because their labor has proved profitable and because their patronage of local businesses has returned much of their incomes to the local economy. However, locals' frustrations over the corporate "externalization of indirect costs" (Hackenberg, 1995, 238)—when the chicken plants do not pay for the social services that their new employees need—has been directed at the Latino newcomers rather than at the employers.

SOCIAL CODING, THE FIXATION OF RACE, AND POLICY FORMATION

At the beginning of this new century, with massive reconfigurations in the structure of the economy, with the devolution of social programs and retreat from Civil Rights, racialized inequalities have shifted, if not worsened. In Sunder Crossings they have found a new target. Economic restructuring has been accompanied by cultural and demographic shifts, including the knowledge that in many cities and states whites will soon become minority populations, and these have brought about new discourses and practices of fear and exclusion. Despite some public rhetoric of equality and inclusion, Latinos are often regarded as "problems."[7] Furthermore, these symbolic judgments have often been worked into potentially viable forms of policy and practice. In Sunder Crossings this leads to public construction of what Latinos need and deserve, to restrictive types of "remedies," and to inadequate resource allocation, all of which together reproduce the local subordination of Latinos.

Even though there is a long history of racial discomfort and injustice in the United States, we are presently witnessing a broad deterioration of support for racial equality. This is not to say that race is independent of social class in the production of inequality. Rather, certain economic patterns reinforce race-linked structures of exclusion and displacement. Race often organizes local labor and local politics, and the process of uneven development has contributed to making these differences a durable diversity. The most dangerous, difficult occupations, typically those of low status, are commonly associated with members of an ethnic identity. In Sunder Crossings, like countless other communities in the South impacted by Latino immigrants (e.g., Gainesville, Georgia [Griffith, 1995]), certain low prestige and hazardous jobs become "Mexican-typed jobs" (Tienda, 1989; Hamann, 1999). Sunder Crossings' workplace segmentation extended beyond the work site to the community social spaces.

Despite the unilateral declaration of "A New World Order" and neoconservative claims to "color-blindness," race is not an illusion nor a vestige of the past. On the contrary, there is no indication that race is of fading sociopolitical importance. "In a range of manifestations wider and wilder than the most fertile imaginations could have dreamed up, race continues to operate as a fundamental factor in political and cultural life" (Winant, 1994, 1). The corrosive effects of continuing ideologies of white superiority and nativism hold local democracies hostage. Since its inception, the United States has embodied this fundamental contradiction. It has claimed to support inclusion, equal opportunity, and justice for all, yet simultaneously has excluded certain groups and individuals perceived to be different from the dominant Anglo American population.[8] In North Carolina, this history of racial exclusion still bears bitter fruit. The moral imperatives of the Civil Rights movement have gradually passed out of sight, and many of the laws designed to remedy racial inequality have been undermined. Legal claims of objectivity, meritocracy, and neutrality have obscured, but not blunted, the self-interest of more powerful sectors of society.

Public anxiety due to perceived and/or actual downward social mobility and displacement is increasing nationally, particularly within the context of deindustrialization and the hypermobility of capital. Wealth has been sharply redistributed, even within sectors of the white middle class. "Facing the prospect of not being able to replicate the privileged circumstances of their parents, the baby boomer generation of frustrated and 'angry white males' are struggling to shore up their eroding position" (Harrison, 1998, 16). Through ethnocentric judgements and practices, nonwhite persons and groups are reduced to physical traits believed to characterize a "race," such as skin color or the amount and texture of hair, or reduced to cultural behavior like language. Scapegoating, too, continues to increase in the form of "racialized" ideologies of welfare parasitism, affirmative action as reverse discrimination, immigrant encroachment, and intelligence as a fixed genetic reality. These discourses all have contributed to the deteriorating treatment and material conditions of newcomer Latinos in places such as Sunder Crossings.[9]

Perea (1996, 3) argues that there are two insights that help us understand the history and status of race in the United States. The first is the theory of "Interest Convergence" by Bell (1980). Simply put, this theory states that the interest in achieving racial equality by racial minorities will only be accommodated when it converges with the interests of whites. The second insight is that a major motivation for the proposal and enactment of Civil Rights was the American embarrassment at the mistreatment of its minorities and the Soviet advertisement of those mistreatments during the Cold War. In the absence of Cold War competition, one moral imperative for whites to promote racial equality is gone.

These insights may partially explain the deteriorating concern for racial equality. I do not, however, consider the end of the Cold War and the fading away of the civil rights movement as the only factors. Rather, I claim that today's power structure not only descends directly from historical colonialism, but also that corporate interests reap large profits by giving rise to new scenarios of threat and vulnerability.

Winant's notion of contemporary racial projects helps explain both the processes that reproduce inequality and division, and the processes, interests, and languages of policy formation, which play a central role in that reproduction. "A racial project is simultaneously an interpretation, representation, or explanation of racial dynamics and an effort to organize and distribute resources along particular racial lines" (Winant, 1994, 24). He goes on to explain, "Each racial project is therefore both a discursive and a cultural initiative, an attempt at racial signification and identity formation on the one hand, and a social structural initiative, an attempt at political mobilization and resource redistribution, on the other" (1994, 24). Winant suggests that there are five main racial projects in practice in the United States: far right, new right, neoconservatism, pragmatic liberalism, and radical democracy. Based upon their understandings of race and difference, these racial projects are then aligned with a particular political/pragmatic agenda, which suggests how resources should be distributed and the role that the state should play in this process. All five racial projects had local manifestations in Sunder Crossings, but far right and new right projects were the most visible in whites' racial categorization and in their de facto policy formation.

In Sunder Crossings, various racialized social and economic processes both sustain and, less often, counter Winant's racial projects. For example, "Southern Culture" influences the development of these projects. David Goldfield (1990) describes southern etiquette as a kind of veneer through which racism is allowed to continue, as it encourages acts and appearances of kindness in the face of injustice. Given the addition of a "third race" to a historically biracial southern community, do newcomer Latinos face instances when southern etiquette is at moments suspended, so as to initially enforce the structures of exclusion and displacement? The history of physical violence directed at African Americans in the South reminds us that breaches in etiquette would not be unprecedented. Are the old race-relation conventions perhaps made to fit new demographic configurations, as practices and beliefs of exclusion become legitimized through policy?

The final element at work in racial projects is white privilege. "Studies of whiteness are demonstrating that whites benefit from a host of apparently neutral social arrangements and institutional operations, all of which seem to whites at least to have no racial bias" (Hartigan, 1997, 496). Along with patterns of "racial etiquette," white privilege feeds a social and economic order established centuries ago. Ironically, focusing on "racial problems" gives attention only to racialized groups, obscuring the invisible systems of dominance of whites.

It is crucial to our understanding of education, policy, and the politics of identity in the Latino Diaspora that we partially shift the focus away from Latinos ourselves/themselves, to examine whites as racial subjects. Too often, "race" is equated with subordinate groups. As we step into this new millennium, notions of nationhood, citizenship, and membership/allegiance in a national community have continued to be brought into question. This chapter and several of the others in this volume analyze racial categorizations, while recognizing whiteness as a power relation that accords socioeconomic and cultural privileges.

As larger discourses get appropriated on the local level, of particular importance is the connection of race to nationality, given the increased diversity and transnationalism in such places as Sunder Crossings. Following Williams (1989), attention must be paid to the conjunction of race-making and nation building, to the perception of "white" as the uncontested U.S. national identity. Much of my ethnographic data reveal an interplay between nationalism and racism, such that the national and racial identities of white citizens comprise the unmarked racial/national "Self." Likewise, my ethnographic data suggest popular notions of a rank-ordering of racial groups, in a hierarchy of "givers" or "takers." These orderings facilitate the views of dominating groups as the most deserving of opportunities and resources. One white Sunder Crossings resident described a dominant local understanding of Latinos: "Many people don't like them [Latinos] because of that. They think that although they're working . . . all the while they're really taking from the government without paying or contributing anything. It seems that they just want people to work without opening their mouths, without problems, without enrolling their children in school. . . . I don't know. But yes, they just want the labor, but without helping them in any form or other, without any due benefits." This belief system has become a vehicle of cultural domination whereby whites fit the prototype of "the good citizen." This implicity supports white privilege and generates social behavior (like educational policymaking), whereby those who are not construed as good citizens are viewed as unentitled or less-deserving.

Of course, given the multiracial complexities of Sunder Crossings, white/nonwhite may not always be the most relevant distinction. Jane Gibson (1996) argues that poor whites are racially denigrated in the context of the historically specific social, political, and economic processes that pauperize them. A secondary thesis, important here, is that racial denigration of poor whites intensifies those poor whites' own racism. Poor whites simultaneously fear displacement and articulate an overt racism in order to assert higher status than society seems willing to offer.

Higher status whites gain from white working-class articulations of racism, without having to appear racist themselves (Hamann, 1999). In fact, higher status whites' superficially gracious offer of low-wage jobs to newcomer immigrants is deceptive in its apparent nonracism. White corporate leaders, far from being benevolent and generous in their welcoming gesture, are gaining profit from the expanded labor supply and the successful manipulation of interethnic/interracial tensions within the labor pool. The poultry industry's engagement in ever more comprehensive patterns of labor control is not only accomplished with immigrant labor, but, as Griffith (1995) has pointed out, "the mere presence of immigrant workers in plants serves as an incentive to native workers to submit to the terms of plant-production regimes" (133). A "welcoming" gesture to immigrant laborers that simultaneously constructs poor whites as lower status than Latino newcomers is threatening to working-class whites. The latter then articulate the overtly racist anti-immigration script (Suárez-Orozco, 1998).

In this context, we are seeing regressive educational policy in the new Latino Diaspora, as (typically white) policymakers construct Latinos as less deserving of resources. Further, Latino newcomers are expected to either fully and successfully assimilate into white middle-class culture, or they are blamed for failing or resisting these efforts. In studying this process, we must take into account the "unofficial and occasionally spontaneous normative guidelines developed in diverse social spaces" as well as formal policy (Levinson and Sutton, 2001).

Newcomer students and their families in Sunder Crossings encounter a barrage of confusing and often improvised public policies, many with unintended consequences. Local policy is enacted and created with respect to a socially constructed, hierarchical, insider/outsider binary system. The ways of thinking about and unequally treating Latino students are routinized through institutional policies and practices, and these are seen as "common sense" and "normal" and are thus not open to interrogation.[10]

With regressive educational practices that bar or impede needed educational curricula (e.g., bilingual education or the acknowledgment of newcomers' existing knowledge), Latino Diaspora students get lost, pushed out, and/or subordinated, internalizing those social messages that degrade the language and diversity they bring to the classroom. Under these conditions, the tragic perspective of Guadalupe, a smart young 11-year-old girl, is not difficult to understand. At a special tutoring program one afternoon, she ran up to Miss Betty and apologized "I'm sorry I'm so stupid 'cause I speak Spanish." She really believed it too! Stories like this have led me to the question: "How does it feel to be a *problem?*"

A NEW MULTIRACIAL TOWN

> "Either you get your public officials to get the INS[11] in here and get these illegal immigrants out or you'll lose your homes, you'll lose your schools, you'll lose your way of life."
> —Former KKK grand wizard David Duke speaking on the steps of Sunder Crossings city hall to a crowd of 400 anti-immigration protesters

> "We all come with one single purpose, to work. There are many people from Oaxaca, Michoacán, and Veracruz. This town is very small and there is nowhere to go and have fun, or because we don't know where to go, or don't know English well enough."
> —Mexicana store clerk

The "public sphere" is a site where persons come together to engage in discourse of public concerns (Habermas, 1989). Stimulated by Habermas, as well as several prominent scholars such as Calhoun (1992) and Fraser (1992), there is a building literature on the concept of the public sphere. However, "relatively little ethnographic research has been done to illuminate this aspect of social life" (Holland, Nonini, and Lutz, n.d.).

In order to do ethnographic research on the public sphere, as well as to document the localized effects of globalization in North Carolina, I lived as a full-time ethnographer in Rodham County for more than two years. This chapter portrays one small political and cultural dynamic that was studied as part of a larger collaborative research project that compared public spheres across five North Carolina communities undergoing economic restructuring.[12] The first tasks of that larger project were to collect rich descriptions of the local public spheres, and then to investigate the claims made about (and by) the social groups which best fit the image of "the public" whose interest should be served. The next goal was to trace the degree to which different groups were estranged from voting and other acts of citizenry and from involvement with local public institutions such as schools.

Education, policy, and identity are framed in this chapter in a broad political sense. The chapter describes the larger circuit of cultural production, including race, language, social class, and multiple categories of demographic diversity (Bailyn, 1960), and does not restrict its discussion to just schooling. Further, as a Chicano/Mexicano myself, I focus particularly on how social barriers and the local political economy constrain Latinos' educational access, opportunity, and achievement.

In Sunder Crossings, North Carolina, Mexicano/Latino laborers and their children have been socially constructed by many established residents in the town as "foreign aliens" unentitled to public services, and as disorganized, dirty, and chaotic. I observed scapegoating and other anti-immigrant activity that paralleled that of previous eras, such as that of the Great Depression.[13] Sunder Crossings is characteristic of many small towns throughout the American South, where one can already see the reconstitution of a new "Other." The categorizations of Latinos in the South have reinscribed similar racialized relationships and identities as those long encountered by African Americans. Using the case of Sunder Crossings for illustration, I ask the same question Du Bois did about African Americans: "How does it feel to be a *problem*?" What does it mean to find yourself thousands of miles away from your "home" in Mexico or Central America, among a town of people, most of whom do not regard you as neighbor or even a complete human being?[14] What does it mean to be denied a stake in local democracy, institutions, and governmental policy?

In the small town of Sunder Crossings, the significant changes in racial composition that have taken place have made it a multiracial town. Latino immigrant laborers have filled the local need for unskilled labor. The transformation of occupational structures in the poultry-processing industry has shifted the employment pattern of Latino newcomers from one where male migrant laborers were recruited to work in seasonal and contracted farm labor, to a pattern of permanent and semipermanent settlement by families with year-round employment. This has changed the previous pattern of single-male migration and return. As the 1990s ended, local social service agencies conservatively estimated that Latinos constituted 38% of the population, whereas other estimates put the Latino population at 50% of the town. Many of the transnational Latino *polleros* (poultry workers) were from extremely rural backgrounds. Some had already been living in the United States and have moved to Sunder Crossings from states such as California, Florida, or Texas.

Spanish-speaking laborers in Sunder Crossings, on average, have had less formal schooling and a lower income than the local population. For the most part, they have settled in segregated, historically African American neighborhoods, mostly in rental housing. They have taken on the most difficult, tiring, and hazardous jobs, many with gratitude and even enthusiasm. Latino immigrant laborers' presence can be directly linked to the market forces of the county's economic restructuring. Not since the colonial period and the days of slavery have the "locals" in Rodham County had to deal with any increased demographic diversity due to workforce reconfiguration. In a matter of a short decade, what was basically an "old-time" and "sleepy" biracial southern community has become a globally competitive manufacturing-based town with multiracial residents and continuing acrimony about the place of Latino newcomers.

A plurality of North Carolinians have not approved of Latinos coming into the state. Of 700 adults surveyed (Institute of Research in Social Sciences, 1997), 42 percent disliked the influx of Latinos into the state (1/3 approved, 1/5 were unsure). When asked how their neighbors would feel if Latinos moved into their neighborhood, 54 percent thought people who lived near them would disapprove. Whites in the survey were more likely to say that their neighbors would disapprove. This unease is vague, however. Many North Carolinians have no clear idea of who Latinos are. In the face of this uncertainty there has been a tendency to "racialize" this new group. Most often, the local immigrants have been labeled under the census term of "Hispanic," but in Sunder Crossings, the immigrants have not been any one ethnic group at all, but a mishmash of many different groups, the majority comprised of Mexicans. The label "Hispanic" has obscured the diverse ancestries and range of countries of origin, and has also cloaked profound differences within national origin groups (e.g., differences between Mexican nationals from urban versus rural backgrounds). Agency workers and formal policy makers have been among those with the greatest tendency to conceive of Latinos in unitary terms, rather than in a way that is sensitive to Latin American cultural heterogeneity (Noblit et al., 1995).

In absolute numbers, Latinos and African Americans in Sunder Crossings made up the demographic majority by the end of the research period, yet formal local policymaking power was retained in the hands of the European American minority.[15] Unique racial pressures have grown as the presence of Spanish-speaking immigrant families has added to the ongoing black-white racial tensions. Established residents commonly expressed concern over communicating rules and regulations to newcomer immigrants, and the intermingling of cultural views was impeded by language differences.

Previous research suggests that dominant groups will react negatively if they perceive their share of resources, opportunities, and status jeopardized by those considered to be subordinates. Beck's (1998) study of Ku Klux Klan activity across the South found a significant correlation between KKK activity and the presence of Latino immigrant newcomers. Intriguingly, Beck found no correlation between rates of KKK activity and local percentages of African Americans. Moreover, supremacist activity was less frequent in counties where the portion of aggregate income of blacks and Latinos was growing, meaning perhaps that white supremacists were attracted to areas where subordinate groups were gaining symbolic power rather than wealth.[16] As Beck (4) suggests, the argument is not that white supremacists have given up their disparaging attitudes toward African Americans, but rather that they have expanded their inventory. The antiblack rhetoric and activities are long-standing, while the anti-immigrant and anti-Latino discourses have new appeal in those social spaces where the arrival of Latino immigrants has gained visibility. These trends all strengthen the claim that Sunder Crossings Latinos' experiences of racism and hostility may be typical for the Latino Diaspora across the South.

Not all established residents reacted with racism. Many established residents in Sunder Crossings, via churches and community groups, have responded to the dramatic changes by inviting and recruiting newcomers to join their established local social networks, sponsoring their proposed assimilation into local society. This was commonly referred to as "learning the ropes." A smaller but less paternalistic group of politicized residents, via service agencies, advocacy work, and adult ESL courses, have welcomed and assisted newcomers with the more serious "survival skills" needed to adjust to difficult local conditions. The less tolerant, however, have engaged in discursive violence and/or often simply ignored the new presence. Town officials and policy makers have gone further yet, to "discipline" the Spanish-speaking immigrants through formal institutional and governmental means, forcing adherence to the societal norms of this small town.

In describing different white behaviors ranging from claims of welcome to vehement racism, we can use Suárez-Orozco's (1998) outline of the "proimmigration script" and the "anti-immigration script." The two scripts are apparently opposed "ideal types" that nonetheless need each other. The proimmigration script reaffirms the symbolic order, maintaining optimism by constructing immigrants as virtuous and hardworking. Indeed, it uses immigrants' very arrival as "proof" of the fairness and attractiveness of current conditions, thus becoming an argument for the socioeconomically stratified status quo and against substantive newcomer accommodation. The "anti-immigration script" expresses a sense of panic and rage over loss of control, and constructs immigrants as lacking and criminal. Note that neither script incorporates the voices of immigrants themselves.

In Sunder Crossings, established residents used these scripts, and other cultural ways of knowing, to construct beliefs and practices regarding immigration. Many who claimed to welcome the newcomers nonetheless tried to change them (using awkward presumptions of benevolence) and enjoyed the self-righteousness of not seeming overtly racist. The "cover" provided by the more obviously xenophobic articulators of the anti-immigration script allowed articulators of the proimmigration script to avoid scrutiny. It is the quiet and insidious proimmigration script, however, that most often becomes enshrined in educational and other formal policies, because the proimmigration script is favored by the socioeconomically better off who dominate the public sphere.

THE VIOLENT AND CHAOTIC OTHER

"There is trash all over the yards. We thought littering was against the law. Clothes all over bushes, trees, and walls, wherever they can throw them. Ducks, roosters, and chickens running wild [*sic*]. We deserve more respect than we are given, we were here trying to make our community a better place to live, long before the new arrivals. Our rights are being violated and the new arrivals are basically doing as they please with no restrictions when they infringe on our rights. Although the new arrivals work in our city, they do not pay city and county taxes."

—Petition to town board by local residents

"The Police harass you, they stop you just to see what's your business. And there are many people who don't like Latinos. You can tell when you go to the store, or when you eat at a restaurant. They stare at you, . . . like what's up, what are you doing here?"

—Transnational migrant laborer

Fieldwork revealed "commonsensical" notions shared by many local townspeople that Spanish-speaking immigrants were "by nature" violent and chaotic. In a September, 1995 edition of the local weekly, an article headlined "Statistics Show Latinos More Prone to Violence" appeared prominently. It portrayed

Spanish-speaking immigrants in Sunder Crossings as chaotic in behavior, and being more prone to violence and injury. Although it principally cited social and health "problems" (offering statistics as proof), the underlying assumption was that Latinos are violent. The opening section read: "Living to a ripe old age may not be a reality for Sunder Crossings Latinos (Hispanics). The North Carolina State Center for Health and Environmental statistics reports the top five causes of mortality for Latinos in N.C. are cardiovascular disease, motor vehicle accidents, homicide, non-vehicular accidents, and cancer." It is notable that three of the five causes were behavior-related, cementing the image that the Latino population engaged in more dangerous habits and practices than the population as a whole. The positive explanation that at least some of the injury and sickness was a product of hard work in dangerous environments was not conveyed by the article. Some local advocates picked up on the way the article was framed, and wrote letters-to-the-editor to protest the article's portrayal, but damage in creating a negative image for local readers had already been done.

On an early June morning in 1997, the local Sunder Crossings radio station broadcast as local news the rumor of a driveby threat on the last day of school, by purported gang members. Even though the rumor proved false, the radio station owner and announcer reported the incident as an example that the arrival of Latinos (conflated with gangs and drugs) now marked the end of their "very friendly city," which he laughingly called "Mayberry." He also spoke of the incident as a lost opportunity to call the Immigration and Naturalization Service and "find out who's here illegally." In his exaggerated descriptions, he warned the town folks that with the Spanish-speaking immigrants came all the "bad" from the big cities. He warned that it was coming like a freight train, and that locals had to decide whether to "get out of the way," or "get in the way" and "do something about it." A partial transcript of the news broadcast went as follows:

We had some rather tense moments, I guess you might say, here in [Sunder Crossings] yesterday. As rumors were going around, that there was going to be some kind of trouble on the last day of school. This incident has made both school and local law enforcement officials realize that additional training is needed now in the area of gang activity. Life in the Friendly Little City! You know, there's not much in the big city that we don't have here in Sunder Crossings. And I won't go into detail, but it's all here. So it's coming like a freight train. Are we going to get out of the way, or are we going to get in the way, or are we going to do something about it, or are we just going to sit back . . . uhhhh . . . put our heads in the sand? Well this is MAYBERRY! Nothing bad can ever happen here (laughter). So, a word to the wise is sufficient. However, I suspect we will sit back and do nothing. Not call in the Immigration Services to find out who's here illegally. Not declare WAR on the drugs coming into Sunder Crossings. Not declare WAR on the violence, the people who are getting beat up because they carry money. And other folks are beating up on them to get drugs, probably won't do a thing about any of this, and just let it get worse.

Months later, when the new school year began, the front-page headlines of the weekly read "Police Set Meeting on Gang Activity." The article that followed described the local police's efforts to stop the spread of gang activity and "save Smalltown U.S.A." from all the serious problems that came from "those (large) cities." A part of it read:

One of the downsides of living in a large city, north or south, is the presence of street gangs and their activity. From random acts of violence or vandalism to more serious offenses, they're a problem for police to deal with in those cities. It's enough to make you want to live in a small town like Sunder Crossings, where none of that stuff goes on, isn't it? Guess what. It's not just the big cities. It's here. Smalltown, USA. Right here. And local police say they want to stop its spread before it grows any larger. To that end, says detective Dan Stewart, the police need the community and have organized a public forum to talk about the issue. "Street gangs are here," Stewart says, "and more and more signs of them are popping up. People are starting to see things and ask questions—what are street gangs, who's in them, where do they come from? And the big one: Are they here?"

At the public forum on gangs, sponsored by the Sunder Crossings Police Department and the Community Concerned Citizens, Officer Stewart lectured the audience of more than 130 people that most of the gang culture had been seen where youth concentrate, like ball fields, schools and so forth. He gave anecdotal information like the use of football team colors for dress style and so forth. The officer, to his credit, did say he felt that people were wrong to make this out to be "a racial thing" (meaning genetically or biologically based). He said it was not so. Instead, he argued that it was "a cultural thing." With respect to gangs, he said, "For Hispanics it is very much a cultural thing! . . . Just like Martin Luther King is part of OUR culture, so are gangs part of THEIRS."[17] He added that gang membership was "not the kids' faults, but a function of where they come from."

He declared clearly, "These are NOT our kids!" and then promised "protective" action though anti-Latino racial profiling. In Sunder Crossings, the association of minority youth with violence was so strong that even trained police officers did not distinguish ethnic youth cultures from hard-core criminal activity. Further, if Martin Luther King Jr. was part of "OUR culture," then the asserted association with violence seemed more narrowly applied to only Latinos. That night in the auditorium, other dangerous comments were made, such as: "These kids come from bad environments," and "These children are victims and the product of bad parenting." Such comments indicated a self-righteous attitude. The perceptions and actions of whites trying to "defend" themselves from the possibility of harm, coupled with racist stereotypes and the fear they evoked, seemed credible to established white residents. From their vantage point of privilege, the startling inadequacy of their town's infrastructure was invisible, and they could easily imagine that (false) rumors of a driveby threat/scare on the last day of classes are believably true, and violent gangs likely. As Villenas (this volume) notes, the construction of Latino parents as "bad" parents also served as a social rationale for various educational treatments and nonaccommodations. Latino parent input into the child rearing of Latino youths was unwelcome; the Anglo community "knew" what was necessary.

THE LABOR IS WELCOMED, NOT THE ENTIRE HUMAN BEING

> "Earth's Most Endangered Species: THE WHITE RACE. Help Preserve It."
> —Bumper sticker on Rodham County road sign

> "Everything was fine at first, but when more and more of our people began to arrive . . . from Mexico . . . what was the first thing they did? They raised the rents! And the houses aren't even in good condition. And the poultry plants would pay good wages at first, but now they refuse to give raises and tell you there's a cap-limit to what you can earn."
> —Mexicano *pollero* (poultry worker)

Transnational labor migration is how local industries, particularly poultry, lumber, and textiles, have maintained their globally competitive edge. This is a trend across the South as a whole, as states like North Carolina maintain themselves as low-wage, industry-accommodating states.[18] Employers are among the few who have actually welcomed the new arrivals. This is because the arriving Latinos represent (1) a pool of unskilled and low-wage labor, filling a needed gap in the labor market; (2) individuals not organized under any labor union; and (3) workers enthusiastic for the opportunity to work, despite the harsh working conditions, particularly in poultry-processing, which has the most hazardous jobs in commercial agriculture. As Griffith (1995) has noted, the presence of immigrants in poultry plants "alters the labor-management relations in ways that continue to favor management, especially in light of network recruiting practices that allow plant personnel managers easy access to new Latino workers" (137).

Many economic studies have found that low-skilled immigrants take jobs that others don't want; their presence stimulates the economy and creates new jobs. Nonetheless, media emphasis on the presence and social costs of undocumented laborers facilitates the misperception that all Latinos are "illegal" (Sanchez, 1997) and fails to recognize for example that in 1990 Latinos paid over $29 billion in taxes.[19] Research has also demonstrated that immigrants do not take away more jobs than they actually create (Feagin, 1997, 31). Further, despite the fact that the average income of Mexican migrants has dropped during the decade of the 1990s,[20] Mexican migrants are less likely than poor Americans to receive welfare. Migration does benefit the migrants themselves, who gain access to meager but still better wages than those broadly available in Latin America. But American business people, farmers, and consumers also benefit.

A 1997 study by the U.S. Commission on Immigration Reform concluded that immigration in the short term can be a drag on taxpayers, but, over the long haul, immigrant families more than pay their own way. As a whole, the U.S. economy grows through employment and consumption generated by the migration. Nonetheless, in many particular communities "immigrants are most often in difficult jobs with low pay, poor conditions, and a few benefits—at the bottom of the labor force regardless of whether the local economy was growing or declining" (Lamphere, Stepick and Grenier, 1994, 19).

In poultry processing, occupational injuries such as respiratory illnesses, warts, rashes, cuts, and carpal tunnel syndrome are commonplace. Interviews with Latino *polleros* revealed that, when injured, many did not receive any compensation. Some claimed that many medical doctors worked in cahoots with the poultry companies. Some claimed they had to work extra unpaid hours to keep their jobs. Many said they had been threatened and often fired, both locally and elsewhere, for complaining about hazardous work conditions, particularly if they made an issue of any injuries. Through network recruiting, the utilization of newcomer immigrant labor, and underreporting of injuries, the industry has maintained high-line speeds and expanded the methods of labor control among poultry workers (Griffith, 1995, 145).

Immigrants are clearly the most insecure of all workers. With the poultry companies focusing strictly on the product, employment practices commodify and dehumanize the workers. The economic "flexibility" (i.e., frequent hiring and firing) employed by the companies most commonly means little to no health insurance, no paid vacation, no pension, and no seniority or job security (despite the fact that most employees are full-time workers). The precarious legal status of undocumented *polleros* reinforces corporations' ability to "discipline" and exploit workers and effectively prevent the formation of labor unions. That many are unable to speak or read with any fluency in English also enables exploitation/subordination. Employee protection laws offer little substantive protection. Sunder Crossings has developed a highly perfected racialized form of economic exploitation and violence. A de facto tolerance, or even expectation, in the public sphere that Latinos are exploitable is sustained by these labor practices, with the public sphere simultaneously becoming an arena for the creation and transfer of Latino-related social constructions.

The year-round settlement of entire families in this locale has strained the municipal infrastructure. The corporate practice of "externalizing indirect costs" has been a frequent attribute of meat-packing businesses (Hamann, 1999, 161; Hackenberg, 1995, 238). In Sunder Crossings, the costs of social services, language instruction, and housing were primary examples of this. At the same time, the portions of the host community that do not benefit from corporate profiting (i.e., working-class whites and African Americans) directed their frustration at these costs—not at the companies initiating them, but instead at the newcomers directly, thereby reinforcing the public construction of Latinos as *problems*.

Interviews with immigrant workers and with advocacy group personnel showed that the poultry companies initially advertised their jobs at the U.S./Mexican border. They felt the companies were at fault for the infrastructural stresses, because they had recruited workers and advertised promises, but had not yet facilitated low-cost housing for their recruited workers, nor had they otherwise invested adequately in the local economy. In Sunder Crossings, there has been serious overcrowding and lack of availability of housing, to the point where some people were actually sharing beds by sleeping in shifts. Latino renters reported discriminatory practices, unsafe housing units, including some condemned units with no water or heat. To top it off, there was flagrant price-gouging by local landlords. As one Latino newcomer described it, "They raised the rents! They didn't want more than just 3 or 4 people living together. Before the rents were from $180.00 to $200.00 dollars at most, and now they're at $500.00 dollars . . . and the houses aren't even in good condition, and even when you file a complaint, they don't fix it." Another stated, "[T]wo or 3 years ago, the rents were $250.00 dollars. . . . Now they charge $500.00 dollars, $600.00 dollars." Still another revealed, "There's a lot of trailer parks where the living conditions are horrible, . . . lack of heating, sometimes water, cockroaches, lots of problems . . . yet the rent is very high. Some landlords charge for every person who lives there, and sometimes there's up to 10 people in one trailer due to lack of housing."

The local infrastructure has been burdened with the presence of newly arrived workers, indirect costs and all, and companies have assumed little responsibility. These dynamics help create the limited accepted identity of Latinos. The construction of Latino newcomers as "labor" also makes schooling of immigrant children a publicly contested expense. The same dehumanization seen in the workplace spills over to the amount, type, and quality of education the dominant community is willing to support for newcomers. That is why an examination of the public sphere construction of Latinos (and of Latinos' contestation of that construction) is important in studying education in the Latino diaspora.

PUBLIC GOODS AND DEMOCRACY

> "I am an American citizen, I know for a fact, the government pays the first six months salary for a Hispanic. They do not pay federal tax or social security for three years, just state tax. The American people made this country, but we have been pushed aside."
>
> —Letter to the editor, local newspaper

"Well, I'm scared and full of fear, just like the majority, that the INS will come. When the Americans look at me, it seems that they look at me as being different. But the majority of us come to do honest work, but they don't see that, right? They don't take us into account; they place us in the hardest and most tiresome jobs. They cut us down, set us apart to one side, and don't give us equal treatment. Only the company owners welcome our people, because the owners know that here it's the Mexicans who work hard."

—Mexicano *pollero*

During the time I lived in Sunder Crossings, there was increased anxiety by white established residents over use of public resources, despite the fact that the local economy had been boosted and that newcomers contributed to this. Interviews with longtime residents revealed Sunder Crossings to have been a "ghost town" before the immigrant workers arrived, but newcomers were not credited for its renaissance. There was a popular myth among less-informed longtime citizens that Latinos were getting a free ride, that they did not pay taxes, but instead lived off welfare, and overutilized county social services. Latinos were often thought of and portrayed as problematic, chaotic, dirty, and unintelligent. Local media also circulated these myths.

Nativist backlash in Sunder Crossings, be it by established residents, local governmental officials, radio commentary, or newspaper media, clearly entwined racism with nationalism. Latinos did not fit the prototypical understandings of what it meant to be a "good citizen," despite the fact that they helped the economy with a big boost from their labor. With respect to the local democratic process, Latinos had little voice and little political representation. They were systematically excluded from public life and the common goods available there. There was local white rule and racial subordination, despite the fact that whites were the minority in absolute numbers. Simply stated, there was "taxation without representation."

Nonetheless, the popular construction placed Latinos as "takers," not "givers." This was facilitated by the racial identities of local white citizens as unmarked. Most Latino residents were most often coded as noncitizens, therefore viewed as less human, less entitled, and less deserving. One Rodham County commissioner, on a local social service program, anxiously commented: "Are they legal? I have trouble being asked to spend taxpayer money for programs for illegals. It's tax money, and comes out of OUR pockets." That many were legal was beside the point in this social boundary-marking act.

Fear and profound vulnerability are run throughout many of the interviews with Latino immigrants: fear of local police, of strict poultry employers, of INS raids, deportation, and the splitting of families. Many interviewees described a daily barrage of police harassment, brutality, and unequal treatment. Yet from the point of view of an "American" nationalist ideology, when a Sunder Crossings police officer stopped Latino workers in a car (a fairly routine occurrence), the cause of American nationalism was reinforced.

DO IT OUR (AMERICAN) WAY OR NO WAY AT ALL!

> "It's going to take an effort from everyone who lives or works in Sunder Crossings, even those who don't pay taxes here. They need to clean up their own backyards, in fact that's where a lot of the litter is coming from. Folks are moving to the area and don't appreciate our way of life, or understand our culture, you know where we use trash cans. You know it's folks coming from other places who are not accustomed to our culture. The same people who throw their baby diapers out on the side of the street, and the beer bottles and all that."
>
> —Radio broadcast on local station

> "What happened is that I came undocumented, crossing the mountain range, and they treated me badly in Mexico and did here as well. When I came I was robbed, and then the migra (INS) caught me, they treated me a bit badly. Yes, I just returned again . . . we Mexicans are like that, they deport us and within the half hour we're back."
>
> —Mexicano laborer

One effort to deal with the presence and influx of Spanish-speaking workers to the town had been the creation of the "Commission on Hispanic Affairs" by the local town board. They publicly presented themselves as welcoming and helping Latinos, and published pamphlets and a video. However they received much flak from local advocates who pointed out their pamphlets were racist and full of stereotypes, so much so that they recalled their literature. A portion of their first pamphlet read:

Please do not make excessive noise at any hour. You are not permitted to use radios or TVs after 10 P.M. If you do so, your neighbor will call the police and you'll be investigated. Pets such as dogs and cats are permitted in Sunder Crossings. Keeping chickens or goats within city limits is illegal. It is illegal to have garbage in your yard or to work on your car in the street or in your driveway. Each driver must have his own license. Each vehicle must have a license plate, and you cannot exchange license plates with a friend. Drugs are illegal, and any person who sells or uses them will be arrested. Drugs are bad and very dangerous. In this country, it is completely illegal for a husband to hit his wife or his children for any reason. A man who does this will be sent to jail and may lose his children. The thing that can help you most here is learning English. Anyone who wants to get a better job must learn English.

The statements in this pamphlet reflected the mentality of many leading townsfolk, including government officials. Ironically, many of these stereotypes match classic portrayals of rural working-class people in general. The claims about receptiveness to the newcomers kept the authors from appearing racist. But it was clear the commission was paternalistically attempting to discipline the Spanish-speaking immigrants to follow the societal norms of this small town. The basis of their pamphlet was Latinos as *problems,* with the underlying message: Do it our (American) way or no way at all. As an alternative, one Rodham County commissioner smugly suggested that Latinos could always "just go back home."

WHO PAYS FOR THE PRICE OF GROWTH?

> ". . . and the little Hispanic children that just sit there in school and stare into space. They don't know the language, they can't speak the language, and yet, there they are, sitting right there in the classrooms unable to communicate. And then we teach English as a Second language (ESL), when we should be teaching them English as a Primary language. And then they should pay taxes, learn our language, and you know . . . get with the program. This is MY country!"
>
> —Radio broadcast on local station

In no realm was the attempt to discipline the transnational subject to the expected societal norms any more apparent than the "mediating institution" (Lamphere, 1992) of formal schooling, where hundreds of Latino children contended with a largely monolingual curriculum. Clearly, the local schools were "mediating," in Lamphere's definition, in that the interaction between immigrant newcomers and established residents was hierarchically structured and largely served to channel the broader political and economic forces that constrained their lives. In Sunder Crossings schools, the established residents had "de facto power over immigrants by dint of the structure of the mediating institution itself" (4).[21] Sunder Crossings schools were not anomalous in this regard. Instead, they reflected as well as contributed to the larger public sphere that defined which groups had power and which did not.

At school, the explicit core issue was language, something that was characterized by the chairman of the county school board as: "a serious and extremely difficult problem." By the end of my research period, the local Sunder Crossings schools had jumped from a Latino student population of virtually nothing, to roughly 27 percent. In 2000, several years after my fieldwork was finished, 40 percent of the kindergarten classes were Latino. In 1996–1997 at Sunder

Crossings Elementary School, 28 Latino students were enrolled in kindergarten; in 1997–1998, there were 51 Latinos, 37 African Americans, and 31 white kindergarten students. In the 1997–1998 year, a total of 117 Latino students enrolled for the first time in Sunder Crossings schools. White student enrollment dropped by 83 from 1993 to 1998 (presumably to private academies or less demographically impacted districts).

Locally, there was a strong push for new funding to pay for ESL teachers, bilingual teacher assistants, and related supplies. Recently, the county school system made an additional allocation of $137,000 to pay for three ESL teachers and four bilingual teacher assistants. Adding more ESL teachers, according to one member of the Citizens-Parents Support Team, would: "enhance the development of Spanish-speaking kids without hindering the American kids."[22] This action, however, did not come without prior strife and pressure, namely, the pending litigation from a $20 million class-action lawsuit filed August 10, 1994, against the State Board of Education and the State Superintendent of Public Instruction.[23] That suit alleges that by failing to properly identify Limited-English-Proficient (LEP) students and thus failing to fund legally required educational programs for them, North Carolina has neglected its legal obligation to educate the children. The suit notes that federal law requires individual states to guarantee that local schools make their educational programs open and accessible to all students, even those whose native language is not English.[24]

Interviews with school social workers and counselors revealed that even mentioning the threat of a lawsuit was effective in pressuring the local schools to deal with the Limited-English-Proficient students.[25] One educator revealed:

I've come up with several things, like . . . I said, "This needs to be rectified right now, I want to remind you we have a lawsuit!" . . . and things usually happen quickly because of that. . . . But I think they've just been desperately trying to meet the needs of kids that come in not speaking English. . . . And I think they've been somewhat successful, but not completely successful. . . . We have a long way to go, but people are trying. . . . And trying probably more than many other places.

When asked why there was such high resistance to accommodating the students, another educator commented:

I think the belief here is that "if you teach the kids in Spanish, they're not going to learn English." And that "why should you make exceptions for everybody?" . . . I think a lot of ground is probably lost while kids are making the language transition. . . . Of course, we get every kind of kid here. . . . But a lot of kids are at grade-level when they come in their own language, and that's lost. . . . Others have never been in school, and don't know their alphabet in the 7th grade. . . . We get a lot of those. . . . And then we get kids that are Learning Disabled, but can't be identified as such because their English is so poor, and maybe their Spanish is poor. . . . By the time it's all sorted out, they've probably dropped out.

This interview revealed much more than just resistance—also inadequate resources and the complexity of figuring out what and how to mobilize.

Referring to the black-white racial tension that had been going on for decades, the same interviewee said, "All of a sudden there's the addition of this third thing, it's kind of segregated and treated as a separate thing." Meanwhile, Latino students were left unattended to contend with the largely monolingual English curriculum, while the skirmish about who should pay for English-Language-Learning Latino students remained principally between the county and state governments. The county said that the state had the responsibility to find the needed resources, and the state in turn said the county had to find them on their own. That this stand-off "succeeded" in reducing the resources available for Latino students underlies how it was publicly acceptable in Sunder Crossings for the accommodation of Latino newcomers to be substandard.

The case of Rodham County illustrates the process by which taxpaying residents and citizens have financed the social costs of economic growth that disproportionately benefit a select few. All taxpayers in Sunder Crossings, including Latinos, have been lifting the profits of the poultry industry by directly supporting social and medical services for the hundreds of immigrants poultry companies have lured to the area. The plants rely on extremely low-wage Latino labor but pay proportionately little in commercial taxes that specifically meet the special needs of the workforce (especially health, housing, and education). Legal actions to find adequate resources have only resulted in a skirmish between county and state governments over who should pay for the impact of this new growth. The supposed "devolution" of responsibility for education frees the state and federal governments of responsibility, and county governments clearly lack adequate funds and adequate experience, as well as sufficient will. In the meantime, the industries responsible for recruiting immigrant workers avoid full responsibility for their behavior. If the county considers raising commercial taxes, the industry simply threatens to move its jobs to another of the many low-wealth North Carolina counties that are so eager to entice industry.

Under these conditions, it is difficult to not be somewhat cynical about the intersection of schooling and the local economy, especially since schools themselves are stratified. The internal segmentation of labor markets of the poultry plants begins to mirror the internal differentiation of schools by language, nationality, race, class, and ethnicity (Griffith, 1995). "Mexican-typed jobs" (Tienda, 1989) begin to have a mirror in "Mexican-typed schooling." All the while, the local immigrant community strives to compete for public resources, like a fair and sound education. Yet, the public sphere construction of Latinos as "problematic" and "less deserving" reduces the viability of their claim.

NOTES

1. "American" and "America" are of course contested terms, which disregard hemispheric sensibilities.

2. Although, as this volume indicates, the growth in the Latino population in Georgia has also been substantial.

3. This scholarship is particularly important because we know comparatively little about Latinos in the American South and because we need to grapple with issues of transiency, and the stereotypes of transiency, as well as pursuing more traditional research on permanently resettled families.

4. Many individuals, place-names, and events have been replaced with pseudonyms in order to maintain confidentiality.

5. This number has been steadily rising. Latino workers, as of January 2000, made up about 80 percent of the workforce at these plants.

6. This small town had a semirural population of 5,500 residents and an unemployment rate as low as 2 percent at the time of this study. It also had 18 police officers, 12 doctors, and two poultry-processing plants.

7. Although "public" rhetoric may seemingly remain on a symbolic level, it is not just coincidence that symbolic discourse has also been accompanied by "a steady increase in the disproportionate level of material wealth, economic dislocation, and intergenerational poverty" (McLaren, 1994, 193).

8. M. Goldfield wrote that the "Spirit of 1776" had already developed what W.E.B. DuBois named the "American Blindspot" (1991, 118), that is, the promise of inclusion but the practice of exclusion of groups different from the dominant Anglo population.

9. In one recent example (February 2000), David Duke, the former Ku Klux Klansman who recently founded the New Orleans–based National Organization for European American Rights (NOFEAR), was invited to Sunder Crossings by a local white-supremacist group to stage an anti-immigration rally. Among the crowd of approximately 400 anti-immigrant protesters were a handful who held signs that said "Pollution of Our Population Is Stupid" and "To Hell with the Wretched Refuse."

10. Varenne and McDermott (1998, 15) note that ethnography encompasses "[an] intense gaze on what people do in the detail of their everyday life." They then credit ethnography as "a mode of investigation that is particularly well suited to bringing out aspects of the human condition that the human condition itself always tries to hide." The norms I am describing indeed usually are hidden from explicit consciousness, and I view the exposure and critique of these norms as a primary research responsibility here.

11. The Immigration and Naturalization Service, commonly referred to as "the border patrol" in English and *la migra* in Spanish.

12. I was one of the nine-person research team of the North Carolina Public Spheres project, a collaborative, National Science Foundation funded ethnographic research study (NSF grant # SBR 9514912).

13. Feagin (1997, 13) cites four major anti-immigrant themes that have been stressed historically over the last two centuries: (1) the common complaint that certain "races" are intellectually and culturally inferior and should not be allowed into the

country; (2) that those who have emigrated from the racially and culturally inferior groups are problematic in terms of complete assimilation to the dominant Anglo culture; (3) that immigrants are disrupting the economic conditions (taking jobs); and (4) that immigrants are creating governmental crises such as overloading school and welfare systems.

14. For diasporic populations even the very notion of "home" must be problematized or at least broadly defined. That is, is home somewhere else? Is home more than one place? Does having ties in two or more places feel like having ties to none?

15. During my fieldwork, I found little proof that Latinos and African Americans in Sunder Crossings identified with each other or felt any common cause.

16. Beck's study, however, is not fine grained enough to illustrate whether in some communities where aggregate proportional wealth of Latinos and African Americans is growing the actual incomes of whites are also growing. (This would mean the growth in Latino and African American wealth was an artifact of population growth and not a case of wealth transfer away from whites.)

17. This OUR is startling, given that the officer was not African American. However, the point should not be lost that the OUR referent was a Nobel Peace Prize winner, whereas the THEIR were accused of bringing a cultural disposition to violence.

18. This is one principal reason why the South as a region remains attractive to potentially mobile low-wage industry. The prospect of movement of manufacturing jobs from North to South and then "south of the border" has created unease and has become a rationale for controlling labor costs. Clearly some of the xenophobia documented in Sunder Crossings can be tied to this concern over the prospect of job disappearance. This happens even at a time when jobs are available in greater numbers than before.

19. Numerous advocates I interviewed in town, independent of each other, all cited estimates that Latinos in Sunder Crossings paid 5 to 10 times as much in taxes as the cost of the services that they actually used. I have been unable to substantiate these numbers. Advocates also pointed out that only a fraction of the local immigrant workers who had taxes withheld actually sent in their federal income tax forms; the majority regularly forfeited any taxes they might have been refunded.

20. As reported by the *New York Times* (08/29/97), this study was commissioned by Presidents Clinton and Zedillo in early 1995 and brought together 20 prominent demographers and scholars—10 Mexican and 10 American—for two and a half years of research, fieldwork, and analysis.

21. Lamphere (1992, 4) concedes that although new immigrants and established residents often interact in more fluid and informal settings like on the street, most interaction takes place in formal settings where relationships are defined and circumscribed through well-defined roles. In this case, teachers-administrators are on top and students-parents are at the bottom of the hierarchy.

22. *Rodham News*, December 18, 1997.

23. This Limited English Proficiency (LEP) lawsuit was filed by attorneys for North Carolina legal services, with Latino children and parents from three counties named as plaintiffs.

24. *Rodham News*, August 18, 1994. At the time of the filing, there were believed to be over 10,000 children not receiving any English-as-a-second language instruction in North Carolina, and not even having been identified as LEP, who normally would qualify for special classes after an appropriate LEP identification.

25. This is the school's classification. I prefer the term potentially-english-proficient.

REFERENCES

Applebome, Peter. 1996. *Dixie Rising: How the South Is Shaping American Values, Politics, and Culture*. New York: Times Books.

Bailyn, Bernard. 1960. *Education in the Forming of American Society: Needs and Opportunities for Study*. New York and London: University of North Carolina Press.

Beck, E.M. 1998. "Guess Who's Coming to Town: White Supremacy, Ethnic Competition, and Social Change." Unpublished paper. University of Georgia, Athens.

Bell Jr., Derrick A. 1980. "*Brown v. Board of Education* and the Interest Convergence Dilemma." *Harvard Law Review*. (93):518, 523.

Calhoun, Craig, ed. 1992. *Habermas and the Public Sphere*. Cambridge: Massachusetts Institute of Technology.

DuBois, W.E.B. 1986. *The Souls of Black Folk*. New York: The Library of America.

Feagin, Joe R. 1997. "Old Poison in New Bottles." In *Immigrants OUT!: The New Nativism and the Anti-Immigrant Impulse in the United States*. J.F. Perea, ed. Pp. 13–43. New York and London: New York University Press.

Fraser, Nancy. 1992. "Rethinking the Public Sphere: A Contribution to the Critique of Actually Existing Democracy." In *Habermas and the Public Sphere*. C. Calhoun, ed. Cambridge: Massachusetts Institute of Technology.

Gibson, Jane W. 1996. "The Social Construction of Whiteness in Shellcracker Haven, Florida." *Human Organization*. 55(4):379–389.

Goldfield, David. 1990. *Black, White and Southern: Race Relations and Southern Culture 1940 to the Present*. Baton Rouge: Louisiana State University Press.

Goldfield, Michael. 1991. "The Color of Politics in the United States: White Supremacy as the Main Explanation for the Peculiarities of American Politics from Colonial Times to the Present." In *The Bounds of Race: Perspectives on Hegemony and Resistance*. D. Lacapra, ed. Ithaca and London: Cornell University Press.

Griffith, David. 1995. "*Hay Trabajo*: Poultry Processing, Rural Industrialization, and the Latinization of Low-Wage Labor." In *Any Way You Cut It: Meat-Processing and Small-Town America*. D.D. Stull, M.J. Broadway, and D. Griffith, eds. Pp. 129–151. Lawrence: University Press of Kansas.

Habermas, Jurgen. 1989. *The Structural Transformation of the Public Sphere: An Inquiry into a Category of Bourgeois Society*. Massachusetts Institute of Technology. Original work, 1962, translated by Thomas Burger with the assistance of Frederick Lawrence.

Hackenberg, Robert A. 1995. "Joe Hill Died for Your Sins." In *Any Way You Cut It: Meat-Processing and Small-Town America*. D.D. Stull, M.J. Broadway, and D. Griffith, eds. Pp. 232–264. Lawrence: University Press of Kansas.

Hamann, Edmund T. 1999. "Anglo (Mis)Understandings of Latino Newcomers: A North Georgia Case Study." In *Negotiating Power and Place at the Margins: Selected Papers on Refugees and Immigrants*. J.G. Lipson and L.A. McSpadden, eds. Arlington, VA: American Anthropological Association.

Harrison, Faye V. 1998. "Affirmative Action Is Still Needed (Point—Counterpoint)." *Anthropology Newsletter, American Anthropological Association*. 39(2):16–17.

Hartigan Jr., John. 1997. "Establishing the Fact of Whiteness." *American Anthropologist*. 99(3)September.

Holland, D., D. Nonini, and C.A. Lutz. n.d. "Estrangement from the Public Sphere: Economic Change, Democracy and Social Divisions in North Carolina." Research Proposal for the National Science Foundation.

Hondagneu-Sotelo, Pierrette. 1997. "The History of Mexican Undocumented Settlement in the U.S." In *Challenging Fronteras: Structuring Latina and Latino Lives in the U.S.* M. Romero, P. Hondagneu-Sotelo, and V. Ortiz, eds. Pp. 115–134. New York and London: Routledge.

Institute for Research in the Social Sciences (IRSS). 1997. *Carolina Poll.* University of North Carolina at Chapel Hill.

Lamphere, L., A. Stepick, and G. Grenier, eds. 1994. *Newcomers in the Workplace: Immigrants and the Restructuring of the U.S. Economy.* Philadelphia: Temple University Press.

Lamphere, Louise. 1992. *Structuring Diversity: Ethnographic Perspectives on the New Immigration.* Chicago: University of Chicago Press.

Levinson, Bradley A. and Margaret Sutton. 2001. "Policy as/in Practice: Developing a Sociocultural Approach to the Study of Educational Practice." In *Policy as Practice: Toward a Comparative Sociocultural Analysis of Educational Policy.* M. Sutton and B.A. Levinson, eds. Westport, CT: Ablex Press.

McLaren, Peter. 1994. "Multiculturalism and the Post-Modern Critique: Toward a Pedagogy of Resistence and Transformation." In *Between Borders.* Henry A. Giroux and Peter McLaren, eds. Pp. 192–222. New York: Routledge.

Murillo Jr., Enrique G. and Sofia Villenas. 1995. "East of Aztlán: Typologies of Resistance in North Carolina Communities." Unpublished paper. University of North Carolina, Chapel Hill.

NCPS. North Carolina Public Sphere Project, by L. Bartlett, M. Frederick, T. Guldbrandsen, D. Holland, C. Lutz, D. Nonini, and E.G. Murillo Jr. 1997. "The Cultural Production of Exclusion: Dramas of Contestation and the Public Sphere in the American South." Panel Discussion at the Annual Meeting of the American Anthropological Association. Washington, DC.

Noblit, G., S. Villenas, A. Adkins, G. Givens, and M. McKinney. 1995. "Latino Cultures and Services Study: Perspectives on Children and Families." Final Report of a Frank Porter Graham Child Development Center Small Grant, September 30.

Perea, J.F., ed. 1996. *Immigrants OUT!: The New Nativism and the Anti-Immigrant Impulse in the United States.* New York and London: New York University Press.

Presley, Sue Anne. 2000. "Hispanic Immigration Boom Rattles South." *Washington Post.* March 6.

Sanchez, Rosaura. 1997. "Mapping the Spanish Language along a Multiethnic and Multilingual Border." In *The Latino Studies Reader: Culture, Economy and Society.* A. Darder and R.D. Torres, eds. Malden, MA: Blackwell Publishers.

Suárez-Orozco, Marcelo M. 1998. "State Terrors: Immigrants and Refugees in the Post-National Space." In *Ethnic Identity and Power: Cultural Contexts of Political Action in School and Society.* Y. Zou and E.T. Trueba, eds. Pp. 283–319. Albany: State University of New York Press.

Turner, Victor. 1974. *Dramas, Fields and Metaphors: Symbolic Action in Human Society.* Ithaca: Cornell University Press.

Tienda, Marta. 1989. "Looking at the 1990s: Mexican Immigration in Sociological Perspective." In *Mexican Migration to the United States: Origins, Consequences, and Policy Options.* W.A. Cornelius and J.A. Bustamante, eds. Pp. 109–147. San Diego: Center for U.S./Mexican Studies, University of California.

Varenne, Hervé and Ray McDermott. 1998. *Successful Failure: The School America Builds.* Boulder, CO: Westview Press.

Villenas, Sofia. 1997. "Una Buena Educación: Latino Education and Cultural Conflict in North Carolina." Paper presented at the 96th Annual Meeting of the American Anthropological Association. Washington, DC.

Williams, Brickette F. 1989. "A CLASS ACT: Anthropology and the Race to Nation Across Ethnic Terrain." *Annual Review of* Anthropology. 18:401–444.

Winant, Howard. 1994. *Racial Conditions.* 2nd ed. Minneapolis: University of Minnesota Press.

11

The New Latino Diaspora and Educational Policy

Margaret A. Gibson

As noted by the editors of this volume in chapter 1, "Education and Policy in the New Latino Diaspora," the nine case studies presented herein describe recent demographic changes that have occurred in New Latino Diaspora settings. Drawing upon ethnographic research and policy analysis, the authors describe the micropolitics of educational change occurring in parts of the United States that until recently have had little or no Latino presence.[1] This collection focuses broadly on the challenges faced by Latino children and their families in New Diaspora sites, and on community and school responses to a growing Latino presence in their midst. This concluding commentary has three purposes: (1) to place the demographic changes discussed by the authors within a larger national and sociohistorical context; (2) to summarize key educational issues that emerge from the nine cases; and (3) to address the implications of this body of work for educational policy.

THE CHANGING DEMOGRAPHY

At the midpoint of the past century, immigration into the United States had slowed almost to a trickle, and by 1970 just 4.7 percent of U.S. residents were foreign born, down from 14.7 percent in 1910 (Camarota, 2001). Immigration was viewed as central to our history but only our past history. However, as noted by Rumbaut (2000, 1), "History is forever being ambushed by the unexpected." Once again we have become a nation of immigrants. Today, one in five Americans is either an immigrant or the child of an immigrant.

Since 1970, the total number of foreign-born residents has tripled, and during the past decade, newly arrived immigrants together with the children born to all resident immigrants has accounted for a staggering 69 percent of this country's population growth (Camarota, 2001).[2] Although the large majority of newcomers continues to be concentrated in a few states,[3] all parts of the country have been touched by this latest wave of immigration. Colorado, North Carolina, and Georgia—states discussed in this volume—have experienced especially dramatic immigrant growth rates during the past decade (190 percent, 189 percent, and 99 percent, respectively). Even in states with a limited immigrant presence, we find individual communities undergoing rapid transformation. For example, Grady (this volume) describes a town in Indiana that for the first time since the late 1800s has a significant number of non–English-speaking residents.[4] Likewise, Brunn writes about a rural Illinois community that prior to 1996 was almost entirely European American; today one-fifth of the town's student population is Latino.

Latinos are the fastest growing group in the United States, accounting for 47 percent of this country's total immigrant population. Twenty-eight percent of the foreign born come from Mexico alone (Camarota, 2001). Although previously concentrated in the West and Southwest, immigrants from Mexico are now settling throughout the whole of the United States. The large majority of the immigrants discussed in these cases are of Mexican origin. Their settlement in new locations throughout the country has been spurred by economic globalization. U.S. industries, ranging from meat and poultry processing in New England, the Midwest, and the South to ski resorts in Colorado, are actively and increasingly recruiting low-skilled, low-wage workers from Mexico in order to remain competitive.

Immigrant and migrant workers come with the expectation of a better standard of living for themselves and their families, and most in fact do earn far more here than in their homelands, but they also face enormous hardships. The authors report that Latino newcomers are harassed in stores and restaurants, in the workplace, and when walking down the street. They are accused by long-term host community members of being dirty and violent, of being in this country illegally, and of taking jobs from American citizens. They are criticized for speaking Spanish. Whether direct or indirect, the message is clear: "Act American" or go "back home" (as described in chapters by Martinez, Murillo, and Wortham). Stereotypical myths circulate fueling resentment among white residents and other long-established minorities. Latino workers are accused of getting tax breaks not available to other Americans and receiving "free" social services. In actuality, many Latino laborers work extremely hard in low-paid and dangerous jobs which provide no health benefits, no pensions, and no job security. Their housing is inadequate. As Murillo observes, New Diaspora communities want Latino labor and Latino business but not the full human being.

These conditions found in New Diaspora sites are regrettably all too similar to those in locations where Mexican workers have had a long-term presence. Far from getting a free ride, many work for low pay in backbreaking jobs and receive few benefits. Nationwide, nearly two-thirds of all Mexican immigrants live in or near poverty; over half have no health insurance (Camarota, 2001). U.S. industries import inexpensive Mexican labor, but they do so without adequate plans for how to integrate new workers and their families into their communities. Worse still, Mexicans and other Latino newcomers are faced with anti-Latino, anti-Mexican initiatives designed to limit employment opportunities, along with their access to social services and public schooling. In California, for example, which is home to the largest number of Mexican workers, voters have passed a series of anti-immigrant initiatives in recent years designed to limit use of Spanish in public places by Mexicans, to end bilingual education in the schools, and to deny undocumented workers and their children access to health care and schooling.

THE TRANSFORMATION OF PUBLIC SCHOOLS

U.S. public schools, perhaps more than any other local institutions, are called upon to respond to demographic changes brought about by immigration. Immigrant children, both U.S. and foreign born, account for the rapid increase in K–12 school enrollments in many parts of the country.[5] For example, in six states more than 20 percent of all school-age children have immigrant mothers. California leads the way with 43 percent followed by Florida, New York, Arizona, Texas, and New Jersey (Camarota, 15). Enrollment increases in these states are due, in large measure, to immigration. Latinos today account for more than 25 percent of all students attending central city schools and 14 percent of the public school population nationwide (NCES, February 2000).[6] Over the next 20 years, the number of Latino children ages 5 to 13 will nearly double, and by 2030 Latino students will comprise one-fourth of the total K–12 school population.[7] The rapid growth of school-age Latino children is especially pronounced in traditional Diaspora sites. In California, Latino students, largely of Mexican origin, have already surpassed whites as the largest student group.

EDUCATIONAL PROBLEMS

Although their numbers are rising, their performance in school is not. Children of Mexican descent nationwide are, among the larger subpopulations of this country, the least likely to finish high school and the least likely to complete four years of college (Gándara, 1995; Gutierrez et al., 2000; Ruiz-de-Velasco and Fix, 2000; Vernez and Abrahamse, 1996, 65). U.S. public schools are, for the most part, ill prepared to meet the educational needs of Mexican and other Latino youth. In New Diaspora locations, Latino children regularly encounter a curriculum that fails to build on what they have already learned at home and in their communities. Many Latino children are also English language learners; 40 percent of all Latino students nationwide are identified as "limited English proficient," and in New Diaspora sites where many of the Latino students are newly arrived from Mexico, the percentage may be even higher (Ginorio and Huston, 2001). It is difficult under any circumstances for immigrant students who lack familiarity with the dominant U.S. culture and who speak little or no English to feel comfortable in their school surroundings. Their problems are exacerbated, however, by the fact that many of their teachers have little (or no) preparation for working with Latino immigrant children. Few speak Spanish, and most lack training in working with English-language learners. The net result is that many teachers are unable to communicate effectively with their Latino students. Furthermore, language classes designed to develop Latino students' English skills often occupy the most marginal spaces on a school campus, thus isolating students and restricting their opportunities to practice English with native speakers.

It is not just language training that teachers lack. Unlike teachers in traditional Latino Diaspora locations, few teachers in New Diaspora communities have had any prior exposure to Latino culture or to the most basic realities of the Latino world outside of school. Students' command of Spanish is rarely used as a building block for further instruction, and teachers often center on what students do not know rather than on what they do know. As noted in the chapters by Murillo and Villenas, educators frequently identify Latino students and their families as "the problem," unaware that their own lack of preparedness in working with culturally and linguistically diverse populations is itself a major obstacle and one that needs urgent and sustained attention. These shortcomings, together with inadequate language development policies and the sometimes racist attitudes of non-Latino schoolmates, make learning English and the mastery of subject matter content all the more difficult for Latino immigrant students.

Conflicts between Latino and non-Latino classmates also lead some English language learners to avoid practicing English in front of fluent English-speaking classmates for fear of ridicule and embarrassment (Hurd, 2000). As described in several of the case studies, Latino students may also avoid using Spanish in the presence of monolingual English-speaking peers, knowing that their use of Spanish is considered un-American. As noted in the chapter by Beck and Allexsaht-Snider, the widespread support in many parts of this country to enact "English Only" laws illustrates the political nature of language policy development. Decision makers rarely support the adoption of educational policy that promotes bilingualism, bowing instead to anti-immigrant sentiments and public backlash against the use of any language other than English. The net result is that schools may be pressured to enact language and curricular policies that actually retard Latino students' academic progress and undermine their identity development.

SUBTRACTIVE ACCULTURATION

Assimilationist pressures faced by Latino youth today are in many respects similar to those faced by immigrant children a century ago. In 1911, more than half of all K–12 students in 37 of this country's largest cities had foreign-born parents (Cordasco, 1976). Schools became the primary vehicle for assimilating newcomers, by suppressing or eliminating children's "foreign ways" (Covello, 1967, 411, cited in Cordasco, 1976, 36–37; Olneck, 1995; Olsen, 1990; Tollefson 1989). Few educators saw need for reform in the way schools were structured or in the concept of Americanization that they embodied. Too little has changed.

Although schools today may explicitly advocate respect for cultural differences and provide immigrant students far more specialized instructional assistance than was the case a century ago, the goal in the minds of many educators and policy makers remains one of cultural replacement and eventual assimilation.[8] Few schools place value on Latino children's home culture or encourage them to develop their skills in Spanish. More frequently Latino children are made to feel that at school they must hide their Latino identity and refrain from using Spanish. Under such circumstances, English rapidly replaces Spanish as the dominant language, and a valuable resource is lost not only for the individual but also for the nation as a whole (Portes and Hao, 1998; Rumbaut, 2000). The sorts of assimilationist pressures that immigrant children face in school have been termed variously as subtractive acculturation or replacement acculturation (Gibson, 1988, 1995), deculturation (Spring, 1997), and subtractive schooling (Valenzuela, 1999).[9]

IDENTITY ISSUES

As Villenas notes, schools unwittingly force children into painful dichotomized choices: "the U.S. way or the Mexican way, English or Spanish, mainstream or deficit." Assimilationist pressures, however well intentioned, can have unintended and extremely negative consequences; children may feel forced to choose between their parents' culture, the culture of the white mainstream majority, and their own need to express their "evolving identities" (Brunn, this volume). Wortham's (this volume) case focuses directly on Latino youth, males in particular, who were confronted with such either/or choices. Wishing to preserve their identity, most of the boys resisted the school's rules for success. They rarely worked hard in their classes, and those few who did disguised their efforts lest they be labeled "school boys." Girls, on the other hand, were more able to move between their two worlds without facing a trade-off. They adopted a strategy of accommodation without assimilation (Gibson, 1988).

Similar gender differences in the school engagement and achievement of Latino adolescents are described elsewhere in the literature (Gibson, 1998; Hurt, 2000; Valenzuela, 1999). Research findings suggest that Mexican males may have a more difficult time than Mexican females accommodating themselves to school rules while simultaneously seeking to secure and maintain their reputation within peer networks. Believing their identities threatened, boys more than girls may feel the need to resist school authority and to manifest symbols of an oppositional identity, which in turn places them at greater risk of doing poorly in school.[10] It need not be this way. As illustrated by Grady's case study on lowrider art, Latino peers can be a very positive force for school engagement when activities at school build upon students' out-of-school knowledge and interests.

ADDITIVE ACCULTURATION AS EDUCATIONAL POLICY

Grady (this volume) describes how Latino boys[11] used lowrider art to create and circulate a very different discourse from that of the traditional school curriculum, and in so doing they were able "to resist their marginalization and the stultifying and culturally unresponsive curriculum they faced on most school days." Through their art the students were also to construct and project a visible and positive Latino identity at school. Their lowrider art gave the boys an opportunity to engage in an activity at school which they found meaningful, where they could choose what they wanted to learn and could identify the resources they needed to accomplish their goals. Their art became an integral part of their peer relations and identity development. Grady also describes how one of their teachers observed their artwork and incorporated it into her curriculum. In so doing, she not only validated the boys' knowledge but gave them the opportunity to share it with others. By assigning all her students—Anglo as well as Latino—a lowrider art project, this teacher also exposed non-Latino students to a new aspect of Mexican culture, created an opportunity for students to develop new friendships, and made cultural "border crossing" a two-way process (Erickson, 1987; Phelan et al., 1998).

Grady's study contributes to a growing body of ethnographic research describing immigrant youth who have found ways to remain strongly rooted in the cultures of their families and communities while at the same time developing the skills needed to navigate successfully between their "multiple worlds" (Phelan et al., 1998). There is increasing evidence, moreover, that students who develop bicultural and bilingual skills have advantages over those who lack these abilities. In their large-scale, longitudinal study of immigrant youth in San Diego, Portes and Rumbaut found that high school students who are fluent in two languages receive higher grades than either coethnics who speak only English or white peers (Rumbaut, 1997). Likewise, recent research indicates that students who complete bilingual programs in New York City schools are more likely to finish four years of high school; in addition, they score higher in English on the city's demanding Regents Examination (Steinberg, 2001). Ethnographic research also provides evidence in favor of additive acculturation as educational policy. Students with strong bilingual and bicultural skills have advantages over those who lack the ability to move fluidly across social, linguistic, and cultural borders.[12]

These findings from both quantitative and qualitative research challenge earlier understandings of acculturation and the steps that immigrants must follow in order to move ahead academically and economically. No longer can we assume that cultural assimilation is the surest path to success. In fact, immigrant students who feel they must shed their home cultures and languages may be at greater risk in school than those that who develop strong bilingualism. There are, of course, many other consequences of language and culture loss, not the least of which are the cultural and linguistic resources lost to this country when schools fail to promote students' bilingual and bicultural skills (Rumbaut, 2000).

POLICY DEVELOPMENT AND TEACHER PREPARATION

Building on the evidence at hand, we need to move forward to construct educational policies and programs that will enable children to remain securely anchored in their home communities and cultures while pursuing a strategy of additive acculturation. A major prerequisite is the availability of teachers who are well prepared to work with Latino students, including those who are English language learners. Research indicates that a well-trained, caring teacher who also has an understanding of Latino students' worlds outside of school can have a profound impact on students' lives in school (Bejínez, 1998; Valenzuela, 1999; Yao, 1999). The art teacher described by Grady provides such an example. For the most part, however, and this is particularly true in New Latino Diaspora locations, colleges of education provide prospective teachers with little preparation for working with Latino students. More generally, teachers are prepared to teach middle-class, English-speaking students whose home and school worlds embrace similar values (Phelan et al., 1998). Such is not the case for many Latino children. The values, behaviors and expectations taught at home may be very different from those taught at school.

In order for schools to meet the needs of Latino students, there will need to be a major reorientation of this country's teacher recruitment and preparation programs. There is pressing need to recruit more Latinos into teaching so that the teaching force is more reflective of the student population. At the present time only 4 percent of this nation's teaching force is Latino (NCES, February 2000; Ginorio and Huston, 2001). With nearly 40 percent of all Latino students (K–12) identified as limited English proficient (Ginorio and Huston, 2001), teachers need preparation in the theories and methods of second language acquisition. Strategies must also be developed to address the severe shortage of fully credentialed bilingual teachers. One strategy, as described in this volume (in the chapters by Hamann; Zúñiga et al.) is for U.S. school districts to develop partnerships with Mexican universities and teacher training institutions. Another, somewhat longer-term strategy, is to interest U.S. college students who are Spanish majors to take up teaching as a career. Latino high school students should also be encouraged to enter the teaching profession and given the necessary academic and financial support they need to complete a college degree and teacher credential program.

Drawing from Levinson and Sutton (2001, 17), the chapters by Hamann, Murillo, and Wortham note that educational policy is unique among policy arenas "in its power to determine who has the right to become an 'educated' person." Researchers have found as well that in schools and communities where Latino adults hold positions of political power Latino students do better in school (Meier and Stewart, 1991). All too rarely, however, are Latino parents and community members given real opportunities to be involved in educational policy development. Brunn's case study of collaborative educational decision making provides us with a notable exception.

As detailed by the case studies appearing in this volume, U.S. public schools are failing in large measure to meet the needs of Latino students. The current state of public education presents a crisis not only for Latino children and their families but also for this nation as well. The educational success of Latino students, given their rapidly increasing numbers, will determine the quality of the labor force throughout this country in the years ahead. Solutions to the current crisis can be found, but not without a major investment of resources and the involvement of all the stakeholders.[13] The costs of closing the education gap for Latino students will be high, but the costs of not doing so will be far higher.

NOTES

1. The term Latino, as commonly used, refers to U.S. residents whose families have their origins in Mexico, Central and South America, and the Spanish-speaking Caribbean.

2. For a fuller discussion of these changes, see the Center for Immigration Studies recent report titled "Immigrants in the United States—2000" (Camarota, 2001).

3. California leads the way with 31 percent of this country's immigrant population, followed by New York (13 percent), Florida (10 percent), Texas (9 percent), New Jersey (4 percent), and Illinois (4 percent) (Camarota, Table 4, 2001).

4. When I refer to the contributors by name, or when I reference the "authors" or the "case studies," my citation is always to their chapters in this volume.

5. As used herein, the terms immigrant children and immigrant students refer to all children with immigrant parents, regardless of the their birthplace.

6. If all Latino youth were in school, these numbers would be much higher. As is, more than 40 percent of all immigrant Mexicans ages 16 to 24 are not currently enrolled in school and have not completed 12 years of schooling (NCES, June 2000). Many never attend school and others leave prior to graduation. During this same period, the population of European American children is projected to decrease by 11 percent (U.S. Department of Education 1997, cited in Ginorio and Huston, 2001).

7. During this same period, the overall population of European American children is expected to decline (U.S. Department of Education 1997, cited in Ginorio and Huston, 2001).

8. Assimilation is a process whereby individuals of one society or ethnic group are incorporated or absorbed culturally into another. At the individual level, cultural assimilation implies loss of identification with one's former group.

9. Acculturation is the process of culture change and adaptation that occurs when groups with different cultures come into contact. It need not be a subtractive process. Instead, it may lead to the addition of new traits or the blending or new and old ways.

10. Researchers have observed comparable differences among African American and African Caribbean youth in the United States, Canada, and Britain (Fordham, 1966; Gibson, 1991; Gillborn, 1997; Solomon, 1992; Waters, 1996), and among North African youth in France (van Zanten, 1997).

11. Only one of the student artists discussed in Grady's chapter was female.

12. Such patterns have been documented in studies of academically successful Mexican students (Gándara, 1995; Matute-Bianchi, 1991; Mehan et al., 1994; Suárez-Orozco, 1989; Vigil, 1997; Vigil and Long, 1981), as well as among non-Latino immigrant groups (Gibson, 1988; Gibson and Bhachu, 1991; Hall, 1995; Hoffman, 1988; Zine, 2000; Zhou and Bankston, 1998), and nonimmigrant minority students (Brayboy, 2000; Carter, 1999; Deyhle, 1995; Mehan et al., 1994).

13. See Vernez, Krop, and Rydell (1999) for an analysis of the benefits and costs of closing the education gap for this country's Latino population.

REFERENCES

Bejínez, Livier F. 1998. "Caring, Identity, and Academic Achievement: The Role of the Migrant Education Program in a Racially Mixed High School." Unpublished master's thesis. University of California, Santa Cruz.

Brayboy, Bryan McKinley. 2000. "Climbing Up and Over the Ivy: Examining the Experiences of American Indian Ivy League College Graduates." Unpublished manuscript. College of Education, University of Utah.

Camarota, Steven A. 2001. "Immigrants in the United States—2000: A Snapshot of America's Foreign-Born Population." Washington, DC: Center for Immigration Studies.

Carter, Prudence L. 1999. "Balancing 'Acts': Issues of Identity and Cultural Resistance in the Social and Educational Behaviors of Minority Youth." Unpublished doctoral dissertation. Department of Sociology, Columbia University.

Cordasco, Francesco. 1976. "Immigrant Children in American Schools." Fairfield, NJ: August M. Kelly.

Deyhle, Donna. 1995. "Navajo Youth and Anglo Racism: Cultural Integrity and Resistances." *Harvard Educational Review*. 65(3).

Erickson, Frederick. 1987. "Transformation and School Success: The Politics and Culture of Educational Achievement." *Anthropology and Education Quarterly*. 18(4):335–56.

Fordham, Signithia. 1996. *Blacked Out: Dilemmas of Race, Identity, and Success at Capital High*. Chicago: University of Chicago Press.

Gándara, Patricia. 1995. *Over the Ivy Walls: The Educational Mobility of Low-Income Chicanos*. New York: SUNY Press.

Gibson, M.A. and P.K. Bhachu. 1991. "The Dynamics of Educational Decision Making." In *Minority Status and Schooling: A Comparative Study of Immigrant and Involuntary Minorities*. A. Gibson and J.U. Ogbu, eds. Pp. 63–95. New York: Garland Publishing.

Gibson, Margaret A. 1988. *Accommodation without Assimilation: Sikh Immigrants in an American High School*. Ithaca, NY: Cornell University Press.

———. 1991. "Ethnicity, Gender, and Social Class: The School Adaptation Patterns of West Indian Youths." In *Minority Status and School*. M.A. Gibson and J.U. Ogbu, eds. Pp. 357–387. New York: Garland Publishing.

———. 1995. "Additive Acculturation as a Strategy for School Improvement." In *California's Immigrant Children: Theory, Research, and Implications for Educational Policy*. Rubén G. Rumbaut and Wayne A. Cornelius, eds. Pp. 77–105. La Jolla: Center for U.S.-Mexican Studies, University of California, San Diego.

———. 1998. "Promoting Academic Success among Immigrant Students: Is Acculturation the Issue?" *Educational Policy*. 12(6):615–633.

Gillborn, David. 1997. "Ethnicity and Educational Performance in the United Kingdom: Racism, Ethnicity and Variability in Achievement." *Anthropology and Education Quarterly*. 28(3):375–393.

Ginorio, Angela and Michelle Huston. 2001. *¡Sí, Se Puede! Yes, We Can: Latinas in School*. Washington DC: American Association of University Women.

Gutierrez, Kris, P. Baquendano-Lopez, and H.H. Alvarez. 2000. "The Crisis in Latino Education." In *Charting New Terrains of Chicana(o)/Latina(o) Education*. C. Tejeda, C. Martinez, and Z. Leonardo, eds. Cresskill, NJ: Hampton Press.

Hall, Kathleen. 1995. "'There's a Time to Act English and a Time to Act Indian': The Politics of Identity among British-Sikh Teenagers." In *Children and the Politics of Culture*. Sharon Stephens, ed. Pp. 243–264. Princeton, NJ: Princeton University Press.

Hoffman, Diane M. 1988. "Cross-Cultural Adaptation and Learning: Iranians and Americans at School." In *School and Society*. H. Trueba and C. Delgado-Gaitan, eds. Pp. 163–180. New York: Praeger.

Hurd, Clayton A. 2000. "Belonging in School: The Politics of Race and Emotion Among Mexican-Descent Students at Hillside High." Paper presented at the annual meeting of the American Anthropological Association, San Francisco.

Levinson, Bradley and Margaret Sutton. 2001. "Policy as/in Practice." In *Policy as Practice*. M. Sutton and B. Levinson, eds. Westport, CT: Ablex.

Matute-Bianchi, M.E. 1991. "Situational Ethnicity and Patterns of School Performance among Immigrant and Nonimmigrant Mexican-Descent Students." In *Minority Status and Schooling: A Comparative Study of Immigrant and Involuntary Minorities*. M.A. Gibson and J.U. Ogbu, eds. Pp. 205–247. New York: Garland Publishing.

Mehan, Hugh, L. Hubbard, and I. Villanueva. 1994. "Forming Academic Identities: Accommodation without Assimilation among Involuntary Minorities." *Anthropology and Education Quarterly*. 25:91–117.

Meier, Kenneth and Joseph Stewart. 1991. *The Politics of Hispanic Education.* Albany: SUNY Press.

National Center for Education Statistics, Office of Educational Research and Improvement, U.S. Department of Education. 2000. "Racial and Ethnic Distribution of Elementary and Secondary Students. Indicator of the Month." February (NCES 2000-05).

———. 2000. "High School Dropouts, by Race-Ethnicity and Recency of Migration. Indicator of the Month." June (NCES 2000-009).

Olneck, Michael R. 1995. *Immigrants and Education.* Handbook of Research on Multicultural Education. James Banks and Cherry M. Banks, eds. New York: Simon and Schuster.

Olsen, Laurie. 1990. "Then and Now: A Comparative Perspective on Immigration and School Reform during Two Periods in American History." *California Perspectives.* Vol. 1, Winter.

Phelan, Patricia, Ann L. Davidson, and Hanh Cao Yu. 1998. *Adolescents' Worlds: Negotiating Family, Peer and School.* New York: Teachers College Press.

Portes, Alejandro and L. Hao. 1998. "*E pluribus unum:* Bilingualism and Loss in the Second Generation." *Sociology of Education.*

Ruiz-de-Velasco, Jorge and Michael Fix. 2000. *Overlooked & Underserved: Immigrant Students in U.S. Secondary Schools.* Washington, DC: The Urban Institute.

Rumbaut, Rubén G. 1997. "Paradoxes (and Orthodoxies) of Assimilation." *Sociological Perspectives.* 40(3):483–511.

———. 2000. "Sites of Belonging: Shifts in Ethnic Self-identities among Adolescent Children of Immigrants." Paper prepared for the MacArthur Foundation Conference on Discovering Successful Pathways in Children's Development: Mixed Methods in the Study of Childhood and Family Life. Santa Monica, CA.

Solomon, Patrick. 1992. *Black Resistance in a High School.* New York: SUNY Press.

Spring, J. 1997. *Political Agendas for Education.* Mahwah, NJ: Lawrence Erlbaum.

Steinberg, Jacques. 2001. "Americans Show Little Interest in Building a Bilingual Culture." *San Francisco Chronicle.* 5 January, A12.

Suárez-Orozco, Marcelo. 1989. *Central American Refugees and U.S. High Schools: A Psychosocial Study of Motivation and Achievement.* Stanford, CA: Stanford University Press.

Tollefson, James W. 1989. *Alien Winds: The Reeducation of America's Indochinese Refugees.* Westport, CT: Praeger.

Valenzuela, Angela. 1999. *Subtractive Schooling: U.S.-Mexican Youth and the Politics of Caring.* Albany: SUNY Press.

van Zanten, Agnes. 1997. "Schooling Immigrants in France in the 1990s: Success or Failure of the Republican Model of Integration?" *Anthropology and Education Quarterly.* 29(3):351–374.

Vernez, Georges and A. Abrahamse. 1996. *How Immigrants Fare in U.S. Education.* Santa Monica, CA: RAND Center for Research on Immigration Policy.

Vernez, Georges, Richard A. Krop, and C. Peter Rydell. 1999. *Closing the Education Gap: Benefits and Costs.* Santa Monica, CA: RAND Center for Research on Immigration Policy.

Vigil, James D. 1997. *Personas Mexicanas: Chicano High Schoolers in a Changing Los Angeles.* Fort Worth, TX: Harcourt, Brace and Company.

Vigil, James Diego and J.M. Long. 1981. "Unidirectional or Nativist Acculturation: Chicano Paths to School Achievement." *Human Organization.* 40(3):273–277.

Waters, Mary. 1996. "The Intersection of Gender, Race, and Ethnicity in Identity Development of Caribbean American Teens." In *Urban Girls: Resisting Stereotypes, Creating Identities*. Bonnie Leadbeater and Niobe Way, eds. Pp. 65–81. New York: New York University Press.

Yao, Juliet M. 1999. "Constructing Bridges to Learning: The Role of Care in Student-Teacher Relationships." Unpublished master's thesis. University of California, Santa Cruz.

Zine, Jasmin. 2000. "Redefining Resistance: Towards an Islamic Subculture in Schools." *Race Ethnicity and Education*. 3(3).

Zhou, M. and Bankston, C.L., III. 1998. *Growing Up American: How Vietnamese Children Adapt to Life in the United States*. New York: Russell Sage Foundation.

Index

Accommodation, Latina adolescents, 118, 123–124

Acculturation: additive, 246–247; Clayton CUSD, 211; definition of, 249 n.9; Hope City, 26; subtractive, 245

"Act/Acting white," 117–118, 131, 165

Acuña, Rudolfo, 39

Adolescents: Anglo identity issues, 135–136; Latinas/os, identity issues, 117–118, 122–124, 124–126, 132–138, 245–246

Agua Fria, 145, 151

Al mando, moral education, 27, 29

Al pendiente (vigilant), moral education, 27, 28

Allexsaht-Snider, Martha, 8, 11, 40, 244

Americanization: educational policy, 245; Georgia DOE, 49–50, 52–54

Anderson, Benedict, 122

Anglos, "mainstream cultural order," 8

Anzaldúa, Gloria, 51

Argyris, Chris, 71

Arkansas, Diaspora Latinos, 1

Art: acceptance, 8, 12; curriculum, lowrider art, 184–187, 246

Artists, lowrider art, 179–180, 181–182, 183–184

Assimilation: CPS, 79, 92–93; definition of, 249 n.8; educational policy, 245; Hope City, 26

Avila, Armando, 174–175

Baker, Keith, 50

Banks, James, 189

Barnes, Roy, 59

Beck, E.M., 224

Beck, Scott A.L., 8, 10, 11, 40, 50, 55, 56, 58, 244

Becker, Adeline, 8

Bell, Derrick A., Jr., 218

Bell, Sally Alonzo, 30

Benevolent racism, 7; Havertown, 121; Hope City, 17–18

"Best practices," Diaspora Latinos, 6

Bilingual curriculum, CPS, 72, 80–91

Bilingual curriculum coordinator, CPS, 69–70, 82–83, 84, 86, 87, 88, 90–91

Bilingual education: Clayton CUSD, 197–198, 200; Colorado, 11–12; debates about, 4, 6; as educational method, 38; Georgia DOE, 3, 46, 49–52, 56, 57; Georgia/Mexico partnership, 67–93; misleading assumptions about, 59 n.4; opposition to, 244–245;

politicalization of, 38–39; as second class education, 2; Sunder Crossings schools, 234; value of, 246–247

Bilingual education consultant, Georgia/Mexico partnership, 69–70, 81–82

"Bilingual Transitional Plan," 84–85, 86–87

Bilingualism, elite vs. folk, 47

"Borderization," 102, 104

Bourdieu, Pierre, 39, 44

Bracero program, 99

Broadway, Michael, 121, 122

Brown v. Board of Education, Topeka, Kansas, 41, 59

Brunn, Michael, 10, 12, 242, 248

Buen comportamiento (good conduct), moral education, 18, 24–25

Business community, externalized costs, 5, 216–217, 229–230

Calhoun, Craig, 222

California: Diaspora Latinos, 99, 103, 248 n.3; hostility toward Latinos, 121

Cariño (love), 29

Carpet mills, Diaspora Latinos, 10, 73

Catholicism, Mexican Diaspora, 103

Center for Applied Research in Anthropology (CARA), Latino residents, 102–103

Central American immigrants, in La Sierra County, 145, 147

Changing Relations Project, 2

"Charity magnet," 121

Charvey, Fernando, 101

Chavez, Leo, 122

Chicago, Mexican Diaspora, 101

Chicano, 143, 166 n.1

Child rearing practices: Hope City, 18, 21–30; Latino, 5

Christiana: Latino immigrants, 146–147; ski resort town, 144–145

Civil Rights movement, 218

Clayton, demographic change, 194–195

Clayton Community Unit School District (CUSD): bilingual staff, 198–199, 200; demographic change, 193–194; parental involvement, 196, 197, 198, 199; principals of, 197–198, 200, 212; segregated program, 199–200; structure of,

195–196; "Statement of Principles and Beliefs," 200–212

Coded language, 39, 56, 231

Colorado, Diaspora Latinos, 1, 11–12, 242

Commission on Hispanic Affairs, Sunder Crossings, 232–233

Commission on Immigration Reform study, immigration's value, 229

Communication: Christiana, 146; Georgia Project, 110; parent-child, 29

"Communication gap," CPS, 71, 74

Commuting, Christina, 147

Conasauga: anti-immigrant sentiment, 79; demographic change, 102–103; description of, 102; Georgia Project, 99–102, 107–114

Conasauga Model for Bilingual Education, The, 85–86

Conasauga Public Schools (CPS): demographic changes, 73, 89, 103, 114 n.1; Georgia/Mexico partnership formation, 68–69, 72–75, 79; superintendent's letter, 71, 75–78

Confianza (trust), 29

Consejos (homilies), moral education, 25, 27, 28, 33 n.14

Construction industry, Georgia, 42

Crawford, James, 46

Cuadros, Paul, 42

"Cultivating Gringo Bilingualism with Limited Resources," 50

Cultural defect ideology, 8

Cultural inversion, 7

"Cultural texts," 71

"Cultural wars," 37

Curriculum: CPS bilingual, 72, 80–91; lowrider art, 184–187, 246; Snow Elementary, 160, 164

Dallas, Mexican Diaspora, 101

Delgado-Gaitan, Concha, 5, 10

Dentler, Robert A., 6, 91, 92

Dewey, John, 109

Dialogue, Georgia Project, 110, 111

Diaspora Latinos: anti-immigration script, 221, 224–225; perspectives of, 7–9; as "problems," 4–5, 71, 217, 221, 222, 230,

244; proimmigration script, 7, 79, 93, 221, 224–225

Dicker, S.J., 44, 53

Direct Instruction, CPS, 80, 82, 83, 88, 89, 91, 94 n.10

Discrimination, Havertown, 121

Douglas, William O., 155–156

Dual identities, Latinas, 137, 138

Duke, David, 45

Durand, Jorge, 101

Education: Anglo view of, 3; Diaspora Latinos, 2, 92; Fuentes, Teresa, 131–132; immigrant student needs, 91; Latino view of, 3–4, 139 n.5; policy impact, 244–245; in Southwest, 2; Villalobos, Jesús, 128–130

"Education" services, Hope City, 18, 20–21

Educational policy: additive acculturation, 246–247; Diaspora Latinos, 4, 5–6, 9–10, 106, 221; La Sierra County, 143–144, 153–154, 165; subtractive acculturation, 245; Sunder Crossings, 221

El hogar, 24–25, 28

El Salvadorean immigrants, Rodham County, 216

English as a second language (ESL): Havertown, 119–120; Villalobos, Jesús, 128–129; Snow Elementary, 154; Roseville High, 170, 171–174

English, as official language, 44, 45, 46–47, 56, 58, 121, 244

English for speakers of other languages (ESOL): educational method, 38; Georgia DOE, 47–49, 52–53, 56, 57

"English Language Empowerment Act of 1996," 46

English Language Learners (ELLs): Clayton CUSD, 199; language policy impact, 193, 244

"English: The Language That Unifies U.S.," 53

Entitlement, public goods, 215

Erickson, Frederick, 138

Erickson, Ken, 121, 122

Escamilla, K., 39, 56

Espoused theory, 71; CPS, 71–72

Ethnicity, Mexican Diaspora, 104

Extended family, Havertown absence of, 122

Family loyalty: Fuentes, Teresa, 130; Hope City, 17

Family values, Latinos, 5, 22

Farm labor, Latino immigrants, 41–42

Federal Education Programs "Mega-Conference," 50

Federation for American Immigration Reform (FAIR), immigration to George, 41

Flamming, Douglas, 73

Flores, J., 176

Florida, Mexican Diaspora, 101, 103, 248 n.3

Folk linguistics, 37, 39, 48, 56

Fordham, Signithia, 136, 137

Foucault, Michel, 37, 68, 111–112, 194

Fraser, Nancy, 222

Fuentes, Teresa, 130–132, 136

"Funds of knowledge," 6, 7

Galindo, René, 38–39, 44

Gangs, fear of, 226–227

Gender differences, Latinas/os adolescents, 124–126, 137–138, 246

Gender roles, Latinas/os adolescents, 8, 24–25, 122, 132–137

Georgia: anti-immigration sentiment, 46; Diaspora Latinos, 1, 10, 11, 101; Latino immigration, 41–43, 60 n.6, 102–103, 242

Georgia Department of Education (DOE): anti-immigration sentiment, 46; language policy, 37–40, 47–57; migrant education agencies (MEAs), 54–56, 61 n.19; Migrant Education program, 10, 11, 54–56, 61 n.19; Migrant Education Retreat, 49, 54; resistance to, 57–58, 59

Georgia ESOL Resource Guide, 50–51, 52–53

Georgia/Mexico partnership, bilingual education, 67–93

Georgia Project, 92–102, 107–114

Georgia State University, Latino residents, 102–103

Gibson, Jane, 220

Gibson, Margaret, 12, 132, 137

Gingrich, Newt, 46
Globalization: impact of, 215, 218; Mexican Diaspora, 104, 242; North Carolina, 216
Goldfield, David, 219
Goldman, Dorie, 181
Grady, Karen, 8, 12, 242, 246, 247
Granite School, Clayton CUSD, 197, 198
Great Immigration, 41, 60 n.6, 241
Grief counseling, Snow Elementary, 162
Griffith, David, 127, 220–221, 228
Guatemalan immigrants, Rodham County, 216
Guerra, Juan C., 9

Habermas, Jurgen, 222
Hafner, Anne L., 6, 91, 92
Hall, Kathleen, 8, 137
Hamann, Edmund T., 10, 11, 54, 57, 102, 107, 248
Hatch, Thomas, 71
Havertown: ethnographic background, 119–124; Latina/o adolescents, 118
Health care: externalized costs, 5; poultry factories, 17–18, 229; Sunder Crossings, 216
Heath, Shirley Brice, 74
Hernández-Leon, Rubén, 10, 11
Hispanic Task Force, Hope City, 19–20
Hispanics: Clayton CUSD, 193–194, 195; La Sierra County, 145, 153, 154, 164, 165, 166 n.3; Sunder Crossings, 223–224
Home communities, 9
Hope City, 17–31, 32 n.1. *See also* Sunder Crossings
Hornberger, Nancy H., 68
Housing: Hope City, 21–22; La Sierra County, 145–147, 151–153; Sunder Crossings, 216, 230
Houston, Mexican Diaspora, 101
Hubbard, Lea, 118, 132, 134, 138
Hudak, G., 164
Hunter, Floyd, 72–73

Identity: Diaspora Latinos, 1, 2, 7–8, 117; Fuentes, Teresa, 131–132; La Sierra Latino Diaspora, 164–165; Latina/o adolescents, 117–118, 122–124,
124–126, 132–138, 245–246; lowrider art, 169, 177, 182, 246; Villalobos, Jesús, 128–130
"Ideological role model," 47
Illegal immigrants, 22; La Sierra County, 148, 149; poultry factories, 18–19; host concerns, 6, 231
Illinois, Diaspora Latinos, 1, 10, 12, 99, 242, 248n.3
Imagery, lowrider art, 175, 180–181, 186
Immigration: opposition to, 236 n.13; recent Latino, 41–43, 60 n.6, 99–100, 102–103, 216, 233–235, 241–242
Immigration and Naturalization Service (INS), La Sierra County raids, 149–150
Immigration Reform and Control Act (IRCA), 99, 103
Indiana, Diaspora Latinos, 1, 10, 12, 169, 242
Indiana Department of Education (DOE), Office of Language Minority and Migrant Programs, 171
"Interest Convergence," 218
Iowa, Mexican Diaspora, 101

Juarez, Benito, 186, 188
"Just wage," 147

King, Martin Luther, Jr., 227
Kissam, Ed, 127
Ku Klux Klan, 224

"La Maestra," 161–162
La migra, 150, 236 n.11
La Sierra County: anti-immigrant sentiment, 148–149, 153, 163; demographic changes, 147–148; description of, 145–147; "Latinization" of, 143–144
La Sierra County School District, hostility toward, 163
La Sierra Trailer Park, closure of, 151
Lamphere, Louise, 233
Language: Diaspora Latinos, 2; Hope City schools, 20
Language ideologies, 37, 38, 39, 44
Language policy: Clayton CUSD, 12, 193–194, 200–210; Georgia DOE, 37–40, 47–57

Latino, definition of, 12 n.1, 248 n.1
Latinos: as clients, 20–23, 31; economic value of, 228–229, 237 n.19; hostility toward, 43, 46, 79, 148–149, 153, 163, 236–237 n.13, 242; stereotypes/myths, 120, 225–228, 231, 233, 242; Sunder Crossings, 223
Lau v. Nichols, 49, 52, 59, 155–156
Levinson, Bradley A., 4, 39, 57, 69, 70, 75, 118, 133, 143, 194, 248
Libertades (liberties), moral education, 27
Libertinaje (licentiousness), moral education, 26, 27
Limited-English-proficient (LEP) students: Snow Elementary, 154, 157, 158, 159, 160; Sunder Crossings, 234
"Linguicism," 44
Lipsky, Martin, 23
"Little Mexico," 19
Los Angeles, Mexican Diaspora, 101
Lowrider art: artifact bearers, 181; artists/producers of, 179–180, 181–182, 183–184; consumers of, 181, 182; as curriculum, 184–187, 246; distribution of, 180–181; imagery/symbolism, 175, 180–181; as resistance, 169, 189, 246; social network, 187–189
Lowrider Arte (magazine), 12, 174, 175–176, 180, 181–182, 188; as cognitive resource, 182; and identity, 176–177; and social relationships, 177–179, 182, 183–184, 188
Lowrider magazine, 174–175, 176, 177, 178, 180
Lucas, Tamara, 6

MacLeod, Jay, 136
Mahler, Sarah, 118
Maine, Diaspora Latinos, 1, 101
Manufacturing industry, demographic changes, 104–105, 114 n.2
Martinez, Elias, 10, 11–12
Massey, Douglas S., 30, 101
McKinney, Cynthia, 45
Meat-processing industry: Clayton, 195; Diaspora Latinos, 10, 242; externalizing costs, 229; Havertown, 117, 119; Roseville, 170–171

"Mediating institution," 233
Mediation, Georgia Project, 110–111
Mehan, Hugh, 118, 132, 134, 138
Meier, Kenneth J., 9, 121
"Melting pot," 54
Mexican cuisine, Mexican Diaspora, 103–104
Mexican Diaspora: extent of, 101–103, 117; impact of, 103–107; and Mexican Universities, 113
Mexican immigrants: in Georgia, 41–43, 101, 102–103; in La Sierra County, 145, 148; in Rodham County, 216; in United States, 242
Mexican University. *See* Universidad de Monterray
Mexicanos en el Extranjero, 9
Mexico-United States Binational Migration Study, 101
Meyer, Lois M., 92
Midwest, Diaspora Latinos, 10, 242
Migrant education agencies (MEAs), Georgia DOE, 54–56
Migrant Education Grant, Roseville High, 170, 171
Migrant Education Retreat (1998), Georgia DOE, 49
Minnesota, Mexican Diaspora, 101
Moll, L., 182
Money, Villalobos, Jesús, 127
Monolithic Spanish-speaking (MSS) students, Snow Elementary, 154, 158
Moral education, Hope City, 17, 18, 21, 23–28
Multicultural education, dimensions of, 189
Murillo, Enrique, Jr., 1, 12, 19, 242, 244, 248

National Association of Early Childhood Education (NAECE), 197
National Organization for European American Rights (NOFEAR), 45
Nationalism, and racism, 220, 231–232
Native language instruction (NLI), Snow Elementary, 154, 157
Nativism: La Sierra County, 148–149; Sunder Crossings, 217, 231
Nebraska, Mexican Diaspora, 101

Nespor, J., 182

New England, Diaspora Latinos, 10, 11, 119–124, 242

New Latino Diaspora, 1–3, 117; education policy, 221, 243–244; language policy, 38, 212. *See also* Mexican Diaspora

New York, Mexican Diaspora, 101, 248 n.3

Noble, moral education, 22

Noblit, George, 21, 31

Norms, CPS, 75, 77, 93

North Carolina: Diaspora Latinos, 1, 10, 12, 101, 223–224, 242; economy of, 228; Hope City, 17–31; racial exclusion, 218; Sunder Crossings, 216–218, 220–236

Office of Civil Rights (OCR): Georgia DOE, 52, 55, 57, 59; Snow Elementary, 155

Office of Language Minority and Migrant Programs, Indiana DOE, 171

"Official English" laws, 44, 45, 46–47, 56, 58, 121, 244

Ogbu, John U., 7, 118, 136, 137

"Oppositional" identities, Latinos, 135–136, 137, 165

Oregon, Mexican Diaspora, 101

Parents, education responsibilities, 5, 6, 10–11

Peligro (danger), moral education, 26

Peña, D.C., 58

Perea, J.F., 218

Plyler v. Doe, 48–49, 59

Police: Havertown, 120; La Sierra County, 150; and Mexican Diaspora, 105

Policy: Clayton CUSD debate, 208–210; definition of, 70; Georgia-Mexico project, 11; role of, 4, 194

Policy and Planning Committee, Clayton CUSD, 201–202

"Policy community," 70

Policy formation, 4, 69, 71, 90

"Political technology," 90, 194

Polleros, 223, 229

Portes, Alejandro, 246–247

Portugese students, immigrant experience, 8

Poultry industry: in Georgia, 42, 73, 94 n.4; in Hope City, 18–19; and immigrant labor, 220–221, 228, 242; Sunder Crossings, 216, 223, 229, 230, 235

Principals: Clayton CUSD, 197–198, 200, 212; CPS, 77; La Sierra County, 156, 160–161, 163

Private sector, Georgia/Mexico partnership, 68, 70–71, 72–74, 80, 83–84, 87–88, 92–93, 94 n.5

Proposition 187, 121

Proposition 227, 39, 121

Public goods/resources, distribution of, 215–216, 231, 235–236

Public space, and Mexican Diaspora, 102, 104

Public sphere, definition of, 222

Pugach, Marleen C., 7, 133

Pull-out instruction, Snow Elementary, 163–165

Race, conditions for progress, 218

Racial equality, decline in support for, 217

"Racial etiquette," 219

Racial profiling, anti-Latino, 227

Racial project, definition of, 219

Racial projects, 218–219

Racialization: Hope City, 19–20, 21, 25; host community, 8, 12; North Carolina, 223–224; Sunder Crossings, 218

Racism: biracial system, 43, 224; Diaspora Latinos, 2, 7, 8; Hope City, 17, 18; and nationalism, 220, 231–232

Rasquachismo, 175

Religious faith, moral education, 24

Replacement acculturation, 245

Resort industry: Diaspora Latinos, 10, 242; La Sierra County, 144–147

Respect: moral education, 17, 18; Villalobos, Jesús, 127

Respeto, moral education, 18, 23–24, 29

Respetuosas, moral education, 22

Rocky Mountains, Diaspora Latinos, 10, 144

Rodham County: demographic change, 216; economic growth costs, 235

Role models, school success, 135–136

Roseville High: class schedules, 171–174; demographic change, 171; Latino students, 169

Rumbaut, Rubén, 241, 246–247
Rural locations: Diaspora Latinos, 2–3, 10; Georgia DOE, 56–57, 61 nn. 20, 21, 22

San Miguel, Guadalupe, 5
Sarason, Seymour B., 89, 91
Scapegoating, of Latinos, 218, 222
Schön, Donald A., 71
School success, Latina/o adolescents, 118–119, 124, 126, 134–136
Schooling: Diaspora Latinos, 5–6, 68; goal of, 92
Schools: Diaspora Latinos, 1–2, 7, 105–106, 243, 249 n.6; Havertown, 120–121; Hope City, 20; La Sierra County, 143, 144; mediating role, 233; responsibilities of, 5; role of, 67–68
Schrenko, Linda, 46–54, 56, 58–59
Sending communities, Mexican, 9, 73
Shadduck-Hernández, Janna L., 10, 11
Shannon, S.M., 39, 56
Shipp, Bill, 49
Shor, Ira, 6
Shore, Cris, 4, 68, 70, 71, 90, 93, 111–112, 194
Sikh students, immigrant experience, 8
Sink or swim submersion, educational method, 38, 57, 155, 166 n.5
Ski resorts, 10, 144–147, 242
Snow Mountain Elementary: demographic change, 153, 162–163; dual language program, 157–159; housing pressure impact, 151–152; INS raids impact, 150, 153; pull-out instruction, 163–165; TBE program, 144, 154–157, 158–159, 162
Soccer, Mexican Diaspora, 103
Social class, and Mexican Diaspora, 104–105
Socialization, Clayton CUSD, 211
South: anti-immigration sentiment, 43–46; governing elites, 73; Latino immigrants in, 37–38, 41–43, 215, 242
South Carolina, Mexican Diaspora, 101
"Southern Culture," 219
Southwest, Latino education, 2, 6
"Spanglish," 17
Spanish as a second language (SSL), Snow Elementary, 159

Spanish language: educational policy, 244–245; Georgia Project, 109; Havertown, 119; Mexican Diaspora, 103–104; Roseville High, 176–177; Villalobos, Jesús, 127
Spener, David, 79
"Statement of Principles and Beliefs:" consensus building, 201, 207–208; development of, 200, 202; parent participation, 200, 205–206, 209, 210; program exploration, 201–207; response/ratification, 201, 208, 210; student participation, 200, 205, 206–207, 209, 210; teacher participation, 200, 202–205, 209, 210, 211, 212
Stewart, Joseph, Jr., 9, 121
Stone, Michael Cutler, 176, 180
"Studying through," 70
Stull, Donald, 121, 122
Suárez-Orozco, Carola, 118
Suárez-Orozco, Marcelo M., 6, 7, 79, 135, 164, 224–225
Subtractive acculturation, 245
Summer Institute: CPS staff, 90, 93; Universidad de Monterray, 100
Sunder Crossings: demographic changes, 216, 222–223; economy of, 229; infrastructure impact, 216, 229–230; racial attitudes, 217–221, 224–225; racial stereotypes, 225–228, 231–233; schools, and Latino immigration, 216, 233–235. See also Hope City
"Survival English," 153, 154, 155
Sutton, Margaret, 4, 39, 57, 69, 70, 75, 135, 143, 194, 248
"Symbolic power," 39
"Symbolic violence," 39, 44–45
Symbolism, lowrider art, 175, 180–181, 186

Tapia, J., 182
Teachers: lack of skills, 244; "Statement of Principles and Beliefs," 200, 202–205, 209, 210, 211, 212
Teachers training, Latino Diaspora, 247–248
Tennessee, Mexican Diaspora, 101
Texas, Diaspora Latinos, 99, 103, 248 n.3

Theory-in-use, 71; CPS, 71–72, 88, 91
Tienda, Marta, 134
Title I, Georgia DOE, 47–48, 49, 54–55, 59
Title VII: Georgia DOE, 47, 59; La Sierra County, 144, 156–157; Snow Elementary, 160–161; Washington Elementary, 160
Title VII: Systemwide Bilingual Education, 69
Totten, Leah, 42–43
Trail of Tears, 41
Transitional Bilingual Education (TBE) program, 144, 154–157, 160
"Transnational communities," 9
Transnational laborers: Hope City, 22; Sunder Crossings, 220, 228
Trueba, Henry, 10, 118
"Truncated curriculum," 164

Una buena educación, Hope City, 17–18, 23–26, 28, 30, 31
United States: early immigration, 241; Mexican Diaspora, 101–103; recent immigration to, 41–43, 60 n.6, 99–100, 102–103, 216, 233–235, 241–242
United States Commission on Immigration Reform study, immigration's value, 229
United States Department of Education, Office of Bilingual Education and Minority Language Affairs (OBLEMLA), 154
United States Department of Education, Office of Civil Rights (OCR): Georgia DOE, 52, 55, 57, 59; Snow Elementary, 155
Universidad de Monterray: Georgia Project, 99–100, 107–114; Georgia/Mexico partnership, 74–75, 77–78, 80, 81–82, 85, 88, 89, 92–93; and local leadership, 106
University of Arizona, "funds of knowledge," 6

Unz, Ron, 39
Utah, Mexican Diaspora, 101

Valdés, Guadalupe, 5, 8
Valdéz, María, 45
Valencia, Richard H., 8
Vásquez, Olga, 5
Vicios (vices), moral education, 26
Villalobos, Jesús, 126–130, 136
Villanueva, Irene, 118, 132, 134, 138
Villarreal, María Olina, 10
Villenas, Sofia, 1, 3, 5, 10–11, 121, 227–228, 244
Visiting instructors, CPS, 78, 80, 82, 85, 86, 90, 92, 94 n.9, 95 n.11

White privilege, 219–221
Whitman, K., 182
Whitmore School, Clayton CUSD, 197, 198, 199
Williams, Brickette F., 220
Willis, Paul, 133–134, 137
Winant, Howard, 218–219
Wong Fillmore, Lily, 92
Woodcock-Muñoz English Survey, 171, 172, 173
Work: adolescent choices, 133–134; segmentation of, 217; Villalobos family, 127–128
Work force: La Sierra County, 143; Sunder Crossings, 216
Working class: Diaspora Latinos, 2, 105; English "lads," 133–134; Villalobos, Jesús, 128; White, 220–221
Working conditions: La Sierra County, 147, 148, 152–153; poultry factories, 18–19
Wortham, Stanton, 8, 11, 245, 248
Wright, Susan, 4, 68, 70, 71, 90, 93, 111–112, 194

Yudice, G., 176

Zambrana, Ruth E., 30
Zúñiga, Víctor, 10, 11

About the Editors and Contributors

MARTHA ALLEXSAHT-SNIDER is an associate professor in the Department of Elementary Education at the University of Georgia where she teaches courses on families, schools and communities; language and culture in diverse communities and international contexts; and anthropology and education. She received her Ph.D. from the University of California at Santa Barbara in Crosscultural Education and is a former bilingual teacher and teacher of English for speakers of other languages. Her research interests include family-school linkages in diverse contexts, mathematics education reform and systemic change, and professional development and teacher education in multicultural and multilingual settings.

SCOTT A.L. BECK is a Ph.D. student in Language Education at the University of Georgia. He also is an instructor in the Department of Early Childhood Education and Reading at Georgia Southern University. He has worked among Mexican American migrant farmworkers in the South for over a decade as a health outreach worker, classroom teacher, migrant educator, and curriculum coordinator. His research and teaching interests include the teaching of additional languages, literacy education, multicultural children's literature, social education for democracy and diversity, and the comparative histories of African American and Latino education.

MICHAEL BRUNN has conducted ethnographic research on the juxtaposition of English language learners in mainstream social and educational contexts for many decades. His research is focused on the issues and paradigms of second language acquisition in relation to the majority culture. His most recent work was in the rural Midwest among a newly established Hispanic migrant community. His earlier work was with the Indigenous peoples of Alaska and the Southwest region. He has a number of publications and presentations at national conferences which illuminate the range and depth of his work.

MARGARET A. GIBSON, Professor of Education and Anthropology at the University of California, Santa Cruz, focuses her research on the variability in immigrant and minority students' school achievements. In her fieldwork she has given particular attention to ways in which ethnicity, gender and social class interact to shape students' school adaptation patterns. In addition to ongoing fieldwork in several multiethnic high schools in California, Gibson has conducted field research in the U.S. Virgin Islands, northern India, and Papua New Guinea. Major publications include *Accommodation without Assimilation: Sikh Immigrants in an American High School, Minority Status and Schooling: A Comparative Study of Immigrant and Involuntary Minorities,* co-edited with John Ogbu, and *Ethnicity and School Performance: Complicating the Immigrant/Involuntary Minority Typology.* Gibson is one of the founding editors of *Race, Ethnicity and Education;* she also serves on the Board of Directors, Council on Anthropology and Education.

KAREN GRADY is Assistant Professor at Illinois State University in the Curriculum and Instruction department. She previously taught English as a second language in the California public schools for 14 years. Her research interests include school reform at the secondary level and the social contexts of second language acquisition and literacy.

EDMUND T. HAMANN is a Research and Evaluation Specialist at the Education Alliance at Brown University. In that capacity, he studies the links between equity and diversity issues, notably the accommodation of English Language Learners, and comprehensive school reform. His recent fieldwork has been primarily in Maine, Puerto Rico, and Georgia. He has a Ph.D. in Education from the University of Pennsylvania's Graduate School of Education and an M.A. in cultural anthropology from the University of Kansas. His published work has focused on the evolving understandings and resulting actions of educational leaders in response to increasing student diversity, particularly the rise in Latino enrollment. He has also authored technical reports on the implementation of the federally funded Comprehensive School Reform Demonstration project (a.k.a. Obey-Porter) in Puerto Rico and Maine and on the limited success of that program so far to overtly consider the needs and proclivities of English Language Learners. Current research projects include an effort to develop a theory of personalized learning applicable to secondary school reform and an effort to define and describe the educational needs of "sojourner students"—economically marginal, transnational students. Previously Dr. Hamann has taught qualitative research methods, cultural anthropology, writing, and intercultural communication at the university level and has coordinated and taught in a bilingual family literacy program. He has helped school districts obtain Title VII funding and evaluated Title VII implementation at the state level.

RUBÉN HERNÁNDEZ-LEÓN is a Fogarty Postdoctoral Fellow with the Mexican Migration Project at the Population Studies Center at the University of Pennsylvania. He has a Ph.D. in Sociology from the State University of New York at Binghamton. He was a member of the faculty in the Department of

Humanities at Universidad de Monterrey in Monterrey, Mexico (1997–1999), and a research associate with the Center for Immigration Research at the University of Houston (1995–1999). At Universidad de Monterrey, he was the research director of The Georgia Project. His current areas of research are new destinations of Mexican immigration in the United States, urban and metropolitan origins of the Mexico-U.S. migration, and the social and political management and construction of the U.S.-Mexico border. He has also conducted research on youth issues and urban poverty in Mexico. The results of his research have been published in several journals and edited books. He is currently editing a volume on new destinations of Mexican migration in the United States.

ELIAS MARTINEZ is a faculty member in the School of Education and Human Development at the State University of New York at Binghamton, where he conducts research on the contextual factors that affect the academic achievement of Latino students in secondary schools. Dr. Martinez received his Ph.D. from the University of Colorado at Boulder and is interested in how school contexts affect identity and achievement.

ENRIQUE G. MURILLO JR. is a faculty member in the College of Education at California State University San Bernardino. He is a first generation Chicano, born and raised in the greater East side of Los Angeles, and a native bilingual speaker of Spanish and English. He completed his Ph.D. in the Social Foundations of Education program at the University of North Carolina at Chapel Hill. Enrique previously taught elementary school as a bilingual instructor in inner-city South-Central Los Angeles. Prior to that, he served as a coordinator, instructor and community organizer in various community-based organizations. During graduate school, Enrique served as a research associate for the North Carolina Public Spheres project, a collaborative, National Science Foundation funded research project. Enrique has received several awards, including the Southern Oral History Award and the 2000 Outstanding Dissertation Award from Phi Delta Kappa. He has published articles in various academic journals, including *Educational Foundations, The Urban Review,* and the *International Journal of Qualitative Studies in Education.* He is co-editor and contributing author of several forthcoming books. He is also the founding editor of the *Journal of Latinos and Education.*

JANNA L. SHADDUCK-HERNÁNDEZ is the national representative and coordinator of the refugee and immigrant issues network of the American Friends Service Committee. She received a Master's degree in education from the Center for International Education at the University of Massachusetts at Amherst, where she focused on the workplace education needs of Vietnamese refugee women in the United States. She conducted doctoral work at the same university, concentrating on community/university partnerships with refugee and immigrant communities. At UMass, she was also a research associate with a statewide community development project, CIRCLE (Center for Immigrant and Refugee Community Leadership and Empowerment), funded by the Massachusetts Office of Refugees and Immigrants. She has conducted academic and applied research on adult education, community development, immigration and human rights issues in Vietnam, Mexico, and the Northeast and Southeast regions of the United States.

MARÍA OLIVIA VILLARREAL has served as Exchange Coordinator and research assistant for the Georgia Project since it began in 1996. With an M.S. in sociology from the University of Texas-PanAmerican, she currently is an Associate Professor in the Humanities Department of the Universidad de Monterrey in Monterrey, Mexico. Villarreal has specialized in the area of U.S./Mexico border relations and roles of women in the labor force. She has written on Mexican women textile workers in south Texas and on Anglo-Hispanic relations in schools in that region and north Georgia.

SOFIA VILLENAS is assistant professor in the Department of Education, Culture and Society and the Ethnic Studies Program at The University of Utah. Her research centers on investigating Latino home and community education within the dynamics of racial/cultural community politics. She specifically focuses on Latina mothers' roles as educators in the family and community while simultaneously studying their racialization as women and transnational laborers. Dr. Villenas also explores ethnographic methodological issues of positionality and location, as well as issues in multicultural education. Her work appears in *Harvard Educational Review, Curriculum Inquiry, Educational Theory,* and *Anthropology and Education Quarterly.* She is also co-editor with Laurence Parker and Donna Deyhle of *Race Is . . . Race Isn't: Critical Race Theory and Qualitative Studies in Education.*

STANTON WORTHAM teaches in the Educational Leadership Division at the University of Pennsylvania Graduate School of Education, in the "Education, Culture & Society" specialization. His doctorate is from the Committee on Human Development at the University of Chicago. He is a linguistic anthropologist of education whose work explores how the sociocultural aspects of language use can facilitate learning and identity development in educational settings. He has also developed discourse analytic methods for studying the interactional functions of language use. His first book, *Acting Out Participant Examples in the Classroom* (1994), analyzes the use of examples in urban high school English and history classrooms. His second book, *Narratives in Action* (2001), analyzes the construction of self in autobiographical narrative discourse. He has also studied media bias, through detailed examination of network news coverage of U.S. Presidential campaigns.

VÍCTOR ZÚÑIGA is a professor of sociology at Universidad de Monterrey and a visiting professor at Université de Versailles. He is a specialist on Mexican/U.S. migration cultural issues. He has published more than 60 articles, chapters and books on these issues. He has also been Director of the Georgia Project from 1997 to the present and a member of the Sistema Nacional de Investigadores since 1989.